New Perspectives on State Government Fiscal Challenges

New Perspectives on State Government Fiscal Challenges

Edited by
Barry W. Poulson and John Merrifield

LEXINGTON BOOKS
Lanham • Boulder • New York • London

Published by Lexington Books
An imprint of The Rowman & Littlefield Publishing Group, Inc.
4501 Forbes Boulevard, Suite 200, Lanham, Maryland 20706
www.rowman.com

86-90 Paul Street, London EC2A 4NE

British Library Cataloguing in Publication Information Available

Library of Congress Cataloging-in-Publication Data

Names: Poulson, Barry Warren, 1937- editor. | Merrifield, John, 1955- editor.
Title: New perspectives on state government fiscal challenges / edited by Barry W. Poulson and John Merrifield.
Description: Lanham, Maryland : Lexington Books, 2023. | Includes bibliographical references and index.
Identifiers: LCCN 2023013892 (print) | LCCN 2023013893 (ebook) | ISBN 9781666932034 (cloth) | ISBN 9781666932041 (epub)
Subjects: LCSH: Finance, Public—United States—States. | Local finance—United States. | Intergovernmental fiscal relations—United States. | State governments—United States
Classification: LCC HJ275 .N48 2023 (print) | LCC HJ275 (ebook) | DDC 336/.010973—dc23/eng/20230517
LC record available at https://lccn.loc.gov/2023013892
LC ebook record available at https://lccn.loc.gov/2023013893

Contents

List of Figures

List of Tables

Introduction

John Merrifield and Barry W. Poulson

The COVID-19 pandemic is a tail event that had an unprecedented impact on the economy. The United States had the worst economic downturn since the Great Depression. The economy recovered more rapidly than originally forecast, due primarily to the massive fiscal stimulus policies pursued in 2020. Tail events like the COVID-19 pandemic require unprecedented coordination of monetary and fiscal policy to provide the macroeconomic policy response required for stabilization. Large purchases of financial assets by the Federal Reserve created the fiscal space required for countercyclical fiscal policy. Monetary or fiscal policy alone could not have provided the level of support deemed necessary in responding to the crisis.

As the COVID-19 pandemic waned, the burning question was when and how to restore normal monetary and fiscal policies. The coordination of monetary and fiscal policy works only if the credibility of the two commitments to stable prices and sustainable debt levels is not questioned. During the "Great Moderation" of the late 1980s and 1990s, the United States made significant progress in fulfilling those conditions. In those years, John Taylor and others formalized benchmarks for prudent monetary and fiscal policy. While Taylor-style monetary and fiscal rules were never adopted as formal rules, they served as benchmarks for prudent policy. Empirical studies reveal that fiscal and monetary policies approximated, and in some years exceeded, those benchmarks.

However, over the past two decades monetary and fiscal policies no longer approximated the rules-based policies pursued during the "Great Moderation." The major discontinuity in monetary policy occurred during the 2008 financial crisis, when the Fed placed a check on the excess reserves that their emergency operations created. Since then, not only has the Fed failed to normalize monetary policy, it greatly expanded its balance sheet, and left the crisis-era operating system in place. The Fed's policy response to the

COVID-19 pandemic further blurred the lines between monetary and fiscal policy. The Fed is in danger of becoming a pawn of Congress, forced to finance government expenditures in a manner that endangers the legitimacy of both monetary and fiscal policy.

The commitment to sustainable debt ended long before the COVID-19 pandemic. During the 2008 financial crisis, debt roughly doubled from $5 trillion to $10 trillion, and doubled again to $20 trillion in the years prior to the pandemic that pushed formal debt to nearly $30 trillion. The Congressional Budget Office says that current law will cause the 2050 debt to exceed 200% of GDP. And many elected officials want massive new spending programs that would require even more debt, and many of them insist that the Fed buy more treasury bonds or "print" the sovereign currency required to finance those programs.

Over the past two decades, many state and local governments have added to the federally induced debt fatigue, allowing debt to rise more rapidly than state gross domestic product. Much of that increased state debt has been off the radar, because much of it is "off budget." The most rapid rise in state and local debt has been in unfunded liabilities in pension and Other Post Employment Benefit (OPEB) plans.

A major challenge for the states is a comprehensive measure of total long-term liabilities. The Government Accounting Standards Board (GASB) set new standards for government financial reporting in the Comprehensive Annual Financial Reports (CAFR). These standards required reporting unfunded liabilities in government employee pension and health-care plan. However, states are given wide leeway in how they measure and report these unfunded liabilities. Despite some improvement, states continue to underestimate and underreport unfunded liabilities in their CAFR, and as a result they continue to be underfunded. This book addresses those state-level issues, and offers strategies for reporting long-term liabilities, and managing them.

Some of the rise in state and local debt is linked to federal bailouts during the 2008 financial crisis and the COVID-19 pandemic. In addition to direct aid to state and local government, the federal government supported their bond issues. The Fed was allocated $429 billion in Cares Act money to finance their pandemic lending facilities. The Fed made only $25 billion in loans and other commitments because businesses and municipalities could borrow more cheaply in the private credit market. Democrats wanted to use the Fed's lending facility to fund more bailouts, but Republicans were successful in terminating the Fed Lending facility, as called for in the Cares Act.

Federal bailouts allowed state and local governments to issue hundreds of billions of dollars in bonds, backed by Fed purchases and guarantees. The Fed bailouts created all the wrong incentives for state and local governments. The fiscal commitment problem requires that state and local governments, as well as the federal government, pursue fiscal policies consistent with sustainable debt. Debt fatigue at all levels of government means that the commitment to sustainable debt is now questioned.

Debt solvency is an area of economics where conceptual clarity meets practical fuzziness. Conceptually, public debt cannot exceed the present value of all future surpluses (net of interest payments). But, in practice, predicting future budget surpluses is uncertain, and in the near term servicing the debt may expose state and local governments to insolvency risk. Indeed, recent empirical studies suggest that many states allowed their total debt to reach levels that exposes them to the risk of insolvency and default.

There is an extensive literature exploring the reason for the bias toward deficits and debt. Indeed, Yared (2019) argues, "normative economic theories cannot deliver a complete justification for the rise in public debt across all advanced economies, which suggests that the widespread increase in debt partly represents a political failure."[1] The public choice literature says the culprit is time inconsistency. Politicians, focusing on the next election, find that expenditures yielding immediate benefits for their constituents are more valuable than future expenditures, or present outlays whose benefits are visible in the future. Government budgets are ultimately the translation of a political platform. This means that fiscal policy is determined by political factors that make it difficult to solve the "commitment problem." Given the bias toward deficits and debt, the question is how to constrain fiscal policy decisions to achieve sustainable debt.

This book is a starting point in understanding how state and local governments can normalize their fiscal policies in the post–COVID-19 era. It offers new ways to think about the macroeconomic frameworks needed to solve the "commitment problem." State and local governments must maintain or achieve policy credibility while showing resilience in meeting the challenge of economic shocks. Constraining policymakers' discretion will be even more important in this new era than it was during the "Great Moderation." The recent economic crises have provided a learning experience for state and local governments, and the rules-based macroeconomic framework required for this new era may be significantly different than that of the past.

The first section of the book creates a framework for exploring the "commitment problem" of states. The Powers chapter provides a comprehensive framework for understanding state debt in the modern era. The chapter by Horpedahl reviews problem of state insolvency and default in the nineteenth and early twentieth centuries. Savidge examines unfunded liabilities in state pension plans. The chapter by Gonzalez takes a holistic approach in assessing state fiscal sustainability, using a Fiscal Condition Index (FCI).

The second section of the book explores other dimensions of fiscal rules and fiscal policy in the states. Historically state and local governments constrained fiscal policy by incorporating balanced budget rules and debt limits in constitutional or statutory provisions. In the 1970s, when those traditional fiscal rules proved to be ineffective, citizens and elected officials enacted new fiscal rules and institutions to solve the "commitment problem." Amazingly, saving for a "rainy day" is not yet a well-developed or widespread element of government budgets. Gary Wagner's chapter examines how careful rainy day fund (most often formally designated as budget stabilization funds) design can reduce the fiscal stress that underlies much ratcheting up of state spending and enhance budget stability over the business cycle. The success or failure of fiscal rules is often linked to other institutions governing fiscal policy in the states. The chapter by Mitchell traces the background of anti-subsidy provisions in state constitutions, an important perspective for understanding the current debate about state and local government bailouts. Other institutional reforms are explored in chapters by Stuart on "privatization," and Broughel on "zero based regulation."

The outcome of debt fatigue at all levels of government has been a deterioration in the federalist system. Tax and spending power has shifted dramatically from state and local governments to the federal government; and state and local governments have become increasingly dependent on direct transfers and bailouts from the federal government. It will be difficult for the federal government to solve the "commitment problem" if state and local governments continue to depend upon massive federal transfers, and bailouts in response to economic shocks. The chapter by Thomas and Thomas is a Nebraska case study that traces how the concentration of fiscal power in the federal government constrains states' economic options. The Edwards chapter provides a comprehensive perspective on fiscal federalism, and proposes a wide range of reforms designed to restore a strong federalist system. The average planned federal deficit over the years preceding the pandemic approximately equal federal aid to state and local governments; something Edwards argues should be cut even if unsustainable federal debt does not force us to cut it. The chapter by Lee makes a strong case for reverse revenue sharing as a way to restore the balance of power between the federal government and the states envisioned in the Constitution; most explicitly by the tenth amendment of the Bill of Rights. Ultimately, fiscal sustainability depends upon the willingness of citizens and elected representatives to seek and accept effective fiscal rules and sustainable fiscal policies. The final chapter by Holcombe explores how citizens and elected officials in a conservative state, Florida, provided the support necessary to solve the "commitment problem."

NOTE

1. Yared, Pierre (2019), "Rising Government Debt: Causes and Solutions for a Decades-old Trend," *Journal of Economic Perspectives*, 33(2): 115–40.

Part I

STATE DEBT AND FISCAL STABILIZATION

Chapter 1

State Debt and Liabilities

A Holistic Approach

Thurston Powers

INTRODUCTION

State and municipal governments have faced greater scrutiny of their fiscal health in the wake of the Great Recession. Most of their liabilities fall into four categories: (1) bonds (American Legislative Exchange Council 2019); (2) government employee pensions (Center for Retirement Research at Boston College 2020); (3) government employee retirement healthcare (American Legislative Exchange Council 2019); and (4) deferred infrastructure repairs (The Volcker Alliance 2019). At the state level, those liabilities total to approximately \$1.2 trillion, \$6 trillion, \$1 trillion dollars, and \$0.9 trillion dollars, respectively. This chapter will outline the challenges governments face from each type of liability, strategies for improving reporting, and how best to manage them going forward.

CHALLENGES FACING STATE GOVERNMENTS LEADING INTO THE 2020S

State Pensions

State pension systems have recently become the largest and most troubling state liability. From 2002 to 2018, self-reported unfunded actuarial accrued liabilities (UAAL) rose from \$101 billion to \$1.25 trillion (Center for Retirement Research at Boston College 2020). Using a risk-free rate, the UAAL rose from \$2.2 trillion to \$6 trillion. Leading factors contributing to the rise included explicit underfunding, underestimation of liabilities and thus inadvertent underfunding, and improvements in actuarial estimates of public pension liabilities. Central to these factors, and thus pension reform, is the discount rate used by public pension plans in estimating their pension liabilities.

Explicit Underfunding

After the 2001 recession, explicit underfunding of state pension plans became a common practice. The Governmental Accounting Standards Board (GASB) recommends amortizing unfunded retirement benefit liabilities over a 30-year time horizon through annual payments consisting of payments to current retirees and toward any unfunded pension liabilities. The Actuarially Recommended or Determined [annual] Cost (ARC) is calculated based on the estimated liability. The ARC consists of two components, the estimated annual cost of current retirees and the cost of amortizing pension promises made to active employees and vested, former employees who have not yet retired. Employer (state) contributions below 100% of the ARC contribute to UAAL.

In 2005 and 2010, the median state contributions reached lows of 79% and 84% of the ARC, respectively. Explicit underfunding has been one of the primary contributors to the accumulation of UAAL over the past two decades. However, since 2016 states contributed about 100% of the ARC; see figures 1.1 and 1.2. Additionally, the distribution of percent ARC paid fell over the past two decades. These changes represent a nationwide effort to reduce state pension UAAL.

Even New Jersey, infamous for under-contributing to their state pension systems, improved their annual contribution rate. Between 2001 and 2018, New Jersey's average percent ARC paid toward their three state pension plans was 40.4%, far below the next lowest, Kansas at 73.7%. The low average is due in part to the lack of pension contributions in the early 2000s. In 1997, New Jersey issued a $2.8 billion pension obligation bond (POB), shifting their pension liability to a bonded liability, in the hopes that the proceeds of the bond would accrete to a greater amount than the interest costs, an outcome that is still uncertain but unlikely (Municipal Securities Rulemaking Board) (American Legislative Exchange Council 2019). After issuing the bond and reaching full funding in 2002, the state dramatically reduced its annual contributions toward its pension system. However, starting in 2011, New Jersey gradually contributed a greater percentage of their ARC, see figure 1.3, rising to 68.7% in 2018. While New Jersey still ranks last in this metric, it has made a significant improvement over its historical performance.

The improvement in annual contributions has likely been driven by three major factors: incremental pension reforms following the 2007 recession, the longest running bull market in American history, and increased scrutiny of pension liabilities by credit rating agencies, investors, public policy

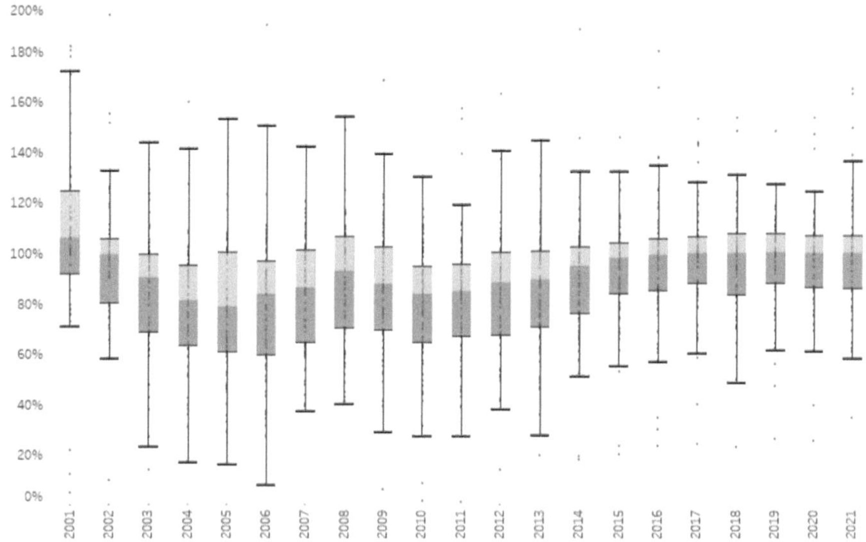

Figure 1.1 Percent ARC Contributed by Plan for All States, 2001–2021. *Note: There are 17 instances of the ARC exceeding 200% that are not visualized in this table, often related to the issuance of pension obligation bonds or other unusual circumstances. *Source*: Calculations based on the Center for Retirement Research at Boston College's public plans database.

Figure 1.2 Standard Deviation of Percent ARC Paid by Plan for All States, 2001–2021. *Source*: Calculations based on the Center for Retirement Research at Boston College's public plans database.

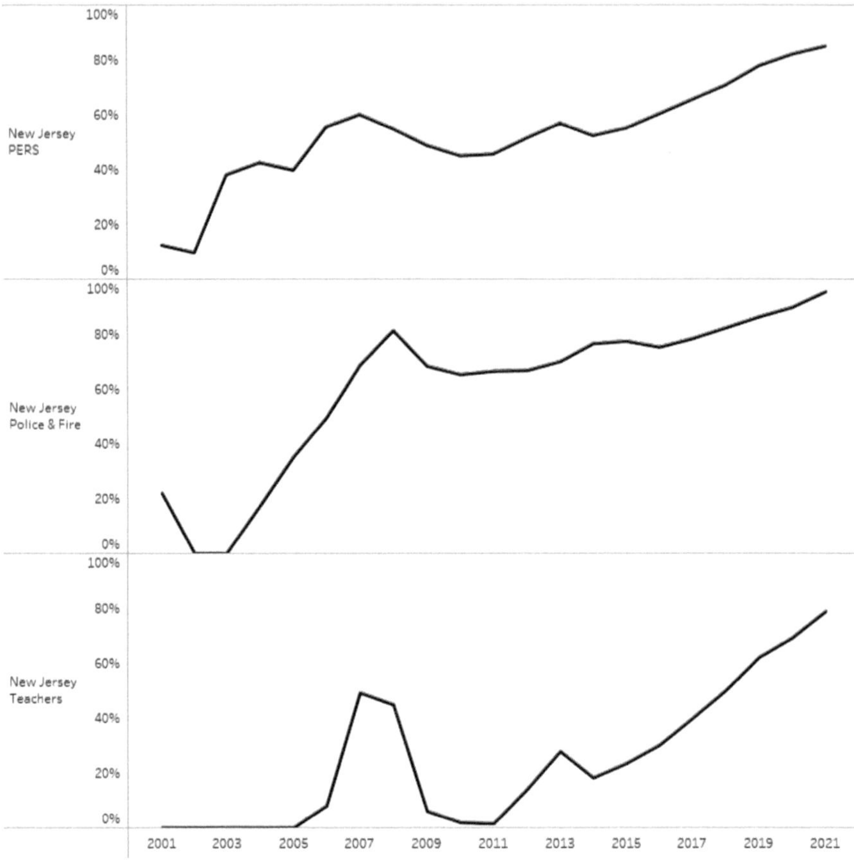

Figure 1.3 Percent ARC Paid for New Jersey's PERS, Police & Fire, and Teacher's Pension Plans, 2001–2021. *Source*: Calculations based on the Center for Retirement Research at Boston College's public plans database.

researchers, and the public. However, if the ARC is underestimated, even governments making full contributions toward their pension obligations will develop unfunded liabilities over time.

Underestimation

Pension liability estimates depend on assumptions about a state's active and retired employees, which include mortality rates, payroll growth, distribution of service years, early retirement rates, disability rates, cost of living adjustments, and investment return rates. The discount rate (rate of return) assumption converts future pension costs into a present value liability, the actuarial accrued liability (AAL). Small changes in the discount rate can dramatically change the unfunded portion, or UAAL. For example, figure 1.4 compares the average discount rate of state pension plans by year, and UAAL as reported by states, to the UAAL rediscounted at different rates. As the discount rate nears 2.25%, the UAAL of 2002 rises from $101 billion to $2,632 trillion. Over-discounting (underestimating) liabilities contributes to underfunding by reducing ARC payments.

There are two main schools of thought for selecting a discount rate, which advise either to set it at long-term investment return rates or at bond interest rates. The investment rate of return method assumes that investments will compound over time at an estimated rate, usually based on historical experience, and thus those future pension investment returns can be deducted

	Avg. discount rate	UAAL	UAAL (4.5% discount rate)	UAAL (2.25% discount rate)
2001	8.03%	41,795,533	-1,056,089,579	-2,132,915,341
2002	8.01%	-91,838,848	-1,343,828,510	-2,575,066,573
2003	7.99%	-219,063,760	-1,533,731,537	-2,838,206,998
2004	7.95%	-261,741,703	-1,664,890,316	-3,069,213,949
2005	7.94%	-339,371,266	-1,861,960,531	-3,386,336,223
2006	7.93%	-361,042,332	-1,979,800,063	-3,603,535,954
2007	7.91%	-358,111,941	-2,090,199,696	-3,830,448,733
2008	7.90%	-432,579,635	-2,259,867,136	-4,100,258,286
2009	7.89%	-660,353,825	-2,574,176,118	-4,508,605,734
2010	7.85%	-753,481,538	-2,705,673,329	-4,705,561,466
2011	7.77%	-831,416,639	-2,780,273,428	-4,830,928,719
2012	7.72%	-930,751,274	-2,923,959,319	-5,038,469,739
2013	7.69%	-990,818,828	-3,049,261,818	-5,243,800,261
2014	7.69%	-989,226,458	-3,134,968,744	-5,433,572,606
2015	7.63%	-1,042,991,074	-3,258,930,186	-5,656,742,871
2016	7.53%	-1,175,802,046	-3,424,379,156	-5,919,916,902
2017	7.37%	-1,216,559,112	-3,467,476,813	-6,040,529,653
2018	7.24%	-1,262,157,914	-3,465,522,391	-6,094,005,750
2019	7.21%	-1,300,171,094	-3,534,071,601	-6,247,754,731
2020	7.15%	-1,332,067,644	-3,584,434,085	-6,360,989,732
2021	7.05%	-898,443,751	-2,305,618,757	-4,123,380,194

Figure 1.4 Unfunded Liabilities with a Range of Discount Rates, 2001–2021. *Source*: Calculations based on the Center for Retirement Research at Boston College's public plans database. Note: The 2021 boom market produced record pension investment gains but faced significant losses in 2022 that erased nearly half the 2021 gains. However, 2022 figures are not yet available in the Public Plans Database.

from pension liabilities. The bond rate method takes the combination of the risk-free rate, usually a U.S. Treasury bond rate, and the risk premium of the obligation, and discounts by that figure. For state and local pension systems, the investment rate of return method is the standard method.

Private-sector pension systems provide an example of both the bond and investment return discounting method. In 2014, a Government Accountability Office report explored the three major categories of U.S. pensions: (1) public employee pensions, (2) private single-employer pensions, and (3) private multiemployer pensions (United States Government Accountability Office 2014). Single-employer pension plans discount using the average interest rate of high-quality corporate bonds, about 3 to 5% depending on the time frame selected.

Multiemployer pension plans use a similar method to public pension plans, discounting by an assumed rate of return on investments, about 7 to 8%. Today, single-employer pension plans have a positive outlook, whereas some multiemployer pension plans are approaching collapse, threatening to take the Pension Benefit Guaranty Corporation (PBGC) down with them (The Heritage Foundation 2019).

Between 2001 and 2018, the interest rate on high-quality market corporate bonds fell from 7.8% to 4%. In turn, single-employer pensions likely raised annual contributions as their calculated ARC rose, making the past two decades more difficult but ultimately placing their pension systems in a favorable position going forward. Multiemployer plans used long-term investment returns to discount their pension liabilities and calculate their contributions, and thus they saw a decline in funding ratios more like public plans—but without having taxpayers to help amortize the UAAL through larger employer contributions. The divergence is likely due in part to their different discounting practices, with discount by the lower, bond-based rate having a superior outcome.

Over the same period, the average discount for state pension plans fell from 8.03% to 7.25%. However, the actual investment returns across state pension systems averaged about 6.4%; see figure 1.5. Expected and actual differ because of the two 2001–2019 recessions. The future average investment return for state pensions is likely a normal distribution centered around 6.4%, based on historical experience. The Pew Research Center and Voya Financial Advisors estimated the same, while J.P. Morgan and Wilshire estimated 6.5% (The Pew Charitable Trusts 2019). If state pension systems were to lower their discount rates to 6.4%, annual costs would increase, and unfunded liabilities would be more likely to amortize within a 30-year period. Unfortunately, state pension managers, state legislatures, and state employee unions have strong incentives to lower their investment return assumption.

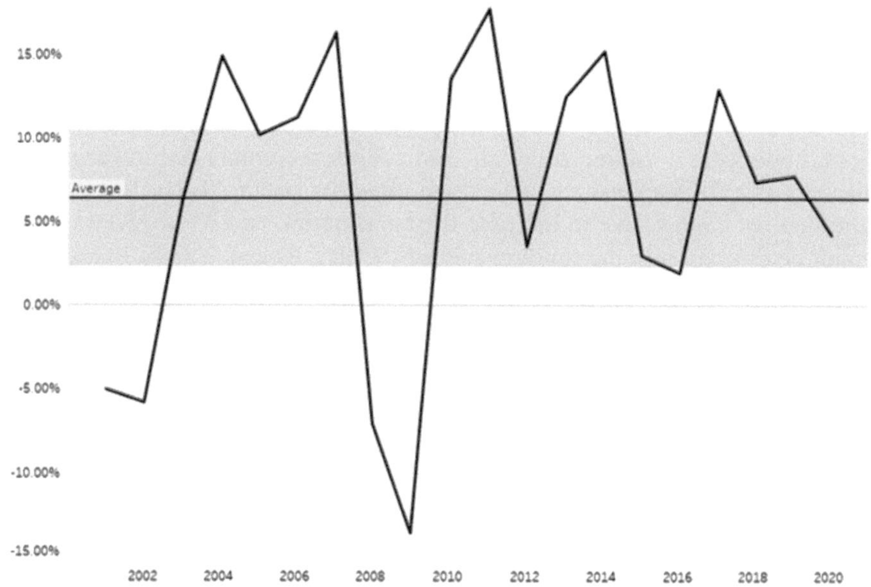

Avg. InvestmentReturn 3yr	6.43%
Avg. InvestmentReturn 5yr	6.76%
Avg. InvestmentReturn 7yr	6.55%
Avg. InvestmentReturn 10yr	8.39%
Avg. InvestmentReturn 15yr	6.85%
Avg. InvestmentReturn 20yr	5.88%

Figure 1.5 State Annual Investment Returns, 2001–2020, and Average Annual Investment Returns for 2020 Using a Range of Time Periods. *Source*: Calculations based on the Center for Retirement Research at Boston College's public plans database. Note: 2021 is excluded from this table due to 2022 data not being available yet. Including the 2021 boom without the subsequent bust in 2022 would skew the averages.

For legislatures, a lower discount rate increases the ARC and presents the legislature with two undesirable choices. First, the legislature can ignore the ARC and overtly underfund the pension, risking a political backlash. Second, the legislature can address it through changes to the state budget, such as allowing pension costs to crowd out other funding priorities or to increase taxes, which also risks a political backlash. By maintaining a high discount rate, legislatures can give the appearance of fully contributing to state pension systems, paying 100% of the ARC, while preserving tax revenue to pursue their own political goals—such as spending or tax cuts promised to constituents. However, this simply pushes the undesirable choices, and thus backlash, onto a future legislature, as was the case for Illinois in 2015 (*Chicago Tribune* 2015).

From a pension manager or treasurer's perspective, lowering the discount rate can create the perception of poor pension management during their stewardship. For example, in 2017 the Mississippi pension fund, PERS of Mississippi, underwent a routine audit, and the auditor recommended lowering the discount rate. In response, the executive directors stated, "I feel 100 percent sure that we would have to increase the contribution rate or we would see a major deterioration in the funding status" (WLBT News). This is likely true, but not because the funding status is deteriorating but instead that the estimate is more accurate.

State employee unions are presented with a similar dilemma. State employee unions seek to secure the best possible salaries and benefits for the employees they represent. Choosing a high discount rate decreases the apparent present value of future retirement benefit and thus reduces the estimated costs of union contracts, strengthening their bargaining position. Maintaining the funds that support those future retirement benefits is a secondary concern due to the legal protections afforded to state pension systems. For example, in Connecticut, unions worked with then-Governor John G. Rowland in 1995 and 1997 to underfund the state employee pension system in order to balance the state budget (Yankee Institute, 2016). The union could agree to this without fear of the state defaulting on its promised benefits due to the pension benefits being protected as property rights.

Given decades of explicit underfunding and the incentives aligned toward underestimating pension benefits, the investment rate of return method has not performed as intended. Furthermore, the investment rate of return method does not reflect the legal protections afforded to state employee pension benefits. To quote Joshua Rauh:

> The logic of financial economics is very clear that measuring the value of a pension promise requires using the yields on bonds that match the risk and duration of that promise. Therefore, to reflect the present value cost of actually delivering on a benefit promise requires the use of a default-free yield curve, such as the Treasury yield curve. Financial economists have spoken in near unison on this point. The fact that the stock market, whose performance drives that of most pension plan investments, has earned high historical returns does not justify the use of these historical returns as a discount rate for measuring pension liabilities. (Rauh, Jonathan D 2018)

From that perspective, the discount rate for state pensions should be a risk-free rate, such as a treasury bond. Applying a risk-free rate increases the estimated state UAAL to about $6 trillion. A discount rate based on high-quality municipal bonds may be more applicable to municipal pension systems, as those jurisdictions may be able to file for bankruptcy.

Hybridization and Self-correction

States and local governments are considering "hybrid" pension plans in place of, or alongside, their traditional pension plans. Hybrid plans usually consist of both a defined benefit (DB) and defined contribution plan (DC). Hybrid plans are often presented as a way of reducing costs or liabilities. However, hybrid plans are not innately more stable or less expensive than DB plans. Rather, the DB portions of hybrid plans tend to be more modern in the design: using lower discount rates, having benefit "spiking" protections, variable employee contribution rates, and other design improvements. One of the most important elements of hybrid plans is the ability for the DC portion of the plan to self-correct and prevent the accumulation of UAAL.

Self-correcting pension systems run by modulating the annual benefits and/or contributions based on the plan's funding ratio. For example, a plan may have a benefit that varies on funding ratio with a benefit floor to protect state employee retirees, depending on the legal definition of the benefit. Alternatively, a plan may automatically raise employee contributions if the funding ratio drops below a threshold, scaling higher as the funding ratio declines. Those approaches are not mutually exclusive. A plan can use a combination of variable benefit and variable contributions.

For most state employee systems, employee contribution rates are fixed by contract of statute. In 2016, the Maine Public Employee Retirement System reformed their pension system to have both variable employee contribution rates and variable benefits, through COLA freezes (Bloomberg 2018). Going forward, municipal and employee contributions can rise as high as 12.5% and 9%, respectively, depending on the health of the pension fund. If the rate increases are insufficient, COLAs are suspended until the fund recovers.

The "risk-sharing" created by reforms like this shifts the political incentives in a positive direction for both liability management and asset management. For state employee unions, the best way to keep their member contributions low is to keep the funding ratio high. As the changes to active employee contributions are automatic, negotiating budget deals where the state underfunds a pension with the understanding that the state must honor their pension promises becomes unpopular with active employees. Furthermore, politically motivated investment strategies, such as divesting industries for political reasons, become less attractive as investment returns on pension assets would matter to state employees.

Wisconsin provides another example of a risk-sharing model. Wisconsin provides two retirement benefits, a relatively small DB paired with a variable benefit. The DB portion of the plan provides a traditional pension, whereas the variable benefit fluctuates based on asset performance. If the stock market declines, the variable benefit also declines. For example, following the 2007 recession, the annual cost of the system declined by more than $4 billion (*Milwaukee Journal Sentinel* 2016). While difficult for some retirees, the decline helped stabilize and replenish Wisconsin's pension fund quickly while other states continued to struggle.

State and Local Bonds

Bonded liability growth is more stable than other state liabilities, highly transparent in terms of disclosure and debt service schedules, and, perhaps most importantly, exposed to market forces. Credit rating agencies and the investment community pressure governments to engage in more fiscally prudent behavior in exchange for high credit ratings and thus less expensive access to capital. However, governments that are desperate for funds often turn to complex bonds with hard-to-estimate future costs. Such bonds are often presented to the public as "cost saving" or "cheap money" rather than the gamble they are.

Purpose of State and Local Bonds

In most state and local financial disclosures, the term "debt" is reserved for general obligation bonds, as those are backed by the full faith and credit of the government. This is a narrow definition of debt, but in recognition of the distinction, other bonds are referred to as "obligations." In 2019, bonded obligations for the most recent state CAFRs and bond disclosures were compiled into the State Bonded Obligations report, estimating that states had accrued an estimated $1.2 trillion in bonded obligations (American Legislative Exchange Council 2019).

Of this $1.2 trillion, general obligation bonds account for $434 billion, governmental activity bonds account for $217 billion, business-type activity bonds accounted for $194 billion, and component unit bonds accounted for $295 billion. Within each of these four categories, there is an immense diversity of maturities, interest rates, debt service structures, and contractual agreements that complicate broad comparisons among states, which are further complicated by the different reporting methodologies of each state.

Bonds allow governments to borrow funds from investors and to repay those funds at an agreed-upon interest rate, structure, and other contractual stipulations found in the covenant. As an example, a state might issue a $5 million general obligation bond for general funding purposes that has a five-year maturity, level debt service, and an interest rate of 5%. The proceeds of the bond could be used to fund various priorities within the general fund so long as it does not violate the covenant or additional terms of the agreement.

Bonds can provide states with the ability to smooth costs. For example, a hypothetical bridge requires annual maintenance, minor rehabilitation every 10 years, and major rehabilitation every 30 years. In years that the state rehabilitates the bridge the annual cost spikes, but tax revenue does not. If the rehabilitation projects are funded via bonds with 10-year maturities, the annual cost will be smoothed. This also applies to reactive expenditures, such as emergency expenditures in response to natural disasters or tax revenue shocks for external forces, such as recessions.

The Cost and Risks of Bonding

Borrowing comes at an interest cost. The interest rate on a bond can vary across time and on different parts of the bond structure. There are fixed and variable interest rate bonds. The former apply a set interest rate to the debt service schedule. Different periods within the debt service schedule have different rates. For some fixed-interest bonds, different series within a bond have different set rates. Variable interest rate bonds have interest rates that fluctuate, usually relative to the LIBOR rate or treasury rate. Variable interest rate bonds add a layer of complexity to the bond where the total cost to the issuer is unknown, leading to potentially disastrous situations.

Variable interest rate bonds have a range of possible total interest costs. Politicians, other public officials, and special interest groups have a strong incentive to focus on the rosier tail of the distribution of potential costs. If these groups can convince the policymakers and/or the public that the cost of bonding is lower than average or below the cost of not funding the project, the bonds are more likely to be approved. Unfortunately, governments that are already experiencing fiscal distress are often drawn into compounding their challenges by the promise of "cheap" money.

For example, between 2003 and 2007, the Chicago Public School system (CPS) issued $1 billion dollars of adjustable-rate bonds with interest-rate swaps. That was proposed as a way of saving $90 million dollars in interest cost relative to traditional, fixed-interest bonds. However, an analysis by the *Chicago Tribune* estimated that it raised the interest cost by over $100 million (*Chicago Tribune* 2014). The initial estimates assumed that interest rates on the "auction-rate" bonds would correlate with the interest-rate swap, meaning that CPS would only pay the fixed interest to the bank. However, the interest rates on the auction-rate bonds rose with the 2007 recession while the interest-rate swap, based on LIBOR, remained low. CPS was liable for the divergence. CPS has a myriad of fiscal challenges, and the additional cost associated with these adjustable-rate bonds did not help.

Variable interest rate bonds are like any other debt instrument; they are tools that can be useful in the right context and with moderation. The bonds issued by CPS underwent an approval process, as most bonds do, but the risk and, ultimately, the cost of the bonds was either not clearly communicated or not identified. If the bonds had been presented to the school board with an analysis of the range of outcomes, based on the historical divergence between LIBOR and municipal bond interest rates, perhaps the amount of variable interest rate debt would not have grown sixfold between 2003 and 2008.

POBs are often presented as cheap, or even free, money through arbitrage. In theory, POBs can lower a state or municipality's net liabilities by issuing the bond at a low interest rate and investing the proceeds of the bond into assets that have a higher average rate of return than the interest on the bond, creating an "expected spread." However, if the investment returns do poorly, the POB compounds the pension liability, increasing the government's net liability. Ideally, governments should limit POBs to a part of a long-term investment strategy, issuing fixed interest rate POBs only when interest rates are at extremely low, as in the case of Oregon in 2009 (Governing 2013).

Unfortunately, states and municipalities facing fiscal duress appear to be the governments most willing to risk compounding their fiscal woes, regardless of timing or strategy—gambling at best, kicking the can down the road at worst (Center for Retirement Research at Boston College 2014). Illinois has struggled with fiscal challenges for decades, in part due to large unfunded liabilities. Rather than address the source of their growing unfunded liabilities, Illinois issued POBs of $10 billion, $3.5 billion, and $3.7 billion in 2003, 2010, and 2011 (Illinois Policy). High-profile POBs issued in response to fiscal distress have largely tarnished the reputation of POBs in both the eyes of investors and the public.

In addition to variable interest cost and bond proceed investment performance, the cost of debt service relative to the anticipated revenues may change a government's ability to pay. A state or municipality may experience decades of fast and steady economic growth, issuing bonds on the assumption that the economy and thus tax revenues will continue to grow rapidly. However, changes in the global economy, technology, demographics, and culture can change the trajectory of even the richest areas of the country, eroding their ability to service their liabilities without decreasing expenditures on other government services (*The Atlantic* 2017).

Market Forces

Unlike pensions, Other Post-Employment Benefits (OPEBs), and deferred transportation maintenance, state and local bonds must be sold to willing investors in the municipal bond market. The municipal bond market pressures governments toward fiscal responsibility through interest costs. Investors provide capital with an interest rate, the perceived combined rate of inflation, risk of default, and a directional risk of future changes in the inflation rate. When a government's fiscal health declines due to an overextension of the government credit, weak economic outlook, or, more commonly, a mixture of both, credit rating agencies, such as Moody's, Standard & Poor's, and Fitch, may issue credit rating downgrades. These downgrades and outlooks signal to the municipal bond market, in addition to their firm's own research, the risk inherent in a government's bonds. As the perception of risk increases, alternative sources of municipal bonds, such as other governments with less risk, become relatively more attractive investments at equal interest rates. Interest costs and political pressures to maintain a stable to positive credit outlook may buffer states and local governments from overextending their bonds, but that is dependent on accurate, timely, and accessible financial disclosures to the public.

Covenants

Covenants create extra contractual obligations for the bond issuer. Covenants are highly flexible, allowing issuers to customize the terms of the bond, limited by existing contractual, legal, and constitutional requirements. Covenants typically exist to create assurances in order to secure the sale of a bond or to lower the interest rate of a bond, such as the promise to not dilute the issuer's credit or exceed an agreed-upon debt service ratio. However, in some cases, covenants are a way a government imposes fiscal responsibility onto future governments.

Connecticut has a long history of underfunding their state pension systems, resulting in the lowest funding ratio in the country as of 2018, controlling for differences in discount rates. In 2007, Connecticut issued a bond that imposed a covenant requiring the state to pay the full actuarial required contribution on the pension liability until the maturity date of the bond to improve the Teacher Retirement System funding ratio. The proceeds of the bond, $2 billion, were invested into the Teacher Retirement System. Even if the bond does not successfully achieve arbitrage by its maturity, its impact on the fiscal health of the state has likely been positive by ensuring that the state contributes the full ARC to the Teacher Retirement System.

In 2018, Connecticut entered another bond covenant aimed at reigning in their bonded obligations, the second highest per capita in the country as of 2019 (American Legislative Exchange Council 2019). Connecticut suffered six credit downgrades between 2016 and 2018, related to the accrual of large unfunded liabilities associated with state employee retirement benefits (CT State Finance 2020). The bond covenant contractually binds Connecticut to a series of fiscal reforms, including a cap on bond issuance and a volatility cap on income tax revenue that contributes excess income tax receipts into the budget stabilization fund (BSF) (CT Mirror 2018).

These covenants were intended to communicate to credit-rating agencies and investors that Connecticut has moved past its perpetual budget crises and is now on a path to fiscal stability. So far, the covenants, along with incremental pension and OPEB reforms in 2018, appear to be successful. In 2019, two credit-rating agencies upgraded their outlook for Connecticut's general obligation bonds, reversing the three-year trend of negative to stable outlooks (*Hartford Courant* 2019).

Alternatives to Bonding

Just as there is a diversity of bonds, there is also a diversity of alternatives to bonding. Three of the most common alternatives are BSFs (see chapter 7), emergency funds, and trusts. Each of these alternatives is best suited to different fiscal challenges that all governments will face at some point.

Since a BSF transfers state revenue from high economic growth years to low growth years, it is ideal for managing tax revenue volatility. Some tax structures are more volatile than others and susceptible to different types of economic shocks. For example, a state that levies high corporate income or capital gains taxes will have more volatile revenue during recessions than one that relies on broad-based sales or other taxes (The Pew Charitable Trusts 2017). Governments should develop BSFs proportional to the historical volatility of their revenue, reducing need to issue bonds during economic downturns and other predictable shocks to their revenue.

For less predictable expenditures, such as natural disasters or pandemics, emergency funds (chapters 5 and 6) can be an effective alternative to issuing bonds. For example, Colorado requires the state and its municipalities to maintain an Emergency Reserve Fund equal to at least 3 percent of fiscal year spending (Nonpartisan Services for Colorado's Legislature 2020). Establishing targets for emergency funds is difficult as the nature, time, and cost of a future disaster are unknown.

Lastly, there are some functions of government that have volatile year-to-year expenditures. Transportation and school construction projects can produce spikes in expenditures that are often smoothed by issuing bonds to fund the project. However, a well-managed trust can provide a similar benefit. Funds are appropriated annually or from a dedicated revenue source to the fund and withdrawn as needed. Instead of having the funds today and servicing debt for five years, funds would be appropriated for five years and then spent. The funds would be invested so that they would benefit from investment returns, as opposed to the government paying interest costs.

State OPEBs

State and local governments often provide retirement benefits in addition to their pension systems, called "other post-employment benefits" (OPEBs), an umbrella term for a diverse set of benefits including health insurance, disability health insurance, supplemental health insurance, vision insurance, dental insurance, and life insurance. A recent estimate places state OPEB liabilities at $1 trillion dollars (American Legislative Exchange Council 2019). Due to the diversity of OPEB plan designs, unfunded liabilities range from $0 to about $18,500 per capita. Furthermore, this range is heavily skewed toward 10 states (see figure 1.5). OPEB plans do not appear to represent a large portion of other states' liabilities, but the benefit structure of most OPEB plans is hard to estimate. In addition to the usual pension risks, OPEB plans must also account for the healthcare trend rate, which is subject to shocks from healthcare utilization, prices, regulations, and coverage changes. The additional variables typically make OPEB obligations a riskier type of obligation than pensions.

Actuarial Estimation for OPEB

As explained above in the state pensions section (subsection Underestimation), actuarial estimates of retirement benefit liabilities are constructed using assumptions about future mortality rates, payroll growth, distribution of service years, early retirement rates, disability rates, cost of living adjustments, investment return rates, and other variables. However, OPEB estimation has an additional variable to contend with, the healthcare trend rate. For most plans' OPEB estimation, the healthcare trend rate is more important than the discount rate.

Table 1.1 Other Post-Employment Benefit Liabilities, 2019

State	*Total Risk-Free Unfunded Liabilities Per Capita*	*Ranking, Descending Order*
Alaska	$18,507.35	50
New Jersey	$14,479.26	49
Hawaii	$12,256.65	48
Delaware	$10,382.89	47
Connecticut	$9,387.12	46
New York	$6,512.50	45
Illinois	$5,029.56	44
Michigan	$4,856.09	43
Vermont	$4,644.04	42
California	$4,213.14	41

Source: Adapted by the author from "Other Post-Employment Benefit Liabilities" (2017, 2019), American Legislative Exchange Council.

There are two primary reasons for that. First, the OPEB plans that operate as pay-as-you-go plans tend to have 0 to 5% funding ratios, paying the annual normal cost and choosing not to fund future obligations. As a result, most OPEB plans apply low discount rates, usually based on their prevailing municipal bond rate in pay-as-you-go, which are closer to normalized, risk-free liabilities when compared to self-reported pension liabilities. Second, variations in the healthcare cost trend often contribute larger actuarial gains and losses on a per point basis. For example, in an actuarial valuation of the New York City Health Benefits Program for fiscal year 2018, a 1% change in the discount rate produced a range of actuarial gain and loss of $34.237 trillion whereas the range for a 1% change in the healthcare trend produced a range of $45.007 trillion (New York City Office of the Actuary 2018).

The healthcare cost trend is, itself, an aggregation of a multitude of factors outside of a state or local government's control. The trend consists of healthcare prices and utilization, which are influenced by gross domestic product, regulation, monetary inflation, and even the national political environment. A 2016 article in the *North American Actuarial Journal* analyzed the errors of the U.S. Office of the Actuary's (OACT) national health expenditures (NHE) (Getzen, Thomas 2016). The author noted:

> The improvement in forecast accuracy since 1995 could be interpreted as indicating possibilities for future methodological gains. Conversely, the rather large errors in "historical" NHE suggest that measurement of health spending is inherently difficult and unstable, so that greater precision may not be possible or meaningful. . . . Given the inherent uncertainty in long-run economic projections, it seems unwise to expect significantly better precision from health spending forecasts.

Put simply, healthcare is an immensely complex industry with an equally complex legal and regulatory regime. Both the industry and its regulation are constantly evolving in new and unexpected directions, making prediction both difficult and potentially impossible to improve. This uncertainty is layered on top of the uncertainty associated with more traditional defined-benefit pensions, which have already proven difficult for most governments to manage thus far.

Limits on Healthcare Trend Rate Growth

Most actuarial models assume a sharp drop in the healthcare trend rate over the next decade. Since healthcare expenditures cannot outpace GDP growth indefinitely, the healthcare expenditure trend will converge to the long-run GDP growth rate.

For example, New York City's New York Health Benefits Program has accrued over $90 billion dollars of unfunded OPEB liabilities, a far larger obligation than most states. In 2013, the New York Health Benefits Program valuation estimated that the healthcare trend rate for pre-Medicare plans would decline from 9.5% to 5% between 2013 and 2023 (New York City Office of the Actuary, 2013). In 2018, the plan's valuation estimated that it would reach 5% in 2028 (New York City Office of the Actuary 2019). In five years, the estimated point where it would reach a healthcare trend rate of 5% had moved up five years.

Even small errors in future benefit cost estimates could dramatically impact OPEB liabilities and present budget challenges for New York City. This is not a criticism of the estimates. They are reasonable from the perspective that healthcare is limited by income and competition with other goods, such as housing, food, transportation, and other costs. In 2018, healthcare accounted for 17.7% of GDP, but the eventual equilibrium rate is unknown; it could be 20 to 30% GDP (Getzen 2016).

State Deferred Maintenance of Capital Projects

In late 2019, a report by the Volcker Alliance's Truth and Integrity in Government Finance initiative, estimated that states had accrued an estimated $873 billion in deferred maintenance (The Volcker Alliance 2019). Although unfunded pension liabilities highlight the importance of conservative actuarial assumptions, and unfunded OPEB liabilities highlight the importance of estimating and limiting the variability of actuarial assumptions, deferred maintenance liabilities highlight the importance of improving our state financial disclosures. Relative to all other liabilities, deferred maintenance liability offers the most fertile ground for reform—and recommendations from the Volcker Alliance provide an excellent framework for it.

New Construction, Maintenance, and Deferred Capital Improvements

States and local governments own capital assets vital to the provision of public services, such as schools, roads, and police stations. Each year, these assets require maintenance and, potentially, improvements. When appropriations or bond proceeds are insufficient to meet these demands, governments develop gaps in the maintenance and/or modernity of their assets.

The quality of these structures, in terms of both modernity and physical integrity, modulate the impact of the taxpayer dollars. For example, a poorly maintained road or a road that lacks modern safety improvements may have a higher rate of accidents and fatalities than a similar road without deferred maintenance or capital improvements.

It is also possible for states and local governments to overextend themselves, such as building roads and bridges that are either underutilized or simply pull traffic from another serviceable road. Worse than either, governments may inadvertently prioritize new, less useful construction over addressing deferred maintenance on heavily utilized assets (Transportation for America 2020).

When state or local governments face fiscal challenges, they tend to restructure their net liabilities to defer their coming due. Examples of this include issuing POBs to reduce or defer annual pension contributions, deficit financing by issuing bonds to cover general purpose revenue shortfalls, and reducing pension contributions to fund other budget priorities. Currently, these actions are identifiable in CAFRs or other supporting documents, such as actuarial valuations and official statements for recently issued bonds.

However, it is much harder to know if a government has deferred maintenance and capital improvements to fund other budget priorities, has fewer demands for new construction or capital improvements, or is restricting its new construction due to a weaker-than-expected economic outlook. In most cases, it is only clear that a state is investing less than it has in the past. Ideally, state governments would conduct regular valuations of their existing assets, retrospective analyses of their utilization, cost, and potential redundancies, and prospective analyses of alternative capital assets, particularly if the utilization trend is falling and costs are rising. They should also differentiate among new construction, maintenance, deferred capital improvements, and deferred maintenance. This would assist with capital investment prioritization and good government advocacy efforts.

POLICY RECOMMENDATIONS FOR STATE DEBT AND LIABILITIES

Recommendations for State Pension Plans

The policy recommendations in this section are presented from most impactful to least. The majority of these recommendations can be implemented in conjunction with one another. Pension reforms yield benefits that can take several years to materialize because they do not reduce liabilities that have already accrued; pension benefits have strong legal, sometimes constitutional, protections. That said, the earlier reforms are implemented, the larger their impact will be.

DC Plans

Many states' pension plans can be closed and replaced with DC plans, in much the same way that private-sector pension plans have been largely supplanted by 401k retirement funds. DB pension plans have some benefits over DC plans, such as risk sharing across vestees and protection from surviving one's retirement savings. However, DB plans both provide greater portability and, most importantly, resolve the incentive challenges.

Transition costs are often cited as a deterrent to switching to a DC plan. GASB supports amortizing the UAAL of a closed pension plan using a shorter time frame than an open pension plan. Doing so raises the ARC, in the same way that choosing a 15-year mortgage instead of a 30-year mortgage increases monthly payments (Reason Foundation 2014). However, the cost of fully funding the state pension system is the same. Furthermore, states are not legally forced to reduce their amortization period.

The transition to a DC plan may reduce or increase annual costs depending on the generosity of the match relative to the generosity of the pension plan. In other words, it's possible to create a DC plan that is more expensive than a DB plan. The greatest boon of transitioning to a DC plan is that it eliminates the state's ability to over-discount future benefit costs and thus under-contribute to their benefit plans. The cost of a DC plan is experienced in the present, in the form of states contributing a contractually or legislatively prescribed match with every paycheck, protecting state employees' retirements and taxpayers in the process.

Bond-Based Discount Rates

State and local governments that continue to provide defined benefits should calculate those benefits using a risk-free, bond-based discount rate. At minimum, states should adhere to the discount practices like those outlined by FASB for single-employer plans, as they have proven to be more robust than the public sector's current approaches, such as discounting by the rate of return of AA municipal bonds with maturities between 10 and 20 years. Ideally, states should discount their pension liabilities relative to their inability to default and apply a discount rate based on the yield on Treasury bonds. A discount rate based on the bond approach would increase the estimated UAAL and, in turn, increase the projected ARC associated with state pension plans. If states increase their ARC payments to match their new estimates, the lower discount rate will result in state pension plans reaching full funding quickly, protecting promised state employee benefits.

Self-Correcting Pension Plans

State and local governments that continue to provide defined benefits should reform their retirement benefits to have self-correcting features. For DB plans, this could include automatic increases in employer and employee contributions depending on the funding status of the plan, as seen in the Maine state employee retirement system. However, hybrid plans have the additional benefit of being able to have flexible payments based on the funding of their plan, as seen with the Wisconsin state employee retirement system. Ideally, the self-correction would have risk-sharing across all stakeholders, meaning the employer, active employees, and retirees, ensuring that all stakeholders share an interest in the fund's health and investment performance.

RECOMMENDATIONS FOR STATE BONDS

BSF Management

BSFs, sometimes referred to as "rainy day funds," can provide protection against the worst types of bonding, such as deficit bonding. Stabilization fund adequacy is best determined by historical tax revenue. BSFs usually have withdrawal conditions, such as a recession (The Pew Charitable Trust 2018). How tightly or loosely defined these conditions are can deny governments access to the fund when there is legitimate cause for withdrawal or erode the fund through continuous withdrawals due to structural budget deficits (The Pew Charitable Trust 2014). In both cases, states and municipal governments are pushed into the municipal bond market due to either being unable to access funds or having already depleted funds when they need them most. Outside of macroeconomic downturns, states and municipalities should be very restrictive against withdrawal from their stabilization funds paired with required contributions to their fund if it is below their volatility-based target. During macroeconomic downturns, the funds should be easily accessible to reduce the probability of deficit bonding or higher or new taxes.

Bond Caps

Bonds can be serviced through involuntary revenue, voluntary revenue, or a mixture of both. Involuntary revenue comes from taxes or mandatory fees; usually general obligation bonds or government activity bonds. Voluntary revenue comes from fees associated with services freely chosen; usually business-type activity bonds or component unit bonds. If the voluntary revenue comes from fees or subscriptions related to a service, bonds backed by voluntary revenue can provide two advantages over those backed by involuntary revenue: they likely adhere to the benefit principle, and they are further exposed to market forces. Thus bonding caps are best applied to tax-supported bonds that are disconnected from the use of the bond proceeds. When bonding caps are applied too broadly, states and municipal governments create alternative debt instruments that tend to have less detailed disclosures.

The transparency required to issue a bond on the municipal bond market and for that bond to be recorded in the MSRB database, EMMA, has value, both in terms of improving market information and for holding governments accountable.

RECOMMENDATIONS FOR OPEB MANAGEMENT

The policy recommendations in this section are again presented in descending order of impact. The majority of these recommendations can again be implemented in conjunction with one another. The earlier reforms are implemented, the larger their impact will be.

Phase-Out OPEB Liabilities

For most state and local governments, estimated OPEB liabilities are already small relative to their budgets. For these governments, it is possible to phase out OPEB for new hires. Most public-sector professionals can retire at a similar age as their private-sector counterparts and thus raising the minimum retirement age to 65 would either eliminate OPEB liabilities or dramatically reduce them. If OPEBs are also either not present for those who are Medicare eligible or phased out beyond the Medicare eligibility, the liability ends.

Alternatively, state and local governments could continue to allow early retirement and access to their health insurance plans but without explicit and/or implicit subsidy. This can be accomplished by increasing the employee portion of the health insurance premiums to the point where the retiree internalizes their full cost to the plan. In 2014 and 2016, respectively, Kansas and South Dakota pursued this reform and eliminated their OPEB liabilities (American Legislative Exchange Council 2019).

Restructure OPEB Liabilities to Be More Predictable

An OPEB plan benefit structure can be changed to be more predictable. The primary goal of this reform would be to remove the need for predicting the healthcare trend rate, with a secondary goal being to limit the benefit to the early retirement window. For example, a government could provide an explicit healthcare subsidy indexed to inflation for individuals who retire before age 65 or meet the criteria for disability retirement. This would reduce the number of relevant variables for estimating the OPEB liability, reducing the risk of underestimating future costs.

In 2015, the New Jersey Pension and Health Benefit Study Commission proposed replacing their OPEB plan with an explicit subsidy. The new subsidy would be equal to the current value of a gold plan or the recently repealed "Cadillac" health insurance tax threshold, indexed to inflation going forward, deposited into a reimbursement retirement account (RRA) (New Jersey Pension and Health Benefit Study Commission 2016). Retirees would use the funds in their account to purchase health insurance of their choice from the healthcare exchange, ideally customized to their individual needs.

The report stressed "a state budget so burdened by employee benefits would not be able to weather a recession or permit the State to do what is necessary to promote the general welfare of its citizens (New Jersey Pension and Health Benefit Study Commission 2015)." For states facing large unfunded liabilities, especially those with large unfunded OPEB liabilities, this is not a trivial concern. In a recent report by the American Legislative Exchange Council, California's total OPEB unfunded liability grew by 66% in a single year (American Legislative Exchange Council 2019). Ideally, liabilities should grow roughly proportionally with the rest of governmental expenditures that should, in turn, grow proportionally with the economy that supports the government.

Prefund OPEB Trusts

In 2017, the majority of OPEB plans operated as pay-as-you-go, with 101 out of 132 state OPEB plans having 0% funding (American Legislative Exchange Council 2019). Governments that choose to continue to provide subsidies and that have restructured those subsidies to be more predictable should establish OPEB trusts, if they have not already, and prefund their liability. Trusts can reduce the cost of providing an OPEB benefit through investment returns. There is potential for a fund performance-based savings for the employer and bonuses for the retiree. For example, a higher than 100% funding ratio could trigger automatic decreases in contributions, with the decreases being rolled back when the fund dips below 100% again. Prefunding also provides states and local governments the ability to smooth over shocks, caused by either actuarial losses due to misestimation or actual losses, such as new regulations or taxes on health insurance.

Create an OPEB/Pension Trade-Off

An early retirement may improve the services of physically demanding public-sector professions. However, health insurance costs before age 65 can act as a significant barrier to early retirement, even when states facilitate early retirement through relatively low service retirement requirements. Furthermore, pension plans often discourage early retirement by using the last two to three years of an employee's earnings to calculate pension benefits. When

OPEB plans have more predictable benefit structures, it is possible to provide early retiree access to OPEB plans without increasing a government's liability through a trade-off. If the present value of the pension penalty is equal to the present value of the OPEB plan, then the trade-off would yield an approximate net OPEB liability of around $0. By increasing the number of years used to calculate an employee's pension benefit, increasing the multiplier to compensate the lower average, and providing the ability to pay for healthcare through their future pension payments, barriers to early retirement can be removed without incurring additional costs to the state or local government.

RECOMMENDATIONS FOR INFRASTRUCTURE NEEDS

This section echoes the call to action set forth in the Volcker Alliance's report *America's Trillion-Dollar Repair Bill*, specifically the standardization and disclosure subsections. In the early 2000s, many states began posting their pension actuarial valuations online, providing good government advocates with low-cost access to detailed reports on state pensions. A decade later, OPEB valuations followed suit, shortly after a report detailing an estimated $1.5 trillion in unfunded state and local OPEB liabilities in 2007 (Credit Suisse 2007). Between 2010 and 2020, there were waves of pension and OPEB reforms, and research built on actuarial valuations played a pivotal role. If, in the early 2020s, states were to improve their financial disclosures related to infrastructure needs in a standardized, comprehensive manner, good government advocates would be able to identify problematic trends in the management of state and local assets.

GASB 34 and 34 Modified Approach

At a minimum, states should disclose what they should have spent on maintenance, what they spent, and how much deferred maintenance they have accrued. These would be similar metrics to the ARC, contribution, and UAAL of pension and OPEB valuations. For the total deferred maintenance, GASB 34—the standard accounting manual for U.S. government operations—recommends that state and local governments present the total value of their assets if in good condition and their current depreciation, often referred to as total capital assets, at historical cost and total accumulated depreciation or some other variant of assets and their depreciation. GASB 34 modified recommends governments set a predetermined condition for their assets, such as a "B" as defined in the ASCE Infrastructure Report Card, and to estimate the annual cost required to maintain that condition (Connecticut Society of Civil Engineers 2018). Nearly half of states use the modified approach for some assets, primarily bridges and roads, and about 6% of local governments are estimated to (GASB 2019). Between knowing how much depreciation is currently outstanding and how much a state is contributing toward its maintenance relative to its target contributions, it would be possible to measure the annual accrual of deferred maintenance (The Volcker Alliance 2019). However, the impact of applying both statements is contingent on the estimates being comprehensive, meaning that it covers all public assets regardless of revenue source, and their definitions of assets and estimation methodology being similar across governments to facilitate comparisons.

Inventory and Prioritization

State and local governments, especially state governments, should develop comprehensive datasets for public assets, including transportation. Each should have its estimated annual cost, annual contribution, current depreciation, and its priority relative to all other capital assets. Priority could be defined as score based on utilization, availability of alternatives, current depreciation as a percentage of predetermined value, percent greater probability of mortality at current depreciation relative to predetermined value, and other indicators deemed important by the government. Supporting documents, such as the most recent valuation of the property, the assumptions used to estimate the value of its current depreciation, and the reasoning behind the priority score should also be available. In theory, the process of quantifying, prioritizing, and publicizing will result in sounder capital management and empower the public to hold policymakers accountable for deferred maintenance.

REFERENCES

Bellis, Rayla. *The Congestion Con.* Transportation for America. 2020. http://t4america.org/wp-content/uploads/2020/03/Congestion-Report-2020-FINAL.pdf.

Blair, Russell. "Second Credit Rating Agency Upgrades Connecticut's Bond Outlook." Hartford Courant. 2019. https://www.courant.com/politics/capitol-watch/hc-pol-connecticut-credit-rating-20190710-jyx6m7gcubaebgf4lrtc3onhx4-story.html.

Braun, Martin. "Public Pensions Adopt Cost Sharing Mechanisms to Stem Volatility." Bloomberg. 2018. https://www.bloomberg.com/news/articles/2018-07-17/public-pensions-adopt-cost-sharing-mechanisms-to-stem-volatility.

Center for Retirement Research at Boston College, Center for State and Local Government Excellence, and National Association of State Retirement Administrators. "Public Plans Data." *2001-2020.* 2020. https://crr.bc.edu/data/public-plans-database/.

Connecticut Society of Civil Engineers. *Report Card for Connecticut's Infrastructure*. 2018. https://www.infrastructurereportcard.org/wp-content/uploads/2016/10/ASCE-CT-report.pdf.

Cournoyer, Caroline. "Pension Obligation Bonds: Risky Gimmick or Smart Investment?" Governing. 2013. https://www.governing.com/topics/finance/gov-pension-obligation-bonds-risky-or-smart.html.

CT State Finance. *CT Bond Ratings*. 2019. http://ctstatefinance.org/bonding/bondratings.

Fitch, Marc. "Union Leaders Approved Underfunding of Connecticut Pensions." Yankee Institute. 2016. https://yankeeinstitute.org/2016/10/04/union-leaders-approved-underfunding-connecticut-pensions/.

GASB. *Capital Assets*. 2019. https://www.gasb.org/jsp/GASB/GASBContent_C/ProjectPage&cid=1176173270952.

Getzen, Thomas E. *Accuracy of Long-Range Actuarial Projections of Health Care Costs*. North American Actuarial Journal. 2016. https://www.soa.org/globalassets/assets/files/research/research-accuracy-long-range-projections.pdf.

Greszler, Rachel. "Union Pension Underfunding is Bankrupting this Government Entity." The Heritage Foundation. 2019. https://www.heritage.org/jobs-and-labor/commentary/union-pension-underfunding-bankrupting-government-entity.

Griffith, Joel. "Pension Obligation Bonds Could Unravel Pension Reform Victory." American Legislative Exchange Council. 2017. https://www.alec.org/article/could-pension-obligation-bonds-unravel-recent-pennsylvania-pension-reform-victory/.

Grotto, Jason and Gillers, Heather. "Risky bonds prove costly for Chicago Public Schools." Chicago Tribune. 2014. https://www.chicagotribune.com/news/watchdog/cpsbonds/ct-chicago-public-schools-bond-deals-met-20141107-story.html.

Illinois Policy. "Illinois' Pension Bonds: The other $26 billion obligation you shouldn't ignore" https://www.illinoispolicy.org/reports/illinois-pension-bonds-the-other-26-billion-obligation-you-shouldnt-ignore/.

McCarthy, Waverly. *State Pension Fund's Future Is Still Uncertain*. WLBT News. 2017. https://www.wlbt.com/story/36245983/state-pension-funds-future-is-still-uncertain/.

Municipal Securities Rulemaking Board, Electronic Municipal Market Access. *State Pension Funding Bonds, Series 1997A-1997C*. 2019. https://emma.msrb.org/MS132411-MS107719-MD208528.pdf.

Munnell, Alicia, Aubry, Jean-Pierre and Cafarelli, Mark "An Update on Pension Obligation Bonds." Center for Retirement Research at Boston College. 2014. https://crr.bc.edu/wp-content/uploads/2014/07/slp_40.pdf.

Murphy, Mary, Zhang, Alexandria and Iyengar, Akshay. *States' Tax Portfolios Drive Differences in Revenue Volatility*. The Pew Charitable Trusts. 2017. https://www.pewtrusts.org/en/research-and-analysis/articles/2017/10/16/states-tax-portfolios-drive-differences-in-revenue-volatility.

New Jersey Pension and Health Benefit Study Commission. *A Roadmap to Resolution*. 2015. https://www.state.nj.us/treasury/pdf/FinalFebruaryCommissionReport.pdf.

New Jersey Pension and Health Benefit Study Commission. *Supplemental Report on Health Benefits*. 2016. https://www.nj.gov/treasury/pensions/documents/pdf/NJPensionCommission-Supplemental-Report-on-Health-Benefits.pdf.

New York City Office of the Actuary. *Fiscal Year 2013 GASB 74/75 Report*. 2013. http://www.nyc.gov/html/actuary/downloads/pdf/OPEB_Report_FY2013.pdf.

New York City Office of the Actuary. *Fiscal Year 2018 GASB 74/75 Report*. 2018. https://www1.nyc.gov/assets/actuary/downloads/pdf/OPEB_GASB_7475_Report_FY2018.pdf.

New York City Office of the Actuary. *Fiscal Year 2019 GASB 74/75 Report*. 2019. https://www1.nyc.gov/assets/actuary/downloads/pdf/OPEB_GASB_7475_Report_FY2019.pdf.

Pearson, Rick and Geiger, Kim. "Illinois Supreme Court rules landmark pension law unconstitutional." Chicago Tribune. 2015. https://www.chicagotribune.com/news/breaking/ct-illinois-pension-law-court-ruling-20150508-story.html.

Phaneuf, Keith. "Connecticut 'locks' into New Budgetary Restraints in Three Weeks." CT Mirror. 2018. https://ctmirror.org/2018/05/25/connecticut-will-lock-new-budgetary-restraints-three-weeks/.

Randazzo, Anthony. "The 'Transition Costs' Myth." Reason Foundation. 2014. https://reason.org/policy-brief/the-transition-costs-myth/.

Rauh, Jonathan D. *Testimony Before the Joint Select Committee on Solvency of Multiemployer Pension Plans*. United States Senate & United States House of Representatives. 2018. https://www.pensions.senate.gov/sites/default/files/25JUL-2018RauhSTMNT.pdf.

Rosewicz, Barb, Moody, Jonathan and Newman, Daniel. *States Make More Progress Rebuilding Rainy Day Funds*. The Pew Charitable Trust. 2018. https://www.pewtrusts.org/en/research-and-analysis/articles/2018/08/29/states-make-more-progress-rebuilding-rainy-day-funds.

Savidge, Thomas, Williams, Jonathan, and Skips, Estates. American Legislative Exchange Council. *State Bonded Obligations, 2019*. 20219. https://www.alec.org/app/uploads/2020/02/Bonded-Obligations-Tax-Publication-02-04-20-web.pdf.

Savidge, Thomas, Williams, Jonathan, and Skips, Estates. American Legislative Exchange Council *Other Post-Employment Benefit Liabilities*. 2019. https://www.alec.org/app/uploads/2020/01/OPEB-Web.pdf.

Sobetski, Greg. *TABOR Emergency Provisions*. Nonpartisan Services for Colorado's Legislature. 2020. https://leg.colorado.gov/sites/default/files/r20-303_tabor_emergency_provisions.pdf.

Stein, Jason. "Wisconsin's Fully Funded Pension System Is One of a Kind." Milwaukee Journal Sentinel. 2016. https://projects.jsonline.com/news/2016/9/26/wisconsins-fully-funded-pension-system-is-one-of-a-kind.html.

The Pew Charitable Trusts. *State Pension Funds Reduce Assumed Rates of Return*. 2019. https://www.pewtrusts.org/en/research-and-analysis/issue-briefs/2019/12/state-pension-funds-reduce-assumed-rates-of-return.

Thompson, Derek. "What on Earth Is Wrong with Connecticut?" The Atlantic. July 5, 2017. https://www.theatlantic.com/business/archive/2017/07/connecticut-tax-inequality-cities/532623/.

United States Government Accountability Office. *Views on Using Multiple Measures to Offer a More Complete Financial Picture*. 2014. https://www.gao.gov/assets/670/666287.pdf.

Urahn, Susan and Ettlinger, Michael. *Building State Rainy Day Funds*. The Pew Charitable Trust. 2014. https://www.pewtrusts.org/-/media/assets/2014/07/sfh_rainy-day-fund-deposit-rules-report_artready_v9.pdf.

Zhao, Jerry Zhirong, Fonseca-Sarmiento, Camila, and Tan, Jie. The Volcker Alliance. *America's Trillion-Dollar Repair Bill*. 2019. https://www.volckeralliance.org/sites/default/files/attachments/Americas%20Trillion-Dollar%20Repair%20Bill%20-%20Capital%20Budgeting%20and%20the%20Disclosure%20of%20State%20Infrastructure%20Needs.pdf.

Zion, David and Varshney, Amit. "You Dropped a Bomb on Me, GASB." Credit Suisse. 2007. http://online.wsj.com/public/resources/documents/DroppedB.pdf.

Chapter 2

U.S. State Debt Defaults and Constitutional Reform in Historical Perspective

Jeremy Horpedahl

INTRODUCTION

Throughout U.S. history, there have been several waves of state debt defaults. These defaults have motivated states to reform their constitutional rules about acquiring debt, usually to make it more difficult for state and local governments to do so. The first wave occurred in the 1840s. Following the Civil War, there were repudiations of debt acquired both during the Civil War and then by Reconstruction governments. During the Great Depression, debt issues were mainly at the local level, as local debt became the primary source of public debt in the decades leading up to the Depression. The local debt did create problems for some state governments, including Arkansas defaulting in the 1930s. In this chapter, I give a summary of this history of debt defaults and the changes to constitutional rules that followed.

While the U.S. government has never defaulted on its debt, dozens of U.S. states, plus thousands of municipalities and other local taxing districts, have defaulted throughout U.S. history. Three major waves of defaults were in the 1840s, the post–Civil War period, and during the Great Depression, and these waves led some states to reform their constitutional rules regarding debt accumulation. In this chapter, I investigate these historical cases for lessons about government debt in general, constitutional change, and whether these post-default reforms changed the form or substance of debt procedures.

As of early August 2022, the total outstanding debt of the U.S. federal government is about $30.6 trillion, and the amount held by the public (rather than other government agencies) is around $24.0 trillion (U.S. Treasury Department 2022). That's over $93,000 per resident, or $73,000 per resident if we use the debt held by the public. Despite this large amount of debt, the U.S. government manages to make the required regular debt service payments (about $352 billion in fiscal year 2021) and has done so since the country was founded.

In addition to the federal debt outstanding, state and local governments also have a large amount of debt outstanding. Total state and local debt in 2019 was around $3.2 trillion, with about 63% of this debt at the local level (U.S. Census Bureau 2022). State and local debt exists in spite of the fact that 49 of the 50 U.S. states have some form of balanced budget requirement, though the stringency varies, and only 38 states prohibit carrying over deficits from year to year (National Conference of State Legislators 2010).

State debt defaults tend to come in waves and near financial crises, with the most prominent periods being the 1840s and 1870s. Local government defaults tend to cluster as well, and for local entities the Great Depression was by far the worst period for default, with over three-quarters of the cumulative 6,298 local defaults taking place during the 1930s.[1] One state, Arkansas, also defaulted during the 1930s, largely through the assumption of local debts, though several states were also in "technical default" by missing payments though the debts were eventually paid in full (Kroll Bond Rating Agency 2011).

State responded to debt defaults by writing new rules about incurring debt, often by amending their constitutions or by writing new constitutions. Specifically, states sought to restrain their own ability to take on debt or to run budget deficits. These constitutional changes are a classic of example of states tying their own hands to prevent future behavior.

In this chapter, I investigate the history of state and local debt defaults, resulting constitutional changes to state debt procedures, and evidence of states often circumventing their own barriers to incurring debt.

OVERVIEW OF HISTORICAL GOVERNMENT DEBT IN THE UNITED STATES

Before recounting the specific waves of debt defaults in the United States, it is useful to get a sense of the changes in U.S. government debt over the long run. Figures 2.1 and 2.2 present data on state, local, and national debt outstanding for selected years since 1841. Figure 2.1 shows debt levels as a percent of GDP, while figure 2.2 shows that same data as a percent of all public debt. The pandemic recession and public response to it has increased public debt even further, with federal debt held by the public now over 100% of GDP, but due to data availability for state and local debt the charts end in 2019.

In the early American republic, the federal government started out with a sizable amount of debt from the Revolutionary War and added to that in the

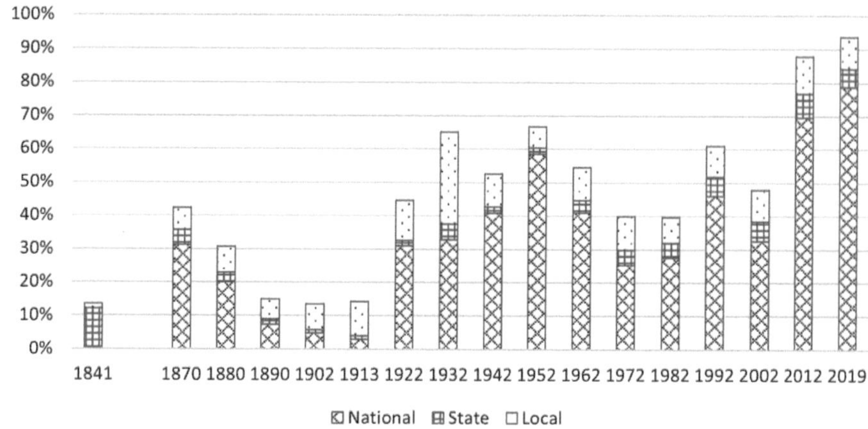

Figure 2.1 National, State, and Local Public Debt as a Percent of GDP in the United States, 1841–2019. *Sources*: Wallis (2000) and US Census Bureau (2018) for debt data, Officer and Williamson (2018) for inflation-adjustment, and Johnston and Williamson (2021) for GDP. National debt only includes debt held by the public.

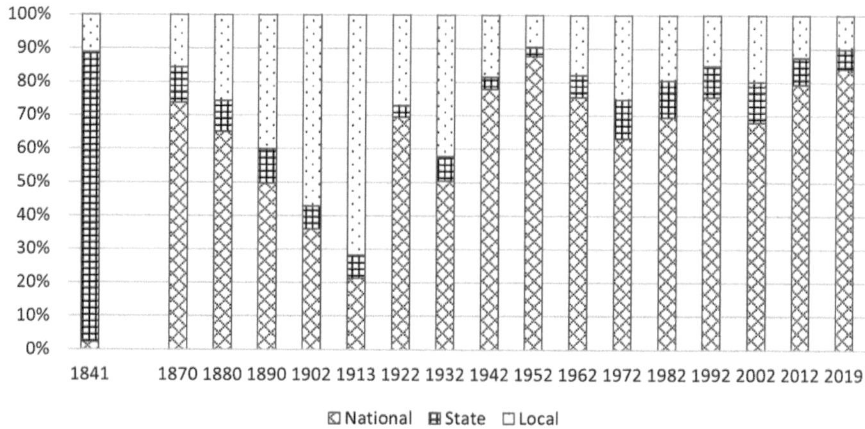

Figure 2.2 National, State, and Local Public Debt as a Share of Public Debt in the United States, 1841–2019. *Sources*: Wallis (2000) and US Census Bureau (2018) for debt data, Officer and Williamson (2018) for inflation-adjustment, and Johnston and Williamson (2021) for GDP. National debt only includes debt held by the public.

War of 1812. Following the War of 1812, the federal government slowly paid down its debt until it was largely paid off in 1834. But as the federal government paid off its debt, state and local governments began to accumulate debt for a variety of projects, such as internal improvements, or infrastructure in modern terminology (roads, canals, and later railroads).

By 1841, state debt accounted for 86.5% of all public debt in the United States, and federal debt was negligible, only about 2% of the total. The peak of state debt in 1841 turned into a debt crisis. At the time, half the union struggled with debt. Of the 26 states, eight defaulted on their debts (along with one territory) and an additional three states barely avoided default.

By 1870, the trend had reversed. The federal government had issued war bonds to finance the Civil War, making it the dominant borrower in the United States, with about three-quarters of the debt. State-level debt declined to just 10% of total public debt. However, this was not because state debt shrunk. On the contrary, in inflation-adjusted terms, it was slightly larger than 1841, though after accounting for population growth it was about half of what it was in 1841.

As detailed below the 1870s saw another wave of debt sweep the nation, with 10 states defaulting (though there were now close to 40 states). There was also the first wave of local debt default in U.S. history, with 159 localities, mostly cities and counties, defaulting in that decade (in the 1840s just four localities did). The defaulting states were concentrated in the South, and they were of a much different nature than the 1840s defaults, as post-Reconstruction Southern states repudiated debts incurred by their Reconstruction governments. Despite having different causes from the debt defaults in the 1840s, the result was similar, with many Southern states amending their constitutions to put further restrictions on debt limits. These 1870s defaults are also closely tied with post–Civil War politics, as well as the repudiation of the debts of the Confederate States incurred during the Civil War. A wave of defaults followed passage of the Fourteenth Amendment to the U.S. Constitution in 1868, although most states repudiated earlier upon reentering the Union (Ratchford 1941, 159–61).

Local debt defaults continued in the decades between 1880 and the Great Depression, with an average of 145 defaults per decade and a high of 258 in the 1890s (Advisory Commission on Intergovernmental Relations 1973). These local defaults were nothing compared with the 1930s when 4,770 local debt defaults occurred. Unlike earlier defaults, over 60% of these local defaults were school districts and "other" districts (such as road building or levee construction districts), rather than cities or counties. In addition, four states were also in serious debt problems, though only one, Arkansas, ultimately defaulted on its debt.

Since the Great Depression and World War II, federal debt has clearly come to be the dominant form of debt, now comprising over three-quarters of all public debt. But this does not mean that state and local debt have disappeared. As a percentage of GDP, state debt in recent years is near its all-time highs, excluding the 1840s debt crisis. Similarly, local debt is also near all-time highs as a percentage of GDP, once again excluding the major local debt crisis of the Great Depression.

None of this is to say that state and local governments are on the verge of another debt crisis. Debt crises have always been the product of particular circumstances, as opposed to a simple relationship between debt and revenue. Rather, I bring this up to suggest that while a variety of restrictions on debt have been imposed over the years, governments have still found ways to incur debt as a part of financing overall spending. I explore this theme further below, asking whether the substance or merely the form of state and local debt has changed.

STATE DEBT DEFAULTS IN THE 1840S

The first major wave of state debt defaults occurred in the 1840s. The causes of the debt crisis are still debated, though the aftermath of the Panic of 1837 is often cited and is surely part of the explanation (English 1996). Sylla and Wallis (1998) do not doubt the impact of the Panic of 1837, but they point to variation in state revenue mechanisms as a proximate cause of default. In short, states that had a stable source of revenue, such as a general property tax, were able to weather the crisis without defaulting. States that relied primarily on asset finance, such as revenues from tolls and canals, saw large drops in revenue following the Panic of 1837 and were the states that eventually defaulted (Wallis 2000). Furthermore, the defaulting states only were able to resume debt payments once they adopted a property tax.

Tables 2.1 and 2.2 provide a sketch of the relevant history for both states that defaulted and those that did not, and whether they made any constitutional changes in the years following the crisis. As table 2.2 makes clear, many states that did not default on their debt, including several new states, chose to put restrictions on debt issue. Even though they had not suffered the consequences of a default, they saw the trouble other states got into and chose to tie their own hands as well.

CASE STUDIES

Maryland

Maryland defaulted on its debt in 1842, but by 1848 had resumed payments as it started to receive revenue from a newly implemented property tax (Sylla and Wallis 1998). When Maryland drafted a new constitution in 1851, it introduced several restrictions on issuing debt. These restrictions are primarily found in Article III, Sec. 22 of Maryland's 1851 constitution. The restrictions

Table 2.1 States Defaulting on Debt, 1841–1842

State	*Default*	*Resolution*	*New or Amend Constitution*	*Debt Restrictions?*
Florida (terr.)	Jan 1841	Repudiated Feb 1842	n/a	N
Louisiana	Feb 1843	Resumed 1844, eventually repudiated	1845	Y
Maryland	Jan 1842	Resumed Jul 1848	1851	Y
Illinois	Jan 1842	Resumed Jul 1846	1848	Y
Arkansas	Jul 1841	Resumed 1869, repudiated part 1884	1846	N
Michigan	Jul 1841	Resumed 1846, repudiated part 1849	1850	Y
Pennsylvania	Aug 1842	Resumed Feb 1845	1857	Y
Mississippi	Mar 1841	Repudiated Feb 1842	n/a	N
Indiana	Jan 1841	Resumed Jul 1847	1851	Y

Sources: Wallis, Sylla, and Grinath (2004), Wallis (2005), and state constitutions.

Table 2.2 Non-Defaulting States and Constitutional Changes

State	*New Constitution Year*	*Debt Restrictions?*
Barely Avoided Default		
New York	1846	Y
Ohio	1851	Y
Alabama	n/a	N
No Default		
Kentucky	1850	Y
Rhode Island	1842	Y
New Jersey	1844	Y
New States		
Iowa	1847	Y
California	1849	Y
Wisconsin	1848	Y

Sources: Wallis, Sylla, and Grinath (2004), Wallis (2005), and state constitutions.

prohibited the issuing of debt unless a tax was also authorized to make the interest payments on the debt and to discharge the debt within 15 years.

Maryland also prohibited using the credit of the state to benefit any individual, association, or corporation, and established that the state shall not be involved, in any mode, with the construction of works of internal improvement. The funding of internal improvements with state debt through private corporations, primarily the Chesapeake and Ohio canal and the Baltimore and Ohio Railroad, was the primary reason Maryland had $15 million in state debt at the time of default. At the time this was the second highest debt load in the country in per capita terms among the states (Wallis 2005).

Debt issues related to internal improvements were also important in the defaulting states of Illinois, Michigan, Pennsylvania, and Indiana, as well as states like New York and Ohio that barely avoided default (English 1996). Not only did all of these states add general provisions restricting debt to their constitutions, Michigan, Pennsylvania, and Ohio placed further restrictions on debt to finance internal improvements.

Louisiana

Louisiana followed a similar pattern to Maryland, but with one important difference. Rather than issuing debt to fund canals and railroads, Louisiana's debt was issued almost exclusively to fund banks. Issuing debt for banks was the common thread among states and territories in the South that incurred a significant amount of debt (Florida Territory, Arkansas, Mississippi, and Alabama), unlike the eastern or frontier states. By the 1840s, Louisiana had issued $24 million in debt, the highest in per capita terms among the states, and more than double Maryland's (Wallis 2005).

Louisiana drafted two new constitutions in 1845 and 1851. Both had two major debt-related features. As stated in Title 6, Art. 114 of Louisiana's 1845 constitution, no debt issued shall exceed $100,000. However, an exception was made if there was a specific tax levied to fund both the interest and retirement of the debt, very similar to Maryland. And to emphasize the link between taxation and debt, the Louisiana constitution went further and made clear that the tax "shall be irrepealable until principal and interest are fully paid and discharged." The 1851 constitution further added the provision (in Title 6, Art. 110) that the aggregate amount of debt of the state shall not exceed $8 million, which was one-third of their outstanding debt in the previous crisis.

Other States

Louisiana was the only Southern state to place debt restrictions in its constitution following the defaults in the 1840s. Arkansas, Florida, and Mississippi did not modify their constitutions regarding public debt. Alabama nearly avoided default but also refused to tie its own hands. Most Northern states did establish restrictions on debt. This lack of debt restriction in Southern states would be an ominous warning for the next wave of debt defaults.

REPUDIATION OF CIVIL WAR AND RECONSTRUCTION DEBTS

The Civil War, Reconstruction, and post-Reconstruction periods are the next important period in U.S. history regarding state debt. During the war, Southern states incurred substantial debt to fight for their right to secede from the Union and maintain the institution of slavery. Near the end of the war, these debts totaled around $96 million and were concentrated in the 11 Confederate States. About two-thirds of this Confederate state debt was in the just four states: Alabama, Georgia, Louisiana, and North Carolina (Ratchford 1941, 151). As a comparison, $96 million was about one-third of the total debt that all U.S. states had incurred by the 1840s.

As the Union army began to take control of Southern states in 1864 and early 1865, they set up new provisional governments, usually with new constitutions. In general, we can refer to these governments, constitutions, and debt incurred with the label Reconstruction, even though official Reconstruction legislation from Congress would not come for a few more years.

In addition to the important racial issues, one of the first tasks of the new Reconstruction governments in their new constitutions was to repudiate the debts incurred to fight the war (Ratchford 1941, 159–61). Thus, we could label this period of defaults as *debt repudiation*, as the defaults were not due to an inability to service the debt, but rather that the debt was rejected as illegitimate by the states repudiating it.

During Reconstruction, the newly readmitted states immediately began issuing debt to rebuild their economies. The overwhelming majority of debt issued was for the construction of railroads, though small amounts were issued for other rebuilding purposes, such as levee construction. However, the debt issued was characterized by widespread fraud, with little of the funds being used to construct infrastructure of any sort. Other debt was issued to authorize conversion bonds from pre-war debt, in some cases to repay some of the repudiated debt from the 1840s (Ratchford 1941, 172–76).

By around 1874, total debt in Southern states was around $247 million, up from about $146 million at the beginning of Reconstruction (Ratchford 1941, 183). Around the same time, many states were retaken by Democrats, and Reconstruction governments were overthrown. Once again, a new round of constitution writing and debt repudiation occurred. But importantly, the new state constitutions of the 1870s also frequently included new restrictions on the issuing of debt by the state itself, and in a few cases by local governments.

The pattern of first repudiating Civil War debt upon reentering the Union in the late 1860s, and then further repudiating Reconstruction debt once Democrats retook control in the 1870s, was common across nearly all Southern states. But the precise time at which new debt restrictions were put in place varied. Some states put them in place before they officially repudiated the Reconstruction debts, others waited until after, and a few put no new restrictions in place. The only state with a different history of debt in this period is Virginia, which had to deal with the unique issue of the new state of West Virginia, carved out of Virginia during the Civil War, and how Virginia's pre-war debts should be apportioned to West Virginia.

CASE STUDIES

Georgia

Georgia incurred one of the largest Civil War debt totals, second only to North Carolina. By the end of the war, Georgia had accumulated over $18 million (Ratchford 1941, 151). When Georgia's first Reconstruction constitution was drafted in October of 1865, repudiating the Civil War debt was one the main accomplishments, other than the obvious changes of abolishing slavery and repealing the secession ordinance (Ratchford 1941, 160).

Another constitution was drafted and approved in 1868, as official Reconstruction began in earnest and Georgia was readmitted to the Union. The 1868 constitution did include one important restriction on the issuing of public debt. Article 3, Sec. 5 of the 1868 Georgia constitution prevented the state from using its credit to aid any private company unless "the whole property of the company shall be bound for the security of the State."

After repudiating its $18 million Civil War debt, Georgia was left with about $2.8 million in other legitimate debts from before the war. By 1868 this had grown to $6.5 million, and despite the restriction mentioned above in the 1868 constitution, the debt further grew to $18 million by the end of Reconstruction (Ratchford 1941, 183).

The majority of the debt in Georgia was issued for the construction of railroads. In just the first three legislative sessions under the 1868 constitution, over $8 million in bonds were issued by the state for the construction of over thirty different railroads (Scott 1969, 98–99). While legislation required that railroads complete 20-mile sections before bonds would be issued, the governor often issued bonds before any construction began, and in many cases, it never began (Ratchford 1941, 173). This pattern of issuing bonds for companies that never constructed much of anything was characteristic of the fraud across the South in this period.

In 1872, Democratic control of the legislature effectively ended Reconstruction. The legislature recognized that many of the bond issues were fraudulent, and some of the debt was repudiated (Scott 1893, 100). However, the issuing of new debt continued until all the debt was repudiated in May of

1877 (Scott 1893, 105–106). With federal Reconstruction officially ending in 1877, Georgia drafted yet another new constitution. It contained several important provisions restricting public debt. Article VII, Sec. III specified that the state could only issue debt for a very limited number of purposes: short-term revenue deficiencies (not to exceed $200,000); defense of the state; and to pay existing public debt (those that had not been repudiated, of course). Article VII, Sec. VII placed a number of restrictions on the issuing of debt by local governments (not to exceed 7% of the assessed value of taxable property), and Section VIII of the same article prohibited the state from assuming any local debts unless incurred for defensive purposes. Georgia owned many railroad assets and, in light of the numerous defaults by railroads, it amended Article VII, Sec. XIII of the constitution to require that any proceeds from selling railroads be applied to the public debt.

South Carolina

South Carolina's sequence of constitution writing and rewriting was similar to Georgia's. Upon secession from the Union, a constitution was ratified in 1861, but this constitution contained no provisions limiting public debt. By the end of the war, South Carolina had accrued about $2.8 million in debt, on the low end among the Confederate states (Ratchford 1941, 151). After the war, South Carolina's first Reconstruction constitution was adopted in 1865. This constitution contained no provisions regarding public debt and did not yet officially repudiate the Civil War debts.

It was not until the 1868 constitution that South Carolina would repudiate its Civil War debt and limit the issue of public debt (Ratchford 1941, 160). By 1868, South Carolina had accumulated $5.8 million in debt, but the bulk of this was debt from before the Civil War, and thus it was still valid. The most notable debt limit in the 1868 constitution was in Article 9, Sec. 7, which allowed the state to issue debt provided that a tax was levied to pay the interest on the debt.

South Carolina proceeded to accrue massive public debt. The debt was issued for so many different purposes, and so much fraud was involved, that there was dispute at the time and among historians as to exactly how much debt existed. One state public debt historian (Ratchford 1941, 182) claimed the correct figure was $23 million, though a state committee found a total of $29 million (Scott 1893, 85), and one contemporary historian put the figure as high as $33 million (Pike 1874, 130).

The exact figure for South Carolina debt is not important for my analysis, but the widespread disagreement shows the extent of debt issued, and the confusion and resulting potential for fraud. Scott (1893, 79–82) lists nine distinct functions for which the debt was issued between 1868 and 1871. These functions included paying interest on previous debt, funding the state bank, aid to private railroad companies, the establishment of a land commission, and various conversion bonds. Despite reassurances from the state legislature in 1872 that all the debt was valid, later that year the governor announced that the interest due could not be paid.

South Carolina remained under the Republican Reconstruction regime until 1877, but by 1873 they saw the need to remedy their self-imposed debt troubles. The legislature attempted to put the debt on solid footing by consolidating all debt into a single issue of bonds, though this was only at 50% of par value, and much of it would be repudiated a few years later under the post-Reconstruction government.

But most important, in 1873, was a constitutional amendment, the first since the constitution was ratified in 1868. The new Article 16 of the constitution prohibited the state from issuing any new debt unless voters approved it by a two-thirds supermajority. When the new Democratic regime wrote a new constitution in 1895, they maintained this restriction on debt and the two-thirds vote of the people requirement (Article X, Sec. 11 of the 1895 South Carolina constitution); these provisions remained in place until a 1977 amendment introduced some significant changes.

Other States

In the midst of the multiple debt repudiations following the Civil War and Reconstruction, most Southern states placed new constitutional restrictions on debt issue. In 1868, North Carolina wrote a new constitution which required popular votes for local debt (Article 7, Sec. 7) and for extending state credit to private corporations (Article 5, Sec. 5), as well as requiring a tax funding any new debt until all old debt had been paid off. The 1868 constitution in North Carolina was the governing document in the state until 1971.

Alabama's 1867 constitution required a two-thirds vote of the legislature for most new debt, including extending the state's credit to any private entities (Article IV, Sec. 32). When Alabama wrote a new constitution in 1875, it prohibited all new debt, except for defense of the state; it maintained the two-thirds vote of the legislature (Article XI, Sec. 3), which was also maintained in the 1901 constitution and is still in force today.

The 1866 Texas constitution established a two-thirds requirement for the legislature to assume new debt (Article VII, Sec. 33), but it also empowered the legislature to guarantee railroad company bonds (also with a two-thirds requirement, Article VII, Sec. 36). The 1869 constitution dropped the two-thirds requirement, the power to guarantee railroad debt, and said the state or counties must create "adequate means for the payment" of any debt incurred (Article 12, Sec. 23). The 1876 Texas constitution finally placed strong restrictions on state debt. No debt could be created except for limited purposes, such as repaying old debt and defensive purposes (Article III, Sec. 49). These strong restrictions were in place until a 1991 constitutional amendment.

Florida had defaulted on its debt as a territory in 1841 but did not put any restrictions on debt following that episode. But following the post–Civil War defaults, Florida's 1875 constitution forbade the state from issuing any bonds, except for defensive purposes or redeeming old debt at a lower interest rate (Article IX, Sec. 6). Further the state could not use tax revenue to pay the debt of private chartered companies (Article IX, Sec. 7).

Tennessee adopted a new constitution in 1870, and it contained a few restrictions on debt, but none strongly restricting state debt. Article II, Sec. 31 prohibited the state from extending its credit to any private entities or municipalities. Article II, Sec. 33 also prohibited the state from issuing any bonds to railroad companies if those companies were in default on any previous bonds.

Most important among the Southern states, however, is one state that did not place strong restrictions on debt: Arkansas. The 1874 constitution of Arkansas did place very tight restrictions on local debt, both prohibiting the issue of local debt in most cases (Article XVI, Sec. 1) and prohibiting the state from assuming local debt (Article XII, Sec. 12). But as we will see in the following section, the prohibition on local debt was significantly relaxed in the 1920s, and the state mostly ignored the prohibition on assuming local debt. One constitutional amendment in Arkansas from this period is notable: an 1884 amendment to their 1874 constitution which repudiated a large part of the state's debt, including some pre–Civil War debts.

DEFAULTS DURING THE GREAT DEPRESSION

As the decades passed between the first two waves of defaults and the Great Depression, an important change to public debt occurred across the United States: a shift from state debt to local debt. By 1870, local debt of cities, counties, and special taxing districts, such as school districts, was already larger than state debt: In that year there was $516 million in local debt and $352 million in state debt.

Up to 1913, state debt remained roughly constant, while local debt exploded to over $4 billion, more than 10 times state debt and 72% of all public debt in the United States, including federal debt (Wallis 2000). Federal debt would of course grow significantly during World War I, but by 1932 local debt was still over 42% of the total, not due to a shrinking of local debt in the aggregate, but due to growth in the federal debt. State debt was comparatively small, such that roughly half of public debt was at the state and local level.

Along with mounting local debt came more local debt defaults. Before the 1870s, local defaults were virtually unknown. However, between the 1870s and 1890s, local defaults became more common, rising from 159 in the

1870s to 258 in the 1890s. But the massive buildup of local debt in the 1920s (roughly doubling in the aggregate) and the onset of the Great Depression made the 1930s by far the worst decade for local debt defaults, with an estimated 4,770 (Advisory Commission on Intergovernmental Relations 1973).

In some sense, it could be said that the restrictions of state debt worked too well. While states tied their own hands regarding debt issue, they largely left local governments free to incur debt. As discussed above, this was not universally true. For example, Georgia and a few other states did place some limitations on the issuing of local debt and prohibited the state from assuming local debt. Arkansas also placed restrictions on local debt, but as will be seen in the case study below, it often ignored those provisions and further amended their constitution to allow local governments to borrow under certain conditions.

As an example, the strong Florida constitutional restrictions discussed in the previous section certainly limited public debt. Florida, along with Nebraska, had virtually no outstanding debt in the 1920s and 1930s. But this obscured an important change: cities, counties, and special districts had accumulated $532 million in debt by 1932. In inflation-adjusted terms, local debt in Florida alone was 40% greater than all the state debts in 1870. By 1932, Florida's $338 per capita was the highest in the country, followed by New Jersey ($279 per capita), New York ($271 per capita), Oregon ($205 per capita), Wyoming ($187 per capita), and California ($186 per capita). For those high-local-debt states, around 85% or more of the debt was at the local level (US Census Bureau 1935).

Because only one state, Arkansas, defaulted during the Great Depression, it is the only state I will use as a case study. In terms of total debt, Arkansas was typical; with $137 in per capita debt in 1932, it was almost exactly at the national aggregate of $141 in per capita debt (U.S. Census Bureau 1935). Arkansas was also typical in how the debt was used, primarily to fund local infrastructure, such as roads and bridges. But Arkansas was the only state to default on its debt during the Great Depression, making it atypical in that sense, and Arkansas's debt started at the local level but was later assumed by the state. By contrast, Tennessee is a good example of a state that mismanaged its debt but was still able to avoid default.

THE TWENTIETH CENTURY DEFAULTS AND THEIR CONSEQUENCES

Arkansas

Arkansas was no stranger to debt defaults. Having defaulted on its debt in 1841, Arkansas made no constitutional changes to limit future debt. Like most Southern states, it defaulted on both its Civil War and Reconstruction debts. Constitutional changes were made in this period, mostly related to the issuing of local debt. The poor credit rating from three defaults in four decades probably also served as a limit to much state borrowing. By the early twentieth century, Arkansas's state debt was down to around $1 million dollars, from highs of over $8 million in the late nineteenth century.

Arkansas's restriction on the issuing of local debt in its 1874 constitution prevented counties, cities, towns, and other municipalities from issuing debt. To get around this prohibition, in the early twentieth century the legislature began approving special improvement districts for the construction of roads in the state. In 1915 the legislature passed the Alexander Road Law which provided a general procedure for creating these local improvement districts, 120 of which had been created by the following year. Another 312 improvement districts were created by special acts through 1920 (Ratchford 1941, 383–85).

The 1920s saw several important changes leading to an eventual debt crisis. First, a 1926 amendment to the constitution allowed city governments to issue debt if approved by voters for a wide variety of purposes, such as roads, sewers, firefighting, public parks, and many other local services (Amendment 13, changing Article XVI, Sec. 1). Next, with many of the road improvement districts in distress, the legislature passed the Martineau Act in 1927, which gave the state the authority to assume over $70 million in local debt (again, despite constitutional prohibitions to doing so). Additional debt was issued by the state to fund highways as well as Confederate pensions, meaning that the state now had over $120 million in debt (Ratchford 1941, 386–87), which would further grow to $164 million by 1932 (US Census Bureau 1935).

As tax revenues declined across the nation with the onset of the Great Depression, Arkansas's available revenue fell from about $22.5 million in 1930 to about $16 million two years later. About half of the decline came in the highway fund, with gasoline and auto license taxes declining by about $3.5 million between 1930 and 1932 (Ratchford 1941, 392–93). By August of 1932, the state of Arkansas defaulted on some payments, and in March 1933 it defaulted on all highway bonds. No payments were made again until 1935, and these were made at a significantly reduced interest rate as the old debt was reissued as new debt with a lower, 3% rate (Ratchford 1941, 394–95).

The most interesting outcomes from our perspective are the constitutional changes that followed the default. Voters approved two important amendments to the constitution in 1934. Amendment 19 dealt with taxes and spending, requiring a three-fourths vote of the legislature (or a majority of voters) to increase any of the taxes in existence at the time and to pass spending bills. Amendment 20 to the Arkansas constitution put strong restrictions on the issuing of debt. Except for refunding old debt and for assuming road district bonds, Amendment 20 prohibited the state from issuing any bonds "for any purpose whatsoever" unless approved by voters. These two amendments taken together limited both the debt that Arkansas could issue and the means to raise revenue to pay for debts and other purposes.

Arkansas's tight restrictions on debt would be loosened to some extent in subsequent years. In 1984 voters approved constitutional Amendment 62, which allowed cities and counties to issue bonds for capital improvements if approved by voters. Two years later in 1986 voters approved another change in Amendment 67 that allowed local governments to issue revenue bonds for capital improvements without a vote of the people in most cases. Then in 2004 voters loosened the restrictions on state debt with Amendment 82, allowing the state to issue bonds to pay for infrastructure for large economic development projects. And in 2016, voters approved a constitutional amendment overhauling the requirements for both the Amendment 62 local bonds and the Amendment 82 state bonds, in both cases making it easier to issue them and to issue them for more purposes than originally defined.

Other States

While no other states defaulted on their debt in the Great Depression, there were widespread concerns with local defaults. Among U.S. regions, only the New England states were spared from having many local government defaults; they had just seven local defaults in the 1930s. All other regions of the United States had at least 200 defaults, and looking over the long sweep of history from 1839 to 1969, except for New England, each region had at least two-thirds of its local defaults happen in just the 1930s (Advisory Commission on Intergovernmental Relations 1973). While the local debt crisis did not lead to many constitutional changes, states such as Michigan, North Carolina, and New Jersey set up state debt commissions to assist local governments that were in trouble and to monitor local debt issues (Kroll Bond Rating Agency 2011). North Carolina appears to be the only state, other than Arkansas, to modify its constitution with respect to debt in the 1930s. The essential change was Amendment 92, allowing for certain kinds of debt to be permitted if approved by voters (previously the legislature had this power).

Other states had difficulties with state debt, even though none made the same mistake as Arkansas by assuming such a large amount of local debt in such a short amount of time. Ratchford (1941, 407–28) singles out Tennessee as having the most significant issues with state debt during the Depression after Arkansas, though Tennessee did not ultimately default. Kroll Bond Rating Agency (2011) also includes Louisiana, South Carolina, and Texas as states that were also near default, and did experience "technical defaults" which were settled in full within 90 days. For example, Louisiana failed to make a payment in March 1933 as their assets were frozen at the time due to bank runs, but they were back making scheduled payments by May.

Ratchford (1941, 433) summarized the basic debt rules of the states as of 1938 by grouping states into three groups. The major divisions were how debt for most purposes could be issued. The three groups were:

1. 18 states required a vote of the electorate and a constitutional amendment
2. 17 states required a vote of the electorate by referendum (usually a lower bar than an amendment)
3. 13 states left it up to the legislature, and of those states 9 had essentially no quantitative limit

HAVE STATE AND LOCAL GOVERNMENTS CHANGED THEIR BORROWING HABITS?

Experience with debt and default throughout U.S. history have clearly produced changes in state constitutions regarding the issuing of debt. In many cases, states that defaulted or nearly defaulted saw fit to tie their own hands, though this was not universally true. States that did not take the opportunity to restrict debt following a crisis often had a repeat crisis further down the road.

However, constitutional restrictions on state debt proved to be an imperfect solution. States shifted to locally issued debt at the dawn of the twentieth century to fulfill many of the same functions that state debt had served in the nineteenth century, primarily financing of internal improvements, infrastructure, public education, and other economic development projects. In fact, if we go back even further in history to the buildup of state debt in the 1830s, one might attribute it to unwillingness of the Jackson administration to fund internal improvements and Jackson's insistence on paying off the national debt. These actions led states to take up the reins of debt and development projects.

What is next for public debt in the United States? The national debt continues to increase, though this is primarily to fund consumption and transfer programs rather than infrastructure. If we look back at figure 2.1, we will see that despite limits placed on state and local debt over the years, state debt today is at essentially its highest level as a percent of GDP since the 1840s, and the combination of state and local debt is higher than any time other than the Great Depression.

State and local governments have indeed continued to use debt to finance activities. In some cases, the debt may be contracted on a much sounder basis, possibly lowering the future risk of default. State budgets are also much larger today than in the past, meaning that there is more slack in the budget, and if states run into financial difficulties they have plenty of other functions to cut back on before incurring debt.

Still, one could speculate about the next evolution in public debt. The next evolution may already be here with unfunded liabilities, such as state pension plans. While estimates of the size of the unfunded liabilities vary, depending on the assumptions about future economic growth, market returns, and demographics, but the number is probably somewhere between $1.4 trillion (Pew Charitable Trusts 2018) and $6 trillion (American Legislative Exchange Council 2017). Whatever the true number, unfunded pension liabilities are certainly comparable to state or local debts in size, and possibly double the two combined.

Of course, unfunded pension liabilities are not the same thing as public bonds, but they do share many similar features. They are promises to pay future funds in exchange for some present consideration, money in the case of bonds and labor services in the case of pensions. In seven states, pensions have constitutional protections, and in most other states they are treated as either contracts or property (only two states, Indiana and Texas, have essentially no legal protections for pensions). Thus pensions have legal status that is similar to bonds in many states (Munnell and Quinby 2012).

It is also likely that state public debt will evolve in some ways we cannot foresee right now, and that it will happen following some critical turning point in history. The wave of debt defaults in the 1840s followed one of the worst economic downturns in the antebellum period, the Panic of 1837. The destruction and turmoil of the Civil War produced the next wave of defaults. And finally, the Great Depression was the catalyst for knocking down the massive local debts.

While history cannot tell us when or if another debt crisis will occur, it does strongly suggest that it will be followed by a new round of constitutional reforms that will change the form of public debt, though perhaps pushing into another sphere rather than diminishing its importance.

NOTE

1. The number of defaults through 1969 are reported by the Advisory Commission on Intergovernmental Relations (1973), and the post-1969 data comes from Moody's (2017).

REFERENCES

Advisory Commission on Intergovernmental Relations. "City Financial Emergencies: The Intergovernmental Division." 1973.

American Legislative Exchange Council. *Unaccountable and Unaffordable 2017*. 2017. https://www.alec.org/app/uploads/2017/12/2017-Unaccountable-and-Unaffordable-FINAL_DEC_WEB.pdf.

English, William B. "Understanding the Costs of Sovereign Default: American State Debts in the 1840's." *The American Economic Review* (1996): 259–75.

Johnston, Louis, and Samuel H. Williamson. "What Was the U.S. GDP Then?" MeasuringWorth, 2021, https://www.measuringworth.com/datasets/usgdp/.

Kroll Bond Rating Agency. "An Analysis of Historical Municipal Bond Defaults: Lessons Learned—The Past as Prologue." 2011.

Moody's Investors Service. "US Municipal Bond Defaults and Recoveries, 1970–2016." 2017.

Munnell, Alicia H. and Laura Quinby. "Legal Constraints on Changes in State and Local Pensions." Center for Retirement Research at Boston College, 2012. http://crr.bc.edu/wp-content/uploads/2012/08/slp_25.pdf.

National Conference of State Legislatures. "State Balanced Budget Provisions." 2010. http://www.ncsl.org/documents/fiscal/StateBalancedBudgetProvisions2010.pdf.

Officer, Lawrence H., and Samuel H. Williamson. "The Annual Consumer Price Index for the United States, 1774–Present." MeasuringWorth, 2021. http://www.measuringworth.com/uscpi/.

Pew Charitable Trusts. "The State Pension Funding Gap: 2016." 2018. https://www.pewtrusts.org/-/media/assets/2018/04/state_pensions_funding_gap_2016_final.pdf.

Pike, James Shepherd. *The prostrate state: South Carolina under Negro Government.* D. Appleton and Company, 1874.

Ratchford, Benjamin Ulysses. *American State Debts.* Duke University Press, 1941.

Scott, William Amasa. *The Repudiation of State Debts: A Study in the Financial History of Mississippi, Florida, Alabama, North Carolina, South Carolina, Georgia, Lousisiana, Arkansas, Tennessee, Minnesota, Michigan, and Virginia.* No. 2. TY Crowell & Company, 1893.

U.S. Census Bureau. "Financial Statistics of State and Local Governments: 1932." 1935.

U.S. Census Bureau. "2019 State & Local Government Finance Historical Datasets and Tables." 2022. https://www.census.gov/data/datasets/2019/econ/local/public-use-datasets.html.

U.S. Treasury Department. "Debt to the Penny." 2022. https://fiscaldata.treasury.gov/datasets/debt-to-the-penny/debt-to-the-penny.

Wallis, John Joseph. "American Government Finance in the Long Run: 1790 to 1990." *Journal of Economic Perspectives* 14, no. 1 (2000): 61–82.

Wallis, John Joseph. "Constitutions, Corporations, and Corruption: American States and Constitutional Change, 1842 to 1852." *The Journal of Economic History* 65, no. 1 (2005): 211–56.

Wallis, John Joseph, Richard Sylla, and Arthur Grinath III. "Sovereign Debt and Repudiation: The Emerging-Market Debt Crisis in the US States, 1839–1843." National Bureau of Economic Research working paper 10753, 2004.

Chapter 3

Pension Liability Stress for State Governments

Thomas Savidge

INTRODUCTION

This chapter explores the role that public pensions play in the growth of state government spending. Most states provide defined-benefit pensions that are not adequately funded or managed by state governments. Poor funding and management have contributed to unfunded pension liabilities reaching nearly $5 trillion in FY 2018. In many states (such as Illinois), these benefits are constitutionally guaranteed, and spending on these retirement payments represents a fixed cost. The more state governments spend on pensions, the less funds are available for essential government services, infrastructure, or opportunities for tax cuts. Fortunately, states such as Wisconsin, Michigan, Maine, and Tennessee offer comprehensive reform solutions to the pension liability stress.

The first section of this chapter discusses the structure of the defined-benefit pension plan, which is the most common type of public pension plan in the United States. The second section discusses how government accounting changes have created transparency and provided a more accurate picture of pension liabilities. The third section shows the differences in risk levels between pension assets and liabilities and then argues why lower discount rates are the best measurement for pension liabilities because they reflect a state's inability to default on pension promises. The fourth section examines public pension liabilities in the United States utilizing data collected by the American Legislative Exchange Council for its annual pension report. The fifth section examines cases of states enacting successful reforms for their respective pension systems. The sixth section concludes with additional recommendations for pension reform.

PUBLIC PENSIONS STRUCTURE: DEFINED BENEFIT PLANS

Most pension plans deliver a defined benefit. In a defined benefit plan, employees (in the case of public pension plans, state workers) and employers (in the case of public pension plans, state governments) contribute funds during the employees' time at work and a specified amount of monthly retirement income is provided to the employee upon retirement. The key elements of the formula underlying the retirement payment include the employee's salary, years of work, age,[1] how long the retiree has been in the public sector, and their final average compensation at retirement. The formula is usually something like this:

$$\textit{Annual Retirement Benefit} = \textit{Benefit Multiplier} \times \textit{Years of Service} \times \textit{Final Average Salary} \quad (1)$$

Dividing the annual retirement benefit by 12 determines how much is paid per month.

Generally, the normal cost (the projected cost to pre-fund retirement promises during the years an employee works) is paid for by employee and employer contributions. Most pension plans are not fully funded. The promised pension benefits that are not covered by plan assets are paid for by the employer and taxpayers (unless the plan is cost sharing, where employees cover these payments as well).

Each year, state governments should make an Actuarially Determined Contribution (ADC). The ADC (previously known as the annual required contribution or ARC) consists of the normal cost and the amortization payment (a catch-up payment for any unfunded liabilities over the past 30 years).[2] If a plan is consistently making 100% of its ADC payments, it is better able to adjust to fluctuating variables (i.e., cost of living adjustments and life expectancy) and pay off its unfunded liabilities in a timely manner.

Illinois has the second largest unfunded pension liabilities in the country at $359 billion—only California has greater unfunded liabilities—and the third largest unfunded liabilities per capita at $28,220 per resident, after Connecticut and Alaska. This is, in part, due to Illinois's pension contributions failing to meet the ADC due to Public Acts 100-0023 and 100-0340 having used a methodology that does not conform with ADC calculation methods set by GASB. Illinois plans always make payments based upon the state statutes and not the ADC.[3] Table 3.1 has been re-created from the American Legislative Exchange Council annual report on public pensions with permission from the authors. Table 3.1 highlights ADC payments for the pension plans in the state of Illinois for fiscal year 2018 (June 30, 2017–July 1, 2018).

Table 3.1 ADC Schedule of Payments for Illinois State Plans

Plan	*ADC*	*ADC Paid*	*Percent ADC Paid*
Illinois General Assembly Retirement System	$32,084,644.00	$21,155,000.00	65.93%
Illinois Judges Retirement System	$168,056,916.00	$135,962,000.00	80.90%
Illinois Municipal Retirement Fund	$947,568,823.00	$947,568,823.00	100.00%
Illinois State Employees Retirement System	$2,739,377,709.00	$1,929,175,044.00	70.42%
Illinois Teachers Retirement System	$7,080,756.00	$4,178,650.00	59.01%
Illinois University Retirement System	$1,862,033.00	$1,607,880.00	86.35%

Source: Williams, Jonathan, et al. *Unaccountable and Unaffordable 2019*. American Legislative Exchange Council. 2020.

The one notable exception, the Illinois MRF (which uses ADC methodology to determine the required contribution), has the highest funding ratio of Illinois plans (a lowly 48.80%) and still has nearly $43 billion in unfunded liabilities. After years of not making the required contributions, liabilities have piled up, making Illinois's plans some of the worst funded pension plans in the country, with nearly $360 billion in unfunded pension liabilities.[4]

Public pension plans have been grossly underfunded, and recent changes in pension reporting (as highlighted in the next section) have shown how poor the funding situation usually is. Generally, pensions are underfunded due to a combination of four major reasons:

1. Intentional underfunding: State policymakers have decided not to pay enough into the fund to meet future obligations, creating debt for future generations. As states fail to make necessary contributions but continue to promise the same benefit payouts, the burden of unfunded liabilities is placed on future generations.

2. Poor management: Overly optimistic investment return goals, open amortization schedules, outdated or unclear actuarial assumptions, and politicized pension boards are just some examples of the mismanagement of pension plans. As will be discussed later, pension plans have drastically increased the risk in their asset portfolios, and investment returns have become increasingly volatile. Later sections will discuss how pension board governance structures relate to investment performance.
3. Market conditions and volatility: Recessions, the long-term decline in interest rates, and pension systems' vulnerability to unexpected market losses are the key market conditions that pension plans must contend with.
4. Benefit design issues: Plans sometimes allow retirees to double-dip (receive two pensions). Recall equation (1) is partially based on the final average salary. In some cases, employees will "spike" their pensions, which is to use raises and bonuses to increase their final average salary, thus increasing their overall annual retirement benefit.

Unfunded pension liabilities totaled anywhere between $1.2–$4.9 trillion for fiscal year 2018.[5] This number varies due to the various discount rates used to estimate the present value of unfunded liabilities. As mentioned above and in the following sections, the discount rate is used to determine the present value of liabilities. As will be recommended and explained, pension plans should use a lower discount rate to determine the value of unfunded liabilities.

CHANGES IN PENSION REPORTING WITH GASB 67 AND 68

State governments have experienced increased pressure in their balance sheets from growing pension liabilities. This pressure is becoming more apparent with improved financial reporting. The Governmental Accounting Standards Board (GASB) statements 67 and 68 went into effect in FY 2014 and 2015, respectively. These statements focus on how pension plans measure assets and liabilities.

The changes declared in GASB 67 require plan assets to be valued each year so pension trustees cannot engage in "asset smoothing." Asset smoothing is a process by which pension investment performance is averaged over a five-year period to "smooth out" swings in market performance. As noted by pension scholars Eileen Norcross and Sheila Weinberg, asset smoothing evens out investment swings and provides plan sponsors with predictability in annual contributions, but simultaneously hides the volatility of pension asset portfolios.[6] Under GASB 67, pension plan officials must provide an actuarial value of assets (AVAs) for that given year, however. This chapter's analysis uses the AVA that is reported in state pension plan actuarial valuations each year.

Under GASB 68, state and local governments were now obligated to report unfunded pension liabilities on state balance sheets as opposed to just the ADC. Norcross and Weinberg also note that under GASB 68, however, state governments can continue a form of asset smoothing. Governments are permitted to defer the recognition of the difference between the return expected on plan assets and the actual return, with this "deferred inflow of resources" occurring over a five-year period. This is the same as asset smoothing, which permits the sponsor to gradually incorporate any changes to the market value of assets that differ from the expected value of assets over time. They note, "The consequences of this practice remain the same [as the consequences of asset smoothing]. Market declines and gains are only gradually recognized, likely increasing the riskiness of sponsor behavior."[7]

The new information required by GASB 67 and 68 is reported in the "Required Supplementary Information" section at the end of each state's comprehensive annual financial report (CAFR) and in actuarial valuation documents for each pension plan. These notes include breakdown of the ADCs, asset valuations, and Fiduciary Net Positions for all pension plans; how the pension plan discount rate is calculated; and information about liability valuations. The net pension liability is shown in equation (2) below:

$$\begin{aligned} Net\ Pension\ Liability &= Actuarial\ Value\ of\ Assets \\ &\quad - Actuarially\ Accrued\ Liabilities \end{aligned} \tag{2}$$

If the value of the Actuarially Accrued Liabilities is greater than the AVAs, the Net Pension Liability will show that there are unfunded pension liabilities. Another important measure of the health of a defined benefit pension plan is the plan's funding ratio. That is expressed in equation 3 below:

$$Funding\ Ratio = \frac{Actuarial\ Value\ of\ Assets}{Actuarial\ Accrued\ Liabilities} \tag{3}$$

The larger the value of liabilities, the lower the funding ratio, and the less "healthy" a defined benefit pension plan. As recommended by the American Academy of Actuaries, plans should strive for a 100% funding ratio or greater.[8] Keeping a pension funding ratio at 100% can be costly. Several states have found solutions and alternatives to unfunded pension liabilities. These states are discussed in "Case Studies for Reform."

Improved reporting and more accurate estimates of state obligations have shed light on the actual value of unfunded pension liabilities. GASB 67 also provided guidance on how liabilities were to be valued. Prior to GASB 67, public pension plans used the expected return on pension assets to assess the value of liabilities. Economists objected to this valuation, stating that legally guaranteed pension promises should be valued with a lower discount rate, as will be described in detail in the next section. Weinberg and Norcross note that GASB 67 attempts to split the difference by valuing liabilities that are covered by pension assets with a higher discount rate and unfunded liabilities with a lower discount rate based on the low-risk return on tax-exempt municipal bonds.[9]

Many of the changes in assumptions based on actuarial experience studies conducted in 2016 to comply with the standards of GASB 67 and 68 (i.e., the inflation assumption remains at 2.25%). The changes include drastically lowered discount rates in some states (such as several Wyoming state pension plans lowering the discount rate from 7.75% to 7.00% in FY 2017). Other plans incrementally decreased discount rates (such as the California Public Employee Retirement Multiemployer Fund, which gradually decreased its discount rate from 7.50% in FY 2016, to 7.25% in FY 2017, and then at 7.00% in FY 2018).[10,11]

Assumptions Matters: Rates of Return and Discount Rates

The discount rate is the rate used to determine the present value of liabilities. Although public plans often use the term "discount rate" and "investment rate of return" interchangeably, the two terms refer to two different aspects of a pension plan. Specifically, the investment rate of return is based on a pension plan's portfolio of investment assets and what those investments will earn. It looks at the risk of the plan's investment assets.[12]

For public pensions, there are different risk levels with pension assets and pension liabilities. Over the past four decades, pension asset funds have changed from low-risk, fixed income investments (such as U.S. Treasury bonds) to an increasingly volatile portfolio of stocks, bonds, and alternative investments such as office buildings and golf courses.[13] This is the result of lower bond yields, the desire to chase higher returns, and politicians and plan managers using pension funds to advance their own economic development or political agendas—a perfect storm of bad incentives.

Figure 3.1 below shows the disparity between assumed rates of return (noted by the dotted line) and the actual annual return on investment (noted by the solid line). As pension plans invest in riskier assets, meeting the assumed rate of return for that year becomes less likely. Some years this pays off, and returns exceed expectations, while other years fall far short of assumed returns.

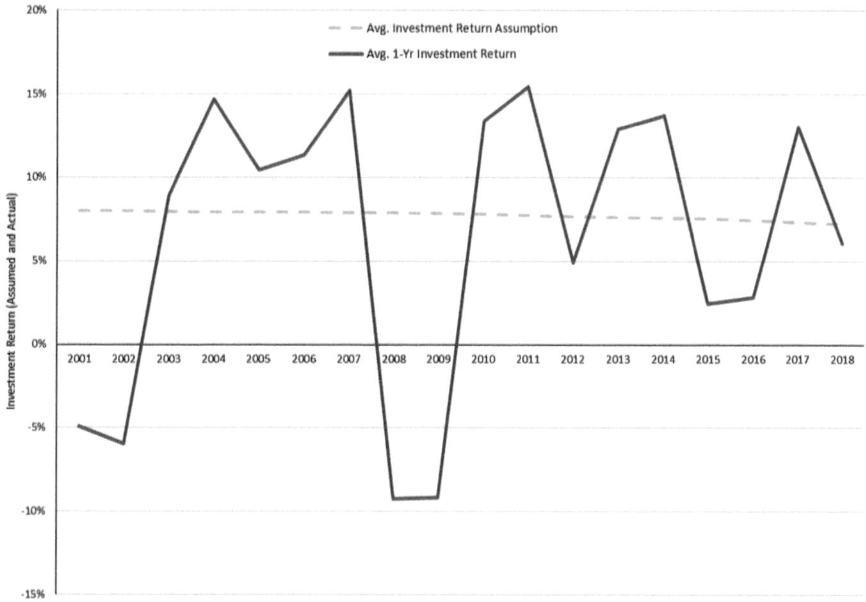

Figure 3.1 Assumed versus Actual Investment Returns, Average of All Public Pension Plans. *Source*: Center for Retirement Research, "Public Plans Data 2001–2018," November 9, 2020.

Average assumed rate of return hovered just below 8% from 2001 to 2007 but steadily declined from 7.99% in 2001 to 7.88% in 2008. That decline continued in 2009 to a lower 7.85% and then steadily declined each year. By 2018, the average assumed rate of return was 7.22%, a 10.7% decline over 18 years. However, as figure 3.1 shows, average actual 1-year returns were much more volatile. During years of recession, investment returns averaged losses of −4.91% in 2001, −6.22% in 2002, −9.49% in 2008, and −9.42% in 2009. Throughout the years measured, 9 of the 18 years measured saw average 1-year investment returns below the average assumed return.

While market conditions contributed to lower funding ratios by lowering the value of assets, the pension crisis is primarily a spending problem that stems from the intentional underfunding of pension plans and the poor management of those plans. The ALEC pension report finds that states with relatively higher tax rates often have *larger* unfunded pension liabilities.[14]

Meanwhile, as stated previously, states are still contractually and constitutionally obligated to pay pension liabilities, so there has been a major divergence between the risk premiums of pension assets and liabilities.

As the Society of Actuaries' Blue-Ribbon Panel on Public Pension Plan funding recommends, "the rate of return assumption should be based primarily on the current risk-free rate plus explicit risk premium or on other similar forward-looking techniques."[15] This is similar to the blended discount rate recommended by GASB.

The most recent example of the inability of states to alter pension payments comes from a ruling in the Illinois State Supreme Court on May 8, 2015. The state of Illinois passed a pension reform in December 2013 that stopped automatic, compounded, yearly cost-of-living increases, extended retirement ages for current state workers, and limited the amount of salary used to calculate pension benefits. Several public-sector unions sued the state of Illinois, and on May 8, 2015, the pension reforms were ruled unconstitutional.[16] After rolling back these pension reforms, unfunded liabilities continued to grow and left Illinois one of the worst funded public pension systems in the United States.

Because U.S. Treasury bonds are insured with the full faith and credit of the U.S. government, the rate of return for these bonds is the best proxy for a risk-free rate. A valuation of liabilities based on a risk-free rate contrasts sharply with the overly optimistic assumptions used by nearly every public-sector pension plan. As economist Joshua Rauh notes:

> The logic of financial economics is very clear that measuring the value of a pension promise requires using the yields on bonds that match the risk and duration of that promise. Therefore, to reflect the present value cost of actually delivering on a benefit promise requires the use of a default-free yield curve, such as the Treasury yield curve. Financial economists have spoken in near unison on this point. The fact that the stock market, whose performance drives that of most pension plan investments, has earned high historical returns does not justify the use of these historical returns as a discount rate for measuring pension liabilities.[17]

For this reason, it is recommended that states use the lower discount rate. In its annual pension report *Unaccountable and Unaffordable*, researchers at the American Legislative Exchange Council use a risk-free rate (based on U.S. treasury bond yields) and a fixed discount rate (4.5%) in comparison to discount rates provided in state financial documents. For the 2019 report, a 15-year midpoint, using a hypothetical 15-year U.S. Treasury Bond yield, is used to derive an estimated risk-free discount rate of 2.96%. This is calculated as the average of the 10-year and 20-year bond yields.[18]

This report uses a more prudent discount rate calculated by averaging 10-year and 20-year U.S. Treasury bond yields to create a hypothetical 15-year bond yield to match the 15-year midpoint of the amortization schedule of pension liabilities. The discount rate calculated from these bond yields is the best proxy for a risk-free rate. The 15-year midpoint comes from GASB noting "the maximum acceptable amortization period [the length of time to pay liabilities] is 30 years," and our assumption that pension plans will take the full 30 years to pay off liabilities.[19]. Research has also shown that the midpoint of the stream of future benefits for a public pension plan is approximately 15 years in the future.[20] Thus the midpoint of the amortization period is used because a lump-sum payment in 15 years can be treated as an approximation of the annual benefit liability owed by the plan.[21]

This methodology was developed by Bob Williams and Andy Biggs when this report was created by State Budget Solutions, which is now a project of the Center State Fiscal Reform at ALEC. It normalizes the liability values across plans and presents a more prudent valuation of liabilities than many state benefits plans with more rosy assumptions (such as higher discount rates). The inclusion of the fixed discount rate of 4.5%, was added by Thurston Powers in *Unaccountable and Unaffordable, 2018.*[22]

Discount rates used for pension plans can vary even among plans within a state. The use of a risk-free discount rate normalizes discount rates across pension plans, providing the means to assess present value of liabilities across plans. This provides a basis of comparison for liabilities and funding ratios across the 50 states. Other variables provided by state financial documents, such as mortality rates, demographics, and health-care costs were assumed to be correct and not normalized across plans.

This is a more prudent discount rate than many plans offer. The formula for calculating a risk-free present value for a liability requires first finding the future value of the liability. That formula, in which "*i*" represents a plan's assumed discount rate, is shown by equation 4[23]:

$$Future\ Value = Actuarial\ Accrued\ Liability \times (1+i)^{15} \qquad (4)$$

The second step is to discount the future value to arrive at the present value of the more reasonably valued liability. That formula is shown in equation 5 below, where "*i*" represents either the risk-free or fixed discount rate[24]:

$$Present\ Value = \frac{Future\ Value}{(1+i)^{15}} \qquad (5)$$

To demonstrate the differences in discount rates, examine the following graphs about three Pennsylvania public pension plans Municipal Retirement Fund (MRF), Public School Employees' Retirement Systems (PSERS), and State Employees' Retirement Systems (SERS) for FY 2018 using various discount rates:

The AVAs is shown on the far left of each chart. Then the chart shows, in appearance from left to right, the present value of liabilities using the

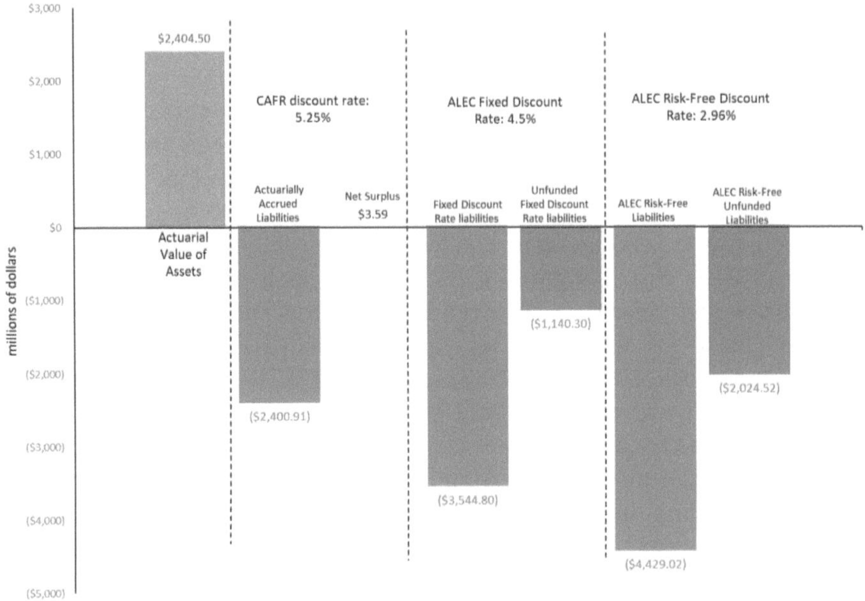

Figure 3.2 Pennsylvania MRF Actuarial Value of Assets and Liabilities. *Source*: Pennsylvania Municipal Retirement System, "Actuarial Valuation as of January 1, 2018," May 2019; Author's calculations.

"blended discount rate" found in the state's CAFR, followed by the present value of liabilities using the ALEC fixed discount rate of 4.5%, and then finally the ALEC FY 2018 risk-free discount rate of 2.96%. All unfunded liabilities are calculated by subtracting the valued liabilities from the AVAs.

Using the blended discount rate, the Pennsylvania MRF shows a net surplus for FY 2018, however, the ALEC fixed and risk-free discount rates show over $1.1 billion and $2 billion in unfunded pension liabilities, respectively. For the PSERS plan, unfunded liabilities are nearly $94 billion under the fixed discount rate and $132 billion under the risk-free discount rate, significantly larger than the $44.9 billion using the state's assumed discount rate of 7.25%. For the SERS plan, unfunded liabilities reach $47.4 billion using the fixed discount rate and $66.5 billion under the risk-free discount rate, far greater than the $22.8 billion using the 7.25% discount rate.

The purpose of these charts is to show that assumptions matter, especially the discount rate. Using lower discount rates do not "add" liabilities, and using higher discount rates do not "take away" liabilities. The discount rate simply shows the value today of liabilities that are owed in the future. Using a more prudent rate of return, such as the ALEC risk-free rate of return, will provide a clearer picture of pension liabilities because, as previously stated, state governments are legally (and often constitutionally) bound to make

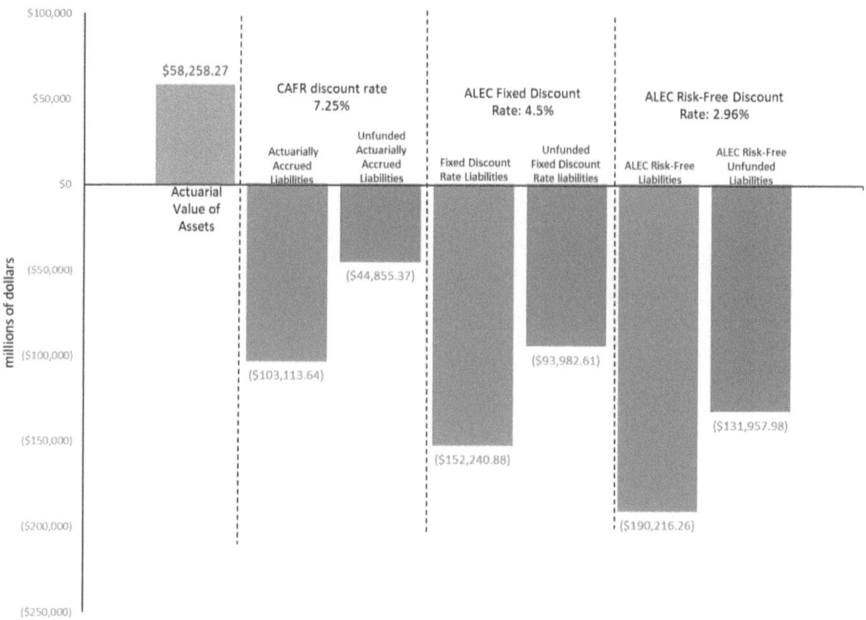

Figure 3.3 Pennsylvania PSERS Actuarial Value of Assets and Liabilities. *Sources*: Pennsylvania Public School Employees' Retirement System, "Actuarial Valuation Report," June 30, 2018; Author's calculations.

those pension payments. The lower discount rate reflects the state government's inability to default on its pension promises.

UNFUNDED LIABILITIES: A NEARLY $5 TRILLION PROBLEM

The ALEC annual report on pensions found that, using a risk-free discount rate, unfunded liabilities totaled $4.9 trillion (a little more than $15,000 per person) for FY 2018.[25] The table in figure 3.5 has been re-created from the ALEC annual report on pensions *Unaccountable and Unaffordable* with permission from the authors:

As one can see, the unfunded liabilities are not evenly dispersed among the 50 states. The 10 states with the largest unfunded liabilities (the bottom 10 states in the ranking) are Georgia, Massachusetts, Michigan, Florida, New Jersey, Pennsylvania, New York, Ohio, Texas, Illinois, and California. Together these states have a combined sum of $2.97 trillion in unfunded liabilities. This sum makes up 60.27% of all unfunded pension liabilities in the country.

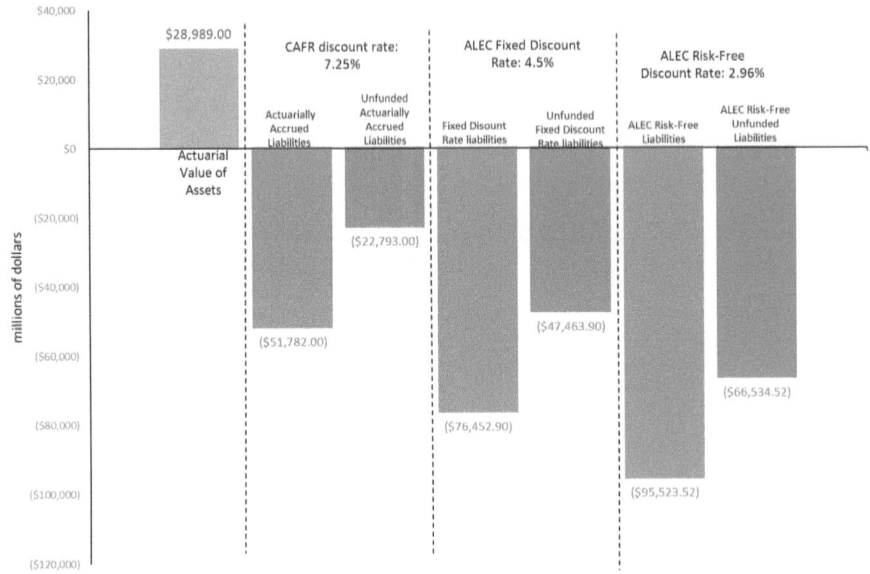

Figure 3.4 Pennsylvania SERS Actuarial Value of Assets and Liabilities. *Sources*: Commonwealth of Pennsylvania State Employees' Retirement System, "2018 Actuarial Report," June 14, 2019; Author's calculations.

To put these unfunded liabilities in context, it is important to examine unfunded liabilities per capita. That measurement shows the unfunded pension liabilities apportioned out to each state resident. Figure 3.6 is re-created from the ALEC annual pension report with permission from the authors:

This measurement is concerning because it shows the personal share of liability for every resident in each state. As economist James M. Buchanan noted, government debt is a cost borne by taxpayers in the future.[26] Each of these unfunded liabilities represents a future tax upon the residents of each state from these unfunded liabilities. States with relatively smaller populations face the largest burdens. Take Illinois for example, where unfunded liabilities are $28,200.06 per capita. That money could pay for tuition, fees, and room and board at Illinois State University for every citizen of every age for the 2020–2021 academic year (just over $25,000) and have some money left over to pay for books and school supplies.[27]

It is also important to note that these unfunded liabilities make up sizeable portions of their respective state GDP measurements. The table in figure 3.7 is recreated from the ALEC annual pension report with permission from the authors:

Unfunded liabilities as a percentage of state GDP shows a state's ability to pay its unfunded liabilities. This measurement highlights the severity of a pension crisis in a relatively smaller economy (such as Kentucky or Mississippi).

State	Risk-Free Unfunded Liabilities	Rank	State	Risk-Free Unfunded Liabilities	Rank
South Dakota	$8,085,638,583.63	1	Alabama	$67,437,993,673.53	26
North Dakota	$8,761,680,266.46	2	South Carolina	$73,081,438,956.47	27
Vermont	$8,954,116,122.98	3	Kentucky	$78,757,474,540.66	28
Delaware	$11,209,552,268.25	4	Louisiana	$82,685,184,739.22	29
Wyoming	$11,735,339,612.67	5	Maryland	$82,750,803,486.58	30
Maine	$14,333,176,211.72	6	Oregon	$85,421,420,280.11	31
Nebraska	$15,762,090,811.49	7	Missouri	$86,896,555,657.34	32
Idaho	$15,778,713,937.19	8	Minnesota	$90,103,122,717.00	33
New Hampshire	$16,459,495,419.35	9	Arizona	$93,703,276,877.31	34
Rhode Island	$16,785,438,870.20	10	Connecticut	$94,864,011,214.24	35
Montana	$22,029,299,834.96	11	Virginia	$95,747,698,172.39	36
Utah	$24,281,056,135.81	12	Washington	$98,108,228,076.09	37
West Virginia	$27,605,493,322.79	13	Colorado	$99,566,298,766.88	38
Alaska	$29,459,806,480.10	14	North Carolina	$101,250,412,082.39	39
Hawaii	$36,692,427,005.98	15	Georgia	$126,271,834,206.80	40
Tennessee	$36,924,390,920.51	16	Massachusetts	$126,363,420,361.63	41
Kansas	$37,662,386,691.31	17	Michigan	$139,167,300,292.42	42
Arkansas	$39,464,841,630.25	18	Florida	$175,122,110,438.56	43
Iowa	$40,866,792,605.31	19	New Jersey	$196,810,498,087.95	44
Wisconsin	$42,706,299,777.93	20	Pennsylvania	$200,517,027,371.72	45
Oklahoma	$44,229,465,695.39	21	New York	$277,576,023,216.62	46
Indiana	$45,352,556,511.16	22	Ohio	$290,905,972,324.24	47
New Mexico	$49,127,169,375.79	23	Texas	$301,219,126,898.18	48
Mississippi	$61,531,351,056.57	24	Illinois	$359,553,997,754.76	49
Nevada	$63,931,899,479.58	25	California	$780,051,066,093.13	50

Figure 3.5 Risk-Free Unfunded Liabilities by State. *Source*: Thomas Savidge, Jonathan Williams, Bob Williams, and Skip Estes, *Unaccountable and Unaffordable, 2019*, American Legislative Exchange Council, June 4, 2020.

However, large unfunded liabilities can even have a significant impact on relatively larger economies such as California, Illinois, and New York.

As previously mentioned, the funding ratio is an important measure of a defined benefit pension plan's health. The table in figure 3.8 is re-created from the ALEC annual pension report with permission from the authors:

Also, as previously mentioned, states must always strive for 100% funding ratio, however most states fell far below that. For 2018, the weighted average funding ratio was 34.8%.[28] This weighted average was taken by multiplying the funding ratio by the frequency which that funding ratio appeared and then dividing the sum of the weighted values by the sum of the frequencies. This is dangerously low for pension plans. The best funded state, Wisconsin, has consistently had the highest funding ratio among the ALEC rankings since FY 2012. Figure 3.9 shows the 3 highest and 3 lowest funding ratios for FY 2018 over time using the ALEC fixed discount rate of 4.5% compared to the weighted average funding ratio for each fiscal year:

The dashed line in figures 3.9 represents the weighted average of all 50 states for each fiscal year. As shown in the chart, the three highest funding ratios for FY 2018 (Wisconsin with 87.92%, South Dakota with 75.37%, and Utah with 70.86%) have consistently performed above the 50 state weighted

State	Unfunded Pension Liability Per Capita	Rank	State	Unfunded Pension Liability Per Capita	Rank
Tennessee	$5,454.11	1	Missouri	$14,183.83	26
Indiana	$6,777.25	2	New York	$14,203.92	27
Wisconsin	$7,345.97	3	Vermont	$14,296.87	28
Utah	$7,681.19	4	South Carolina	$14,374.43	29
Nebraska	$8,169.99	5	West Virginia	$15,284.31	30
Florida	$8,221.96	6	Pennsylvania	$15,656.76	31
Idaho	$8,994.78	7	Rhode Island	$15,875.53	32
South Dakota	$9,164.95	8	Minnesota	$16,057.79	33
North Carolina	$9,750.97	9	Colorado	$17,482.42	34
Texas	$10,494.77	10	Kentucky	$17,625.42	35
Maine	$10,709.16	11	Louisiana	$17,743.69	36
Oklahoma	$11,216.99	12	Massachusetts	$18,307.84	37
Virginia	$11,241.05	13	California	$19,719.65	38
North Dakota	$11,516.75	14	Wyoming	$20,312.60	39
Delaware	$11,590.04	15	Oregon	$20,383.51	40
Georgia	$12,003.63	16	Mississippi	$20,602.96	41
New Hampshire	$12,134.17	17	Montana	$20,737.26	42
Kansas	$12,935.71	18	Nevada	$21,069.10	43
Iowa	$12,948.33	19	New Jersey	$22,092.39	44
Washington	$13,019.31	20	New Mexico	$23,444.93	45
Arizona	$13,065.80	21	Ohio	$24,886.22	46
Arkansas	$13,094.60	22	Hawaii	$25,830.81	47
Maryland	$13,694.30	23	Connecticut	$26,552.73	48
Alabama	$13,797.01	24	Illinois	$28,220.06	49
Michigan	$13,922.42	25	Alaska	$39,948.86	50

Figure 3.6 Unfunded Pension Liability Per Capita by State. *Source*: Thomas Savidge, Jonathan Williams, Bob Williams, and Skip Estes, *Unaccountable and Unaffordable, 2019*, American Legislative Exchange Council, June 4, 2020.

average (indicated by the dashed line) since FY 2012. Illinois and Connecticut have consistently performed below the weighted average since FY 2012, symptoms of underfunding and poor management. West Virginia performed just below the weighted average in FY 2017 but dramatically increased in FY 2018 thanks to high returns on investments increasing the asset value. Vermont steadily decreased from FY 2012 to FY 2018, seeing the largest dip from FY 2014–2015. Year over year, there are only slight changes in pension funding ratios, yet slight changes to assets and liabilities can have large impacts over time. Figure 3.11 below shows the percent change in funding ratios from FY 2012–2018. Figure 3.11 also uses the ALEC fixed discount rate of 4.5% to control for changes in discount rates.

On a positive note, average funding ratios have consistently increased during the period of FY 2012–2018, controlling for discount rates. This is in part due to increasing returns in pension assets as well as some states paying down

State	Unfunded Liabilities as a Percentage of State GDP	Rank	State	Unfunded Liabilities as a Percentage of State GDP	Rank
Tennessee	10.14%	1	California	26.02%	26
Indiana	12.36%	2	Michigan	26.40%	27
Wisconsin	12.70%	3	Colorado	26.78%	28
Nebraska	12.71%	4	Arizona	26.90%	29
Utah	13.63%	5	Vermont	26.92%	30
Delaware	15.25%	6	Missouri	27.25%	31
South Dakota	15.54%	7	Rhode Island	27.70%	32
North Dakota	15.62%	8	Wyoming	30.00%	33
New York	16.63%	9	Alabama	30.41%	34
Texas	16.71%	10	Arkansas	30.73%	35
Florida	16.85%	11	South Carolina	31.24%	36
Washington	17.34%	12	New Jersey	31.64%	37
North Carolina	17.96%	13	Louisiana	32.14%	38
Virginia	17.97%	14	Connecticut	34.41%	39
New Hampshire	19.49%	15	Oregon	35.62%	40
Maryland	20.06%	16	West Virginia	35.65%	41
Idaho	20.48%	17	Nevada	37.76%	42
Georgia	21.32%	18	Kentucky	37.85%	43
Iowa	21.54%	19	Hawaii	39.12%	44
Oklahoma	21.84%	20	Illinois	41.55%	45
Maine	22.10%	21	Ohio	43.04%	46
Massachusetts	22.19%	22	Montana	43.77%	47
Kansas	22.38%	23	New Mexico	48.98%	48
Minnesota	24.43%	24	Mississippi	53.58%	49
Pennsylvania	25.60%	25	Alaska	53.82%	50

Figure 3.7 Unfunded Liabilities as a Percentage of State GDP. *Source*: Thomas Savidge, Jonathan Williams, Bob Williams, and Skip Estes, *Unaccountable and Unaffordable, 2019*, American Legislative Exchange Council, June 4, 2020.

unfunded liabilities and making reforms to make pension systems more sustainable. Notice that slight changes, such as in Wisconsin, do not necessarily mean weak growth. Wisconsin has consistently had the highest funding ratio for all years measured. Funding ratio contraction, such as in the bottom nine states, can mean millions of dollars in unfunded liability growth.

The next section will discuss how Maine, Michigan, Tennessee, and Wisconsin have made effective changes to their pension systems, keeping them sustainable for the future.

CASE STUDIES FOR REFORM: MAINE, MICHIGAN, TENNESSEE, AND WISCONSIN

This section will discuss how the states of Maine, Michigan, Tennessee, and Wisconsin have all made workable reforms to their public pension systems to keep them sustainable for the future. Among these pension reforms, there are many similarities between the state pension systems.

State	Risk-Free Funding Ratio	Rank	State	Risk-Free Funding Ratio	Rank
Wisconsin	70.37%	1	Indiana	38.65%	26
South Dakota	60.32%	2	Ohio	38.64%	27
Utah	56.71%	3	Montana	38.15%	28
New York	54.54%	4	Maryland	37.46%	29
Idaho	51.50%	5	New Mexico	36.70%	30
Tennessee	50.64%	6	Alabama	36.63%	31
North Carolina	49.74%	7	Louisiana	36.33%	32
Delaware	48.21%	8	New Hampshire	35.08%	33
Maine	47.65%	9	Michigan	34.85%	34
Nebraska	47.41%	10	Kansas	34.57%	35
Florida	47.13%	11	Vermont	34.10%	36
Washington	47.01%	12	Arizona	33.93%	37
Iowa	46.55%	13	New Jersey	33.78%	38
Oregon	44.80%	14	Alaska	33.66%	39
Texas	44.64%	15	Rhode Island	32.76%	40
Virginia	44.25%	16	Colorado	32.73%	41
Minnesota	42.80%	17	Massachusetts	31.72%	42
Arkansas	42.74%	18	Mississippi	31.26%	43
Oklahoma	42.69%	19	Hawaii	31.15%	44
Missouri	42.57%	20	Pennsylvania	30.90%	45
Georgia	42.27%	21	South Carolina	30.39%	46
Wyoming	41.94%	22	Kentucky	28.57%	47
Nevada	39.39%	23	Illinois	26.66%	48
California	39.19%	24	Connecticut	26.08%	49
North Dakota	38.84%	25	West Virginia	24.82%	50

Figure 3.8 State Risk-Free Funding Ratios. *Source*: Thomas Savidge, Jonathan Williams, Bob Williams, and Skip Estes, *Unaccountable and Unaffordable, 2019,* American Legislative Exchange Council, June 4, 2020.

Wisconsin, as previously mentioned, has the best-funded pension system in the country at 70.37%, controlling for difference in discount rates, because it has a variable benefit rate, meaning the disbursement varies over time. State retirees are entitled to a low, guaranteed pension payment paired with a variable payment based on the pension system's funding ratio.[29] This means when tax revenue is lower during economic recessions, the fund lowers payments to retirees and allows the fund to recover rather than exhausting the fund or taking on debt to keep making payments.[30] While the plan has been criticized for diminishing benefits during economic downturns, it has succeeded in providing retirement security with few significant changes to the plan since 1975.[31]

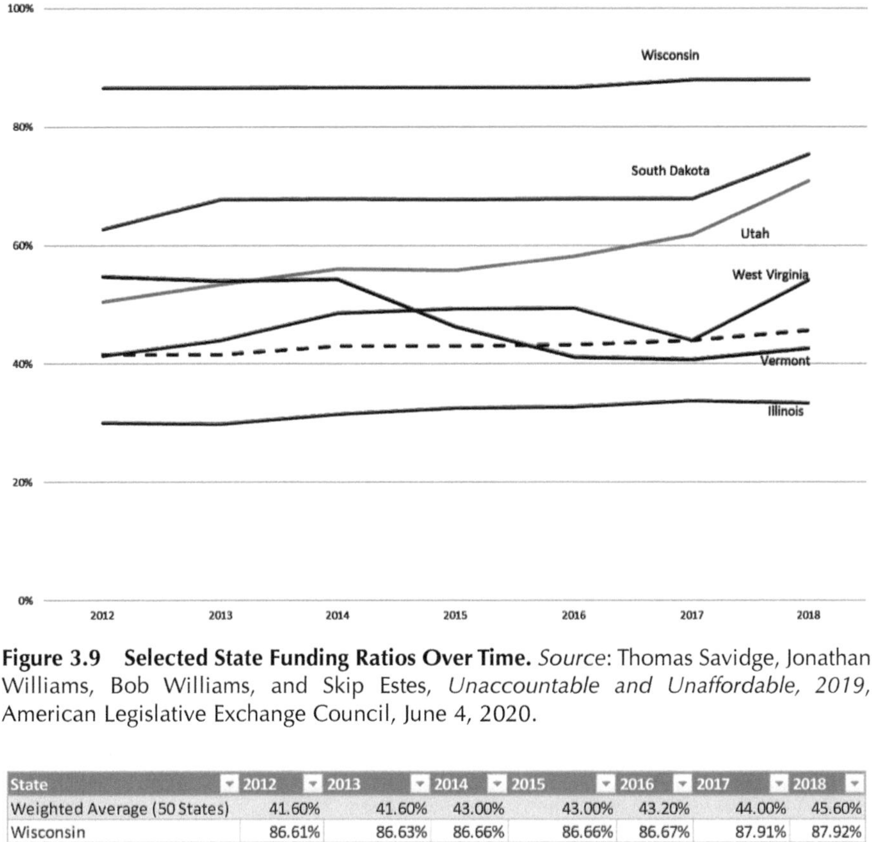

Figure 3.9 Selected State Funding Ratios Over Time. *Source*: Thomas Savidge, Jonathan Williams, Bob Williams, and Skip Estes, *Unaccountable and Unaffordable, 2019*, American Legislative Exchange Council, June 4, 2020.

State	2012	2013	2014	2015	2016	2017	2018
Weighted Average (50 States)	41.60%	41.60%	43.00%	43.00%	43.20%	44.00%	45.60%
Wisconsin	86.61%	86.63%	86.66%	86.66%	86.67%	87.91%	87.92%
South Dakota	62.76%	67.77%	67.79%	67.78%	67.85%	67.79%	75.37%
Utah	50.42%	53.34%	55.90%	55.73%	58.13%	61.79%	70.86%
West Virginia	41.35%	43.98%	48.50%	49.28%	49.40%	43.95%	54.02%
Illinois	29.95%	29.76%	31.45%	32.49%	32.68%	33.71%	33.30%
Vermont	54.69%	53.97%	54.30%	46.21%	41.17%	40.71%	42.61%

Figure 3.10 Selected State Funding Ratios Over Time (in Table Format). *Source*: Thomas Savidge, Jonathan Williams, Bob Williams, and Skip Estes, *Unaccountable and Unaffordable, 2019*, American Legislative Exchange Council, June 4, 2020.

One significant change in Wisconsin occurred in 2011. That year, the Wisconsin legislature and then-Governor Scott Walker signed pension reform Acts 10 and 32.[32] These acts introduced several pension cost- and risk-sharing measures, including requiring Wisconsin Retirement System (WRS) participants to contribute half of the ADC.[33] The ADC payment covers both normal costs for the year and an amortization payment of liabilities from previous years, both of which depend partially on investment returns. By requiring participants and the state to split the ADC payment every year, it incentivizes

Rank	State	Percent Change in Funding Ratio 2012-2018	Rank	State	Percent Change in Funding Ratio 2012-2018
1	Utah	40.55%	26	Illinois	11.21%
2	Arkansas	34.00%	27	Indiana	10.86%
3	Oklahoma	31.00%	28	Mississippi	10.58%
4	West Virginia	30.63%	29	Missouri	10.48%
5	Alaska	27.61%	30	Kentucky	10.37%
6	Kansas	25.46%	31	Connecticut	9.07%
7	North Dakota	25.34%	32	Texas	8.79%
8	Louisiana	23.98%	33	Florida	7.29%
9	New Hampshire	23.47%	34	Delaware	4.48%
10	Nebraska	23.40%	35	New Jersey	4.21%
11	New York	21.13%	36	Colorado	4.17%
12	Virginia	20.60%	37	Wyoming	4.15%
13	South Dakota	20.09%	38	Hawaii	4.09%
14	Montana	18.11%	39	Arizona	2.72%
15	Ohio	17.37%	40	Rhode Island	2.33%
16	Minnesota	16.68%	41	Wisconsin	1.51%
17	Idaho	16.26%	42	Washington	-0.02%
18	Tennessee	16.05%	43	Georgia	-0.73%
19	New Mexico	14.97%	44	Oregon	-2.29%
20	Maryland	14.83%	45	Massachusetts	-2.39%
21	Michigan	14.28%	46	California	-2.96%
22	Nevada	13.68%	47	North Carolina	-3.86%
23	Alabama	13.28%	48	Pennsylvania	-8.61%
24	Iowa	12.35%	49	South Carolina	-11.20%
25	Maine	11.69%	50	Vermont	-22.09%

Figure 3.11 Percent Change in Funding Ratios Over Time. *Source*: Thomas Savidge, Jonathan Williams, Bob Williams, and Skip Estes, *Unaccountable and Unaffordable, 2019*, American Legislative Exchange Council, June 4, 2020.

prudent investment practices to minimize financial risks and annual costs. In addition, Wisconsin also uses a variable benefit rate where retirees receive a low, guaranteed minimum payment and additional payments based on investment performance (known as the Core Fund).[34] If investments underperform, retirees only receive the minimum payment. Results are smoothed over five years to account for market volatility. Public employees can opt into receiving additional benefits from an all-stocks fund (known as the Variable Fund).[35]

In 2016, Maine pursued a series of reforms to implement variable contribution rates.[36] Due to these reforms, in the past two years Maine's unfunded pension liabilities have decreased by almost $10 billion (about 50%). Normally employer contribution rates fluctuate to meet the ADC or other contribution standards, whereas employee contributions are a fixed rate set by contract. Under a "risk-sharing" plan, changes in the ADC result in changes in contributions for both employer and employee.

The models share a key aspect: both Maine and Wisconsin have automatic "triggers," These triggers serve as an objective management tool to ensure pensions are funded. Automatic adjustments based on actuarial science are difficult to argue against, particularly when the potential deviation will underfund the pension system.

In addition, numerous states (e.g., Michigan, Pennsylvania, Wisconsin, and Tennessee) have introduced hybrid pension plans and options for full defined-contribution pensions. In most cases, a hybrid is a relatively small defined-benefit pension plan offered in tandem with a defined-contribution plan. The defined-benefit portion of these hybrids carries all the same risks as traditional pension plans. The risks, however, are mitigated by the smaller size and, often, better contract terms, such as benefit formulas that block spiking (getting large raises or bonuses in the time immediately before retiring in order to get a higher pension payout during retirement) or higher employer contribution rates.

Tennessee currently offers a hybrid pension plan for all state and higher education employees hired on or after July 1, 2014. All state and higher education employees hired before that date have been incorporated in the defined-benefit legacy plan.[37] The hybrid plan incorporates both a defined-benefit plan and the option to set aside money in a 401(k) plan. Tennessee is consistently one of the states with the best funding ratios and the lowest unfunded liabilities per capita in the ALEC pension reports since 2016 (the earliest edition of the *Unaccountable and Unaffordable* report). Unfunded liabilities will continue to fall as more retirees participate in hybrid pension plans and the state legacy pension plan liabilities are paid off.

Similarly, Michigan transitioned its Public School Employee Retirement System (MPSERS) to hybrid pensions for all new hires in 2017. The plan auto-enrolls new hires in a defined-contribution plan, but new teachers have the choice of opting into a hybrid plan with a mix of defined-contribution and defined-benefit plans.[38] The defined-benefit plan splits all costs 50–50 between employers and employees, uses a 10-year amortization schedule, and uses a 6% discount rate. In addition, if the hybrid plan's funding ratio falls below 85% for two consecutive years, the plan is closed to new hires until the funding ratio rises above the 85% threshold for two consecutive years.[39]

In 1996, Michigan was the first state in the nation to close its defined-benefit State Employee Retirement System (MSERS) and enroll new hires in a hybrid plan.[40] However, other state employee plans (such as MPSERS, the State Police Retirement System, State Judges Retirement System, Municipal Employees Retirement System, and the Legislative Retirement System) kept the defined-benefit option open to new hires. Thus unfunded liabilities continue to accumulate in the other Michigan pension plans.[41]

The case of Michigan demonstrates that a transition to defined-contribution plans does not mean unfunded liabilities will disappear overnight or even in one fiscal year. Michigan still ranks 42nd in the nation on unfunded liabilities, but the counterfactual would be much worse. If these reforms were not in place, Michigan would resemble its neighbor to the southeast, Ohio, or nearby Illinois. Ohio (48th in the nation) has $290 billion in unfunded liabilities, while Illinois (49th in the nation) has nearly $360 billion in unfunded liabilities. A study conducted by Richard Dreyfuss and the Mackinac Center found that Michigan's reforms saved taxpayers $167 million in pension liabilities, saved $2.3 billion to $4.3 billion in unfunded liabilities, and improved the political incentives of pension funding.[42] By continuing reforms to transition more pension plans to defined-contribution, Michigan can steadily improve its retirement plans and reduce its unfunded liabilities.

By following the examples of these states, other state pension plans can make improvements to their respective pension systems, keep pensions sustainable for years to come, and lower the burden of pension debt on taxpayers.

Further Recommendations: Protecting Workers and Taxpayers from Growing Debt

As recommended by Poulson and Merrifield, states should set a target for debt (including "soft debt" of pension and benefit liabilities) as a percentage of personal income.[43] This section will explore several specific recommendations to keep pension debt below the target rate: adjusting pension plan board governance structure, changing rules for investment, and enrolling new hires in a defined contribution plan. The first is a more modest adjust while the second is a complete change to the pension plan.

When discussing the governance structure of pension plan boards, it is important to note that not all pension board structures are created equal. Recent research from Aleksandar Andonov, Yael Hochberg, and Joshua Rauh note that the structure of the pension boards strongly correlates with pension asset investment performance. Andonov, Hochberg, and Rauh find that pension funds whose boards have high fractions of ex officio members (i.e., state treasurers) or members appointed by a state official underperform the most, followed by funds whose boards have a high fraction of members elected by participants.[44] The authors noticed that the worst-performing governance structures invest more in riskier assets, such as real estate and certain mutual funds, partially explaining the lower performance. Lack of financial experience among public pension board members partially contributes to poor performance but does not explain the performance of boards with state officials who have expertise on the subject.[45] Political contributions from the finance industry to state officials on pension fund boards are strongly and negatively related to performance, but the authors found it did not fully explain lower performance.[46]

Public pension plans would also benefit from a rule regarding protecting investment returns. In November 2020, the Department of Labor finalized a rule clarifying "investment duties" under Title I of the Employee Retirement Income Security Act of 1974.[47] This rule requires private pension plan managers to make investment decisions solely on the basis of financial considerations relevant to the risk-adjusted economic value of a particular investment or investment course of action.[48] This means that retirement portfolio managers cannot invest in political causes if such investments yield lower returns than a portfolio with optimized risk.

Several states, such as California and Alabama, invest public pension funds using environmental, social, and governance (ESG) investing practices and in economic development. The California Public Employees Retirement System (CalPERS) and the California State Teachers Retirement System (CalSTRS) have had volatile investment returns, costing the pension plans billions of dollars in missed investment returns.[49] Alabama invests public pension funds in questionable economic development projects, such as golf courses and movie theaters, yielding extremely volatile investment returns.[50] These volatile investment returns mean that the state and public employees must make higher ADC payments to make up for lost investments. If states were to issue a rule similar to the Department of Labor's for their respective public pension systems, they could maximize investment returns and increase predictability and stability for pension contributions in the future.

Ultimately the way to ensure that unfunded pension liabilities are cut and large burdens are not placed on taxpayers is to completely transition to defined contribution. In a defined contribution pension plan, employees make contributions to their own personal retirement accounts, and in some cases employers will match retirement contributions up to a certain dollar amount. The funds put into the retirement account are invested in an index fund, and retirement savings accumulate value through investment returns and contributions. Upon retirement, it is up to the retiree to budget what he or she has saved and invested while working.[51] While a defined contribution plan does not promise the annual payments of a defined benefit plan, it offers employees greater flexibility. The employee does not have to wait to be vested in a defined contribution retirement plan, and the plan follows the employee if he or she chooses to change careers. That flexibility can allow a public-sector worker to leave his or her public-sector job for another job (whether in the public or private sector) and not worry about losing retirement savings. The defined contribution will follow him or her wherever their career takes them all the while lowering the cost of retirement payments for taxpayers.

NOTES

1. Jonathan Williams, Kati Siconolfi, Theodore Lafferty, and Elliot Young, "Keeping the Promise: Getting Politics Out of Pensions," American Legislative Exchange Council, December 14, 2016, https://www.alec.org/publication/keeping-the-promise-getting-politics-out-of-pensions/

2. Sheila Weinberg and Eileen Norcross, "GASB 67 and GASB 68: What the New Accounting Standards Mean for Public Pension Reporting," Mercatus Policy Briefs, June 15, 2017, https://www.mercatus.org/publications/urban-economics/gasb-67-and-gasb-68-what-new-accounting-standards-mean-public-pension

3. The State of Illinois "Notes to Required Supplementary Information," in The State of Illinois Comprehensive Annual Financial Report for the Fiscal Year Ended June 30, 2018, August 31, 2018, https://www.trsil.org/sites/default/files/documents/CAFR-FY2018_1.pdf

4. Thomas Savidge, Jonathan Williams, Bob Williams, and Skip Estes, Unaccountable and Unaffordable, 2019, American Legislative Exchange Council, June 4, 2020, https://www.alec.org/publication/unaccountable-and-unaffordable-2019/

5. Savidge, et al. *Unaccountable and Unaffordable.*

6. Weinberg and Norcross, "GASB 67 and GASB 68."

7. Ibid.

8. American Academy of Actuaries, "The 80% Pension Funding Standard Myth," American Academy of Actuaries Issue Brief, July 2012,https://www.actuary.org/sites/default/files/files/80_Percent_Funding_IB_071912.pdf

9. Weinberg and Norcross, "GASB 67 and GASB 68."

10. Wyoming Retirement System, "Wyoming Air Guard Firefighters' Retirement System Actuarial Valuation Report for the Year Beginning January 1, 2019," April 18, 2019, https://retirement.wyo.gov/About/Reports?Label=Actuarial+Valuations&Sort=Most+Recent&Page=1

11. California Public Employees' Retirement System (CalPERS), "State Actuarial Valuation As of June 30, 2018," October 2019, https://www.calpers.ca.gov/docs/forms-publications/2018-state-valuation.pdf

12. Savidge, et al. *Unaccountable and Unaffordable 2019.*

13. Williams, et al. "Keeping the Promise."

14. Savidge, et al. *Unaccountable and Unaffordable 2019.*

15. Society of Actuaries, *Report of the Blue-Ribbon Panel on Public Pension Plan Funding*, 2014, https://www.soa.org/brpreport364/

16. *In re Pension Reform Litigation*, 118585 IL. 2015. Retrieved from: https://courts.illinois.gov/Opinions/SupremeCourt/2015/118585.pdf

17. Joshua Rauh, "Testimony Before the Joint Select Committee on Solvency of Multiemployer Pension Plans. United States Senate & United States House of Representatives," July 25, 2018, https://www.pensions.senate.gov/sites/default/files/25JUL2018RauhSTMNT.pdf

18. Savidge, et al. *Unaccountable and Unaffordable 2019.*

19. Governmental Accounting Standards Board (GASB), "Statement No. 27: Accounting for Pensions by State and Local Governmental Employers," November 1994, https://www.gasb.org/resources/ccurl/44/286/GASBS-27.pdf

20. Barton M. Waring, "Liability-Relative Investing," *The Journal of Portfolio Management*, 30, no 4 (Summer 2004): 8–20, https://jpm.pm-research.com/content/30/4/8

21. Eileen Norcross, "Getting an Accurate Picture of State Pension Liabilities," Mercatus Center at George Mason University, December 2010, https://www.mercatus.org/system/files/Getting-an-Accurate-Picture-of-State-Pension-Liablilities.Norcross.12.13.10.pdf

22. Thurston Powers, Christine Smith, Bob Williams, and Jonathan Williams, Unaccountable and Unaffordable 2018, American Legislative Exchange Council, 2018, https://www.alec.org/publication/unaccountable-and-unaffordable-2018/

23. Savidge, et al. *Unaccountable and Unaffordable 2019.*

24. Ibid.

25. Ibid.

26. James M. Buchanan, *The Collected Works of James M. Buchanan Volume 2: Public Principles of Public Debt: A Defense and Restatement*, Indianapolis: Liberty Fund, 1999, p. 22.

27. Financial Aid Office of Illinois State University, "Cost of Attendance Tables: New, undergraduate students for Fall 2020, Spring 2021, or Summer 2021," March 2020, https://financialaid.illinoisstate.edu/paying/cost/table-group-7.php

28. Savidge, et al. *Unaccountable and Unaffordable 2019.*

29. Seyfert, Kerri. "The Wisconsin Retirement System Is Fully Funded." Reason Foundation. Jan. 2020.

30. Ibid.

31. Jason Stein, "Wisconsin's Fully Funded Pension System Is One of a Kind," Milwaukee Journal Sentinel, September 26, 2016, https://projects.jsonline.com/news/2016/9/26/wisconsins-fully-funded-pension-system-is-one-of-a-kind.html

32. Act 32 modifies the cost-sharing provisions of Act 10, covering municipal police and fire employers as well as state employers of troopers and vehicle inspectors.

33. Kerri Seyfert, "The Wisconsin Retirement System Is Fully Funded and a Model for Other States," *Reason Foundation*, January 14, 2020, https://reason.org/commentary/the-wisconsin-retirement-system-is-fully-funded-and-a-model-for-other-states/.

34. Wisconsin Retirement System, "Core Trust Fund and Variable Trust Fund," https://etf.wi.gov/wrs-performance/core-trust-fund-and-variable-trust-fund

35. Ibid.

36. Martin Z. Braun, "Public Pensions Adopt Cost Sharing Mechanisms to Stem Volatility," Bloomberg, July 17, 2018, https://www.bloomberg.com/news/articles/2018-07-17/public-pensions-adopt-cost-sharing-mechanisms-to-stem-volatility

37. Tennessee Department of Treasury, "GASB and Actuarial Information," Updated 2019, https://treasury.tn.gov/Retirement/Boards-and-Governance/GASB-and-Actuarial-Information

38. Leonard Gilroy, Anthony Randazzo, and Daniel Takash. "Michigan Adopts Most Innovative Teacher Pension Reform in the Nation," Reason Foundation, June 16, 2017, Retrieved from: https://reason.org/commentary/michigan-adopts-most-innovative-teacher-pension-reform-in-the-nation/

39. Ibid.

40. Anthony Randazzo, "Pension Reform Case Study: Michigan 2016 Update," Reason Foundation August 2016, https://reason.org/wp-content/uploads/files/pension_reform_michigan.pdf

41. Ibid.

42. Richard C. Dreyfuss, "Policy Brief: Estimated Savings from Michigan's 1997 State Employees Pension Plan Reform," Mackinac Center for Public Policy, June 23, 2011, https://www.mackinac.org/15672

43. Merrifield, John and Poulson, Barry. "Debt Fatigue in the States: Red States, Blue States, Zombie States." See Chapter 6.

44. Aleksandar Andonov, Yael V. Hochberg; and Joshua D. Rauh, "Pension Fund Board Composition and Investment Performance: Evidence from Private Equity," Hoover Institution Economics Working Papers, March 2016, https://www.hoover.org/sites/default/files/research/docs/16104_-_pension_fund_board_composition_and_investment_performance_-_andonov_hochberg_and_rauh.pdf

45. Ibid.

46. Ibid.

47. Employee Benefits Security Administration of the U.S. Department of Labor, "Financial Factors in Selecting Plan Investments," November 13, 2020, https://www.federalregister.gov/documents/2020/11/13/2020-24515/financial-factors-in-selecting-plan-investments.

48. Ibid.

49. Jonathon Hauenschild, Jonathan Williams, and Thomas Savidge, "Comment 0723 American Legislative Exchange Council 07302020," Employee Benefit Security Administration, August 6, 2020,https://beta.regulations.gov/document/EBSA-2020-0004-0717

50. John A. Dove and Daniel J. Smith "Alabama at the Crossroads: An Economic Guide to a Fiscally Sustainable Future," The Mercatus Center at George Mason University, March 22, 2016, https://www.mercatus.org/publications/urban-economics/alabama-crossroads-economic-guide-fiscally-sustainable-future

51. Savidge, et al. *Unaccountable and Unaffordable 2019.*

Chapter 4

Preparing State Finances for a Time of Crisis

Olivia Gonzalez

Our new fiscal environment reinforces the importance of sustainability. Although it is too soon to know the full extent of the COVID-19 pandemic's impact, experience thus far shows that it could be the greatest shock to the U.S. economy in nearly a century (Buckley 2020, McKinsey Global Institute 2020, White 2020, Maher, Hoang and Hindery 2020). The United States' growth rate declined by 31.4% between quarter one and quarter two of 2020 alone (Bureau of Economic Analysis n.d.). This was the nationwide impact, whereas the experience by state differed; the percentage change in real Gross Domestic Product (GDP) in quarter two ranged from −20.9% in Delaware to −42.2% in Hawaii and Nevada. It is clear that despite this range, state economies across the U.S. suffered.

Following lockdowns in 2020, as a result of the economic shock, many state and local governments suffered severe fiscal stress. This took place through declines in tax revenues and an increased demand for public services (McDonald and Larson 2020, National Conference of State Legislatures 2018, McNichol and Leachman 2020, Peter G. Foundation 2020, Peter G. Foundation 2020, The Pew Charitable Trusts 2020, Larson and McDonald 2020). The total state budget shortfalls that resulted stand to be the largest on record (Center on Budget and Policy Priorities 2020). This crisis begs the question: Could state governments have done anything to prepare?

The answer lies in the reason behind one factor that can significantly influence how well states manage their finances following an economic shock. This factor is the role that fiscal institutions play. It is true that state economies suffered, but how that translated into the actual budgets and finances of state governments varied. Most states suffered to some degree, but the magnitude of the fiscal stress was not uniform. Some states faced drastic revenue shortfalls, while others experienced small surpluses (Cantlon 2021, Maher, Hoang and Hindery 2020).

Looking at what could have potentially led to this diverse range of experiences following the initial start of the pandemic in the United States can help us learn how to prepare for the future. The pandemic provided a wake-up call for governments to rethink and reform their approaches to fiscal sustainability (Maher, Hoang and Hindery 2020). It drew attention to the importance of addressing long-standing issues even before an emergency hits. Sustainability includes being able to respond to crises while also meeting ongoing financial obligations, without over-reliance on debt or other fiscally imprudent practices.

One specific way that state governments can prepare for a crisis is to make deposits into the government's version of a savings account: a budget stabilization fund (BSF). BSFs, also known as rainy-day funds, are accounts where states can set aside surplus revenue to save for when they experience unexpected budget deficits. The goal is to set aside funds when times are good to access when finances are struggling, usually following economic shocks. 49 states have a formal BSF, but the balances and rules surrounding deposits and withdrawals vary substantially.

This chapter explores the role that BSFs play in influencing a state's fiscal health and sustainability. It also provides a review of the research on BSFs to date. I'll start by providing a brief overview of what makes a state fiscally healthy by summarizing one common measure that has been operationalized by the Mercatus Center at George Mason University: the fiscal condition index (FCI) (Arnett 2014, Norcross 2015, Norcross and Gonzalez 2016, Norcross and Gonzalez 2017, Norcross and Gonzalez 2018). The FCI draws from state financial reports to calculate financial indicators that are then aggregated into one final rank of fiscal condition.

In the 2018 edition of our Mercatus Center study, Eileen Norcross and I calculated the fiscal condition ranks for all states from 2006 to 2016 (Norcross and Gonzalez 2018). This provides us with a way to quickly assess how states compare fiscally over time. These numbers provide a helpful starting point, but in order to better understand how each state is doing objectively, we recommend diving deeper into the numbers and comparing them with external information that provides important context. One such external criterion we recommend is the BSF institution.

It is important to directly compare the FCI and its underlying financial indicators with BSFs because the former gives us a picture of each state's fiscal health, whereas the latter helps us understand the factors that created this picture. BSFs are just one essential tool in driving fiscal health and for preparing states for times of crisis. Other important things to take into consideration are the state's economy, tax system structure, budget, pensions systems, and other fiscal institutions. Fiscal health in any given year translates into sustainability in the long-run when institutions encourage fiscal management practices that are prudent on a consistent basis.

In this chapter, I make a case for well-designed BSFs as one essential tool among many that states can better utilize to prepare for times of uncertainty. I show that BSF balances and rules are associated with state fiscal health between 2006 and 2016. As states work to rebuild the next few years, they should keep in mind that instead of aiming for some sort of "optimal" savings balance, a lot more can be gained from improving the rules that influence BSF governance and management. Taking this approach will help states better prepare for the unfortunate, but inevitable, occurrence of recessions in the future.

WHAT MAKES A STATE FISCAL HEALTHY?

Financial indicators are helpful statistics that summarize the status of an organization or governing body. Similar to how financial indicators are used to assess the profitability of publicly traded companies, they can be applied to assess the fiscal health, or solvency, of governments. This is the idea behind much of the research devoted to assessing the fiscal condition of governments. Fiscal health, solvency, and condition are all terms that are used synonymously to describe the ability of a state to meet its short- and long-term obligations without incurring excessive debt, engaging in budget gimmicks, or using other evasive tactics. Although the focus of financial indicators will change by institutional context, the intuition behind this type of analytical approach remains the same.

We are more limited in our ability to assess the fiscal condition of a government than a private company because the former has less of a rational basis in economic calculation shaping its financial decisions. This leads analysis of a company's fiscal health to focus more on profitability, whereas a public governing body's analysis will entail more of a focus on cash and liability metrics, but the goal for both is the same: to help analysts assess the governing entity's financial health and long-term viability.

The FCI is an analytical approach that utilizes financial indicators in order to summarize the fiscal condition of state governments. It is based on research that has evolved from Wang, Dennis, and Tu's (2007) solvency test. Under the FCI, financial indicators are grouped together by the area of fiscal condition that they assess. To date, the main areas of fiscal solvency developed in the literature are (1) cash solvency, (2) budget solvency, (3) long-run solvency, (4) service-level, and (5) trust fund solvency. Each solvency area is associated with various financial indicators that can be calculated by drawing from a state's financial statements.

Solvency areas 1 through 4 were first developed by Groves, Godsey, and Shulman (1981) and then operationalized by XiaoHu Wang, Lynda Dennis, and Yuan Sen (Jeff) Tu (Groves, Godsey and Shulman 1981, Wang, Dennis and Tu 2007). Mercatus Center researchers extended this approach to measuring fiscal condition to produce a ranking of the states on the basis of their relative performance (Arnett 2014). In her 2015 publication utilizing this approach, Eileen Norcross stressed the importance of adding the fifth area, trust fund solvency, to ensure that pension and other post-employment benefit (OPEB) liabilities are also included when assessing financial condition (Norcross 2015). Follow-up studies from the Mercatus Center further developed this with improvements upon the methodology of the FCI in each edition (Norcross and Gonzalez 2016, Norcross and Gonzalez 2017, Norcross and Gonzalez 2018).

In the 2018 edition of our fiscal rankings study, we applied the FCI to ten years of data (Norcross and Gonzalez, Ranking the States by Fiscal Condition, 2018 Edition 2018). Doing so allowed us to benefit from the structure of the FCI in identifying which financial ratios to focus on, while also benefiting from time series analysis that is absent from cross-sectional FCI studies. We recommend that analysts use the overall FCI scores and ratio analysis on the financial indicators within the FCI. Pivoting between the two can be a more robust approach than solely relying on one or the other.

Table 4.1 provides an overview of the 13 financial indicators that are used to calculate the FCI and, ultimately, to measure the fiscal condition of the states. It also includes what solvency area each indicator is a part of. Each solvency area essentially portrays the different components that go into a state's entire fiscal condition. Ideally, it is important to know how a state's short- and long-term fiscal components are doing. The short-term components are those that are more urgent and likely to influence policymakers' decisions within one year. For example, the cash and budget area solvencies are most pertinent in the short-term. Knowing how much revenue a state has to cover expenses, as calculated through the operating ratio, will help tell state policymakers how financially sound their current budget is.

The long-run and trust-fund solvency areas—on the other hand—capture financial obligations that are less urgent, but must be dealt with eventually. The long-term liabilities per capita ratio, for example, tells a state policymaker how many financial obligations they must pay for at some point, but they are not as urgent as the state's operating budget.

The service-level solvency area is unique in that it has short- and long-term components. By looking at how large taxes, revenues, and state spending are as a percentage of state personal income, state policymakers can see how much "fiscal slack" they have to increase spending if citizens demand more services. A state that has high taxes and spending, for example, does not have

Table 4.1 Financial Indicators Used to Measure Fiscal Condition

	Financial Indicator	*Definition*	*Solvency Area*
1	Cash ratio	(Cash + cash equivalents + investments)/current liabilities	Cash
2	Quick ratio	(Cash + cash equivalents + investments + receivables)/current liabilities	Cash
3	Current ratio	Current assets/current liabilities	Cash
4	Operating ratio	Total revenues/total expenses	Budget
5	Surplus (or deficit) per capita	Change in net assets/ population	Budget
6	Net asset ratio	Restricted and unrestricted net assets/total assets	Long-run
7	Long-term liability ratio	Long-term liabilities/total assets	Long-run
8	Long-term liability per capita	Long-term liabilities/population	Long-run
9	Tax-to-income ratio	Total taxes/state personal income	Service-level
10	Revenue-to-income ratio	Total revenues/state personal income	Service-level
11	Expenses-to-income ratio	Total expenses/state personal income	Service-level
12	Pension-to-income ratio	Unfunded pension liability/ state personal income	Trust fund
13	OPEB-to-income ratio	OPEB/state personal income	Trust fund

Note: OPEB = other post-employment benefits.
Source: Eileen Norcross and Olivia Gonzalez, *Ranking the States by Fiscal Condition, 2018 edition* (Arlington, VA: Mercatus Center at George Mason University, 2018). https://www.mercatus.org/publications/urban-economics/state-fiscal-rankings.

a lot of room to increase funding for more public services, at least if they wish to be fiscally healthy.

All of these solvency areas are important for understanding what makes a state fiscally healthy. I summarize the key lessons for states into the following bullet points. I also include the solvency area of the FCI that helps us assess states under each lesson. States that are fiscally healthy:

- Have enough cash on hand to cover urgent bills that might come up—*cash solvency indicators*
- Have enough revenues to cover expenses—*budget solvency indicators*
- Have long-term liabilities that are not too large—*long-term solvency indicators*
- Do not consistently issue debt in order to cover short-term expenses—*long-term solvency indicators*

- Have enough "fiscal slack"—low taxes, revenues, and expenses—to leave room for new public service demand—*service-level solvency indicators*
- Don't have significantly underfunded pension and OPEB obligations—*trust fund solvency indicators*

Most importantly, a state is most fiscally sustainable when they have strong financial indicators across all these areas over a consistent period of time, not just one year.

Table 4.2 displays the descriptive statistics for the different financial indicators that go into these solvency areas between 2006 and 2016. I look at this time period because it is the most comprehensive collection of state financial data at the time of writing this chapter. It's important to look at a range of years because financial performance can fluctuate year to year. Looking at just one year would be limiting in our pursuit of understanding how states generally perform according to the FCI financial indicators.

On average, states during this period have enough cash on hand to cover liabilities, but there is considerable variation in this area. Although the average cash ratio of 1.82 is above the industry standard of one, a standard deviation of 1.96 puts many states above and below this depending on the year, with the worst cash metrics primarily being a result of the 2008 recession. The same goes for the operating ratio average of 1.04; most states on average

Table 4.2 Descriptive Statistics of Fiscal Condition Indicators, 2006–2016

Financial Indicator	*N*	*Average*	*Std. Dev.*	*Min*	*Max*
Cash Ratio	550	1.82	1.96	0.32	21.86
Quick Ratio	550	2.55	2.06	0.24	22.25
Current Ratio	550	2.81	2.08	0.86	22.78
Operating Ratio	550	1.04	0.12	0.32	2.08
Surplus (or deficit) per capita	550	$270	$1,432	-$10,380	$14,528
Net asset ratio	550	0.02	0.45	-2.98	0.85
Long-term liabilities ratio	550	0.40	0.45	0.01	3.88
Long-term liabilities per capita	550	$2,792	$2,514	$104	$18,928
Tax to income ratio	550	0.06	0.02	0.00	0.25
Revenues to income ratio	550	0.14	0.05	0.07	0.53
Expenses to income ratio	550	0.13	0.04	0.06	0.30
Unfunded pensions to income ratio	550	0.29	0.15	0.03	0.98
OPEB to income ratio	550	0.04	0.06	0.00	0.44

Source: Author's calculations based on Eileen Norcross and Olivia Gonzalez, *Ranking the States by Fiscal Condition, 2018 edition* (Arlington, VA: Mercatus Center at George Mason University, 2018). https://www.mercatus.org/publications/urban-economics/state-fiscal-rankings.

brought in more revenues than expenditures between 2006 and 2016, but with substantial variation.

A long-term liability ratio is calculated by dividing total long-term liabilities by total assets. It helps assess whether a state has a healthy amount of assets on hand to cushion against potential shocks or long-term fiscal risks. The larger long-term liabilities are, or the smaller assets are, the more at risk the state is of not being able to pay for long-term obligations in the future. This ratio captures liabilities like outstanding bonds, loans, and compensated employee absences.

The average long-term liability ratio of 0.40 is noteworthy considering how the benchmark standard for this ratio is 0.50 (Finkler 2012, 480). Financial management textbooks recommend not going above a long-term liability ratio of 0.50 because it can cause an organization to become overly reliant on debt. This ratio for the states has on average been on a steady increase over the years (Norcross and Gonzalez 2018, 30). These ratios, as well as the pension-to-income and net asset ratios will be especially important to keep an eye on in the years to come.

THE INTUITION BEHIND BSFS

BSFs have increasingly become an essential tool for states only in recent history. Twelve states had BSFs in 1982, but by 1994 forty-four states had them (Sobel and Holcombe 1996). This trend can at least in some part be attributed to the 1980–1982 recession (Wagner 2003). During this time, states found BSFs very attractive. Although those that hadn't built one up yet could not use a BSF to help recover from this recession, many hoped starting one could help prevent the recurrence of fiscal crises in the future.

Other researchers expand on this motivation behind BSF adoption: the general fear behind being unprepared for recessions (Gold 1984, Y. Hou 2004, Douglas and Gaddie 2002). Revenue volatility even more broadly speaking, however, is another big motivating factor (Grizzle, Stewart and Phillips 2015). It is unclear how much of BSF adoption by states was entirely motivated by these factors, but they at least play some part. Although recessions may have made finding tools for promoting sustainability more crucial, it could have also been the case that many states just did not know where to start. As a result, after a few states started leading the charge to adopt BSFs, other less certain states started following in their steps. Whether a state implements a BSF because of a desire to strategically stabilize their budget or merely to emulate their neighbors, it is clear that BSFs have benefits.

The crucial, yet simple, intuition behind BSFs is founded in a concern for fiscal sustainability. The reality of state revenues is that they are going to fluctuate. Although many factors go into revenue dynamics, the most concerning one is an unexpected economic shock. An economic shock, especially one ignited by a global pandemic, can be enough to throw a state's budget off course. Even shocks of smaller degrees are concerning to state policymakers. When actual revenues fall short of projected revenues, state policymakers are left to figure out how to make ends meet. This only adds to the many spending commitments and priorities that they are managing on a daily basis.

Given the reality of revenue fluctuations, a lot of state fiscal policy is drafted to counteract the risk they bring about. BSFs are just one fiscal policy tool intended to address the tendency for state revenues to fluctuate, or to be cyclical. This is why BSFs, and other policy tools like tax and expenditure limits, are deemed "countercyclical" policy tools.

Tax and expenditure limits are statutes that state policymakers implement to essentially tie their own hands (Stallmann, et al. 2017). These statutes restrict the amount that they can tax or spend. The main appeal of these limits is their ability to constrain government, if designed well. However, how they are operationalized often means they act as a countercyclical tool as well. Although tax and expenditure limits can take on many forms, the countercyclical goal is for them to constrain growth in government spending in boom times in order to mitigate the deleterious effects of budget shortfalls following economic downturns.

Colorado's Taxpayer Bill of Rights (TABOR), for example, is a TEL that requires that higher-than-expected tax revenues each year be refunded to taxpayers. Colorado's TABOR was adopted by voters in 1992 and it essentially restricts revenues by prohibiting any tax or spending increases without voter approval.

TELs and BSFs are two sides of the state fiscal sustainability coin. They are both intended to stabilize state finances, but they operate from different sides of the budget equation: one attempts to introduce stability through limiting spending (tax and expenditure limits) and the other does so through encouraging saving (BSFs) (Mitchell 2010).[1] In fact, robust BSFs that improve saving behavior are even more attractive when a state's spending rules are inadequate (Sunjoo 2014). It's recommended that states employ a fiscal strategy that combines the utilization of tax and expenditure limits and BSFs in order to stabilize and constrain spending (Merrifield and Poulson 2014).

THE "OPTIMAL" SIZE OF BSFS

Rainy-day fund balances have been going up over time on average. Figure 4.1 shows BSFs as a percentage of general funds for the average state between 2006 and 2016. On average, states only had 10% of general fund expenditures covered by BSFs in 2016. This doesn't mean they actually used these funds for this purpose, it just means that if they were to experience a budget

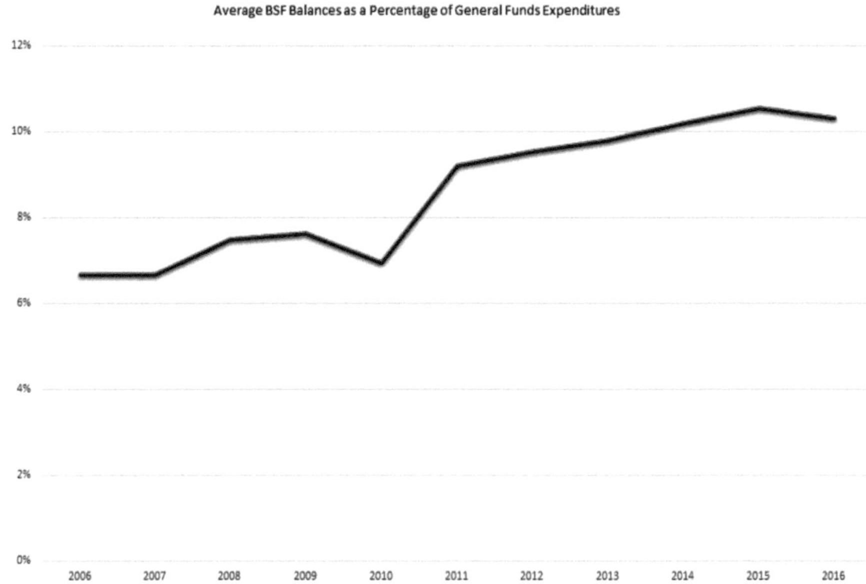

Figure 4.1 How Much of General Funds to BSFs Cover, on Average? *Source*: The Pew Charitable Trusts, *Fiscal 50: State Trends and Analysis* (Accessed February 2021). https://www.pewtrusts.org/en/research-and-analysis/data-visualizations/2014/fiscal-50#ind5.

shortfall due to unexpected revenue declines, they could only cover 10% of their general expenses with their savings. For a state in a situation like this, they'd likely have to raise taxes or cut expenditures to make up for shortfalls.

Although figure 4.1 displays the average trend, there has been a wide range of experiences across the states. Between 2006 and 2016, the typical BSF held $743 million, which amounted to about 9% of general fund expenditures. However, balances varied between $0 and $16.3 billion; this translated to a range of 0 to 238% of general fund expenditures. Fluctuations in BSFs over time are expected considering how their purpose is to augment state finances in times of crisis, which also fluctuate.

Balances should also differ state by state to some degree, considering the unique characteristics of each state, but the question: to what degree?

As discussed in the previous section, BSFs help smooth state spending across business cycles. They do so by providing states the option to draw on reserves during times of fiscal distress instead of raising taxes or lowering expenditures. States should have BSFs to offset revenue shortfalls, but the exact magnitude of how much to save will vary. Just like what's in your savings account will depend on where you are at in life and what your goals are, state BSFs should vary based on different risk factors. Some research has debated the efficacy of a one-size-fits-all guideline of saving 5% of funds

(Joyce 2002). A more conservative estimate suggests that states save at least 30% of total revenues (Kriz 2002). Over time, researchers have moved away from advising rule-of-thumb savings rates and instead suggest that states should set aside amounts that correspond to the unique makeup and volatility of their revenues (Zhao 2016).

Public finance researcher Kenneth A. Kriz suggests that how much is saved in a BSF is "strongly dependent on a jurisdiction's revenue history and revenue mix, its desire for future expenditure growth, and its success in producing interest earnings on its fund balances." This necessitates taking a closer look at each state's unique fiscal context and goals. Taking into account a state's risk factors or revenue portfolio that influence its expected revenue shortfalls, for example, can shape how much it should deposit into its BSF (Ray and Cornea 2004).

One approach that economist Erick Elder recommends is to save the amount necessary to help cover a state's expected revenue shortfall during a recession of average size (Elder 2016). He calculates how prepared each state is according to this rule of thumb by estimating how large revenue shortfalls would be for each state during hypothetical recessions of various sizes. At the time of his study in 2016, Elder found that the majority of states had not saved enough in their rainy-day funds to weather recessions of many sizes.

According to Elder's estimates in 2016, states have been under-saving, but some are more prepared than others. He identified Alaska, West Virginia, South Dakota, Nebraska, and Wyoming as being the five most prepared states for the next recession when it comes to covering revenue shortfalls. Arkansas, Kansas, Montana, New Jersey, Pennsylvania, and Wisconsin, by contrast, were highlighted as the least prepared.

Two of the states that Elder highlighted as being more prepared for recessions—Alaska and Wyoming—are rated by the Pew Charitable Trusts as having the most volatile revenue streams between 2000 and 2019 (The Pew Charitable Trusts 2020). Pew ranks Alaska, North Dakota, and Wyoming as the three states with the most revenue volatility. This is primarily because of their large reliance on oil production in their tax system.

Each of these states rely on oil tax revenues as their primary income source. It is normal for state economies to differ, but designing a tax system that relies largely on any one industry is risky. Doing so narrows the tax base and violates principles of sound tax policy (Tax Foundation 2012). One such principle is the goal of keeping tax systems neutral, where not any one industry is favored or harmed disproportionately. Broad tax bases—where a tax is applied to all goods and services equally—helps maintain neutrality and make a tax system more efficient. This approach makes it easier to raise more revenue in an equitable way that also leaves room to keep tax rates low. The most important takeaway from this is that broad-based taxes are more likely to produce relatively stable tax revenues year to year.

Having volatile revenue sources and a narrow tax base are concerning enough issues when they exist separately. When both features are present in a state budget, like in Alaska, they introduce even more risk together. States in situations like this should be especially careful about restraining spending and making efforts to save. More comprehensive reforms would reconsider the structural reliance on volatile revenue sources and tax system inefficiencies.

The good news is that states that tend to more heavily rely on severance taxes, which are highly volatile, also went into the pandemic with the largest year-end BSF balances as a percentage of their general fund (Cantlon 2021).

Whether you're in a state that faces budget risks as severe as Alaska's or not, you're going to face revenue volatility to some degree. In either case, it is important to set aside money for a rainy day. As public administration researcher Philip Joyce (2002) aptly concludes, the most we can say about the "optimal" size of a BSF is that it should be above zero (Joyce 2002, 87). Where to go beyond this largely depends on a state's unique context. This, paired with an eye toward the structure of a BSF, are the guideposts that can better ensure a state's path to sustainability.

BSFS AND FISCAL HEALTH

When a state moderates its budget cycles by using a BSF, this has larger implications for its fiscal health. As discussed earlier, cash, budget, long-run, service-level, and trust fund financial indicators matter for assessing a state's fiscal health. Strong financial indicators across all of these categories and over time translate into more robust fiscal health. Fiscal stress, on the other hand, occurs when a state is weak in any of these areas. Researchers often focus on budget shortfalls in particular when assessing the degree of a state's fiscal stress. BSFs have been found to ease state fiscal stress following the 1990, 2000, and 2008 U.S. economic crises (Sobel and Holcombe 1996, Douglas and Gaddie 2002, Chen, Chou and Lu 2018). A less researched area is the connection between overall fiscal health, as measured by the FCI, and state BSFs.

Figure 4.2 helps us visualize this larger association. It shows that, on average, states with larger BSF balances as a percentage of their general fund expenditures are more likely to rank higher on the FCI. This isn't saying that increasing your state's BSF balance guarantees better fiscal health. This is especially true because the rankings are relative; if every state put the same amount of money in their BSF tomorrow, this wouldn't change the relative rankings in the FCI. There are also many other factors that influence a state's

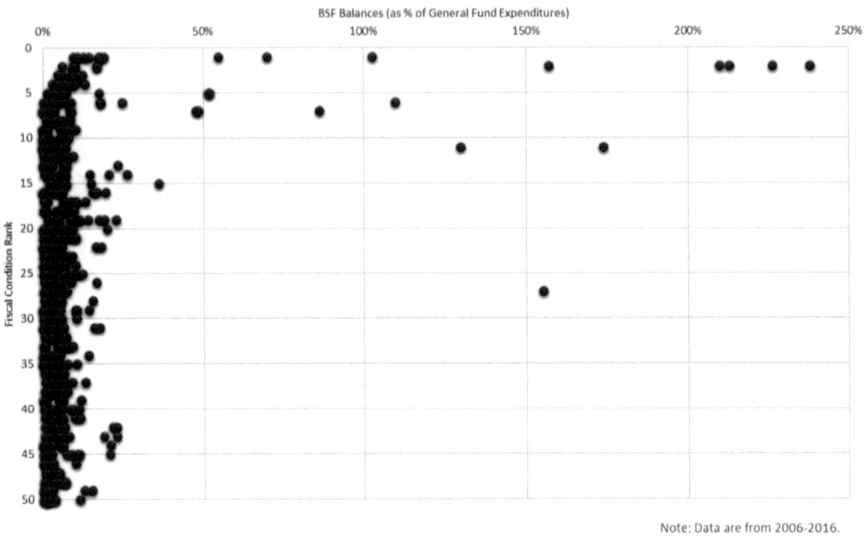

Figure 4.2 States with BSFs Are More Likely to Rank Higher in Fiscal Health. *Source*: Authors calculations based on Eileen Norcross and Olivia Gonzalez, *Ranking the States by Fiscal Condition, 2018 edition* (Arlington, VA: Mercatus Center at George Mason University, 2018). https://www.mercatus.org/publications/urban-economics/state-fiscal-rankings. The Pew Charitable Trusts, *Fiscal 50: State Trends and Analysis* (Accessed February 2021). https://www.pewtrusts.org/en/research-and-analysis/data-visualizations/2014/fiscal-50#ind5.

Table 4.3 Associations between Fiscal Condition Solvency Area and BSFs

	Rainy-Day Fund Balances as % of General Fund Expenditures
Overall Fiscal Condition Rank	−0.257
Cash rank	−0.298
Long-run rank	−0.312
Budget rank	−0.182
Service-level rank	0.193
Trust fund rank	0.185

Source: Authors calculations based on Eileen Norcross and Olivia Gonzalez, *Ranking the States by Fiscal Condition, 2018 edition* (Arlington, VA: Mercatus Center at George Mason University, 2018). https://www.mercatus.org/publications/urban-economics/state-fiscal-rankings. The Pew Charitable Trusts, *Fiscal 50: State Trends and Analysis* (Accessed February 2021). https://www.pewtrusts.org/en/research-and-analysis/data-visualizations/2014/fiscal-50#ind5.

fiscal health. On average, however, states with more robust BSF balances are more likely to be ranked higher along fiscal health dimensions.

Table 4.3 portrays another way of looking at the association between the FCI and BSF balances. It displays the correlation coefficients between BSF balances and the Fiscal Condition rank, along with each of its solvency areas. Correlation coefficients help us capture the degree and direction of an association between two variables. Values can range between −1 and 1, where a value of 1 is interpreted as a perfect positive correlation between two variables: as one variable increases, the other variable also tends to increase. A value of −1 implies a perfect negative correlation: as one variable increases, the other decreases by the same degree. Values closer to zero mean that the association between the two variables is less strong in magnitude.

As table 4.3 displays, the correlation coefficient between the overall FCI rank and BSF balances (as a percentage of general fund expenditures) is −0.257. This means that the magnitude of the association is not very strong, but it is a negative one nevertheless, as predicted by figure 4.2. Remember that moving higher in the fiscal condition rankings means an improvement in fiscal health. So when we say that there is a negative association between the FCI ranking and BSF balance percentages, this means that as a state's BSF balance increases, they are more likely to get a smaller Fiscal Condition Rank. Numerically, this is a reduction in rank, which develops the negative correlation. But the interpretation is that a reduction in rank translates into *better* fiscal health.

This correlation does not take into consideration other factors that could be influencing a state's fiscal health. A state's population size, economic environment, and income, for example, all affect the fiscal environment that a state faces. For this reason, I calculate a new coefficient that captures the association between the FCI overall rank with BSF balances, after factoring in state GDP per capita and state personal income. I find that a one percentage increase in BSF balances is associated with about a 1.85 improvement in fiscal condition rank.[2]

Public administration researcher Yilin Hou examines the association between BSF balances and the gap between actual annual expenditures and "ideal" smoother trends. When actual expenditures end up falling below a state's ideal projected trend, this produces what Hou calls a negative expenditure gap. In his (2003) paper, he finds that a one percentage point increase in BSF balances as a percent of general fund expenditures reduces negative expenditure gaps by a quarter percentage point (Y. Hou 2003).

If states utilized BSFs more effectively, the association with fiscal health would likely be even stronger. Following the 2008 recession, states utilized various policy tools for closing their budget gaps, but using BSFs and other similar reserves only accounted for 9% of efforts (Campbell and Sances 2013). Spending cuts, on the other hand, dominated the response of states, accounting for 45% of states' total budget gap-closing efforts between 2008 and 2012. Emergency federal aid, increases in taxes and fees, and securitization of tobacco settlement payments accounted for 24, 16, and 7% of response efforts, respectively. About half of the 46 states that had BSFs at the start of 2008 drew on their funds at the peak of the recession. Over time, BSFs have become more popular. Following the 2008 recession many states strategized to build up their reserves more and this provided some more flexibility when they were hit by the revenue fallout brought about by the COVID-19 pandemic (Cantlon 2021).

In fiscal year 2020, nearly half of states withdrew from their BSFs in order to balance budgets or in anticipation of spending plans for 2021 (Cantlon 2021). States are still learning to live with the new fiscal environment brought about by the COVID-19 pandemic, but the trend suggests BSFs have been increasing in popularity since the 1980s. As the fiscal environment ahead remains uncertain, BSFs will continue to be an essential tool.

In their research, economists Russell S. Sobel and Randall G. Holcombe found that it wasn't the mere existence of BSFs that reduced state fiscal stress (Sobel and Holcombe 1996). Instead, states that had BSFs with rules that mandated deposits were more effective at reducing fiscal stress. This may sound straightforward, but surprisingly not all states have strong rules surrounding deposits and withdrawals for the BSFs.

RULES AND STRUCTURE MATTER

Forty-nine states currently have BSFs. The exception is Colorado, which technically does not have an official BSF. There wouldn't be much more to say if the presence of reserves was all that was needed. Aside from what Colorado could do to develop a more formal BSF, many states have room to improve when it comes to the management of their funds. It's not the mere presence of a BSF that translates to a better approach to budget shortfalls or to fiscal health more broadly. What is even more crucial is the structure and rules surrounding how BSFs are managed. Having adequate reserves becomes a by-product of this.

The four common elements present in what shapes a BSF's structure are (1) methods deciding deposits, (2) rules governing withdrawals, (3) provisions for repayment, and (4) caps on how much money can be in the fund (National Conference of State Legislatures 2018). This chapter focuses on the first two elements of deposit and withdrawal rules, but the other elements are also important and are covered by others (Merrifield and Poulson 2014, Zhao 2016).

The stringency of these rules can significantly impact the effectiveness of a BSF. The hard part is developing measures of these rules that allow us to compare the states systematically.

Wagner classifies BSF deposit and withdrawal requirements according to their level of strictness using a scale of 1 to 4, with higher values indicating stricter requirements (Wagner 2003). States with a value of 1 do not have any explicit deposit (or withdrawal) rule. Instead, decision-makers in these states can make deposits (or withdrawals) at their discretion through appropriation. A value of 2 for a state's deposit rules means that it is required to deposit a portion of its general fund surplus into its BSF. The same value for the state's withdrawal rules implies that it is allowed to withdraw some portion of any revenue shortfall it encounters.

The last two values in Wagner's scale—3 and 4—are the most stringent. For deposits, a value of 3 means that the state is required to make a designated deposit each year. For withdrawals, it implies that a supermajority is required to withdraw any funds. Lastly, a value of 4 indicates that a state follows a pre-established formula to designate when withdrawals and deposits are made. This is the strictest approach because it removes the discretion of policymakers. During economic booms, this means tying the hands of policymakers so that they do not devote excessive amounts of surplus funds to new spending priorities. Strict withdrawal rules, if properly structured, help guarantee that inappropriate withdrawals are not made.

Wagner's work suggests that states that have stricter rules also save more (Knight and Levinson 1999, Wagner 2003). Saving more money translates into strong fiscal health. Having more savings increases the amount that a state has on hand in the case of an emergency, which helps cover expenses should there be an unexpected drop in revenues. This also allows a state to continue to make payments on their financial responsibilities. Each of these dynamics are captured by the FCI that we have been looking at in this chapter.

To investigate this further, I calculate more coefficients that provide preliminary assessments of the relationship between BSF rule stringency and state fiscal health. Using Wagner's measure, further advanced by researcher Isabel Rodriguez-Tejedo, I focus on the stringency of withdrawal and deposit rules (Rodriguez-Tejedo 2012).[3]

I find that the stringency of deposit and withdrawal rules are both significantly associated with stronger fiscal health over the 2006 to 2016 time period. A one-unit rise in a state's Wagner deposit rule stringency value is associated with about a 1.63 improvement in its rank in the FCI. The same increase in a state's withdrawal stringency is associated with a 1.75 improvement in its rank.[4]

Using well-defined deposit and withdrawal rules, often structured as formulas, is an approach advocated by the Pew Research Center and many researchers (The Pew Charitable Trusts 2020). Using formulas helps prevent budget gimmicks or political manipulation of BSFs. When deposits and withdrawals are left to the discretion of politicians, states tend to have less robust BSF balances (Rose 2008).

This is because politicians have an incentive to be short-sighted. Researcher Shanna Rose finds that between 1989 and 2005 lawmakers across the states withdrew more from BSFs during election years (Rose 2008). This effect is even stronger when politicians who make these decisions are up for re-election on the horizon. It also means deposits into BSFs are less likely to be made during good times because politicians, when left to their own discretion, have the incentive to devote surpluses to new programs. Rose recommends increasing the number of people involved in approving BSF withdrawals or deposits; this would allow opportunities for vetoes to put a check on politically motivated BSF management.

Whether BSFs are used properly or used opportunistically depends on how much fund management is left to discretion. Allowing for more discretion has led to cases where BSFs have been used to avoid the restrictions imposed by other institutions, like tax and expenditure limits or balanced budget requirements (Wagner 2003, Rodriguez-Tejedo 2012). Poor fiscal conditions can only exacerbate the incentive for politicians to use budget gimmicks. Not only do evasive budget practices take place when it comes to BSF management, they also occur in the forecasting of revenues and expenditures, one-time actions to balance budgets, funding of public pensions and other post-employment benefits, and in the reporting of financial information (Hendrick and Hu 2020).

For these reasons, it's important to explore the role that BSF deposit and withdrawal rule stringency plays in state fiscal health. Building on my other calculations so far, I constructed a new estimate of BSF stringency. I develop a binary variable that equals one if a state uses formulas for determining when deposits and withdrawals can be made. Both a state's withdrawal and deposit rules—as measured by values of 4 in Wagner's stringency scale—have to be determined by formulas to meet this standard. All other cases are captured by a value of 0 for this binary variable.

Then, I calculate how this newly constructed measure—the BSF formula variable—is associated with state fiscal health. I find that having formulas determining both withdrawals and deposits is associated with an improvement of 3.31 ranks in the FCI.[5]

Table 4.4 displays each coefficient discussed so far. It shows that stringent BSF withdrawal and deposit rules are significantly associated with improvements in state fiscal health. Having strict deposit *and* withdrawal formulas—not just for one of these categories—appears to have an even larger effect.

This demonstrates that a state's BSF balance is not the only thing that matters for a state's fiscal health. The rules or institutions that shape how resources come and go are just as, if not more, important. Comparing the coefficients from table 4.4 with my results in the previous section illustrates that strict formulas surrounding BSF deposit and withdrawals have a larger impact on a state's FCI ranking than BSF balances alone. The former improves a state's FCI position by 3.31 ranks on average, whereas the latter is associated with a 1.85 improvement.

Taking the formula approach to designate when withdrawals and deposits have the main benefits. The first is that it minimizes the opportunities for

Table 4.4 Strict BSF Withdrawal and Deposit Rules Are Associated with Fiscal Health

	BSF Stringency Category		
	Deposit Rules	*Withdrawal Rules*	*Deposit and Withdrawals Both Use Formulas*
An increase in a state's BSF stringency score improves its FCI rank by	1.63	1.75	3.31

Source: Author's calculations based on Eileen Norcross and Olivia Gonzalez, *Ranking the States by Fiscal Condition, 2018 edition* (Arlington, VA: Mercatus Center at George Mason University, 2018). https://www.mercatus.org/publications/urban-economics/state-fiscal-rankings. BSF stringency ratings are based on Wagner (2003) and Rodriguez- (2012). State GDP per capita and personal income are drawn from the Bureau of Economic Analysis Regional Economic Accounts. https://www.bea.gov/data/economic-accounts/regional.

Note: This table displays the coefficients produced by OLS regressions where Wagner's BSF stringency ratings are the independent variable and the Fiscal Condition Index rank is the dependent variable. All of these coefficients are significant at the $p<0.01$ level. State GDP per capita and personal income are used as control variables.

BSF funds to be used for political gain and at the expense of the state's fiscal health. Even if opportunistic fiscal practices were not a concern, there still lies the difficulty—if not the impossibility—of predicting the future. Models developed by researchers have improved by incorporating the unique context of each state's fiscal and business cycle environment. However, every prediction is still imperfect. We do not know when the next recession will hit with certainty, and with what severity. Defining rules that take into consideration each state's volatility and market risk do require some judgments, however, they do not require re-assessments every budget cycle. Setting them far enough in advance and sticking to them removes the political and knowledge constraints that are exacerbated during a recession.

NEXT STEPS

In 2012, Scott Pattison, executive director of the National Association of State Budget Officers, made a call for states to reevaluate their BSF rules (Pattison 2012). At that time, the worst of the 2008 downturn for the states was over. This offered a prime opportunity for states to reevaluate their approach in preparation for the next downturn. States will be facing a similar opportunity within the next few years.

This chapter summarizes the role of BSFs and institutions in shaping fiscal sustainability. Corroborating previous research, I find that BSF balances and structure are significantly associated with fiscal health. When it comes to practically applying this to fiscal analysis and management, it is important to remember that rankings can only tell us so much. To comprehensively assess how prepared a state is for a fiscal crisis, it is crucial to take a deeper look at the metrics that comprise its FCI ranking. These include the financial indicators that make up each fiscal solvency area listed in table 4.1.

In a similar fashion, it is important for each state to look at the unique structure of their BSF in order to find out how to improve their emergency preparedness. Although different fiscal and economic environments can necessitate differences in BSF balance and structure, there are still margins for states to improve BSF rules as they currently stand. Moving toward formula-based deposit and withdrawal rules can help states be more accountable so that they have the funds they need when the next economic shock hits.

States should keep in mind that surplus revenue in good economic times is unexpected revenue. It cannot be guaranteed to be delivered again in the future. Therefore, these funds should not be consistently directed toward ongoing operating costs or for developing new programs. Instead, surpluses are meant for BSF funds, one-time capital expenditures, or for temporary tax relief (Schunk and Woodward 2005). BSF formulas are the way to ensure that this happens. During good and bad fiscal times, there is political pressure to not think about long-term consequences. Having preset formulas help take off the pressure and ensures that deposits and withdrawals are made when appropriate.

As states take steps to evaluate how to improve their finances in the coming years, something that will help in this process is to see how BSF assessment fits in the larger picture of fiscal sustainability. The associations I've calculated between BSFs and fiscal health demonstrate broad trends that have occurred on average across the states. When it comes to assessing each state individually, I recommend taking a step-by-step as follows:

1. Start with calculating the financial indicators of the FCI for your state.
2. Factor in the soundness of reporting requirements, as these can have a significant influence on the accuracy of certain budget items, especially for public pensions (Biggs 2011, Weinberg and Norcros 2017).[6]
3. Supplement the analysis from steps 1 and 2 with measures not included in state financial reports. This includes variables like GDP per capita, personal income, and a state's bond ratings.
4. Pair all collected metrics with the state's institutional context. This includes the presence and structure of tax and expenditure limits, balanced budget requirements, tax structure, among other factors.
5. Bring everything to life with case studies.

Steps 1 through 3 explore the quantitative measures of fiscal sustainability, while steps 4 and 5 are qualitative measures. Robust fiscal analysis considers all of those factors. The final step is essential for bringing together all the knowledge gained from steps 1 through 4. Developing case studies, or looking at your state's experiences from the past can help make sense of the many different factors that go into influencing its fiscal health. Being more financially prepared for a crisis is not the result of one tried and true, one-size-fits-all, approach. Instead, it results from understanding how these many different components interact with each other. Sustainable solutions are fostered from this understanding.

When going through these steps to assess your state's fiscal sustainability, BSFs are one institution to keep in mind. BSFs are not meant to solve all of a state's problems, but well-designed BSFs can certainly help cope with recessions.

NOTES

1. Some tax and expenditure limits are designed to limit revenues as well, although this is considered less effective at meeting their goal of limiting government spending growth.
2. I utilize a standard OLS regression where BSF balance is the independent variable and the FCI rank is the dependent variable. The coefficient of −1.85 is significant at the $p<0.01$ level. I control for each state's GDP per capita and personal income, and I use robust standard errors. GDP and income data are drawn from the Bureau of Economic Analysis Regional Economic Accounts.
3. Like Rodriguez-Tejedo, I only include states that adopted BSFs as of 2000 as determined by her definition of a BSF: "institutionalized budgetary tools that allow for the accumulation of funds during expansions that can be used during recessions," p. 377. 45 states meet this benchmark. Alabama, Colorado, and Oregon had reserve funds as of 2000, but they were either restricted to usage in the case of natural disasters or for education spending. Arkansas and Montana did not have any BSF or reserve funds established by 2000. Restricting the sample of BSF enactment to this time period allows us to only look at those states that had time to build up their BSFs by 2006, the first year of the sample period for the FCI examined in this chapter. All of these states have since implemented BSFs.
4. I estimate these coefficients using standard OLS regressions where Wagner's stringency ratings are the independent variable and the FCI rank is the dependent variable. All of these coefficients are significant at the $p<0.01$ level. I control for each state's GDP per capita and personal income, and I use robust standard errors.
5. This coefficient is significant at the $p<0.01$ level.
6. A further discussion of these issues can be found in chapter 3 of this volume, authored by Thomas Savidge.

REFERENCES

Arnett, Sarah. 2014. *State Fiscal Condition: Ranking the 50 States.* Mercatus Center at George Mason University.

Biggs, Andrew. 2011. "Proposed GASB rules show why only market valuation fully captures public pension liabilities." *Financial Analysts Journal* 67 (2): 18–22.

Buckley, Patricia. 2020. "U.S. policy response to COVID-19 aims to set the stage for recovery." *Deloitte Insights.*

Bureau of Economic Analysis. n.d. *Gross Domestic Product by State, 2nd Quarter 2020.* https://www.bea.gov/news/2020/gross-domestic-product-state-2nd-quarter-2020.

Campbell, Andrea Louise, and Michael W. Sances. 2013. "State fiscal policy during the Great Recession: Budgetary impacts and policy responses." *The ANNALS of the American Academy of Political and Social Science* 650 (1): 252–273.

Cantlon, McKenzie. 2021. *Rainy Days Are Here: States Tap Reserve Funds to Plug Budget Holes.* National Conference of State Legislatures.

Center on Budget and Policy Priorities. 2020. "*States Need Significantly More Fiscal Relief to Slow the Emerging Deep Recession.*" https://www.cbpp.org/research/state-budget-and-tax/states-need-significantly-more-fiscal-relief-to-slow-the-emerging.

Chen, Hsuan-Chi, Robin K. Chou, and Chien-Lin Lu. 2018. "Saving for a rainy day: Evidence from the 2000 dot-com crash and the 2008 credit crisis." *Journal of Corporate Finance* 48: 680–699.

Douglas, James W., and Ronald K. Gaddie. 2002. "State rainy day funds and fiscal crises: Rainy day funds and the 1990-1991 recession revisited." *Public Budgeting & Finance* 22 (1): 19–30.

Elder, Erick M. 2016. *Weathering the Next Recession: How Prepared are the 50 States?* Mercatus Center at George Mason University.

Finkler, Steven. 2012. *Financial Management for Public, Health, and Not-for-Profit Organizations.* Upper Saddle River, NJ: Prentice Hall.

Gold, S. D. 1984. "Contingency measures and fiscal limitations: The real world significance of some recent state budget innovations." *National Tax Journal* 37 (3): 421–432.

Grizzle, Cleopatra, LaShonda Stewart, and Jeremy Phillips. 2015. "Rainy day fund adoption in U.S. states: a case of learning or emulation." *International Review of Public Administration* 20 (1): 17–33.

Groves, Sanford M., Maureen W. Godsey, and Martha A. Shulman. 1981. "Financial Indicators for Local Government." *Public Budgeting & Finance* 1 (2): 5–19.

Hendrick, Rebecca, and Xiaoyan Hu. 2020. "Beyond truth and integrity in state budgeting: Why state governments use budget balancing maneuvers (or gimmicks)?" *Public Budgeting & Finance* 40 (4): 104–127.

Hou, Y. 2004. "Budget stabilization fund." *Encyclopedia of Public Administration and Public Policy, First Update Supplement* 34–43.

Hou, Yilin. 2003. "What stabilizes state general fund expenditures in downturn years—Budget stabilization fund or general fund unreserved undesignated balance?" *Budget Budgeting & Finance* 650 (1): 64–91.
Joyce, Phillip G. 2002. "What's so magical about 5 percent? A nationwide look at factors that influence the optimal size of state rainy day funds." *Public Budgeting & Finance* 21 (2): 62–87.
Knight, Brian, and Arik Levinson. 1999. "Rainy day funds and state government savings." *National Tax Journal* 52 (3): 459–472.
Kriz, Kenneth A. 2002. "The optimal level of local government fund balances: A simulation approach." *Annual Conference on Taxation and Minutes of the Annual Meeting of the National Tax Association*. National Tax Association. 78–84.
Larson, Sarah E., and Bruce D. McDonald. 2020. "When the beaches close: Impact of COVID-19 upon county fiscal health in Florida." *SSRN*.
Maher, Craig, Trang Hoang, and Anne Hindery. 2020. "Fiscal responses to COVID-19: Evidence from local governments and nonprofits." *Public Administration Review* 644–650.
McDonald, Bruce D. III, and Sarah E. Larson. 2020. "Implications of the coronavirus on sales tax revenue and local government fiscal health." *Journal of Public and Nonprofit Affairs* 6 (3): 377–400.
McKinsey Global Institute. 2020. "*Beyond Coronavirus: The Path to the Next Normal*." https://www.mckinsey.com/industries/healthcare/our-insights/beyond-coronavirus-the-path-to-the-next-normal.
McNichol, Elizabeth, and Michael Leachman. 2020. *States Continue to Face Large Shortfalls Due to COVID-19 Effects*. Washington, DC: Center for Budget and Policy Priorities.
Merrifield, John, and Barry W. Poulson. 2014. "State fiscal policies for budget stabilization and economic growth: A dynamic scoring analysis." *Cato Journal* 34 (1): 47.
Mitchell, Matthew D. 2010. "TEL it like it is: Do state tax and expenditure limits actually limit spending?" *Mercatus Center Working Paper* 10-71.
National Conference of State Legislatures. 2020. "*Coronavirus (COVID-19): Revised State Revenue Projections*." https://www.ncsl.org/elections-and-campaigns/coronavirus-covid-19-revised-state-revenue-projections.
National Conference of State Legislatures. 2018. "Rainy day fund structures."
Norcross, Eileen. 2015. *Ranking the States by Fiscal Condition*. Mercatus Center at George Mason University.
Norcross, Eileen, and Olivia Gonzalez. 2016. *Ranking the States by Fiscal Condition, 2016 Edition*. Mercatus Center at George Mason University.
Norcross, Eileen, and Olivia Gonzalez. 2017. *Ranking the States by Fiscal Condition, 2017 Edition*. Mercatus Center at George Mason University.
Norcross, Eileen, and Olivia Gonzalez. 2018. *Ranking the States by Fiscal Condition, 2018 Edition*. Mercatus Center at George Mason University.
Pattison, Scott. 2012. "A time to reevaluate the rules for rainy day funds." *Public Administration Review* 72 (3): 386–387.

Peter G. Foundation. 2020. "*Pandemic Budget Crunch Could Force States to Slash Social Services, Education, Police Budgets, and More*." https://www.pgpf.org/blog/2020/07/pandemic-budget-crunch-could-force-states-to-slash-social-services-education-police-budgets-and-more.

Ray, Nelson D., and Gary C. Cornea. 2004. "Determining the optimal size of rainy day funds using value at risk." *Annual Conference on Taxation and Minutes of the Annual Meetings of the National Tax Association*. National Tax Association. 80–87.

Rodriguez-Tejedo, Isabel. 2012. "The determinants of the structure of rainy day funds." *Public Administration Review* 72 (3): 376–386.

Rose, Shanna. 2008. "The political manipulations of US state rainy day funds under rules versus discretion." *State Politics & Policy Quarterly* 8 (2): 150–176.

Schunk, Donald, and Douglas Woodward. 2005. "Spending stabilization rules: A solution to recurring state budget crises?" *Public Budgeting & Finance* 25 (4): 105–124.

Sobel, Russel S., and Randall G. Holcombe. 1996. "The impact of state rainy day funds in easing state fiscal crises during the 1990–1991 recession." *Public Budgeting & Finance* 16 (3): 28–48.

Stallmann, Judith I., Craig S. Maher, Steven C. Deller, and Sungho Park. 2017. "Surveying the effects of limitations on taxes and expenditures: What do/don't we know?" *Journal of Public and Nonprofit Affairs* 3 (2): 197–222.

Sunjoo, Kwak. 2014. "The dynamics of state fiscal behavior over the business cycle: Are state fiscal policies procyclical?" *The American Review of Public Administration* 44 (5): 550–574.

Tax Foundation. 2012. "*The Principles of Sound Tax Policy*." https://taxfoundation.org/principles/#:~:text=All%20Tax%20Foundation%20research%20is,for%20policymakers%20and%20taxpayers%20everywhere.

The Pew Charitable Trusts. 2020. "*Governors' 2020 Priorities in Their Own Words*." https://www.pewtrusts.org/en/research-and-analysis/data-visualizations/2020/governors-2020-priorities-in-their-own-words.

The Pew Charitable Trusts. 2020. "*How to Effectively Use State Rainy Day Funds: Best Practices for Spending, Replenishing Reserves*."

Wagner, Gary A. 2003. "Are state budget stabilization funds only the illusion of savings? Evidence from stationary panel data." *The Quarterly Review of Economics and Finance* 43 (2): 213–238.

Wang, Xiaohu, Lynda Dennis, and Yuan Sen Tu. 2007. "Measuring financial condition: A study of US states." *Public Budgeting & Finance* 27 (2): 1–21.

Weinberg, Sheila, and Eileen Norcros. 2017. "A judge in their own cause: GASB 67/68 and the continued mismeasurement of public sector pension liabilities." *Journal of Law, Economics, and Policy* 14: 61.

White, Kathryn. 2020. *State Fiscal Outlook: Pre- & Post-COVID-19*. National Association of State Budget Officers.

Zhao, Bo. 2016. "Saving for a rainy day: Estimating the needed size of US state budget stabilization funds." *Regional Science and Urban Economics* 61: 130–152.

Chapter 5

Debt Fatigue in the States

Red States, Blue States, and Zombie States

John Merrifield and Barry W. Poulson

INTRODUCTION

The United States is in its worst crisis since World War II. The crisis relentlessly attacking America is debt fatigue; the slowing of economic growth, and the ever-present threat of a financial crisis induced by default risk and tax increases, and or outburst of debilitating inflation.

During World War II, the national debt rose above GDP. Politicians knew that the huge debt was unsustainable. So, in the years after World War II, they reduced debt below half of GDP. In that era, nearly all state and local governments also maintained sustainable levels of debt.

Over the past half century, governments at all levels have suffered debt fatigue. Our federal government has again raised debt above GDP. Much of that debt resulted from responses to the 2008 financial crisis and the 2020–2021 pandemic. But the slowdown in economic growth that is the key symptom of debt fatigue is also a major cause of our declared debt crisis. Alongside the debt growth, we've seen a decline in GDP growth.

Although the federal debt crisis is well known, less well understood is the state and local government debt crisis. In part, this is due to problems in measuring and reporting total long-term liabilities. The Government Accounting Standards Board allows states much leeway in how they measure and report long-term liabilities, especially in how they report unfunded liabilities in government employee pension and health-care plans.[1] In this study we take a pragmatic approach in using the measure of long-term liabilities reported in state CAFRs, recognizing the limitations of this measure. This measure should be referred to as "GASB" debt to distinguish it from other measures of total state debt.

Over the past five decades, many state governments allowed their GASB debt to top 10% of personal income, a debt level that exposes them and bond buyers to default risk. Unfunded liabilities in pension and other post-employment benefit (OPEB) plans underlie most of the recent jump in state and local debt.

Massive federal bailouts have kept some states from defaulting on their debt. In response to the 2008 financial crisis, and now the coronavirus pandemic, the federal government extended trillions of dollars in state aid. The Federal Reserve allowed the states to designate municipal governments and public enterprises for direct access to emergency lending. The massive bailout of state and local governments significantly increased already unsustainable federal debt growth.

State debt has grown rapidly over the past two decades, despite the limitations imposed by most state constitutions. Fiscal rules designed to more effectively constrain debt growth are one approach to many states' unsustainable debt growth. This chapter proposes rules for establishing debt brakes. Other countries successfully use debt brakes to reduce debt at the national, state, and local levels. To understand the rationale for a debt brake, we begin with a discussion of debt solvency and sustainability.

DEBT SOLVENCY AND SUSTAINABILITY

Solvency simply means the ability to meet financial obligations in full and on time. When individuals and private firms become insolvent, they may face legal sanctions or bankruptcy. Governments can also become insolvent when they fail to meet their financial obligations.[2]

We dismiss the proposition of modern monetary theory that sovereign governments are immune to insolvency.[3] MMT implies that sovereign governments can meet their debt obligations without negative consequences simply by printing money. U.S. states cannot issue their own currency, but the assumption in modern monetary theory is that the federal government can print money to bail out the states and avoid insolvency. We have seen the outcome when sovereign governments print money without constraint; hyperinflation in Germany after World War I, and more recently in Venezuela.[4]

An alternative view of solvency arises from a mathematical proposition. If the rate of economic growth tops the rate of interest, debt can grow without limit. Just the U.S. debt owned by the public exceeds GDP, and modern Keynesians argue that even if it grows to some multiple of GDP, it is still not a problem as long as economic growth exceeds the rate of interest. Unfortunately, higher debt levels impact both economic growth and the rate of interest. Indeed, the Congressional Budget Office (CBO 2018) projected that if the debt to GDP ratio continues to rise, we will see higher interest rates and lower rates of economic growth. The CBO also argues that printing more money is not a solution to our debt crisis.

The literature suggests an alternative approach to solvency, the market discipline hypothesis.[5] It says there is a nonlinear relationship between borrowing costs and debt levels. Costs eventually rise steeply, culminating in loss of access to credit. Bayoumi and co-authors (1995) find that the yield on state debt rises by 23 basis points per percentage point rise in debt. At debt levels one standard deviation above the mean, borrowing costs are 35 basis points greater. In their preferred equation, the maximum debt level before states begin to struggle to access credit is 8–9% of gross state product. Demonstrating the significance of debt premiums, they estimate a 50 basis-point drop in the borrowing costs of states with effective constitutional debt limits, and Bayoumi and co-authors find that such limits significantly reduce borrowing costs. Cyclical factors also affect the probability of default.[6]

Based on this research, we set a debt tolerance level at 10% of personal income. For most states, that debt level exceeds state revenue. States with prudent fiscal policies keep their debt/personal income ratio well below the 10% tolerance level, or they move quickly to lower debt to below 10% of personal income.

DEBT FATIGUE IN THE STATES

We designed fiscal rules to include debt brakes that restore sustainable debt levels through slower spending growth. We explore the potential impact of the debt brakes in some red states, blue states, and zombie states—our name for states that are federal bailout dependent. That is, Zombie states' debt level is so high that the combination of low interest rates and federal bailout/subsidy is all that stands between them and insolvency.

Most red states have debt/personal income ratios well below the 10% debt tolerance level. Red states have not suffered the debt fatigue that occurs when the debt/personal income ratio tops the 10% debt tolerance level. Some red states saw a sharp rise in the debt/personal income ratio during the 2008 financial crisis and the coronavirus pandemic. But they avoided debt fatigue. They responded to the economic shocks with policies that reduced the debt/personal income ratio well below the 10% debt tolerance level. Texas, for example, consistently pursued prudent fiscal policies. While the debt/personal income ratio rose in Texas, it is still well below the debt tolerance level. Likewise, Utah and Florida responded to debt increase with policies that restored sustainable debt levels, as discussed in the last chapter of this volume.

But red Kansas and purple Colorado saw a sharp increase in the debt/personal income ratio during the 2008 financial crisis, and during the coronavirus pandemic. The debt/personal income ratio rose above the debt tolerance level, and is projected to continue to rise in the forecast period.

Many blue states suffer debt fatigue. They failed to restore sustainable debt levels. Zombie states are a special category of blue states. Zombie states have had debt fatigue for many years. Those states' fiscal policies sustain debt/personal income ratios well above the 10% tolerance level. Illinois and Connecticut have had debt above the tolerance level for two decades and expect it to grow larger. The major source of their increased debt is unfunded liabilities in state pension and other OPEB plans. Zombie state politicians promised public employees improved benefits without funding them.

Zombie state debt fatigue creates a high default risk, which yields poor bond ratings. Illinois, for example, struggles to get credit at rates readily available to most states. This is a vicious cycle in which higher interest costs add to unsustainable debt levels that culminated in some zombie states temporarily losing access to credit markets. They regained access when the federal government guaranteed repayment. Without such federal bailouts, some zombie states would have defaulted on their debt.

Such federal bailouts create perverse incentives. The bailouts eliminate the incentive to enact prudent fiscal policies, such as effective fiscal rules. The potential for federal bailouts distorts credit agency ratings. Zombie states expect each economic crisis to yield another bailout; they expect an infusion of federal dollars to jolt them back to life. But unsustainable federal debt will end this Ponzi scheme, in which the federal government borrows money to bailout nearly bankrupt state governments.

States suffering debt fatigue and expecting bailouts lose their aversion to debt. Indeed, elected officials become ever more dependent on ever more costly debt. Even if they avoid default, high debt levels negatively affect their state's fiscal health. More state revenue is spent on debt service, leaving less for productive uses. In areas such as education, more revenue is spent on unfunded pension and OPEB liabilities, leaving less revenue for classroom use and school construction. Debt fatigue negatively affects all citizens, including interest groups that benefit from more government spending. Teachers, firefighters, and the police have found that debt fatigue threatens their jobs and livelihood, and they are beginning to challenge imprudent fiscal policies that result in unsustainable debt. Debt fatigue also means that a state is less able to respond to economic shocks such as the 2008 financial crisis and the coronavirus pandemic.

DESIGNING A DEBT BRAKE TO SOLVE THE STATE DEBT CRISIS

Solving a state debt crisis may require fiscal rules and policies focused on achieving the desired debt level. The debt brake we propose follows the precedent set in the countries that have successfully enacted debt brakes to reduce debt to sustainable levels.[7] The most successful of those is the Swiss debt brake used to cut debt levels at both the national and cantonal level. The EU uses the Swiss debt brake as a model for new fiscal rules. Debt brakes have achieved debt sustainability in countries such as Germany, Norway, Sweden, and Switzerland because they had broad public support across political parties and traditional coalitions.

We propose adopting a Swiss-style debt brake.[8] Use of a brake assumes a cap on the rate of growth in state outlays. Our debt brake gives policymakers cap options. Our research revealed that a cap set at the rate of inflation plus the rate of growth in population is more stringent than other caps on spending that the states have previously set. It can be made less stringent through a spending cap multiplier. A multiplier greater than 1 sets the cap above the rate of inflation plus the rate of population growth while avoiding the increased instability that results from using caps based on personal income growth. In this study, we explore the impact of a spending cap multiplier equal to 1.2, as well as having no multiplier.

The debt brake is linked to a cap on spending growth. Approaching the 10% debt to income tolerance level triggers the debt brake. We chose a debt threshold at 80% of the debt tolerance level. So, when the ratio of debt to personal income tops 8%, debt braking begins. Triggering the debt brake lowers the spending cap. The surplus revenue is then earmarked for debt reduction. Braking continues as long as the debt/personal income ratio tops 8%.

Other fiscal rules complement the debt brake. An emergency fund provides for increased spending in response to natural disasters such as the coronavirus pandemic. A budget stabilization fund sets revenue aside to offset revenue shortfalls during recessions, such as the financial crisis. A capital investment fund exists to prioritize infrastructure investments. Flexibility is introduced by allowing policymakers to adjust the caps on each of these funds.

Surplus revenue above the spending cap goes to the emergency fund, the budget stabilization fund (next chapter), and the capital fund. When the cap on each of these funds is reached, remaining surplus revenue is allocated equally between debt reduction and taxpayer relief. Taxpayer relief occurs through taxpayer rebates and/or tax rate cuts. An Appendix contains simulation model details. More detailed information for the parameter values used in the simulation model are available upon request.

The debt brake should be refined to reflect the unique debt experience and fiscal institutions in each state. Historically, the goal in some red states was to eliminate debt entirely. Today that is more likely to be perceived as an aspirational goal, rather than the basis for fiscal rules or fiscal policies. A more pragmatic approach for such states is to set a debt tolerance level well below the ratio of debt to personal income that exposes the state to risk of default.

Based on the recent trends in some red states, we explore the impact of fiscal rules with a debt tolerance level of 6%, as well as 10%.

For blue states, the debt brake reduces and maintains the debt/personal income ratio below the 10% debt tolerance level. For most blue states, the debt brake can achieve this sustainable debt level within several years. But since zombie states have suffered debt fatigue for many years, achieving a sustainable debt level may take several decades.

DYNAMIC SIMULATION OF THE DEBT BRAKE

To explore the potential impact of the debt brake on state budgets and the economy, we simulate our fiscal rules in a red state, a blue state, and a Zombie state: Florida, Colorado, and Illinois, respectively. Our dynamic simulation analysis compares four different fiscal rule designs:

Case 1. Basic Rule: The basic rule design sets the debt tolerance level at 10%. The cap on state spending growth is set equal to the rates of inflation and population growth. The expenditure rule multiplier is set equal to 1.

Case 2. Increased Expenditures Multiplier: A higher expenditures cap multiplier allows state spending to rise more rapidly than inflation plus population growth, with the cap multiplier set at 1.2.

Case 3. Debt Brake with a 10% Debt Tolerance Level: A debt brake is triggered when the ratio of debt to personal income exceeds a debt threshold. We assume a 10% debt tolerance level, and a braking threshold at 80% of that debt tolerance level, that is, 0.08. Triggering the debt brake reduces the expenditures cap below the sum of inflation plus population.

Case 4. Debt Brake with a 6% Debt Tolerance Level:

A 6% debt tolerance level is used, and a braking threshold is set at 80% of that level, that is, 0.048.

The focus of the simulation analysis is on closing the fiscal gap (i.e., stabilizing and reducing the debt/personal income ratio below the debt tolerance level). The rules give legislators several options in achieving this goal. In some cases, the debt tolerance level is not reached and the debt brake is not triggered; and in some cases the debt brake is triggered but the impact is quite small. In the case of Illinois, which has the highest debt/personal income ratio, the debt brake is triggered at both debt tolerance levels, and the impact of applying the debt brake is quite significant. This explains some differences in the graphical results of the simulation analysis.

The dynamic simulation model captures the modest supply-side effects of the debt brake. The dynamic simulation model assumes an opportunity cost of 6% when resources are shifted from the private sector to the public sector.

With the proposed fiscal rules in place, the growth in simulated personal income is higher than the growth in actual personal income.

EVEN A FISCALLY CONSERVATIVE STATE SUCH AS FLORIDA NEEDS A DEBT BRAKE

Historically, Florida has been considered a fiscally conservative state. Its fiscal policies have effectively constrained the state spending growth (see chapter 13). Florida's debt has been well below the debt tolerance levels that would expose the state to the risk of default. However, Florida's fiscal rules are not effective constraints on state spending growth, as discussed in the previous chapter. The fiscal crisis in 2009, and the more recent coronavirus pandemic have been accompanied by a big jump in debt. Florida has seen some debt fatigue, with evidence that debt has become a structural problem. Debt has risen more rapidly than personal income, which has begun to expose Florida to default risk. Much of the new debt is off-budget, in the form of unfunded liability in state pension and OPEB benefits.

Since Florida may not be able to achieve a sustainable debt level with its existing, non-binding fiscal rule, we propose a more binding cap plus our debt brake proposal that follows the precedent set in other countries that have successfully enacted debt brakes to reduce debt to sustainable levels. Our dynamic simulation model estimates the impact of such a debt brake on the budget and economy of Florida for 2002–2019.[9]

State Debt

Actual debt rose over the period from $17 billion to $70 billion. Simulated debt rises at a slower rate with fiscal rules in each of the three cases. With our basic fiscal rules in place, debt would have risen to a little more than $60 billion; to $65 billion with the higher expenditures cap multiplier in case 2.

When high debt triggers the debt brake, it imposes a more stringent cap on the growth in spending, resulting in less debt accumulation. With the debt brake and a 6% debt tolerance level, debt would have risen to a little more than $60 billion. With a 10% debt tolerance level the debt brake is not triggered, and it has no impact on the growth of debt over the period.

The most important measure of debt sustainability is the debt/personal income ratio, which saw a recent dramatic shift. Florida began the twenty-first century with a relatively low state debt burden, and for several years state debt rose less rapidly than personal income. The debt/personal income ratio fell from 3.2% in 2002 to 1.2% in 2004 and remained below 3% until 2008, when the ensuing financial crisis pushed Florida's debt to 8.3% of personal income. For the first time in recent history, Florida was exposed to the risk of state debt default.

Florida reduced the state debt burden to 5.5% of personal income in 2014, but it rebounded to 7% in 2016 and 2017 and 6% in 2018 and 2019. In those years, a major source of the greater debt burden was unfunded liabilities in state pension and OPEB plans.

State Spending

Prior to the financial crisis in 2008, Florida pursued prudent fiscal policies consistent with fiscal conservatism. General fund spending rose from $19 billion in 2002 to $28 billion in 2008. In those years, general fund spending grew at roughly the same rate as personal income. The ratio of general fund spending to personal income varied between 3.5% and 4.0%.

Florida responded to the fiscal stress of the financial crisis with a sharp reduction in general fund spending. General fund spending fell from $28 billion in 2008 to $21 billion in 2010. General fund spending relative to personal income fell below 3% in 2010. Despite that fiscal consolidation, Florida experienced a sharp increase in the debt burden in those years.

From 2010 to 2019, general fund spending in Florida rose from $21 billion to $33 billion. The growth in general fund spending in these years was comparable to the growth in personal income; the ratio of general fund spending to personal income was roughly constant at about 3%.

The simulation analysis reveals how the proposed debt brake reduces the rate of growth in general fund spending in the long run. With the basic rule in place, general fund spending increases to $26 billion in 2008. In 2010, simulated general fund spending is about the same as actual spending. In the decade after the financial crisis, the basic rule significantly reduced the growth in general fund spending. Those trends are also seen in the lower ratio of general fund spending to personal income.

A higher expenditures cap multiplier allows for a slightly higher rate of growth in spending in the pre-financial crisis and post-financial crisis years. The debt brake is triggered with a 6% debt tolerance level, but not with a 10% debt tolerance level. With the 6% debt tolerance level the debt brake is triggered in 2011, reducing the rate of growth in general fund spending by a small margin in subsequent years.

Supply-Side Effects of the Debt Brake

The fiscal rules reduce the growth in state spending, providing a modest boost to economic growth. By the end of the period, simulated personal income with the fiscal rules in place exceeds actual personal income by about 0.1%. The modest rise in personal income is accompanied by a comparable boost in state revenue.

There has been a disconnection between general fund spending and debt in Florida over the past decade. This reflects the fact that much of Florida's new debt is off budget. Florida created unfunded commitments to state pension and OPEB plans. That's why new fiscal rules that include debt brakes are important in states such as Florida.

COLORADO: A RED STATE CAPTURED BY RENT SEEKERS

Over the past two decades, Colorado's fiscal policies shifted dramatically from those of a red state to those of a blue state. In the twentieth century, Colorado was a conservative state pursuing prudent fiscal policies. The fiscal rules in place effectively constrained the growth in state spending. While a rising share of debt was shifted off budget, debt was still well below the debt tolerance levels that would have exposed the state to default risk. Over the past two decades, however, fiscal rules became less effective constraints on state spending growth. The financial crisis in 2009, and the coronavirus pandemic in 2020, were accompanied by a sharp increase in debt. But the growth in debt in Colorado is a structural as well as cyclical problem. Over the past two decades, the state has felt some debt fatigue. Debt rose more rapidly than personal income, which exposed the state to default risk. Like Florida, much of Colorado's new debt is unfunded liabilities in state pension and OPEB plans.

We used our dynamic simulation model to estimate the impact of the debt brake on the state budget and economy in Colorado for 2007–2021.[10] We assumed a stringent cap on the rate of growth in state spending in Colorado for several reasons. Colorado revenue is very volatile because the state relies heavily on its income tax. And, though Colorado has become more diversified, it is still impacted by volatility in prices for oil and natural gas. Again, our dynamic simulation analysis examines four different fiscal rule designs.

State Debt

Actual debt rose over the period from $4.3 billion to $32.8 billion. Simulated debt increases at a slower rate with fiscal rules in each of the four cases. With just the basic fiscal rules, debt rises to only $20.8 billion. With the higher expenditures cap multiplier, debt grows to a significantly higher level compared to the other fiscal rules, $24.1 billion.

When the debt brake is triggered, it imposes a more stringent cap on the growth in spending, resulting in less debt accumulation. With the debt brake and a 6% debt tolerance level, debt rises to a little less than $20.8 billion. With a 10% tolerance level, the debt brake is not triggered, and has no impact on the growth of debt.

The key debt sustainability measure is the debt/personal income ratio. Colorado began the twenty-first century with a relatively low state debt burden, and for several years state debt grew at about the same rate as personal income. The debt/personal income ratio stayed below 3% until 2013.

The financial crisis and the coronavirus pandemic had a major impact on Colorado's debt burden. But the major cause of the higher debt/personal income ratio is the increase in unfunded liabilities in state pension and OPEB plans. Because these unfunded liabilities have only been reported in the state CAFR in recent years, the data show a discontinuous increase beginning in FY 2013. Since then, state debt has been increasing more rapidly than personal income and is projected to continue to do so in the forecast period.

In FY 2017, the actual debt/personal income ratio exceeded the 8% debt threshold, and for the first time Colorado was exposed to the risk of default on its debt. The actual debt/personal income ratio is projected to increase to nearly 9% in the forecast period.

Our simulations revealed that in all four cases the simulated debt/personal income ratio stayed below the 8% debt threshold throughout the period. With a 10% debt tolerance level the debt brake is not triggered. With a 6% debt tolerance level the debt brake was triggered in FY 2016. The debt brake has a modest impact on debt over this period. But, given the projections of a continued increased in actual debt, the debt brake would have a more significant impact on debt in the long run in Colorado.

The 10% debt tolerance level is a low bar to achieve for a state with a long history of conservative fiscal policies. Setting a 6% debt tolerance level is more consistent with that historical tradition. Using the fiscal rules to reduce the debt/personal income ratio below a 6% debt tolerance level would take many years. The simulation analysis reveals how dramatic the recent shift in fiscal policies has been.

State Spending

Actual spending grew from $5.8 billion to $14.0 billion. With just the basic fiscal rule, general fund spending rises to only $9.5 billion. With a higher expenditures cap multiplier in case 2, state spending would have grown to $10.1 billion.

In case 3, with a debt tolerance level of 6%, the debt bake is triggered, resulting in a slightly lower growth in state spending. In case four, with a

10% debt tolerance level, the debt brake is not triggered, so it has no impact on the growth in state spending.

Over the period as a whole, general fund spending rose at about the same rate as personal income. The actual general fund spending/personal income ratio varied between 3% and 4%.

With the fiscal rules in place the general fund spending/personal income ratio drops. With just the basic rule, the general fund spending/personal income ratio falls to 2.5%. In case 2, with the higher expenditures cap multiplier, the ratio drops to 2.7%.

With the 6% debt tolerance level in case 3, the debt brake is triggered, and the general fund spending/personal income ratio falls slightly compared to the other fiscal rules. With the 10% debt tolerance level the debt brake is not triggered and has no impact on the ratio.

There has been a disconnect between general fund spending and debt in Colorado over the past decade. This reflects the fact that much of the debt incurred in Colorado is now off-budget. The growth in unfunded liabilities in state pension and OPEB plans is the major source of this increased debt. Solving the debt crisis in Colorado will require reforms in state pension and OPEB plans to reduce unfunded liabilities.

Solving the debt crisis in Colorado will require a significant reduction in the rate of growth in total state spending, including spending for pension and OPEB plans, and considerable downsizing of the state government relative to the private sector. This should not be surprising after two decades of debt fatigue. Enacting fiscal rules today to achieve a sustainable debt level will be a difficult task. Even with the proposed fiscal rules in place, it will take several years to reduce debt in Colorado below the debt threshold that exposes the state to risk of default. Restoring the prudent fiscal policies that Colorado pursued historically will take many years.

Supply-Side Effects of the Debt Brake

The dynamic simulation model captures the modest supply-side effects of the debt brake. With the proposed fiscal rules in place, the growth in simulated personal income is higher than the growth in actual personal income. The dynamic simulation model assumes an opportunity cost of 6% when resources move from the private sector to the public sector. The fiscal rules reduce the growth in state spending, thus providing a modest boost to economic growth. By the end of the period, simulated personal income with the fiscal rules in place exceeds actual personal income by 0.2% to 0.3%. The modest rise in personal income is accompanied by a comparable boost in state revenue.

ILLINOIS: A HALF CENTURY OF DEBT FATIGUE

Illinois has suffered debt fatigue for half a century, and it emerged in the twenty-first century as one of the most indebted states in the nation. Debt is way above tolerance levels and looks poised to continue rising under current law. That makes Illinois a zombie state. Even with the most stringent fiscal rules in place, Illinois could not have reduced debt below the debt tolerance level over the last two decades. Enacting fiscal rules today to gradually achieve a sustainable debt level will be a daunting task.

State Debt

Actual debt rises over the 2005–2019 period from $67 billion to $169 billion. Simulated debt grows at a slower rate with fiscal rules in each of the three cases. With just our basic fiscal rules, debt rises to "only" $113 billion. With the higher expenditures cap multiplier in case 2, debt reaches a significantly higher level, $120 billion.

The debt brake imposes a more stringent cap on the rate of growth in spending, resulting in less debt accumulation. With the 10% debt tolerance level, debt rises to $110 billion. With the 6% debt tolerance level, debt rises to $105 billion. The actual debt/personal income ratio increases from 14% to 23% over the period.

With just the basic rule in place, the ratio of debt to personal income rises to 15%. The higher expenditures cap multiplier in case 2 allows the ratio to increase to 16%. The debt brake results in less increase in the debt/personal income ratio. With a 10% debt tolerance level, the ratio rises to 15%. With a 6% debt tolerance level, the ratio rises to 14%.

The simulation analysis reveals that even with these fiscal rules in place over the last two decades, Illinois could not have maintained a debt/personal income ratio below the 10% debt tolerance level. Enacting the fiscal rules to achieve a sustainable debt level today is a still more difficult challenge. It would now take several decades to reduce the debt/personal income ratio below the 10% debt tolerance level.

State Spending

Actual spending grew from about $17 billion to $36 billion. With just the basic fiscal rule in place, 2019 spending reaches only $24 billion. In case 2, with a higher expenditures cap multiplier, general fund spending grows to about $26 billion. The debt brake imposed a more stringent cap on spending growth. With a 10% debt tolerance level, general fund spending grows to $23 billion. With the 6% debt tolerance level, 2019 spending reaches $22 billion.

The actual general fund spending/personal income ratio rose from 3.7% to 4.8% over the period. With just the basic rule in place, the general fund spending/personal income ratio drops to 3.2%. In case 2, with the higher expenditures cap multiplier, the general fund spending/personal income ratio falls to 3.4%. The debt brake results in a more rapid decrease in the ratio of spending to personal income. With the 10% debt tolerance level, the ratio drops to 3.1%. With the 6% debt tolerance level, the ratio falls to 3.0%.

Supply-Side Effects of the Debt Brake

The fiscal rules reduce the growth in state spending, providing a modest boost to economic growth. By the end of the period, simulated personal income with the fiscal rules in place exceeds actual personal income by 0.4% to 0.5%. The modest increase in personal income yields a comparable boost in state revenue.

It is clear that solving the debt crisis in Illinois will require a significant reduction in the rate of growth in state spending, and considerable downsizing of the state government relative to the private sector. This should not be surprising after half a century of debt fatigue. Enacting fiscal rules today to achieve a sustainable debt level will be a difficult task. Even with the proposed fiscal rules in place, it will take several decades to reduce debt in Illinois below the debt tolerance level that exposes the state to risk of default.

CONCLUSION

This study reveals how debt fatigue can be hazardous to a state's health. Until the last two decades, most states pursued fiscal policies that yielded sustainable debt levels. But, over the past two decades, elected officials have allowed state debt to grow at an unsustainable rate. Many states shifted rapidly from a red state to a blue state. Debt has been increasing more rapidly than personal income and is projected to continue to do so in coming years. As the debt/personal income ratio continues to increase above the 8% debt brake threshold, these states are increasingly exposed to default in the state debt.

Debt fatigue is hurting citizens. More state revenue is spent on debt service, leaving less revenue for productive expenditures. The state is less able to respond to economic shocks and is increasingly dependent on federal bailouts to sustain even basic services during recessions.

Some politicians want to convince citizens to stop worrying; we can live with our debt, they claim. But citizens should not, like Wile E. Coyote, continue to run headlong toward a fiscal cliff. States often rely on very volatile income tax and energy tax revenues. Recessions, such as the financial crisis in 2008 and the current coronavirus pandemic, yield revenue shortfalls that require huge state spending cuts and create default risk. The hidden debts that states accumulate off-budget, mostly unfunded liabilities in state pension and health benefits for public employees, become increasingly more difficult to repay.

The most recent version of Keynesian economics—modern monetary theory—reinforces some politicians' sanguine attitude toward debt. Citizens should reject this excuse for accumulating debt at unsustainable rates. Such wishful thinking is just an excuse to print more money, something that the Federal Reserve readily accommodates.[11]

Other OECD countries, such as Switzerland, enacted fiscal rules to successfully address their debt crisis. The Swiss debt brake has been adopted in a few other countries to reduce debt to a sustainable level at both the state and national level. The United States has not enacted effective fiscal rules and shows no sign that it is likely to do so. Each year that we continue along this path of accumulating more debt, it becomes more difficult to exit the debt crisis. A debt brake can reduce debt to sustainable levels in the United States just as it has in other countries.

We simulated a Swiss-style debt brake for three states, Florida, Colorado, and Illinois. Had Florida and Colorado enacted the proposed debt brakes, they would have reduced spending growth enough to hold the debt/personal income ratio below the debt tolerance level. Enacting the debt brakes today would allow those states to reduce debt and maintain the debt/personal income ratio below the debt tolerance level.

Enacting the proposed debt brakes in zombie states, such as Illinois, would not reduce spending enough to lower the debt/personal income ratios below the debt tolerance level. Enacting the debt brakes today would reduce the debt/personal income ratio, but it would take several decades to reduce that ratio below the debt tolerance level.

Critics will argue that a debt brake requires draconian cuts in state spending. In fact, a debt brake only requires a reduction in the rate of growth of state spending until the state achieves a sustainable debt level. By inserting a debt brake in the constitution, citizens would replace wholly discretionary fiscal policies with a rules-based fiscal regime in which lawmakers must prioritize the use of slowly, steadily rising spending cap amount.

The simulation analysis reveals that overcoming debt fatigue and addressing the debt crisis becomes more difficult each year. After years of debt fatigue, it will take many years for states to recover. There is no alternative to the fiscal austerity and government downsizing now required to solve the debt crisis in many of our states.

A debt brake enacted in red states such as Florida, with a history of fiscal discipline, could set an example for other states and for the federal government. That would follow the Swiss precedent where some cantons were the first to enact debt brakes. Inter-cantonal competition forced the more profligate cantons to end unsustainable practices. With a track record of fiscal discipline at the cantonal level, Swiss citizens enacted a debt brake for their national government. To be enacted and work in the United States, a debt brake must have this broad citizen support across political parties and interest groups seen in Switzerland.

NOTES

1. For a discussion of these measurement and reporting problems in state CAF Rs see the chapter by Thurston Powers in this book.
2. Rules for Sustainable Fiscal Policy 2019.
3. Wray 2015.
4. During the recent financial crisis the federal government bailed out the states by subsidizing their bond issues, and through direct transfers. However, it is not clear that the federal government now has the fiscal space to bail out the states (Merrifield and Poulson 2017a).
5. For example: Jaffee and Russell (1976); Stiglitz and Weiss (1981); Eaton and Gersovitz (1981); Bishop et al. (1989); Bayoumi et al. (1995).
6. Liu and Thakor 1984
7. Merrifield and Poulson 2014, 2016a, 2016b, 2016c, 2017a, 2017b.
8. Chapter 8 [also Merrifield and Poulson 2016a] describes key differences.
9. Data is from the Florida annual Comprehensive Annual Report (CAFR).
10. The 2020–2021 data come from a state forecast. Data for personal income, population, and fiscal data is from the annual Colorado Legislative Staff "Economic and Revenue Forecast." Data for debt is from the Colorado Comprehensive Annual Financial Report (CAFR). Total Colorado debt includes bonds payable, certificates of participation (COPs), other debt, unfunded liabilities in the state pension plan (PERA), and Other Post-employment Benefits (OPEB).
11. Taylor 1993.

REFERENCES

Bayoumi, T., M. Goldstein, and G. Woglom. 1995. Do Credit Markets Discipline Sovereign Borrowers? Evidence from U.S. States, *Journal of Money Credit and Banking*, 27, no. 4 (November 1995), Part I.

Bishop, G., D. Damrau, and M. Miller. 1989. *1992 and Beyond: Market Discipline Can Work in the EC Monetary Union*. Salomon Brothers, London.

Congressional Budget Office. 2018. *Long Term Budget Outlook*, Washington, DC.

Eaton, J., and M. Gersovitz. 1981. Debt with Potential Repudiation: A Theoretical and Empirical Analysis. *Review of Economic Studies* 49 (April): 289–309.

Jaffee, D., and T. Russell. 1976. Imperfect Information, Uncertainty, and Credit Rationing. *Quarterly Journal of Economics* 90: 651–66.

Liu, P., and A. Thakor. 1984. Interest Yields, Credit Ratings, and Economic Characteristics of State Bond: An Empirical Analysis. *Journal of Money Credit and Banking* 16 (August): 345–50.

Merrifield, J., and B. Poulson. 2014. State Fiscal Policies for Budget Stabilization and Economic Growth: a Dynamic Scoring Analysis. *Cato Journal* 34: 1.

Merrifield, J., and B. Poulson. 2016a. The Swedish and Swiss Fiscal Rule Outcomes Contain Key Lessons for the U.S. *Independent Review* 21, no. 2: 251–75.

Merrifield, J., and B. Poulson. 2016b. *Can the Debt Growth be Stopped? Rules Based Policy Options for Addressing the Federal Fiscal Crisis*. Lexington Books, New York.

Merrifield, J., and B. Poulson 2016c. A Dynamic Scoring Analysis of How TEL Design Choice Impact Government Expansion. *Journal of Economic and Financial Studies* 4, no. 2: 60–68.

Merrifield, J., and B. Poulson. 2017a. *Restoring America's Fiscal Constitution*. Lexington Books, New York.

Merrifield, J., and B. Poulson. 2017b. New Constitutional Debt Brakes for Euroland Revisited. *Journal of Applied Business and Economics* 19, no. 8: 110–32.

Poulson, B. 2004a. *Colorado's TABOR Amendment: Recent Trends and Future Prospects*. Americans for Prosperity Foundation, Washington, DC.

Poulson, B. 2004b. Tax and Spending Limits: Theory, Analysis, and Policy. *Issue Paper* 2- 2004, Independence Institute, Golden, CO, January 31.

Stiglitz, J., and A. Weiss. 1981. Credit Rationing in Markets with Imperfect Information, *American Economic Review* 73: 393–410.

Taylor, J. 1993. Discretion versus Policy Rules in Practice. *Carnegie Conference Series on Public Policy* 39, no.1: 195–214.

Wray, L. 2015. *Modern Monetary Theory* (2nd Edition). Palgrave Macmillan, Basingstoke, ZULU.

APPENDIX: VARIABLE DEFINITIONS, PARAMETERS, AND EQUATIONS FOR THE STATE CALCULATOR

Numbers Shown Are Default Values

$EMERG_0 = 0.2 \times SP_0$; Average Annual Certifiable Emergency Cost to the State

EFCAPRT = 0.2; Emergency Fund Account Balance Cap as a share of State Spending (SP). CCRT = 0.5; countercyclical spending rate increase, as a share of Revenue (REV).

BSFCAPRT = 0.1; Budget Stabilization Fund Account Balance Cap as a share of State Spending.

BSFSPRT = 0.7; limit on share of BSF spendable in one year. $BSFEAR_t = 0$, revenue, in millions earmarked for BSF deposit.
KCAPRT = 0.05; Capital Improvement Fund Account Balance Cap as a share of State Spending.

KSPRT = 0.7; limit on share of Capital Improvement Fund Account spendable in one year. KSHSURP = 0.25; Capital Improvement Fund Share of remaining surplus.
CSLRT = 1.0; multiplier for Pop + Infl growth limit on Discretionary Spending Growth. GRCHG = 1.0; growth rate adjustment parameter.
RECESSt = 0; recession size in year t.

$EXOGTAXCH_t = 0$; exogenous tax rate change starting in year t.

OCR = 0.06; marginal opportunity cost rate for shifting resources from private to public use. MTR = Average Tax Rate = REV0/PI0
RMTR = 0.00251

DEBTTOL = 0.1; limit on sustainable total state debt tolerance; share of PI DEFTOL = 0.02; deficit-level intolerance; share of PI
TOLPROX = 0.8; deficit- or debt-based spending growth braking commences with RDEBT/RPI > (0.8)DEBTTOL or (0.8)DEFTOL

DEBTBRT = 1.0; debt-based braking rate; rate of debt-based reduction in CSLRT. DEFBRT = 1.0; deficit-based braking rate; rate of deficit-based reduction in CSLRT. TRCT = 0; equals "1" for a surplus-based Tax Rate Cut Trigger.
NCYC = 0.2 when TRCT = 1; the weighted drop in MTR for Tax1 that will result from the size of SURPLUS/SP when SURPLUS > 0.

EQUATIONS

$API_t = (((PI_t - PI_{t-1})/PI_{t-1}) \times API_{t-1}) + API_{t-1}$—Adjusted Personal Income Users can choose replacement values for GRCHG and RECESSt default values.

$API_0 = PI_0$ Note: the zero subscript denotes the first data point; the last "real" number. All other data are user-supplied projections or computed values. t = 1 is the first calculated value.

$RPI_0 = PI_0$ Revised Personal Income starts equal to actual personal income. $RDEBT_{-1} = RDEBT_0 = DEBT_0$ Simulation revised debt.
$RDEFPI_{-1} = RDEFPI_0 = 0$ Debt as a share of personal income.
$EFINT_0 = 0$ Emergency Fund Interest
Earned $BSF_0 = 0$ Initial Budget Stabilization Fund Balance

$BSFINT_0 = 0$ Initial Budget Stabilization Fund Balance

$EF_0 = 0$ Initial Emergency Fund Balance

$RREV_0 = REV_0$ Simulation Revised Revenue

$RSP_0 = SP_0$ Simulation Revised Spending

$CCBUMP_0 = 0$ Initial Countercyclical Spending
Bump $AMTR1_0 = MTR1$ Initial Adjusted Marginal Tax Rate
$SURP118_0 = 0$ Initial Surplus after EF and BSF deposits
$SGBASE_0 = SP_0$ Initial "Steady Growth" Base—no ratchet down

$BASE_0 = SP_0$ Initial Spending Growth Base—subject to ratchet

$RDEBTPI_0 = RDEBT_0/PI_0$ Initial Simulation Revised Debt to PI ratio.
$REVREST_t = REV_t - REV1_t - REV2_t$
$AMTR1_t = IF(TRCT = 0, MTR1, IF((RREV_{t-1} - RSP_{t-1}) > 0, (1 - ((RREV_{t-1} /REV1_{t-1}) \times NCYC \times ((RREV_{t-1} - RSP_{t-1})/RREV_{t-1})) \times AMTR_{t-1})), AMTR1_{t-1}))$
$GA_t = (RMTR \times (EXOGTAXCH_t + (AMTR1_t - AMTR1_{t-1})) \times 100) + 1$ Economic Growth Rate Adjustment

$RPI_t = (RPI_{t-1} \text{ x } GA_t) + (API_t - API_{t-1}) + (OCR \text{ x } ((RREV_t - RSP_t) - EMERG_t))$ Simulation Revised PI

$MTR1 = REV1_0/PI_0$ Initial REV1 Tax (e.g., income tax) Marginal Tax Rate
$MTR2 = REV2_0/PI_0$ Initial REV2 Tax (e.g., income tax) Marginal Tax Rate
$MTRREST = (REV_0 - REV1_0 - REV2_0)/PI_0$

$STATSH_t = (EXOGTAXCH_t/MTR1) \times (REV1_t/REV_t)$ Static Revenue Share for REV1 Tax

$RREV_t = (REV_t \times (1 - STATSH_t)) + ((RPI_t - API_t) \times (AMTR1_t + MTR2 + MTRREST)) + EFINT_{t-1} + BSFINT_{t-1}$

$POPGR_t = ((POP_{t-2}/POP_{t-3}) - 1)$ Population Growth Rate

$RDEFPI_t = IF(RDEBT_{t-2} = 0, 0, IF((RDEBT_{t-1} - RDEBT_{t-2}) < 0, 0, (RDEBT_{t-1} - RDEBT_{t-2})/RPI_{t-1}))$
$RDEBTPI_t = RDEBT_{t-1}/RPI_{t-1}$
$DEBTBRK_t = IF(RDEBTPI_t < (TOLPROX * DEBTTOL), 1, IF(((RDEBTPI_{t-1}/ DEBTTOL * (RDEBTPI_{t-1} - (TOLPROX * DEBTTOL))) * DEBTBRT > 1, 0, 1 - ((RDEBTPI_{t-1}/ DEBTTOL) * (RDEBTPI_{t-1} - (TOLPROX * DEBTTOL))) * DEBTBRT))$
$DEFBRK_t = IF(RDEFPI_t < (TOLPROX * DEFTOL), 1, IF(((RDEFPI_{t-1}/ DEFTOL * (RDEFPI_{t-1} - (TOLPROX * DEFTOL))) * DEFBRT > 1, 0,$

$1 - ((RDEFPI_{t-1}/DEFTOL) * (RDEFPI_{t-1} - (TOLPROX * DEFTOL))) * DEFBRT))$

$SGBASE_t = SGBASE_{t-1} \times ((1 + POPGR_t + INFL_t) \times CSLRT)$

$BASE_t = IF(SG = 1, SGBASE_{t-1} \times (((1 + POPGR_t + INFL_t) \times CSLRT) \times DEFBRK_t \times DEBTBRK_t), ((RSP_{t-1} - CCBUMP_{t-1}) \times (((1 + POPGR_t + INFL_t) \times CSLRT) \times DEFBRK_t \times DEBTBRK_t)))$

$CCB1_t = IF((BSF_{t-1} \times BSFSPRT) - (BASE_t - RREV_t) > 0, (BSF_{t-1} \times BSFSPRT) - (BASE_t - RREV_t), 0)$

$CCB2_t = IF((BSF_{t-1} \times BSFSPRT) - (BASE_t - RREV_t) > (CCRT \times (RREV_{t-1} - RREV_t)), CCB1_t))$

$CCB3_t = IF((STATSH_t \times 0.9) > STATSH_{t-1}, 0, CCB2_t)$

$CCBUMP_t = IF(RREV_t > RREV_{t-1}, 0, CCB3_t)$ Calculated in five stages; too many "IF"s for single, long "CCBUMP =" equation.

$RSP_t = IF(BASE_t + CCBUMP_t < RREV_t, BASE_t + CCBUMP_t, IF((BSF_{t-1} \times BSFSPRT) > (BASE_t + CCBUMP_t - RREV_t), BASE_t + CCBUMP_t, RREV_t + (BSF_{t-1} \times BSFSPRT)))$

$EXPSP_t = (((1 + POPGR_t + INFL_t) \times CSLRT) \times DEBTBRK_t) \times (RSP_t - CCBUMP_t)$

Expect Spending

$EFMAX_t = EFCAPRT \times EXPSP_t$ Maximum Emergency Fund Balance $EFINT_t = EF_{t-1} \times STINT_t$

$EF2_t = IF((EF_{t-1} - EMERG_t) < EFMAX_t, EFMAX_t, EF_{t-1} - EMERG_t)$

$EF3_t = IF((RREV_t - RSP_t) > 0, RREV_t - RSP_t + EF_{t-1} - EMERG_t, EF_{t-1} - EMERG_t)$

$EF_t = IF((RREV_t - RSP_t) > (EFMAX_t - EF_{t-1} + EMERG_t), EF2_t, EF3_t) + EFINT_t$

Emergency Fund Balance. Calculated in 3 stages; too many "IF"s for single, long "EF =" equation.

$BSFDEB_t = IF(RSP_t > RREV_t, IF((BSF_{t-1} \times BSFSPRT) > (RSP_t - RREV_t), (RSP_t - RREV_t), (BSF_{t-1} \times BSFSPRT)), 0)$

$BSFMAX_t = BSFCAPRT \times XPSP_t$ $BSFINT_t = BSF_{t-1} \times STINT_t$

$SURP117_t = IF(EF_t > EFMAX_{t-1}, IF((RREV_t - RSP_t) - (EF_t - (EF_{t-1} \times (1 + STINT_t)) > 0,$

$(RREV_t - RSP_t) - (EF_t - (EF_{t-1} \times (1 + STINT_t)), 0), 0)$ Surplus remaining after EF deposit.

$BSF2_t = IF((BSF_{t-1} + SURP117_t - BSFDEB_t) > 0, (BSF_{t-1} + SURP117_t - BSFDEB_t), 0)$ $BSF3_t = IF((BSF_{t-1} + SURP117_t - BSFDEB_t) < BSFMAX_t, BSF2t, BSFMAX_t)$

$BSF4_t$ = IF((BSF_{t-1} – $BSFDEB_t$) > 0, BSF_{t-1} – $BSFDEB_t$, 0) $BSF5_t$ = IF(BSF_{t-1} > $BSFMAX_t$, $BSF4_t$, $BSF3_t$)
BSF_t = IF(EF_t < $EFMAX_t$, $BSF4_t$, $BSF5_t$) + $BSFINT_t$+ $BSFEAR_t$ Budget Stabilization Fund Balance

Calculated in five stages; too many "IF"s for single, long "BSF =" equation.

$PICHTEN_t$ = ((PI_{t-2}/PI_{t-12})^0.1) – 1 – $INFL_t$ Average growth rate for PI for last ten known years. $PICHONE_t$ = (PI_{t-2}/PI_{t-3}) – 1 – $INFL_t$ Average growth rate for PI for last known year.
$TENONEDIF_t$ = $PICHTEN_t$ – $PICHONE_t$

$TENVSONE_t$ = IF($TENONEDIF_t$ > 0, $TENONEDIF_t$, 0)

$CCKSH_t$ = IF($TENVSONE_t$ =0, 0, IF($TENVSONE_t$ > $PICHTEN_t$, KSPRT, ($TENVSONE_t$/$PICHTEN_t$ x KSPRT)) Capital fund spending in slow growth years.

$SURP118_t$ = IF($SURP117_t$ = 0, 0, IF(($SURP117_t$ – (BSF_t – BSF_{t-1})) > 0, ($SURP117_t$ – (BSF_t – BSF_{t-1})), 0))

$KDEBCRED_t$ = IF($TENVSONE_t$ = 0, IF(KF_{t-1} < (KCAPRT × $EXPSP_t$), (($SURP118_t$ × KSHSURP) + (KF_{t-1} × $STINT_t$)), 0), (((-1) × (($CCKSH_t$ × KF_{t-1}) – ((1– $CCKSH_t$) × KF_{t-1} × $STINT_t$)))))
Debit or deposit into Capital Fund.

KF_t = KF_{t-1} + $KDEBCRED_t$

$SGCAP_t$ = (($SGCAP_{t-1}$ – $CCBUMP_t$) × ((1 + $POPGR_t$ + $INFL_t$) × CSLRT)) + $CCBUMP_t$
Spending cap with no ratchet down allowed; growth based on previous cap.

$RDEBT_t$ = $RDEBT_{t-1}$ – IF($SURP118_t$ = 0, 0, IF($SURP118_t$ < $RDEBT_{t-1}$, $SURP118_t$, $RDEBT_{t-1}$)) + ($DEBT_t$ – $DEBT_{t-1}$) Simulation-revised debt.

REB_t = IF(($SURP118_t$ – $RDEBT_{t-1}$) > 0, ($SURP118_t$ – $RDEBT_{t-1}$), 0) Rebate Amount

$PIBUMP_t$ = RPI_t/PI_t Simulation-based PI change.
$SMALLER_t$ = (RSP_t/RPI_t)/(SP_t/PI_t) TEL-induced drop in spending share of PI.
$SGGAP_t$ = RSP_t/$SGBASE_t$ Ratchet down amount.

$EPREP_t$ = EF_t/$EFMAX_t$ Emergency Preparedness Rate.

$EFSIZE_t$ = EF_t/RPI_t EF size relative to PI.

$BSFPREP_t = BSF_t/BSFMAX_t$ Budget stabilization funds relative to max allowed.
$BSFSIZE_t = BSF_t/RPI_t$ BSF size relative to PI
$SPSH_t = RSP_t/RPI_t$ Spending size relative to PI

$REVSH_t = RREV_t/RPI_t$ Revenue size relative to PI

Part II

STATE FISCAL INSTITUTIONS

Chapter 6

Budget Stabilization Funds

Gary A. Wagner and Erick M. Elder

INTRODUCTION

Unlike the federal government, nearly every state has some type of balanced budget requirement;[1] despite the differences in the structure of these requirements across the states, balanced budget requirements still impose constraints upon state governments that the federal government does not experience. The amount of revenue state governments collect is cyclical; it naturally declines during economic downturns. The decline in revenue that occurs during an economic downturn, coupled with a balanced budget requirement, potentially necessitates tax increases and/or spending cuts. During the Great Recession, 42 states cut their spending in 2009, 39 states made mid-year budget cuts in 2010, and 38 states enacted revenue increases in 2010.[2] As the name implies, a rainy-day fund (also known as a budget stabilization fund, BSF) gives a state a savings mechanism that can be used to mitigate tax increases or spending cuts that might otherwise manifest as revenue declines during economic contractions. An important question for states is how much savings they should accumulate to avoid tax increases and/or spending cuts during an economic downturn.

In this chapter, we follow the methodology Wagner and Elder (2007) introduced to estimate state-specific business cycle characteristics (the length and severity of economic expansions and contractions), and then use these estimates to accomplish two goals. (1) We construct a probability distribution of revenue shortfalls for each state; and (2) we use the parameter estimates to estimate the amount each state would need to save during economic expansions in order to be confident in having a sufficient amount of savings to weather a certain proportion of potential recessions. We will now briefly introduce each goal in turn.

First, a probability distribution of potential revenue shortfalls relates the probability that an economic contraction lasting a specific number of months will have a corresponding revenue shortfall.[3] A state does not know with certainty how much savings they should accumulate to weather a revenue shortfall associated with a recession since the duration and severity of the business cycle phases are unknown beforehand. Therefore, how much revenue will decline during an economic contraction cannot be characterized by a single number. It must be characterized by a distribution of possible outcomes associated with the probabilities that each one of those outcomes actually occurs. Knowing the distribution of potential revenue shortfalls allows policymakers to make more informed decisions concerning the likelihood that a given stock of accumulated savings will allow a state to weather the next recession without increasing taxes and/or reducing government spending. As mentioned, the distribution for each state depends on the state-specific business cycle characteristics. With this distribution, it is possible to make statements concerning the average revenue shortfall a state may experience, the median shortfall a state may experience, as well as other potential revenue shortfalls based on various confidence levels. Once the distributions are established, we use data concerning how much each state has currently accumulated to assess their ability to weather a recession. Additionally, policymakers can use these results to make informed decisions concerning how much more they may need to save to weather a certain proportion, such as 75% or 90%, of all possible recessions they are likely to face, and hence can be that confident they have sufficient savings to avoid tax increases/spending decreases during the next recession.

For our second goal, we introduce parameter estimates of the amount that each state would need to save during economic expansions in order to be confident in having a sufficient amount of savings to weather a certain proportion of potential recessions. Clearly it is important for legislators to know how likely they are to avoid the fiscal stress brought on by declining revenues during a recession, but in our opinion, it is at least equally important to give policymakers a roadmap to accumulating the desired savings goals, which is why the calculation of savings rates is useful and important.

Prior to the Great Recession, states had accumulated savings equal to 11.5% of their total 2006 expenditures.[4] Despite the fact that this amount was almost double the historical average, the severity of the Great Recession virtually wiped out the savings that states had accumulated. The total amount that states had accumulated by 2019 is nearly 14% of their expenditures.[5] Based on the number of states that enacted spending cuts/tax increases during the Great Recession, the amount of savings states had accumulated was clearly insufficient to buffer against the ensuing revenue declines. Nonetheless, questions remain concerning the sufficiency of the new, higher level of accumulated savings in terms of just how severe a recession the current level of accumulated savings is capable of buffering; how severe a recession is the current, higher level of savings sufficient for?

Though the states in aggregate have accumulated such a large stock of savings, these aggregated numbers obviously do not tell the complete story. In both 2006 and 2019, the distribution of accumulated savings across the states is quite large. In 2006, nineteen states had savings of 10% or less of their expenditures, while only nine states had savings greater than 20% of their expenditures. Currently, a dozen states have accumulated savings of 10% or less of their expenditures, while a dozen states have accumulated savings greater than 20% of their expenditures. In addition to vast differences across states in terms of their accumulated savings, there are also large differences across states in terms of their business cycles with respect to how long expansions and contractions generally last as well as how much states expand and contract during their business cycles.

One relevant question is whether the states that are saving more than others are actually the states that need to be saving more than the others based on their state-specific business cycle characteristics. Obviously it could be the case that the states are saving enough as a group to weather a mild recession but when the numbers are disaggregated and we look at each state separately, some of them have accumulated enough savings to weather a severe recession while others have not saved enough to weather even a very mild recession.

Although the COVID-19 pandemic recession was roughly twice as severe in terms of jobs losses for the average state than 2008 recession, it has not revealed tremendous insights into the role these larger BSFs may play in helping states to avoid the need for spending reductions or tax increases. The major reason for this is that state coffers, and subsequently their BSF balances, have been significantly boosted by several rounds of extended federal unemployment benefits and direct COVID-related aid. If this sets a new precedent were large federal bailouts to states become more of the norm post-pandemic, then the role BSFs *should* play in state fiscal matters becomes even less clear.

Brief Summary of Results

Based on the results presented below, we find that the average amount states need to save to weather an average economic downturn without reducing spending equal is almost 4% of revenue, but this amount varies considerably from state to state. Interestingly, the distribution is severely skewed to the right so much that for many states, the average revenue shortfall is very similar to the 75th percentile revenue shortfall.

The following sections review the previous literature on the appropriate size of an BSF, offer a brief description of how the distribution of potential shortfalls and savings rates are calculated, a discussion of the data and statistical methodology, a discussion of the results, and concluding remarks.

PREVIOUS LITERATURE

The issue of how large a BSF should be has attracted much attention. In 1983, the National Conference of State Legislators issued a report recommending a balance of 5% of revenue. This recommendation is problematic for a number of reasons. First, as mentioned above, as a group, states had accumulated savings over double this amount, and it proved insufficient during the Great Recession. Granted, the Great Recession was the most severe recession since the Great Depression, but the 5% recommendation is also problematic because it prescribes the same goal for all states despite the fact that each state has differing tax bases and tax structures, and hence each state will likely experience differing revenue declines during a recession, so a one-size-fits-all approach clearly is not informative to state legislators.[6] More recently, in 2009, the Government Finance Officers Administration suggested states accumulate savings equal to two months of their operating revenues. Even though this target was much larger than the 5% target, it is still a one-size-fits-all approach.

The early academic literature on the appropriate size of an BSF estimated how much a state might need to save by estimating the deviations of revenue collections from a trend during economic downturns, but these studies were for single states.[7] Additionally, only single point estimates of the budget shortfalls are reported. This is important because it makes it difficult to assess how prepared a given state might be with their current stock of savings. Cornia and Nelson overcome this issue by using a value-at-risk approach to estimate a distribution of potential shortfalls for Utah. One problem with this approach is that it estimates the potential shortfalls over some fixed period of time such as one year instead of over an economic downturn or over a complete business cycle.

All of the studies cited above use actual revenue data. The problem with using those data is that there are policy changes that quite likely obscure the statistical inferences. Zhao (2014) corrects this problem by adjusting the reported revenue collections by the estimated effect that the policy changes have on the revenue collections. Multiple problems exist with Zhao's approach. First, the data in the analysis are annual revenue collections, making it very likely that at least some of the fluctuations in the revenue series are being smoothed out since it is highly unlikely that revenue fluctuations follow the calendar or fiscal year. And Zhao only reports the mean and median shortfalls, again making it difficult for policymakers to make meaningful inferences concerning how prepared their state might be with their current stock of savings.

We believe the approach taken in this chapter overcomes all of the above-mentioned shortcomings. First, we provide a much more thorough description of the distribution of revenue shortfalls by providing the 10th, 25th· 50th, 75th, and 90th percentiles (along with the expected value). Furthermore, we estimate the cyclical characteristics for each state from the coincident index developed by Crone (2002) and reported by the Philadelphia Federal Reserve.[8] After we estimate the cyclical characteristics for each state, we scale the expansion and contraction growth rates by the elasticity of a state's total revenue with respect to economic activity. That approach ensures that policy changes don't influence the estimates of cyclical characteristics of revenue. Finally, the coincident indices are reported monthly resulting in more accurate measures of the cyclical characteristics because they are not being smoothed out as a result of using lower frequency data.

DISTRIBUTION OF REVENUE SHORTFALLS AND SAVINGS RATES

Distribution of Revenue Shortfalls

Although government spending and revenue collections are both influenced by the phases of the business cycle, in the analysis below, we focus on the volatility of revenue collections. Revenue collections are procyclical, increasing during the expansionary phase of the business cycle and declining during the contractionary phases of the business cycle. In the analysis below, we assume the economic activity (and hence government revenue collections) is in one of two possible phases; it is either expanding or contracting. When the economy is in an expansionary phase of the business cycle, it expands at a rate of μ_H; when the economy is in a contractionary phase of the business cycle it grows at a rate of μ_L (generally, $\mu_L < 0$). If the economy is in an expansionary phase then there is some probability, P_{HH}, that it remains in an expansionary phase, and the probability it switches to a contractionary phase the following month is denoted P_{HL} (where $P_{HL} = 1-P_{HH}$). Likewise, if the economy is currently in a contractionary phase then there is some probability P_{LL} that it remains in a contractionary phase next month, P_{LL}, and there is some probability, P_{LH}, that it switches to an expansionary phase the following month.[9] It can be shown that the probability a contraction lasts for exactly t_L month is $P(t_L) = P_{LL}^{t_L-1} - P_{LL}^{t_L}$. As previously mentioned, we assume that the pattern of revenue collections follows the pattern of economic activity with revenue collections increasing when the economy expands and revenue collections decreasing when the economy contracts. Depending upon the specific tax structure of a state, tax collections may be more or less volatile than overall economic activity. The parameter φ denotes the sensitivity of tax collections to economic activity, so tax collections grow at rate g_H ($=\varphi * \mu_H$).[10] The total revenue shortfall, relative to pre-contraction revenue, associated with an economic contraction can be shown to be $\pi(t_L) = t_L - \sum_{i=1}^{t_L} (1+g_L)^i$. For example, if pre-contraction revenue is 100 and if $g_L = -1\%$ then after the first month of contracting, revenue is 99 and the shortfall is 1. If the contraction lasts two months then revenue in the second month of the contraction is 98 (technically it is 98.01) and the total shortfall from the start of the contraction is 3. If the contraction lasts another month, revenue in the third month is 97 (again, technically it is is 97.03) and the total shortfall through three months is 6. Therefore, the distribution of revenue shortfalls shows the likelihood an economic contraction lasts one month along with the revenue shortfall that would occur if an economic contraction lasts one month, the likelihood an economic contraction lasts two months along with the revenue shortfall that would occur if the economic contractions lasts two months, and so on.

Savings Rates

The above section discussed the distribution of potential revenue shortfalls, but an equally important issue is the *rate* at which states need to save to cover a given shortfall by a given time. Again, denoting the probability that an economic expansion persists from one month to the next as P_{HH}, the probability that an expansion lasts exactly t_H months is $P_H(t_H) = P_{HH}^{t_H-1} - P_{HH}^{t_H}$. It is then possible to calculate the probability that an expansion will last any number of months as well as the probability that an expansion will last *at least* a certain number of months. Therefore, a state first needs to decide how large a revenue shortfall they would like to save for, and then they can determine at what *rate* they need to save each month to achieve the desired accumulated savings based on their own risk preferences and the amount of currently accumulated savings. For example, if a state decided that they wanted to accumulate total savings equal to 6% of their revenue, and they also knew that there was a 75% chance their expansion would last at least three years, then if they saved 2% of their revenue each year, they could be 75% sure they could achieve their target level of savings of 6% (assuming their current savings is equal to zero).

The parameter estimates necessary to estimate the distributions of revenue shortfalls and savings rates are P_{HH}, P_{LL}, μ_H, μ_L, and φ for each state. The first four are estimated using the regime-switching model popularized by

Hamilton (1989). The elasticity is estimated for each state by regressing the log difference in (annual) total revenue on a constant and the log difference in (annual) state GDP.

RESULTS

Regression Estimates

The results from estimating the regime-switching regression are presented below. As mentioned above, a one-size-fits-all recommendation for the size of an BSF makes no sense because of the potential differences among states in terms of their business cycle characteristics. Some states grow faster during expansions than others; some states have longer expansions or contractions; and some states have significantly more overall volatility in their business cycles. These differences can be seen by looking at the parameter estimates of the business cycle characteristics in table 6.1. As can be seen, the parameter estimates for the high- and low-growth-regime growth rates as well as the transition parameters vary considerably. This is strong evidence against the one-size-fits-all approach for the appropriate size since the cyclical characteristics are very state-specific. For the high-growth regime, the average growth rate is 0.286, but it varies from a maximum of 0.437 (Alaska) to a minimum of 0.114 (Louisiana). For the low-growth regime, the average growth rate is −0.45; four states actually have a positive growth rate, whereas three states have low-growth-regime growth rates over 1% (per month) with Louisiana at −4.6 and West Virginia at −2.4. The transition probabilities, P_{HH} and P_{LL}, also differ considerably across the states. The transition probabilities determine the expected length of the economic expansions and contractions.[11] The average duration of an expansion is 72 months, and the average contraction lasts 10.5 months, but again, there is considerable variation across the states. Louisiana has both the longest average expansion and the shortest average contraction. Fifteen states have an average expansion of at least 83 months, but 16 states have an average expansion of 60 months or less. Calculating the average growth rate for each state, again, there is considerable differences among the states with 12 states having an average growth rate of 0.25% (per month) led by Nevada, Arizona, and Utah with average growth rates over 0.30% while eight states have average growth rates below 0.15% with Michigan, West Virginia, and Louisiana all below 0.10%. Finally, in terms of the volatility of the business cycle, there are enormous differences among the states. The states with the most volatile business cycles, Michigan, Louisiana, and West Virginia, have a volatility approximately five times that of the least volatile states, Arkansas, Nebraska, and Georgia. In general, the states that have more (less) volatile business cycles tend to the ones with the

Table 6.1 Markov Switching Regression Estimated Parameters and Estimated Elasticity

State	μ_H	μ_L	P_{HH}	P_{LL}	$E(t_H)$	$E(t_L)$	*Elasticity*
Alabama	0.273	-0.681	0.987	0.883	76.9	8.5	2.03
Alaska	0.437	0.082	0.868	0.98	7.6	50.0	4.32
Arizona	0.435	-0.267	0.982	0.912	55.6	11.4	1.74
Arkansas	0.222	-0.006	0.988	0.91	83.3	11.1	0.89
California	0.355	-0.094	0.984	0.93	62.5	14.3	2.26
Colorado	0.34	0.025	0.984	0.933	62.5	14.9	1.91
Connecticut	0.282	-0.142	0.978	0.936	45.5	15.6	1.45
Delaware	0.245	-0.819	0.992	0.832	125.0	6.0	0.99
Florida	0.335	-0.005	0.985	0.929	66.7	14.1	2.39
Georgia	0.31	0.062	0.98	0.873	50.0	7.9	1.48
Hawaii	0.252	-0.321	0.979	0.878	47.6	8.2	1.29
Idaho	0.318	-0.292	0.989	0.873	90.9	7.9	2.06
Illinois	0.237	-0.401	0.985	0.902	66.7	10.2	1.78
Indiana	0.25	-0.353	0.987	0.906	76.9	10.6	0.99
Iowa	0.21	-0.641	0.991	0.85	111.1	6.7	1.05
Kansas	0.226	-0.565	0.988	0.871	83.3	7.8	1.09
Kentucky	0.287	-0.742	0.982	0.882	55.6	8.5	1.79
Louisiana	0.114	-4.616	0.996	0.749	250.0	4.0	2.27
Maine	0.238	-0.601	0.986	0.854	71.4	6.8	0.59
Maryland	0.317	-0.467	0.983	0.888	58.8	8.9	2.17
Massachusetts	0.357	-0.323	0.985	0.932	66.7	14.7	1.91
Michigan	0.254	-1.251	0.981	0.838	52.6	6.2	2.21
Minnesota	0.281	-0.365	0.988	0.886	83.3	8.8	1.58
Mississippi	0.195	-0.182	0.98	0.873	50.0	7.9	1.82
Missouri	0.215	-0.235	0.982	0.889	55.6	9.0	1.34
Montana	0.251	-0.51	0.984	0.899	62.5	9.9	3.37
Nebraska	0.23	-0.023	0.985	0.896	66.7	9.6	1.53
Nevada	0.401	-0.245	0.988	0.912	83.3	11.4	1.57
New Hampshire	0.347	-0.235	0.986	0.902	71.4	10.2	0.72

New Jersey	0.233	-0.109	0.983	0.908	58.8	10.9	1.54
New Mexico	0.273	-0.323	0.988	0.88	83.3	8.3	2.03
New York	0.236	-0.21	0.98	0.903	50.0	10.3	2.21
North Carolina	0.297	-0.071	0.984	0.903	62.5	10.3	1.60
North Dakota	0.341	-0.151	0.97	0.891	33.3	9.2	1.99
Ohio	0.211	-0.451	0.986	0.883	71.4	8.5	2.73
Oklahoma	0.237	-0.305	0.983	0.855	58.8	6.9	1.99
Oregon	0.323	-0.346	0.986	0.873	71.4	7.9	3.41
Pennsylvania	0.217	-0.366	0.987	0.895	76.9	9.5	1.56
Rhode Island	0.266	-0.411	0.988	0.928	83.3	13.9	1.36
South Carolina	0.33	-0.379	0.982	0.876	55.6	8.1	2.13
South Dakota	0.294	-0.668	0.991	0.868	111.1	7.6	0.56
Tennessee	0.363	-0.439	0.977	0.887	43.5	8.8	1.92
Texas	0.323	0.014	0.987	0.919	76.9	12.3	1.51
Utah	0.368	-0.077	0.987	0.909	76.9	11.0	1.75
Vermont	0.288	-0.387	0.988	0.896	83.3	9.6	1.12
Virginia	0.293	-0.039	0.984	0.93	62.5	14.3	2.45
Washington	0.342	-0.199	0.985	0.909	66.7	11.0	0.77
West Virginia	0.306	-2.359	0.988	0.868	83.3	7.6	0.94
Wisconsin	0.24	-0.366	0.988	0.887	83.3	8.8	1.04
Wyoming	0.22	-0.652	0.988	0.867	83.3	7.5	2.20
Mean	0.28	-0.45	0.98	0.891	72.3	10.5	1.75
Median	0.28	-0.32	0.99	0.89	66.7	9.1	1.74
Max	0.44	0.08	1.00	0.98	250.0	50.0	4.32
Min	0.11	-4.62	0.87	0.75	7.6	4.0	0.56

Source: Created by the authors.

lowest (highest) average growth rate; in other words, there is a strongly negative correlation, −0.51, between the average growth rate and the variance of their growth. Texas, Colorado, and Florida are both in the top ten in average growth rate and each is in the top ten with the lowest volatility. On the flip side, Montana, Kentucky, Michigan, Louisiana, and West Virginia are all in the bottom ten in terms of their average growth rate and have one of the top ten highest volatility measures.

Shortfall Results

After the discussion in the previous section, it should be no surprise that states' revenue shortfalls differ significantly. The shortfall results in table 6.2 are expressed as a percentage of pre-contraction annual revenue. For example, the expected revenue shortfall for Kentucky is 7.24%, meaning that if Kentucky accumulates 7.24% of their current annual revenue, they would have a sufficient amount of savings to weather an average economic contraction without needing to raise taxes or cut their spending when their economy contracts and revenue collections decrease. Because the duration of an economic contraction is unknown with certainty before it starts, the revenue shortfall that may occur is necessarily characterized by a distribution of possible outcomes along with the associated probabilities that each of those outcomes actually occurs. Table 6.2 reports four points along that distribution along with the expected value. The four points that are reported are the 25th, 50th, 75th, and 90th percentiles. The 75th percentile revenue shortfall for Arizona is 5.13%, meaning that when Arizona experiences an economic contraction and associated revenue shortfall, their total revenue shortfall will be 5.13% or less in 75% of all possible economic contractions they might experience, given their estimated business cycle characteristics. In general, it might be useful to think of the 25th percentile numbers as representative of a very mild recession whereas the 90th percentile numbers might be thought of as a relatively severe one.

First, the expected revenue shortfall (which can be thought of as the average revenue shortfall) is much larger than the median shortfall. The reason for this is because the estimated P_{LL}s (the likelihood of remaining in an economic contraction) are so high. The average P_{LL} is 0.891. Table 6.1 demonstrates the distribution of potential revenue shortfalls.[12] Based on this number, the likelihood than an economic contraction lasts six months or less is 50%. If the contraction lasts for six months or less, then the total revenue shortfall will be relatively small. Using the average low-growth-regime growth rate of −0.45 and the average elasticity of revenue to economic activity of 1.75, if a contraction lasts six months then the total revenue shortfall is only 1.36% of pre-contraction revenue (so there is a 50% chance the revenue shortfall will

Table 6.2 Estimated Revenue Shortfalls

State	*Exp. Value*	*25%*	*50%*	*75%*	*90%*
Alabama	7.61	0.68	2.36	8.53	20.14
Alaska	0.00	0.00	0.00	0.00	0.00
Arizona	4.76	0.38	1.38	5.13	12.10
Arkansas	0.05	0.00	0.02	0.05	0.14
California	3.51	0.18	0.97	3.66	9.13
Colorado	0.00	0.00	0.00	0.00	0.00
Connecticut	4.07	0.26	1.13	3.92	10.58
Delaware	2.31	0.20	0.67	2.39	5.97
Florida	0.20	0.01	0.05	0.19	0.52
Georgia	0.00	0.00	0.00	0.00	0.00
Hawaii	2.25	0.21	0.72	2.25	5.76
Idaho	2.98	0.30	1.04	3.24	7.41
Illinois	5.80	0.35	1.64	6.04	15.55
Indiana	3.19	0.17	1.04	3.44	8.52
Iowa	2.40	0.17	0.83	2.48	6.53
Kansas	2.96	0.31	1.07	3.32	7.61
Kentucky	7.24	0.66	2.28	8.24	19.47
Louisiana	10.54	0.87	4.87	11.38	24.80
Maine	1.35	0.09	0.44	1.31	3.48
Maryland	6.24	0.50	1.75	6.35	16.66
Massachusetts	10.25	0.76	2.77	10.38	27.02
Michigan	7.67	0.68	2.24	7.77	21.49
Minnesota	3.54	0.29	1.00	3.67	9.73
Mississippi	1.67	0.17	0.58	1.80	4.15
Missouri	2.08	0.16	0.55	2.02	5.40
Montana	12.17	0.85	3.87	13.97	32.22
Nebraska	0.27	0.02	0.08	0.27	0.68
Nevada	3.98	0.32	1.14	4.27	10.09
New Hampshire	1.44	0.08	0.39	1.47	3.83
New Jersey	1.63	0.08	0.50	1.67	4.15
New Mexico	3.63	0.33	1.14	3.53	10.00
New York	3.93	0.23	1.07	3.97	10.30
North Carolina	0.99	0.06	0.26	0.99	2.58
North Dakota	2.06	0.15	0.70	2.25	5.16
Ohio	6.86	0.61	2.11	7.66	18.14
Oklahoma	2.32	0.15	0.75	2.24	5.89
Oregon	5.64	0.59	2.03	6.25	14.15
Pennsylvania	4.10	0.28	1.31	4.22	10.55
Rhode Island	8.37	0.46	2.52	8.55	21.83
South Carolina	4.13	0.40	1.39	4.31	10.97
South Dakota	1.76	0.19	0.47	1.70	4.70
Tennessee	5.15	0.42	1.45	5.30	13.96
Texas	0.00	0.00	0.00	0.00	0.00
Utah	1.33	0.11	0.40	1.34	3.60
Vermont	3.23	0.22	1.01	3.24	8.13
Virginia	1.60	0.08	0.44	1.66	4.16
Washington	1.52	0.13	0.46	1.52	4.10
West Virginia	9.28	1.10	2.70	9.54	25.26

(Continued)

Table 6.2 Continued

State	*Exp. Value*	*25%*	*50%*	*75%*	*90%*
Wisconsin	2.40	0.19	0.66	2.43	6.48
Wyoming	6.17	0.71	1.76	6.29	16.93
Mean	3.73	0.30	1.16	3.92	9.80
Median	3.09	0.21	1.00	3.28	7.87
Max	12.17	1.10	4.87	13.97	32.22
Min	0.00	0.00	0.00	0.00	0.00

Source: Created by the authors.

be 1.36% or less). Alternatively, there is only 25% chance the economic contraction lasts more than 12 months, but the revenue shortfall associated with an economic contraction lasting 12 months is almost 5%, and every month the contraction lasts, the extra revenue shortfall associated with an additional month of economic contraction gets larger and larger. Therefore, even though long recessions (such as one lasting 12 months or longer) are relatively rare, the revenue shortfalls associated with these longer recessions are very severe. In fact, the average (or expected value of the) revenue shortfall is generally approximately equal to 75th percentile revenue shortfall for most states.

Thirty-six states have an average revenue shortfall of 5% or less, indicating that the NCSL's 5% recommendation may have been appropriate for those states. Yet three states have an average shortfall of 10% or more. If legislators want to be more cautious by accumulating more savings, thus avoiding tax increases or spending cuts during recessions, then they may want to accumulate a savings level equal to or greater than the 90th percentile numbers. For this level of savings, 21 states have potential revenue shortfalls of 10% or more, with seven states having 90th percentile revenue shortfalls in excess of 20%.

One additional point to note concerns the four states that have a positive low-growth-regime growth rate. Based on our methodology, these states seemingly do not need to accumulate any savings because a revenue shortfall does not appear to be possible. This doubtful conclusion owes to the methodology used to calculate revenue shortfall. In our methodology, we use the *point* estimate for the low-growth-regime growth rate to calculate potential revenue shortfalls. Such an approach can produce the illusion that states in the positive low-growth-regime growth rate cohort cannot run deficits because *their low-growth-regime growth rates are positive and hence will not experience any revenue shortfalls during economic contractions*. An alternative strategy for computing the potential revenue shortfalls would be to pull values for the low-growth-regime growth rate from the distribution of the estimate. Although more technically correct, the cost of using this methodology is the ability to offer an intuitive explanation of the results is diminished. Therefore, although the results presented in table

6.2 suggest these four states do not need to accumulate much savings, they should take this as a recommendation that they do not need to accumulate very much in savings.

Ability to Weather Recession

Most states have accumulated savings in their BSFs. Table 6.3 reports the accumulated savings in BSFs as of 2019.[13] Wyoming has by far the largest BSF as a percentage of their annual revenue, with a fund size of 122%. The average state has accumulated savings of 11.2% of revenue, but taking Wyoming out reduces this number to 8.9%, and if the number two state, Alaska, is also exempted, it reduces the average to 7.3%; the median among all the states is 7.1%. Fifteen states have accumulated savings of 10% or more, while 15 states have accumulated savings less than 5%, with five states that have less than 2% accumulated savings in their BSF. As mentioned above though, the question naturally arises whether the states that have accumulated a significant amount of savings are actually the states that need to do so.

To calculate how ready states are to weather an economic contraction, it is possible to compare the amount that each state has accumulated in their BSF with that state's distribution of revenue shortfalls. For example, Hawaii has accumulated 4.8% of its current annual revenue in its BSF. Its 75th percentile revenue shortfall is 2.2%, while its 90th percentile revenue shortfall is 5.8%. Therefore, it can clearly weather somewhere between 75 and 90% of all revenue shortfalls it may experience. Based on its complete distribution of revenue shortfalls, Hawaii can weather 87.5% of all possible revenue shortfalls it may experience. Specifically, based on the methodology used in this essay, Hawaii has enough savings to weather an economic contraction lasting 15 months or less. Overall, 26 states have accumulated enough savings to cover 90% or more of all the possible revenue shortfalls they may experience. On the other hand, six states have accumulated savings sufficient to cover *less than* 50% of their possible revenue shortfalls, and 12 states have insufficient funds to cover the revenue shortfall associated with an average economic contraction.

Savings Rates

Once a state has determined the appropriate level of total savings to target based on its risk preferences and the distributions described in table 6.2, the next question is how much to save each month in order to accumulate that amount of total savings. As mentioned above, based on how likely each state is to remain in an expansion (i.e., their estimated P_{HH}), it is possible to form a distribution of how long their expansion is likely to persist. As an example,

Table 6.3 Rainy-Day Fund Balances and Ability to Weather a Revenue Shortfall

State	*BSF Size*	*% of Potential Shortfalls*
Alabama	9.1	77.5
Alaska	86.9	99.9
Arizona	4.1	72.5
Arkansas	2.6	100.0
California	15.2	94.9
Colorado	9.1	100.0
Connecticut	12.8	91.9
Delaware	5.2	89.0
Florida	4.3	99.9
Georgia	11.0	100.0
Hawaii	4.8	87.5
Idaho	11.3	94.2
Illinois	0.0	9.8
Indiana	8.6	90.6
Iowa	9.7	94.6
Kansas	0.0	0.0
Kentucky	1.1	39.5
Louisiana	4.0	43.9
Maine	8.0	97.3
Maryland	4.8	69.5
Massachusetts	9.9	73.8
Michigan	10.8	79.6
Minnesota	10.3	91.1
Mississippi	5.9	93.4
Missouri	6.8	92.5
Montana	2.3	41.3
Nebraska	6.8	99.9
Nevada	7.1	84.2
New Hampshire	7.1	95.9
New Jersey	1.1	68.6
New Mexico	13.8	94.0
New York	2.9	67.4
North Carolina	5.1	96.2
North Dakota	5.9	91.1
Ohio	8.0	77.5
Oklahoma	10.5	95.6
Oregon	11.1	85.1
Pennsylvania	0.1	10.5
Rhode Island	5.1	64.9
South Carolina	6.0	82.1
South Dakota	10.4	97.1
Tennessee	5.7	76.3
Texas	18.8	100.0
Utah	9.2	97.8
Vermont	13.3	94.8
Virginia	3.7	88.7
Washington	7.3	95.7
West Virginia	15.8	84.1

(Continued)

Table 6.3 Continued

State	BSF Size	% of Potential Shortfalls
Wisconsin	3.7	83.4
Wyoming	122.2	99.9
Mean	11.18	81.11
Median	7.09	90.88
Max	122.24	100.00
Min	0.00	0.00

Source: Created by the authors.

suppose $P_{HH} = 0.97$; the probability distribution describing the duration of an expansion is shown in table 6.4. The first column of table 6.4 shows the various durations; the second column shows the likelihood that an expansion will last *exactly* a certain number of months; and column three shows the likelihood that an expansion will last *at least* a certain number of months. For instance, there is a 91.3% chance that an expansion will last at least four months and a 76.0% chance that an expansion will last at least 10 months. Therefore, if a state sets a target for total accumulated savings equal to 5% of their annual revenue, and if the state wants to be 75% sure to accumulate that amount, then they know that they should accumulate that amount in 10 months, which means they must save 6% of their revenue each month. In general, to achieve a target level of savings of X percent of annual revenue in T months, the savings rate is $12X/T$ (this simple calculation ignores revenue growth).[14]

Table 6.5 reports the distribution of the duration of expansionary months based on each state's estimated value of P_{HH} given in table 6.1. For example, Alabama has an estimated probability of 0.987. Based on this probability, on average, an expansion will last 73 months. There is a 90% chance that an expansion will last at least nine months, a 75% chance an expansion will last 22 months, and a 50% chance an expansion will last 53 months. Therefore, suppose Alabama has decided to accumulate total savings equal to 7.61% of their annual amount of revenue (this corresponds to the expected shortfall level reported in table 6.2). If they want to be 90% sure to accumulate this amount of savings, then they should attempt to accumulate this amount in 9 months or less. This could be accomplished by saving 10.1% of their revenue each month.[15] Alternatively, if Alabama wanted to be 75% sure to accumulate the 7.61% of annual revenues then they would have 22 months to accumulate this amount and could do so if they save 4.1% of their revenue each month. The average duration of the expansion for Alabama is 73 months and median expansion lasts for at least 53 months. Therefore, based on the expected duration of an expansion, if Alabama saved 1.25% of their revenue each month then, on average, they would accumulate their target level of savings of 7.61% of revenues. Finally, if Alabama saved 1.7% of their revenue each month, then in half of the

Table 6.4 Distribution of Expansion Duration with PHH = 0.97

Months	*Probability*	*Cumulative Probability*
1	0.0300	1.000
2	0.0291	0.970
3	0.0282	0.941
4	0.0274	0.913
5	0.0266	0.885
6	0.0258	0.859
7	0.0250	0.833
8	0.0242	0.808
9	0.0235	0.784
10	0.0228	0.760
11	0.0221	0.737
12	0.0215	0.715
13	0.0208	0.694
14	0.0202	0.673
15	0.0196	0.653
16	0.0190	0.633
17	0.0184	0.614
18	0.0179	0.596
19	0.0173	0.578
20	0.0168	0.561
21	0.0163	0.544
22	0.0158	0.527
23	0.0153	0.512
24	0.0149	0.496
25	0.0144	0.481
26	0.0140	0.467
27	0.0136	0.453
28	0.0132	0.439
29	0.0128	0.426
30	0.0124	0.413
31	0.0120	0.401
32	0.0117	0.389
33	0.0113	0.377
34	0.0110	0.366
35	0.0107	0.355
36	0.0103	0.344
37	0.0100	0.334
38	0.0097	0.324
39	0.0094	0.314
40	0.0091	0.305
41	0.0089	0.296
42	0.0086	0.287
43	0.0083	0.278
44	0.0081	0.270
45	0.0079	0.262
46	0.0076	0.254
47	0.0074	0.246

(Continued)

Table 6.4 Continued

Months	*Probability*	*Cumulative Probability*
48	0.0072	0.239
49	0.0070	0.232
50	0.0067	0.225

Source: Created by the authors.

expansions they would accumulate their target level of total savings of 7.6% of annual revenue. In general, states need to first choose the total amount they would like to accumulate in savings based on the distributions in table 6.2, and then the distributions in table 6.5 tell states the number of months they have to accumulate that amount of total savings if they want to have a certain level of confidence in accumulating their target level of total savings.

CONCLUSION

Because the revenue that states collect is procyclical, it is virtually inevitable that revenue will decline during months of economic contraction. If states with a balanced budged requirement do not have enough savings, they must raise tax rates or reduce spending during economic contractions and associated revenue declines. Rainy-day funds are a common way to accumulate savings during expansions. But without knowledge about the severity and duration of the phases of the business cycle, it is impossible to know how much to save. Furthermore, since every state has different business cycle characteristics (expansion and contraction growth rates as well as durations) and different tax bases and tax structures (making the sensitivity of revenue collections to economic activity different in each state), a one-size-fits-all approach simply makes no sense. Not only that, but deriving point estimates of how much of a revenue shortfall a state may experience is not necessarily very useful since, again, the duration and severity of the business cycle phases are unknown beforehand. In this chapter, we have accomplished a number of tasks. First, we have calculated the distribution of revenue shortfalls for each state based on their state-specific business cycle characteristics. This distribution is useful because when combined with their current level of savings, it tells legislators how prepared they are currently. Additionally, this distribution can inform them of savings goals based on their own preferences for avoiding tax increases or spending reductions during an economic contraction. Furthermore, we have assessed how prepared each state is currently by comparing the distribution of potential revenue shortfalls with each state's accumulated savings in their BSF. Finally, we have laid out a roadmap

Table 6.5 Savings Rates

State	Expected Value	90%	75%	50%	25%
Alabama	73	9	22	53	106
Alaska	8	1	3	5	10
Arizona	55	6	16	39	77
Arkansas	78	9	24	58	115
California	61	7	18	43	86
Colorado	61	7	18	43	86
Connecticut	45	5	13	32	63
Delaware	98	14	36	87	173
Florida	65	7	20	46	92
Georgia	50	6	15	35	69
Hawaii	47	5	14	33	66
Idaho	82	10	27	63	126
Illinois	65	7	20	46	92
Indiana	73	9	22	53	106
Iowa	93	12	32	77	154
Kansas	78	9	24	58	115
Kentucky	55	6	16	39	77
Louisiana	106	27	72	173	346
Maine	69	8	21	50	99
Maryland	58	7	17	41	81
Massachusetts	65	7	20	46	92
Michigan	52	6	15	37	73
Minnesota	78	9	24	58	115
Mississippi	50	6	15	35	69
Missouri	55	6	16	39	77
Montana	61	7	18	43	86
Nebraska	65	7	20	46	92
Nevada	78	9	24	58	115
New Hampshire	69	8	21	50	99
New Jersey	58	7	17	41	81
New Mexico	78	9	24	58	115
New York	50	6	15	35	69
North Carolina	61	7	18	43	86
North Dakota	33	4	10	23	46
Ohio	69	8	21	50	99
Oklahoma	58	7	17	41	81
Oregon	69	8	21	50	99
Pennsylvania	73	9	22	53	106
Rhode Island	78	9	24	58	115
South Carolina	55	6	16	39	77
South Dakota	93	12	32	77	154
Tennessee	43	5	13	30	60
Texas	73	9	22	53	106
Utah	73	9	22	53	106
Vermont	78	9	24	58	115
Virginia	61	7	18	43	86
Washington	65	7	20	46	92

(Continued)

Table 6.5 Continued

State	*Expected Value*	*90%*	*75%*	*50%*	*25%*
West Virginia	78	9	24	58	115
Wisconsin	78	9	24	58	115
Wyoming	78	9	24	58	115

Source: Created by the authors.

concerning the rate at which each state could save to accumulate a sufficient amount of savings which may be at least of equal importance relative to just having goals for total accumulated savings.

NOTES

1. Vermont being the only exception.
2. *Fiscal Survey of States*, fall 2010.
3. Using monthly data, T = 360.
4. This total includes amounts in BSF's as well as general fund balances.
5. *Fiscal Survey of States*, Fall 2019.
6. Owyang, Piger, Wall (2005) estimate business cycle characteristics for each state.
7. Navin and Navin (1997) and Pollock and Suyderhoud (1986).
8. The data are from 1979:09 to 2019:12.
9. In technical terms, we are assuming the growth rate of economic activity follows a first-order Markov process.
10. If $\varphi > 1$ then tax collections are more volatile than overall economic activity and if $\varphi < 1$ then tax collections are less volatile than overall economic activity.
11. The expected duration, E(ti) = (1–Pii)–1 for i=H and L.
12. Based on the average low-growth regime growth rate and average elasticity.
13. Based on the *Fiscal Survey of States*, Spring 2020 from the National Association of State Budget Officers.
14. Ignoring the growth of revenue over time, the formula used to calculate the percent of *monthly* revenue that needs to be saved in *T* months to accumulate *X* percent of *annual* revenue is simply *12X/T*. Taking growth into consideration, the formula becomes .
15. Note that if Alabama saves at this rate each month, they will accumulate an amount of savings $\frac{X \sum_{i=T-11}^{T} (1+g_H)^i}{\sum_{j=1}^{T} (1+g_H)^j}$ that is equal to 7.61% of their annual revenue in 9 months; there is a 90% chance the expansion will last longer than 9 months so Alabama could discontinue adding to their savings (and just save enough to maintain their desired percentage) or could continue to save (albeit at a lower rate) which would increase their total accumulated savings and therefore their ability to weather more severe economic downturns.

REFERENCES

Navin, John, and Leo Navin. "The Optimal Size of Countercyclical Bud-get Stabilization Funds: A Case Study of Ohio." *Public Budgeting and Finance* 17, No. 2 (June, 1997): 114–27.

Pollock, Richard, and Jack Suyderhoud. "The Role of Rainy Day Funds in Achieving Fiscal Stability." *National Tax Journal* 39, No. 4 (December, 1986): 485–97.

Chapter 7

Anti-Aid Provisions in State Constitutions

Matthew Mitchell, Jonathan Riches, Veronica Lucero, and Anne Philpot

INTRODUCTION

Policymakers are keenly interested in promoting economic growth, and targeted economic development incentives are an especially popular strategy.[1] These selective privileges are offered to particular firms or industries and can include targeted tax relief, targeted regulatory relief, cash subsidies, loans and loan guarantees, in-kind donations of land and other valuable goods and services, or some combination of the above.

By one estimate, states and localities spend about $95 billion per year on targeted economic development subsidies.[2] As a share of industry contributions to GDP, incentives have tripled since 1990 (Bartik 2017, 2–3).

Unfortunately, the economic case for targeted subsidies is rather weak.[3] Theoretically, a subsidy might boost net economic development in a region if the government manages to subsidize firms with positive externalities using revenue derived from taxes on activities without positive externalities or from taxes on activities with negative externalities.[4] It is not clear, however, that policymakers have either the knowledge or the incentive to do this properly.[5]

More often, the public case for subsidies rests only on the jobs and economic activity the subsidized firm promises to create. For example, in 2017, Wisconsin offered up to $3.46 billion to Foxconn Technology Group to locate a plant in southeast Wisconsin. The company commissioned a study concluding that the plant would add more than $62.4 billion to Wisconsin's GDP over 15 years.[6] Though widely cited in the debate over the subsidy, this estimate overstates the expected economic benefits attributable to the subsidy and ignores the costs.

The estimate overstates the benefits due to the subsidy because it implicitly assumes that the plant would not locate in Wisconsin without it. A recent review of 34 academic studies concluded, however, that subsidies "probably tip somewhere between 2 percent and 25 percent of incented firms toward making a decision favoring the location providing the incentives."[7] Firms are often unswayed by subsidies—even very large ones—because other factors loom larger. Labor costs, business logistics, and access to location-specific resources tend to have a bigger effect on profit. For example, local labor costs are typically about 14 times larger than state and local business tax costs.[8] A mere 2% wage difference can offset as much as a 40% difference in taxes.[9]

If subsidies are decisive between 2 and 25% of the time, we should revise downward the expected gross benefits attributable to any given subsidy. If a bet pays $100 with a 25% probability of winning, it is only worth $25. Similarly, if a subsidized factory is expected to add $62.4 billion to Wisconsin's economy over 15 years and we assume a 25% chance that the subsidy was decisive, then the value of the subsidy is $15.6 billion, not $62.4 billion. If we assume a 76% chance the subsidy was decisive (which might be more realistic for a large subsidy), then the expected gross benefit of the subsidy is $47.4 billion over 15 years.[10]

Still, this ignores the other side of the ledger: the cost of the subsidy. All else being equal, the Foxconn subsidy will require Wisconsin to keep taxes 1.08% higher than they otherwise would be over the next 15 years. According to the range of estimates, if a state raises taxes by 10%, then over the long run, economic activity will tend to decline by about 5%, with a plausible range between 1.5 and 8.5%.[11] Thus, the Foxconn subsidies may cost the state about $29 billion, with a plausible range between $8.7 and $49.5 billion.[12] With gross benefits ranging from $15.6 to $47.4 billion and gross costs ranging from $8.7 to $49.5 billion, it is entirely possible that the expected *net benefits* of the Foxconn subsidy are negative. This conclusion is bolstered when one considers that subsidies likely entail a host of other difficult-to-quantify costs, including rent-seeking,[13] unproductive entrepreneurship (Baumol 1990; Murphy, Shleifer, and Vishny 1991) and the long-run costs of anticompetitive policy (Leibenstein 1966; Mitchell 2012).

The theoretical case against subsidies is supported by the empirical record. Since 1990 there have been more than 100 academic studies of targeted subsidies.[14] Most of these studies evaluate subsidies in light of their effects on the privileged firms, regions, or industries. But subsidies are rarely sold as a means to boost the well-being of these narrowly targeted interest groups. Instead, subsidies are typically sold as a means to benefit the communities paying for them.[15] Among those studies that evaluate subsidies in light of their effects on these broader communities, the vast majority find little to no support for subsidies.[16]

Yet despite the economic case against them, subsidies persist. Public choice models explain why.[17] Subsidies confer highly visible benefits on concentrated, politically organized special interests, while their costs are less obvious and spread across diffuse, politically unorganized taxpayers, consumers, and small businesses.[18] This pattern of concentrated benefits and diffuse costs explains the persistence of many inefficient policies (Olson 1965; Lowi 1969; Schuck 2014). The problem is compounded because voters are often ignorant or confused about the technical aspects of economic development policy.[19] As a result, political leaders may misclassify costs as benefits and believe that a project is more valuable because it involves a large investment or requires a large workforce (Weingast, Shepsle, and Johnsen 1981).

Given the persistence and prevalence of targeted subsidies despite the economic case against them, institutional constraints—such as state anti-aid provisions—are needed to limit their use.

THE RISE OF FAVORITISM IN THE UNITED STATES

Governments have favored particular firms, industries, and interests for centuries. For almost as long, economists have been critical of the practice.[20] At the time of the American founding, the mercantile system had dominated European economic policy for nearly three centuries. Yet despite its long and entrenched practice, early U.S. policymakers showed ambivalence toward mercantilism, especially at the national level. Congress rejected Hamilton's plan to promote manufacturing through tariffs and subsidies in 1791, and when it later resurfaced as Henry Clay's "American system," that too was largely rejected. Thus, for the first several decades of the republic, neither the states nor the federal government actively promoted particular firms or industries.[21]

Starting in the 1820s, the size and scope of state spending changed. First, states—especially southern states—began to invest in private banks (Wallis 2000, 67; Rodden 2006, 58). Then, following the rejection at the national level of John Quincy Adams's proposals to spend heavily on "internal improvements" (modeled on Henry Clay's "American system"), some states began funding infrastructure projects on their own.

The success of the publicly funded Erie Canal, completed in 1825, provided further impetus. It inspired two decades of state-supported railroads, turnpikes, and canals across the nation (Briffault 2002, 911). State governments hoped to stimulate their economies through investment in private firms, especially as interstate competition for economic development escalated (Briffault 2002, 911). During this era, "railroad promoters encouraged towns to bid against each other for influence in locating the railroads" (Libgober 2016, 13). And towns obliged because railroads were believed to have "great potential for public benefit" (Houpt 2011, 381) and to be "critical for economic development since the existence of the railroad would attract other economic enterprise" (Schaefer 1996, 342). Given the Jacksonian era's disdain for national spending on such projects, it was the states that took the lead (See, for example, Jackson's famous veto of the Maysville Road. The president not only noted that the project was "purely local" but also warned of "artful expedients to shift upon the Government the losses of unsuccessful private speculation" (Jackson 1830)). But, as Columbia Law School's Richard Briffault notes, "Many of these projects blurred public and private lines, with states investing in private firms, or providing grants, loans and loan guarantees to private companies."[22]

Though the political appetite for locally funded infrastructure was high, the appetite for taxes to pay for it was low. Early on, states had relied on property taxes (Wallis 2000, 67). As they began earning income on private projects, however, confidence in infrastructure investments grew, and some states cut or eliminated their property taxes. By 1835, Alabama, Georgia, Maryland, Massachusetts, New York, Rhode Island, Pennsylvania, and South Carolina had all eliminated state property taxes (Wallis 2000, 67). Direct taxation—including property, poll, and income taxation—had all but disappeared (Rodden 2006, 57). In its place, the key sources of state revenue became sales of public lands, returns on private investments, and proceeds from issuing bank charters.[23] The economic historian John Joseph Wallis termed this the era of "taxless finance" (Wallis 2005, 213). Reminiscent of modern loan guarantees, under taxless finance, tax-payers took a loss on projects such as canals, roads, or banks only if they failed (Wallis 2005, 213). And evidently, policymakers everywhere believed that failure was impossible. A delegate to the Maryland Reform Convention reflected two decades later, "Every man dreamed he was about to reach a new *El Dorado*. Taxation was to exist no longer—public debt was to become an obsolete idea" (Quoted in Goodrich 1950, 153).

State debt did not become an obsolete idea. In fact, it grew substantially. At the beginning of the 1820s, most states had little or no debt (Rodden 2006, 57). But between 1836 and 1839, states incurred more debt than they had in their entire previous histories (Rodden 2006, 58). Between 1810 and 1840, state debt per capita rose 144%.[24] By the late 1830s, state debt soared to eight times all federal and local debts combined.[25] In 1830, Arkansas, Florida, Illinois, Indiana, Michigan, and Mississippi had no debt. But a decade later, their combined general obligation debt was more than $44 million (in current dollars) (Rubin 1993, 156). As collateral against these debts, states relied on the federal government's implied support and the option of resuming property tax collection.[26]

Because these ventures permitted private actors to gamble with public money—privatizing gains and socializing losses—there was a strong incentive to pursue risky projects. According to Rutgers University law professor David Pinsky,

> there was practically no public control over the planning of the railroad project[s] or over the actual expenditures of publicly contributed funds. These functions were completely delegated to private corporate officials. To phrase it more dramatically, but no less accurately, there was a total abdication of public responsibility. Not infrequently, railroad planning was so speculatively conceived and incompetently executed that the proposed line was never completed. Waste and dishonesty in the expenditure of funds led to corporate insolvency and abandonment of routes (Pinsky 1963, 280).

The unsustainable nature of these public investments in private ventures was laid bare by the panic of 1837 and the significant recession that lasted from 1839 to 1843 (Rodden 2006, 58). As the economy contracted, infrastructure projects across the country—marked "by waste, overbuilding, and mismanagement"—failed to generate expected revenues (Briffault 2002, 911). By 1842, eight states and one territory had defaulted.[27] Four states—Arkansas, Florida, Michigan, and Mississippi—repudiated nearly $14 million in debt.(Ratchford 1941, 114 As Joshua Bates, the umpire of the Anglo-American claims convention of 1853 put it: "It is to be hoped that sooner or later the people of Florida will discover that honesty is the best policy; and that no State can be called respectable that does not honorably fulfill its engagements" 111). Out of these circumstances, the first wave of state constitutional anti-aid provisions was born.

ANTI-AID CLAUSES

As state fiscal positions eroded, support for federal assumption of state debts grew, especially among politicians representing the most heavily indebted states. Ultimately, however, the assumption proposal was tabled. Unable to shift their debts onto federal taxpayers, states were left to clean up their own messes. And one important consequence was that citizens and local leaders mobilized to prevent future messes. A particularly important strategy was to adopt constitutional limitations on public aid to private entities. (These approaches were not mutually exclusive. Rhode Island's debt clause read: "The general assembly shall have no power hereafter, without the express consent of the people, to incur state debt to an amount exceeding 50,000 dollars, except in time of war, or in case of insurrection; Nor shall they in any case, without such consent, pledge the faith of the state for the payment of the obligations of others" *Rhode Island Constitution of 1842*, n.d.). As law professor Dale Rubin notes, "The impetus for the adoption of both state and local constitutional aid limitation provisions was the untrammeled and indiscriminate borrowing by governmental entities and the ruthless profiteering by private corporations and individuals" (Rubin 1993, 156).

Moreover, the aim of public aid limitations was, as one delegate to the Ohio conventions of 1850 and 1851 put it, "to see the State Government brought back to its simple and appropriate functions, [leaving] railroad, canal, turnpike and other corporate associations, to get along on their own credit, without any connection or partnership with the State whatever" (Quoted in Hall and Karsten 2008, 103–4). And as Josiah Scott of the Ohio Supreme Court put it, these provisions aimed to prohibit the union of public and private capital: "The mischief which this section interdicts is a business partnership between a municipality or subdivision of the State, and individuals or private corporations or associations. It forbids the union of public and private capital or credit in any enterprise whatever" (Scott 1871).

Despite their early adoption by a few states in the 1840s, it took more than a decade for a majority of states to adopt anti-aid provisions (Rubin 1993, 144 N. 5). These provisions generally took three forms. The most common was a *credit clause*, which forbade the government from loaning credit to a private individual, association, or corporation. A variant of this clause first appeared in the Rhode Island Constitution of 1842, requiring electoral approval for such deals. Shortly thereafter, New Jersey (1844) and New York (1846) adopted credit clauses that forbade lending credit with or without electoral approval (Pinsky 1963, 278 N. 70). The second type of anti-aid provision was a *stock clause*, which forbade the government from becoming a stockholder in any corporation. This was pioneered by Iowa in 1846 (Pinsky 1963, 278 N. 71). The final provision was a *gift clause*, which forbade the government from granting loans or donations to any individual, association, or corporation. This provision first appeared in Pennsylvania's 1873 constitution (Pinsky 1963, 279 N. 77).

The spread of anti-aid provisions was by no means uniform. Some states adopted just one provision, some two, and others all three. Moreover, especially in their earliest iterations, anti-aid provisions did not necessarily apply to substate governments, such as counties, cities, or school districts (Pinsky 1963, 280). Despite these variations, however, by 1900 some form of public aid limitation had been adopted by a large majority of states (Pinsky 1963, 280). Even those that had withstood the panic of 1837 without defaulting adopted these provisions to avoid the fate of their neighbors (Tarr 1998, 112).

In the decades following the advent of these anti-aid provisions, state aid to private corporations did not end altogether, but it was sharply curtailed (Wallis 2000, 70). As Wallis notes, "The tide of events had turned against state activity" (Wallis 2000, 70). Following the adoption of these provisions, there was a dramatic change in state and local fiscal policy; states reduced their reliance on debt finance, and more activity shifted from state to local governments (Wallis 2000, 66–70). In 1841, the states' share of all government debt was 86.4%, but by 1902, it was 7.0% (Wallis 2000, 66).

ANTI-AID PROVISIONS APPLIED TO LOCALITIES

The first wave of anti-aid provisions did not always apply to localities (Houpt 2011, 381; Pinsky 1963, 278–80). Consequently, as states curtailed their direct support of private interests, localities ramped it up. In many cases, local governments began to take on the sorts of risks that states had once assumed. Sometimes states abetted this local circumvention of anti-aid provisions. Constitutional scholar Alan Tarr writes, "From 1866 to 1873, legislatures approved over eight hundred proposals to grant local aid to railroad companies. New York, Illinois, and Missouri together authorized over $70 million worth of aid" (Tarr 1998, 114).

As with the state aid that had preceded it, much of this local aid was financed through government borrowing or guarantees of private debt. Thus, as the states' share of all government debt was declining, localities' share rose, going from 11.4% in 1841 to 57.1% in 1902 (Wallis 2000, 66). Similarly, while local government revenue per capita was about 40% greater than state revenue per capita in 1840, by 1902 it was 260% greater (Wallis 2000, 70).

As before, the precarious fiscal position of governments—this time, local governments—was laid bare by a national economic contraction. As the panic of 1873 gave way to a deep and lasting economic depression, property values plummeted, and railroads began to default on their debts. By 1874, about 25% of all railroad bonds were in default (Dove 2014, 76). Next, municipalities that had guaranteed many of these debts began to default on their own obligations en masse. It is estimated that roughly 20% of all municipal debt obligations were defaulted on in the 1870s (Chatters 1933; Hillhouse 1936; Dove 2014).

These defaults prompted a second wave of constitutional reforms that extended anti-aid provisions to local governments (Tarr 1998, 114; Briffault 2002, 912). Indiana [1851], Nevada [1864], Georgia [1868], and Illinois [1870]) quickly extended their anti-aid provisions to localities. The 1870s municipal debt crisis prompted more than a dozen other states to also do so over the course of the next 15 years (Credit and stock clauses were applied to local governments by Arkansas, New York, and Pennsylvania in 1874; Alabama, Florida, and Missouri in 1875; Colorado and Texas in 1876;

Connecticut and New Hampshire in 1877; Maine in 1878; California in 1879; and Montana and Washington in 1889. Dove 2014, 77).

The second wave of anti-aid provisions was more successful than the first. With the municipal fiscal crisis fresh in mind and the framers' intentions abundantly clear, courts were active over the next half century in policing governments that overstepped the bounds of anti-aid clauses, certainly more active than they would come to be as the twentieth century wore on. Importantly, early courts understood that the framers of these provisions intended them to limit public aid to private interests regardless of the aid's purpose.[28]

Courts were, however, not rigorous in policing state and local violations of anti-aid provisions (Rubin 1993, 161). Over time, legislatures circumvented these rules while courts invented new doctrines that vitiated these provisions. Nevertheless, the case history of this period shows that—for a time—in geographically and politically diverse regions of the country, courts were willing to stop the elected branches when they transgressed constitutional anti-aid provisions (Rubin 1993, 161).

What was the result? While it is impossible to determine a causal relationship or to disentangle the effects of these provisions from those of other reforms adopted at this time, anti-aid provisions did coincide with improved policy. First, the financial footing of government grew stronger. Figure 7.1 shows state, local, and combined state and local debt as a share of national income from 1838 through 1913. Immediately following the first wave of reforms, state debts as a share of national income began to fall. Given the local loophole, however, local debt as a share of income rose. Following the second wave of reforms, local debt as a share of GDP also began to fall and then leveled off. By the end of the nineteenth century, combined state and local debt stood as a smaller share of national income than at any previous point since the crisis of the early 1840s. Second, as their fiscal positions improved, municipalities found themselves facing lower borrowing costs. Economist John Dove analyzed the prices of bonds issued by dozens of U.S. cities in the latter decades of the nineteenth century (Dove 2014). He found that among those cities that had defaulted during the 1870s, those that subsequently adopted either a credit or stock clause faced borrowing costs that were between 170 and 249 basis points lower. (His analysis is based on an OLS regression that includes a large set of control variables that account for other socioeconomic factors that might affect borrowing costs. Dove 2014, 92.) Finally, as state and local governments curtailed their use of targeted economic development subsidies, the U.S. economy entered a period of prolonged and robust economic expansion (Romer 1986).

Researchers have found that well into the latter half of the twentieth century these constitutional prohibitions were influencing the types of incentives governments offered, making gifts of land and money the least-used (Gray

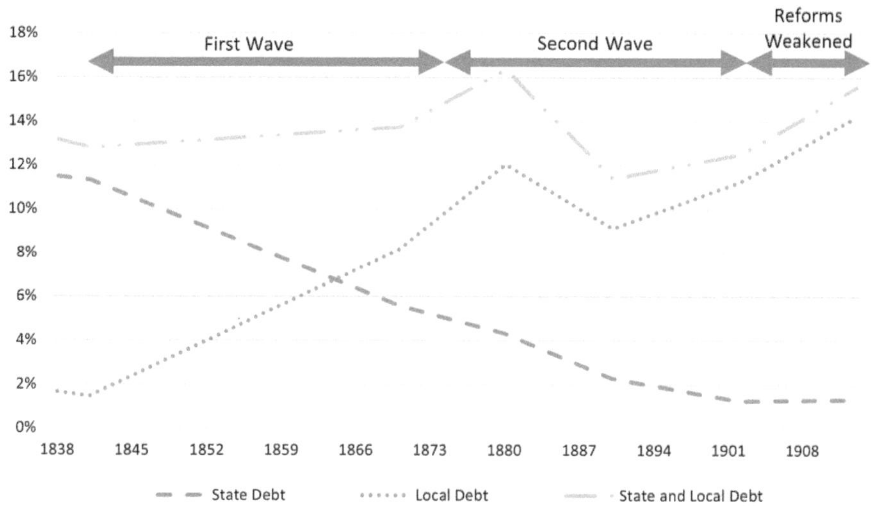

Figure 7.1 Government Debt as a Share of National Income. *Sources*: Debt figures are reported in John Joseph Wallis, "American Government Finance in the Long Run: 1790 to 1990," *Journal of Economic Perspectives* 14, no. 1 (2000). National income figures are from US Department of Commerce, Bureau of the Census, *Historical Statistics of the United States 1789–1945: A Supplement to the Statistical Abstract of the United States*, Washington, DC, June 1949, 14. National income figures are not available for every year, and some data are interpolated.

and Spina 1980, 528). More recently, economist Carlianne Patrick has developed an index measuring the strength of constitutional aid limits (Patrick 2014). Places with weaker limits—and therefore more subsidies to private businesses—experience significantly lower levels of rural employment in the medium term. In subsequent work, she has found that states with weaker anti-aid provisions tend to subsidize capital, causing firms to substitute such capital as computers and robots for labor. She finds that this decreases employment density and causes an employment shift from labor-intensive to capital-intensive industries (Patrick 2015).

THE WEAKENING OF ANTI-AID PROVISIONS

Courts have weakened constitutional anti-aid provisions over the past century.[29] They did so largely by turning the judicially created Public Purpose Doctrine on its head. The doctrine dates back to an 1853 case called *Sharpless v. Mayor of Philadelphia*, (Sharpless v. Mayor of Philadelphia 1853) which was decided two decades before an anti-aid provision was added to the Pennsylvania Constitution (Dove 2014, 77). In the 1840s and 1850s, the Pennsylvania legislature authorized Philadelphia to use debt to pay for shares in two private railroads (Gillman, Graber, and Whittington 2013, 1). A Philadelphia taxpayer named William P. Sharpless brought suit claiming that the state had no authority to use the public taxing power to support a private interest.

At least in principle, the Pennsylvania Supreme Court agreed: "It is said that this is a taking of *private* property for *private* use. If this be so, it is palpably unconstitutional." Though the constitution had no "express inhibition" against such legislation, the court said that the assembly had no authority "to take one man's property and give it to another."[30] Thus was born the Public Purpose Doctrine: the state may only tax to fund projects that are in the public interest; projects that benefit private interests are forbidden. In 1874, the U.S. Supreme Court issued its first Public Purpose Doctrine ruling, finding that state legislatures may confer to municipalities the right to levy taxes, but only if those taxes serve a public purpose (Loan Association v. Topeka 1874). By 1917, the Court had incorporated the doctrine into the 14th Amendment (Jones v. City of Portland 1917).

On its face, the Public Purpose Doctrine seems to complement state constitutional anti-aid provisions. Like those provisions, it bans the expenditure of public resources in service of private interests. In practice, however, it has come to thwart anti-aid provisions for two reasons. First, from the beginning, courts have shown an extraordinary tendency to broadly construe "public purpose." Even in *Sharpless* itself, the court did *not* side with the taxpayer. Instead, the court concluded that, even though the railroad was private, the railroad subsidy nevertheless served a public purpose: "It cannot be denied that a railroad company is a private corporation. But the right to tax depends on the ultimate use, purpose, and object for which the fund is raised, and not on the nature or character of the person or corporation whose intermediate agency is to be used in applying it."[31]

In other words, the court said that the government could buy shares in a private corporation so long as the goal was to serve a public purpose. Then, decades later, courts would come to see the Public Purpose Doctrine as an *exception* to anti-aid provisions rather than a *complement* to them. In the 1918 case of *Georgia v. Cincinnati Southern Railway*, for example, the U.S. Supreme Court held that Georgia could grant a right-of-way to a railroad despite the constitutional bar against "any donation or gratuity in favor of any person, corporation or association," because a "conveyance in aid of a public purpose from which great benefits are expected is not within the class of evils that the constitution intended to prevent" (Georgia v. Cincinnati Southern Railway 1874). Courts reached similar conclusions in several other states.[32]

In all of these cases, courts found that the judicially created Public Purpose Doctrine was an exception to constitutional anti-aid provisions. (For a fuller discussion, see Rubin 1993.) They viewed the doctrine as a justification for public aid to private enterprise so long as the expenditure served some public or quasi-public purpose. This interpretation contradicts the doctrine's initial articulation as a *restraint* on government expenditures, requiring all public projects to serve purely public purposes. It also contradicts the plain language of anti-aid provisions, which forbid government aid to private firms or individuals regardless of the aid's purpose.

Another problem with this interpretation is that the Public Purpose Doctrine was first adumbrated in *Sharpless* in 1853, decades *before* most states adopted anti-aid provisions. As Rubin notes, "Since most of the aid limitation provisions were adopted *after* the Public Purpose Doctrine was judicially enunciated, the courts could not have conceived the doctrine either as an exception or as a doctrine devised to preempt such limitations" (Rubin 1993, 166 Emphasis original).

In the landmark *Munn* decision of 1876, the U.S. Supreme Court held that the government could regulate economic arrangements that were "affected with a public interest."[33] Following this decision, state constitutions written in the ensuing decades, and legislation enacted during this period, began using "public interest" phraseology.[34]

Government involvement with and regulation of private enterprise increased dramatically during the Great Depression. Economists, legal theorists, and policymakers challenged long-held beliefs about the proper role of government in the private economy.[35] Aware that courts saw the Public Purpose Doctrine as an exception to anti-aid provisions, state legislatures were careful to include the words "public purpose" in subsidy legislation. This practice dates back to Mississippi's famous 1936 Balance Agriculture with Industry (BAWI) program, which is widely seen as the beginning of the modern era of targeted economic development subsidies. The BAWI program permitted local governments to hold bond elections to purchase land, build factories, and rent these facilities to private manufacturers at low cost (Eisinger 1989; Bennett 2015, 80). In the preamble to the act, legislators wrote that the "general welfare of its citizens demand, as a public purpose, the development within Mississippi of industrial and manufacturing enterprises" (Quoted in Cobb 1982, 14). As economist James Bennett states, "By invoking those magic words, those constitutional talismans *general welfare* and *public purpose*, this act, which plainly violated the state charter of the Magnolia State, became kosher" (Bennett 2015, 83). When the BAWI program came before the Mississippi Supreme Court, a majority of justices said it didn't violate the state's anti-aid provision, because "in all its parts it contemplates that the proposed industry shall be operated for the accomplishment of the purposes outlined therein" (Albritton v. City of Winona 1938). Justice Anderson's blistering dissent, said the decision "drove a steam shovel through our constitution."[36] The U.S. Supreme Court dismissed an appeal of the case and thus, in the words of two scholars, "closed the door on federal court review of the basic principles underlying industrial development bond financing" (Gray and Spina 1980, 538).

The evolution of anti-aid provisions in many states progressed from strict enforcement after they were first adopted to subsequent approval of subsidies for low-income housing (or "slum clearance") programs and other support for the poor, then to approval of industrial manufacturing projects, and finally to approval of all manner of economic development schemes.[37]

In time, courts came to take what Briffault describes as "a posture of extreme deference to state legislatures, finding that a broad range of goals fall under the rubric of public purpose, and that legislative determinations that a spending, loan, or tax incentive program will promote the public purpose are to be accepted as long as they are 'not . . . irrational'" (Briffault 2002, 914 Quoting Delogu v. State, 720 A.2d 1153 (Me. 1998)).

In so doing, they forgot or ignored the initial aim of the provisions—namely, as the Arizona Supreme Court declared, "to prevent governmental bodies from depleting the public treasury by giving advantages to special interests or by engaging in non-public enterprises."[38] The purpose of these provisions is no less relevant today, especially in the context of prolific public aid to private businesses for the so-called public purpose of economic development (despite the fact that the public is no better off for it).[39]

Following the BAWI program and the courts' acceptance of it, other southern states initiated their own targeted economic development programs, and in the years following World War II, the practice became all but universal. Even when courts did not defer to legislative judgments and declared subsidies unconstitutional, state legislators reacted by amending their constitutions to once again permit subsidies. For example, in 1987, Texas amended its constitution to read as follows: "Notwithstanding any other provision of this constitution, the legislature may provide for the creation of programs and the making of loans and grants of public money . . . for the public purposes of development and diversification of the economy of the state" (*Texas State Constitution, Art 3, Sec. 52-a* 1987). In some cases, courts appealed to such extraconstitutional considerations as interstate economic competition as a rationale for upholding subsidies. (For a thorough discussion of this and citations, see Schaefer 1996.) As North Carolina's Justice Robert Orr stated in a 1996 dissent, the judicial philosophy in these cases seems to boil down to "everybody's doing it."[40]

Briffault reports, "By the end of the [20th] century virtually every state supreme court had upheld at least some economic development programs that involved direct assistance—including cash grants, low-interest loans, and tax breaks—to individual firms" (Briffault 2002, 913).

THE CURRENT STATE OF ANTI-AID PROVISIONS

Currently, 45 states have anti-aid provisions that prohibit public financing of private entities through credit, stock, or gift clauses (see figure 7.2):[41] 44 have a credit clause prohibiting government bodies from lending money or credit

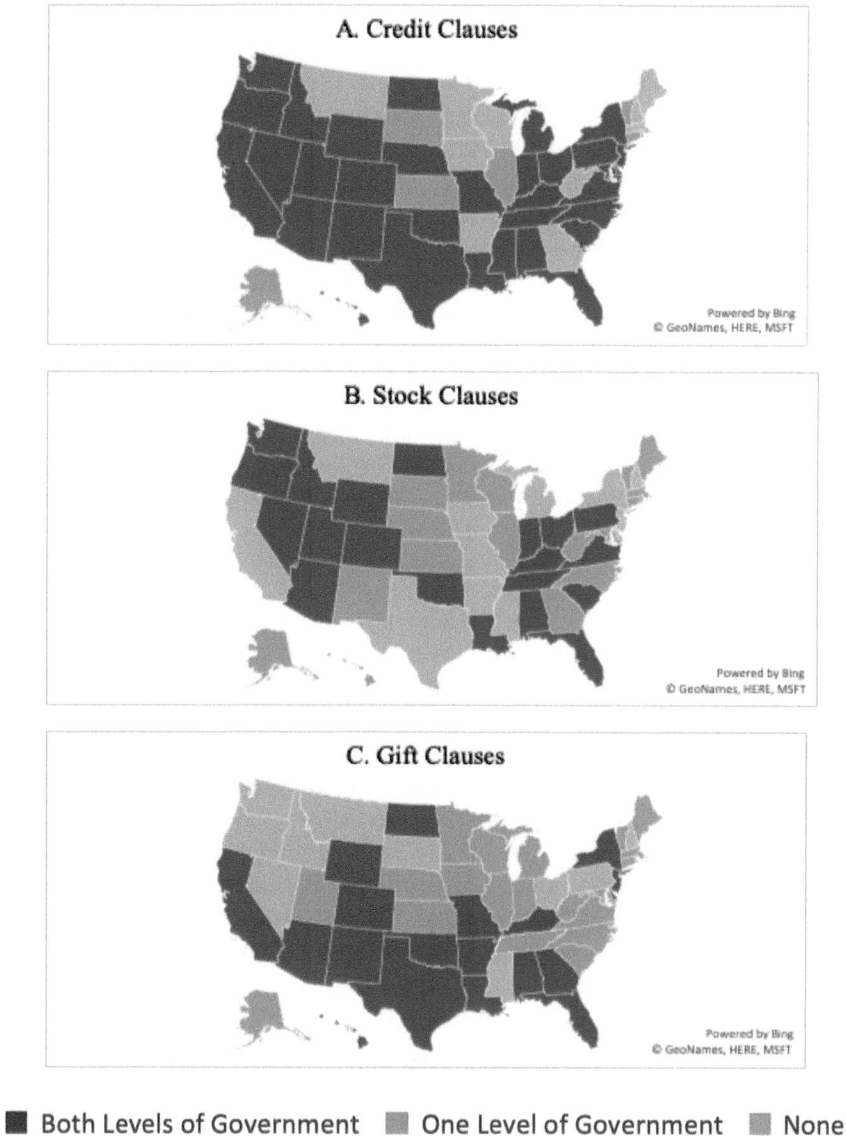

Figure 7.2 The Current State of Anti-Aid Provisions. *Source*: Created by the author.

for nonpublic uses; 32 have a stock clause prohibiting stock subscription in and joint ownership of private ventures;. and 29 have a gift clause prohibiting expenditures of public money for which the government fails to receive anything valuable (i.e., consideration) in exchange, rendering the expenditure a mere gratuity.

Because individual anti-aid provisions are, as Pinsky puts it, a product of "specific evils which had manifested themselves" in the different states during the industrial expansion of the nineteenth century, some state constitutions forbid only one form of public aid, while others forbid two or all three.[42] Likewise, some anti-aid provisions apply to the state, others apply to political subdivisions of the state, and some apply to both levels of government. In addition, some anti-aid limitations are contained within a single clause, while others are found in two or more separate clauses.

Nine state constitutions expressly prohibit both levels of government from aiding private entities in any of the three forms discussed above.[43] For example, Arizona's anti-aid provision provides:

> Neither the state, nor any county, city, town, municipality, or other subdivision of the state shall ever give or loan its credit in the aid of, or make any donation or grant, by subsidy or otherwise, to any individual, association, or corporation, or become a subscriber to, or a shareholder in, any company or corporation, or become a joint owner with any person, company, or corporation, except as to such ownerships as may accrue to the state by operation or provision of law or as authorized by law solely for investment of the monies in the various funds of the state.[44]

Arizona's anti-aid clause is textually stronger than provisions in most other states because it applies to both levels of government, prohibits all three forms of aid, and allows only two exceptions, both related to legitimate government functions.[45] Most of the other nine constitutions that prohibit all three forms of aid at both levels of government also contain textual exceptions (e.g., Oklahoma and Wyoming permit support for economic development).[46]

In comparison, anti-aid provisions in 36 states likewise have various textual exceptions but either fail to address both levels of government or fail to limit all three forms of public aid. Other provisions contain few exceptions, apply to both levels of government, and prohibit more than one form of public aid. Logically, those that contain fewer textual exceptions, address more varieties of aid, and apply to both levels of government tend to be stronger. Most anti-aid provisions fall somewhere in between.

Despite being weakened by textual exceptions and gutted by judicial interpretation, anti-aid provisions have recovered some of their former strength in a few states, and this jurisprudence provides hope for resuscitating failed provisions in other states. For example, Arizona's seminal gift clause case, *Turken v. Gordon*, clarified that public purpose alone cannot justify an expenditure of public money that benefits private interests; instead, the government must receive something sufficiently valuable in return for the expenditure (i.e., it must obtain consideration).[47] If the government receives consideration that is "grossly disproportionate" to what it spent (i.e., if it spends a lot of money but gets very little or nothing in return), the expenditure is an illegal subsidy.

Even better, the court found that *indirect* benefits—such as anticipated tax revenue and employment opportunities for city residents—are not valid consideration if private entities are not contractually required to provide these benefits.[48] Thus, in Arizona, public spending on economic development is unconstitutional unless the government receives valuable and direct (arising from the private entity's obligation) consideration in return. Before the *Turken* case, government bodies had successfully argued that indirect public benefits resulting from an expenditure suffice to justify public aid to private interests.[49] This argument is especially problematic given the tendency of policymakers to rely on the indirect gross multipliers associated with new economic activity, which they often overestimate, while ignoring the negative effects of the taxes that pay for these subsidies. *Turken*'s rejection of that overly lax theory illustrates that it is possible—with strategically litigated cases—to realign anti-aid jurisprudence with the intended purpose of these provisions. In short, it is possible to prevent the application of public money to private purposes.

Other states with relatively strong anti-aid provisions also require that government bodies receive a fair return for an expenditure of public funds. In Oklahoma, economic development has a public purpose only if the government receives adequate consideration for the expenditure and there is accountability or control over the expenditure.[50] And in Mississippi, the state supreme court recently, and without discussing public purpose, held that a city cannot lawfully pay the attorney fees of a mayoral candidate in an election contest because the expenditure lacks consideration and is therefore a donation or gratuity to the candidate.[51]

Some state courts have created tests that strengthen anti-aid clauses. In those states where courts have not already adopted these tests, state legislatures can strengthen their anti-aid clauses by explicitly requiring courts to do so. To prevent the enrichment of private interests at public expense, three criteria should be satisfied for every expenditure of public funds:

1) The public expenditure should be primarily for a public purpose.
2) The government should maintain sufficient control over the expenditure to ensure its public purpose is accomplished.
3) The public should receive direct, ascertainable, obligatory, and proportional consideration for every outlay of public resources.

As noted, these requirements should apply to both the state government and political subdivisions and prohibit all three varieties of aid (gifts, stocks, and credit). Additional safeguards can also ensure that the provisions are as widely applicable as possible by including revenue bonds, industrial development bonds, and special districts.

CONCLUSION

Economic development subsidies do not work as advertised. Both economic theory and experience suggest that, on net, subsidies are more likely to undermine than enhance a region's economic development. There are a number of reasons for this. Among other things, firms tend to collect subsidies for doing what they would have done anyway, subsidies involve significant opportunity costs, and subsidies invite a host of economic problems, including rent-seeking losses and anticompetitive effects.

Despite the problems with subsidies, the incentive for policymakers to dispense them is strong. Consequently, state policymakers have periodically attempted to bind their own hands by outlawing subsidies through various constitutional anti-aid provisions. Our review suggests that anti-aid provisions can affect the size and scope of subsidies, reducing their negative economic and social effects. But the details matter, and some provisions are stronger than others. Moreover, these provisions must be strengthened periodically.

The strongest anti-aid provisions apply to both state and local governments and restrict government extensions of credit, stock purchases, and gifts. These provisions are more effective if courts apply three tests. First, courts should require public expenditures to primarily serve public purposes. Second, they should require the government to maintain sufficient control over expenditures to ensure their public purpose is accomplished. And third, they should ensure that the public has received direct, ascertainable, obligatory, and proportional consideration in return for expenditures. Anti-aid clause litigation is most likely to be successful in states where these tests, or portions of them, are applied. And in states where courts do not currently apply these tests, legislators can strengthen statutory restraints by requiring that all public expenditures satisfy these criteria.

NOTES

1. This is not the only strategy. Another tactic is to create an environment that is conducive to growth by, for example, ensuring some degree of economic freedom.

2. There have been various estimates of annual state and local spending on targeted economic development subsidies (Thomas (2011), Story (2012), Bartik (2017), Thomas (2019), Slattery and Zidar (2020). Among these, the most comprehensive estimate is Thomas (2011). Adjusting for inflation, it is equivalent to $95 billion in 2020 dollars. Cailin Slattery and Owen Zidar, "Evaluating State and Local Business Tax Incentives," *Journal of Economic Perspectives* 34, no. 2 (2020): 90–118; Kenneth Thomas, Investment Incentives and the Global Competition for Capital (London: Palgrave Macmillan, 2011); Timothy J. Bartik, A New Panel Database on Business Incentives for Economic Development Offered by State and Local Governments in the United States (Kalamazoo, MI: W.E. Upjohn Institute for Employment Research, February 2017); Kenneth Thomas, "The State of State and Local Subsidies to Business" (Mercatus Policy Brief, Mercatus Center at George Mason University, Arlington, VA, October 2019); Louise Story, "As Companies Seek Tax Deals, Governments Pay High Price," *New York Times*, December 1, 2012.

3. Matthew D. Mitchell, Michael D. Farren, Jeremy Horpedahl, and Olivia J. Gonzalez, "The Economics of a Targeted Economic Development Subsidy" (Mercatus Special Study, Mercatus Center at George Mason University, Arlington, VA, 2019).

4. Industrial clusters are an often-cited positive externality. However, as Michael Porter, an originator of cluster theory has put it, "Most clusters form independently of government action—and sometimes inspite of it." Michael E. Porter, "Clusters and the New Economics of Competition." *Harvard Business Review* 76, no. 6 (December 11, 1998): 77–90, 89.

5. Christopher J. Coyne and Lotta Moberg, "The Political Economy of State-Provided Targeted Benefits," *Review of Austrian Economics* 28, no. 3 (September 1, 2015): 337–56.

6. EY Quantitative Economics and Statistics, "Quantifying Project Flying Eagle's Potential Economic Impacts in Wisconsin," *EY*, July 2017.

7. Bartik, Timothy J. "'But For' Percentages for Economic Development Incentives: What Percentage Estimates Are Plausible Based on the Research Literature?" Working Paper, W.E. Upjohn Institute for Employment Research, Kalamazoo, MI, July 1, 2018.

8. Timothy J. Bartik, Who Benefits from State and Local Economic Development Policies? (Kalamazoo, MI: W.E. Upjohn Institute, 1991), 61; these figures likely vary by sector. See James Papke, "Interjurisdictional Business Tax Cost Differentials: Convergence, Divergence and Significance," Tax Notes 9, no. 4 (1995): 1701–11.

9. Leah Beth Curran et al., "Economic Wellbeing and Where We Live: Accounting for Geographical Cost-of-Living Differences in the US," *Urban Studies* 43, no. 13 (December 1, 2006): 2443–66; G. Cornia, W. Testa, and F. Stocker, "State-Local Fiscal Incentives and Economic Development" (Urban and Regional Development Series Number 4, Academy of Contemporary Problems, Columbus, OH, 1978).

10. Mitchell et al. "The Economics of a Targeted Economic Development Subsidy."

11. Timothy J. Bartik, *Who Benefits from Economic Development Incentives? How Incentive Effects on Local Incomes and the Income Distribution Bary with Different*

Assuptions about Incentive Policy and the Local Economy (Kalamazoo, MI: W.E. Upjohn Institute, 2018), 11.

12. Mitchell et al. "The Economics of a Targeted Economic Development Subsidy."

13. Gordon Tullock, "The Welfare Costs of Tariffs, Monopolies, and Theft," *Economic Inquiry* 5, no. 3 (June 1, 1967): 224–32; Matthew D. Mitchell, "Rent Seeking at 52: An Introduction to a Special Issue of *Public Choice*," *Public Choice* 181, no. 1 (October 1, 2019): 1–4.

14. Matthew D. Mitchell, Jeremy Horpedahl, and Olivia J. Gonzalez, "Do Targeted Economic Development Incentives Work as Advertised?" (Mercatus Working Paper, Mercatus Center at George Mason University, Arlington, VA, forthcoming).

15. See Mitchell, Horpedahl, and Gonzalez, "Work as Advertised," for more details. But note that from Alexander Hamilton to Donald Trump, policymakers who advocate for subsidies almost universally speak of the benefits to the broader community.

16. Again, see Mitchell, Horpedahl, and Gonzalez, "Work as Advertised." Among those studies that evaluate subsidies for their effects on the broader community, about two-thirds find either mixed or insignificant effects. Just 16% find positive effects, while 20% find negative effects for the broader community.

17. Public choice is the economic study of political markets. For an overview, see (Simmons 2011; Mitchell and Boettke 2017).

18. As the economists Robert Ekelund and Robert Tollison have put it, "The undergirding principle of the interest-group approach is nonetheless organizational costs. The theory begins and ends with this principle. Organized groups gain political wealth transfers at the expense of unorganized or less-well-organized groups" (Ekelund and Tollison 2001).

19. Because their votes are unlikely to make a difference in any election, voters tend to be rationally ignorant about policy and its effects. Worse, they have little incentive to spend time thinking about public policy, causing irrational notions to persist (Downs 1957; Caplan 2008).

20. For an early critique, see Adam Smith's *Wealth of Nations*. For more recent critiques, see (Smith 1776; North, Wallis, and Weingast 2009; Acemoglu and Robinson 2012).

21. Some of this opposition likely arose from the unique circumstances of the American founding. The much-reviled Tea Act of 1773, for example, was a mercantilist tax privilege for the East India Tea Company, a British government-chartered firm that already enjoyed several regulatory privileges. The founding era also coincided with the birth of classical economics, which rejected the earlier mercantilist theories.

22. Briffault, "Disfavored Constitution," 911.

23. Rodden, 57.

24. Wallis, "American Government Finance," 61, 65.

25. Wallis, "American Government Finance," 62.

26. The federal government had bailed out state Revolutionary War debts in 1790 and again repaid some state debts following the War of 1812. Then, in 1836,

Congress agreed to pay $1.5 million in debts incurred by the District of Columbia. Many believe that these actions caused creditors to assume that the federal government would always bail out state governments (Rodden 2006, 58); Thomas J. Sargent, "Nobel Lecture: United States Then, Europe Now," *Journal of Political Economy* 120, no. 1 (February 2012): 15.

27. The defaulting states were Arkansas, Illinois, Indiana, Louisiana, Maryland, Michigan, Mississippi, Pennsylvania, and the territory of Florida (Rodden 2006, 59).

28. See, for example, *Adams v. Jackson Elec. Ry., Light & Power Co.*, 30 So. 58, 59 (Miss. 1901) (invalidating expenditure with no discussion of public purpose); *State ex rel. Bd. of Control of St. Louis Sch. & Museum of Fine Arts v. City of St. Louis*, 115 S.W. 534, 548 (Mo. 1908) (invalidating expenditure despite claim of public purpose and discussing history of provisions); *Wyscaver v. Adkins*, 37 Ohio St. 80 (1881) (striking down a statute authorizing a township to raise $20,000 to make a private railway and finding that the state's anti-aid clause "forbids the union of public and private capital or credit in any enterprise whatever"); (*Counterman v. Dublin Township* 1882; *Taylor v. Comm'rs of Ross County* 1872); (*Pleasant Township v. Aetna Life Ins. Co.* 1891); (*Counterman v. Dublin Township* 1882; *Alter v. Cincinnati* 1897) *(State v. City of St. Louis* 1908) (invalidating a statute that permitted St. Louis to levy a tax that benefited a private corporation, the St. Louis School and Museum of Fine Arts); (*Garland v. Board of Revenue of Montgomery County* 1889) (invalidating a municipal proposal to build a bridge for a railroad); (*Mayor of Jersey City v. North Jersey St. Ry. Co.* 1909) (holding that failure to collect licensing fee from railroad for 30 years was a violation of the state's anti-aid clause).

29. State legislatures have also done much to circumvent constitutional restrictions and provide public resources for private purposes. Though it is beyond the scope of the current analysis, state legislatures frequently circumvent anti-aid clauses through the creation of revenue bonds, moral obligation bonds, and special districts. Governments typically issue revenue bonds to finance the purchase of property that they then lease to private firms. Unlike a general obligation bond, a revenue bond is not backed by government credit or taxing authority; the bond is only secured by the property and by the rental payments from the firm, sparing taxpayers the risk and making it similar in function to a private bond. Because of this, these bonds have not been found to run afoul of state credit clauses. Federal taxpayers do bear a cost, however, because the interest on revenue bonds is exempt from federal income taxation. Moreover, many states exempt the projects financed through these bonds from state and local property taxes because they deem the property to be owned by the public and not by the private entity that occupies it. See (Rubin 1993, 161; Gray and Spina 1980, 533–37).

30. *Sharpless* (*Sharpless v. Mayor of Philadelphia* 1853, 167).

31. *Sharpless* (*Sharpless v. Mayor of Philadelphia* 1853, 169).

32. (*City of Oakland v. Garrison* 1924); (*Alameda County v. Janssen* 1940); (*Brazoria County v. Perry* 1976); (*City of Charlottesville v. Dehaan* 1984); (*Hayes v. State Property and Buildings Comm'n* 1987); (*City of Aurora v. Public Utilities Comm'n* 1990).

33. *Munn v. People of State of Illinois*, 94 U.S. 113, 126, 24 L. Ed. 77 (1876).

34. Timothy Sandefur, "A Natural Rights Perspective on Eminent Domain in California: A Rationale for Meaningful Judicial Scrutiny of 'Public Use,'" *Southwestern University Law Review* 32 (2003): 648–51.

35. Robert Higgs, *Crisis and Leviathan: Critical Episodes in the Growth of American Government*, 25th anniv. ed. (Oakland, CA: Independent Institute, 1987); Price Fishback, *Government and the American Economy: A New History* (Chicago: University Of Chicago Press, 2007).

36. 178 So. at 812 (Anderson, J., dissenting).

37. See, for example, *Humphrey v. City of Phoenix*, 55 Ariz. 374 (1940) (upholding revenue bonds to finance a slum clearance project); In re Constitutionality of ORS 456.720, 272 Or. 398 (1975) (same); Opinion to the Governor, 112 R.I. 151, 155–56 (1973) ("The elimination of overcrowded, unsanitary and dangerous dwelling accommodations and the assisting in making available decent, safe and sanitary housing for people whose income would make such an acquisition impossible unquestionably serves a public purpose."); *Utah Hous. Fin. Agency v. Smart*, 561 P.2d 1052, 1054 (Utah 1977) ("It cannot be said that the finding of the legislature that a public purpose is served by increasing the availability of financing for construction, purchase, and rehabilitation of low and moderate income housing, is incorrect or unreasonable on its face."); *Suber v. Alaska State Bond Comm.*, 414 P.2d 546, 552 (Alaska 1966) (public purpose for relief and support of the poor); *Wright v. City of Palmer*, 468 P.2d 326, 330–31 (Alaska 1985) (public purpose for improvement program to encourage industrial development); *Carruthers v. Port of Astoria*, 249 Or. 329, 336 (1968) (listing several cases in which revenue bonds for industrial development were upheld as a public purpose); *Maready v. City of Winston-Salem*, 342 N.C. 708, 725 (1996) (listing 46 states that have upheld economic development as a public purpose).

38. *Wistuber v. Paradise Valley Unified Sch. Dist.*, 141 Ariz. 346, 349 (1984). See also *Bannon v. Port of Palm Beach District*, 246 So. 2d 737, 741 (Fla. 1971) (to "protect public funds and resources from being exploited in assisting or promoting private ventures when the public would be at most only incidentally benefited"); *Idaho Falls Consolidated Hospitals v. Bingham County Board of Commissioners*, 102 Idaho 838 (1982) (apparent that framers "were primarily concerned about private interests gaining advantage at the expense of the taxpayer"); *Lawrence v. Schellstede*, 348 P.2d 1078, 1081–82 (Okla. 1960) (to prevent the investment of public funds in private enterprises).

39. See section II above.

40. *(Maready v. City of Winston-Salem* 1996*)* 342 N.C. at 739 (Orr, J., dissenting).

41. The exceptions are Alaska, Connecticut, Illinois, Kansas, and Vermont. South Dakota has a state credit clause, but it permits lending of credit with a supermajority of the legislature.

42. Pinsky, "State Constitutional Limitations," 280.

43. These are Arizona, Colorado, Florida, Kentucky, Louisiana, Montana, North Dakota, Oklahoma, and Wyoming.

44. Ariz. Const. art. 9, § 7. The exception at the end of the clause is meant to permit state investment of public funds, such as pension funds or rainy-day funds. Ideally, these funds will have their own statutory restraints that require the fund

managers to be fiduciaries so that investments are made in the public's interest and not in anyone's private interest.

45. However, Arizona amended its constitution in 1940 to exempt "irrigation, power, electrical, agricultural improvement, drainage, and flood control districts, and tax levying public improvement districts" from the anti-aid provision. See Ariz. Const. art. 13, § 7.

46. Okla. Const. art. 10, § 15(B); Wyo. Const. art. 16, § 12.

47. *Turken v. Gordon*, 223 Ariz. 342, 348 (2010) (holding that consideration cannot be "grossly disproportionate to what is received in return").

48. *Turken*, 350.

49. *Turken*, 351–52.

50. *Burkhardt v. City of Enid*, 771 P.2d 608, 611 (Okla. 1989).

51. *McAdams v. Perkins*, 204 So. 3d 1257, 1265 (Miss. 2016).

Chapter 8

Competition, Networks, and Public-Private Partnerships

Contributions to State Governance

Austill Stuart

INTRODUCTION: STATE GOVERNMENTS—SQUEEZED FROM ALL SIDES

Both federal and local (county, municipal, regional, special districts) governments undertake functions that can be identified as providing services and overseeing the delivery of services by subordinate entities. State governments, existing between higher (federal) and lower (local) governments in U.S. governmental hierarchy, occupy a space at the heart of many of the decisions involving critical infrastructure in the country, whether as the responsible provider for the infrastructure and related services themselves, or as a regulator over infrastructure and services provided by local governments.

For every category of major infrastructure or service individuals would identify as "public," from criminal and civil justice to corrections facilities, to energy generation and transmission, to health-care services, highways, solid waste pickup, and water and sewer systems, state governments provide critical functions as the providers of goods and services and the overseers of local government providers.

The flow of grant funding from the federal government makes its way into both types of functions. For highways and corrections, state agencies receive funding via formula-based and discretionary grants and then disburse those funds to state government projects.[1] State governments also receive federal grants for water, sewer, and solid waste services, and they must decide how those funds get disbursed to the lower-level entities managing those functions. In addition to serving as a grant "middleman" between federal and local governments, state governments also make direct grants to lower-level governments.

Grants between governments often come with conditions designed to ensure funding gets devoted to intended uses but can also create significant uses of valuable resources in order to ensure compliance. Both receiving and disbursing grant monies come with inherent risks: Dedicating resources to receive grants come with opportunity costs, and state governments may disburse grants to lower governments based on flawed, or overly burdensome considerations that lead to suboptimal outcomes.

Just as state governments encounter numerous risks in the pursuit and the disbursement of grants, they also encounter numerous risks concerning the management and oversight of infrastructure and services. For both types of cases, private entities have filled critical roles to improve managing infrastructure and services, and in a more forward-looking manner that seeks to avoid repetition of practices that have led to the issues government infrastructure management faces.

This chapter shows how increased competition and private-sector participation can help create additional taxpayer value relative to more hierarchical regimes that prohibit (through regulatory or other means) or under-utilize such practices. Building on Kenneth Boulding's work in the grants economy, the application to government agencies in a federalist hierarchy shows how agencies can help and harm each other through grant conditions. Through most of the twentieth century, narrowly focused management practices in project funding valued up-front development costs over the long-term lifecycles of infrastructure assets, leading to deferred maintenance problems of more recent years.

Through adopting a greater lifecycle focus to infrastructure management as well as a more "networked" approach to governance that includes the use of contracting with outside organizations (private companies and nonprofits as well as other governments) agencies have found ways of more effectively managing deferred maintenance and regulatory compliance risks that improves infrastructure performance.

Highways and municipal water systems provide examples of how the networked approach to government has led to more outsourcing and public-private partnerships (PPPs), which provide innovative ways for agencies to manage risks through transfer to partner organizations. Both water and highway infrastructure suffers from deferred maintenance issues that private-sector organizations are better equipped to address not just through building new and replacing old infrastructure but managing infrastructure through its effective lifecycle. Through working with a committed partner held accountable for performance over infrastructure projects' entire lifecycles, agencies are able to introduce innovative infrastructure management practices that agencies would be hard-pressed to deliver without the ability to enter P3 agreements.

A partner committed to decades-long management of infrastructure will have much greater incentive than an agency acting alone under no contractual agreement to provide consistent maintenance to avoid premature degradation in the infrastructure and unneeded repair costs. Those advancements are important as infrastructure ages and federal grants both shrink (in terms of relative share funding for projects) and come with conditions that require regulated agencies to do more with less.

The chapter also looks at corrections, where improvement has been marginal, but also consistent with improvement coming through a more networked approach that is open to private-sector solutions. Good and bad examples of contracting abound in corrections, but most functions handled by private corrections companies and organizations are the result of corrections agencies seeking them out, which usually points to a lack of internal (within the agency) means of handling the functions contracted out. While the 1990s "tough on crime" mentality did result in greater use of private prisons, their widespread blame for greater incarceration amounts to the equivalent of shooting the messenger, as private prison companies have very limited ability to affect sentencing and criminalization. While corrections conditions will continue to face myriad problems, the presence of for-profit companies in the space of corrections is in itself not bad, and the reliance on private organizations to provide myriad corrections services suggests agencies themselves are ill-equipped to produce outcomes that equal or better their chosen partners.

The chapter closes by examining common objections to outsourcing, privatization, and PPPs, which suffer from applying a morality framework that fails to grasp the reality of providing public infrastructure and services, while often accusing private providers from the same type of shortsightedness that has led state agencies to seek private actors in the first place. While contracting, P3, and privatization outcomes can be both good and bad, the ability to enter partnerships with private organizations has provided risk management opportunities otherwise unavailable to agencies, making blanket arguments to dismiss the practice as morally wrong wanting.

GOVERNMENTS AND THE GRANTS ECONOMY: GIVE-AND-TAKE THROUGH LOVE, FEAR, AND IGNORANCE

The late economist Kenneth Boulding's work in grants economics stems from a common observable fact: A significant portion of goods and services in a nation's economic output will come not from two-way exchanges where both parties seek to improve their condition, but from one-way transfers, or "grants" where, in the purest of terms, a grantor gives something of value to a grantee, with no expectation of any reciprocating compensation, in whole, or part ("benevolence"). Rather than giving such distributions separate treatment, grants should be incorporated into exchange economics. Even further, grants and exchanges are often hard to separate:

> An exchange, if it is not in some sense an exchange of "equal values," contains a grant element. Just what constitutes equal values, however, is often hard to say, and is the source of much controversy. If I buy potatoes from the farmer above the market price because I am fond of him, there is clearly a grant element in this transaction.[2]

The reverse also holds true: Just as transactions deemed "exchanges" often contain a "grant" element, transactions deemed "grants" often contain an exchange element. Individuals often pay more for products deemed to be produced by firms and organizations that adopt production processes, sourcing, and other practices that introduce considerations into products that differentiate themselves well beyond the proverbial "widget" where differentiation is minimal to nonexistent and final purchase cost is the overriding concern. Conversely, individuals look to avoid patronizing goods and services from producers who fall short of the buyer's concerns outside of the price and quantity demanded. Through the lens of the grants economy, if two options for a good or service have the same utility for an average buyer, but the option from a producer A meets the specific buyer's ethical concerns, and rival producer B's option does not meet them, then the premium may constitute a grant.[3]

A seemingly paradoxical revelation of the grants economy is the diversity of sources that drive grant-making, which Boulding boiled down to three categories: "love, fear, and ignorance." Though U.S. intergovernmental grants may seem a topic mostly devoid of much emotion or passion, the three categories can be found, at least in a sense, in intergovernmental grants. If "rule of law" can be defined at the heart of all transfers between governments, then dedication to preserving the "rule of law" in guiding transfers can be seen as a component of "love," the guiding principle that ensures exchanges are acceptable, and predictable. But just as parents' feelings toward their children's behavior can swing widely between affection and (loving) fury, and their attitudes toward giving their children autonomy and freedom can vary from fear to blind acceptance (sometimes out of ignorance), grants from higher-level governments to lower-level governments can be made out of a genuine concern to provide needed funding, withheld as punishment for bad behavior (a "negative bad," in Boulding's verbiage), provided under restrictive terms that reveal a lack of trust in the grantee, or under few restrictions, reflecting trust (or possibly, ignorance).

To the extent they are divorced from the exchange economy, grants will not be driven by the robust feedback loops that drive economic activity. If a grantor finds that their recipient, despite following guidelines provided by originator, fails to address problems that the grantor nonetheless sees problematic, a funding relationship based largely on trust can devolve into one more based on fear, where the grantor looks to punish poor outcomes through "negative bads," or otherwise placing additional resources on much tighter restraints that make grants behave more like conditional exchanges, or in extreme cases, micro-management conditions (which can be seen as grants in themselves back to the original "grantor") of grantees imposed by grantors.

Another issue arises with repeat "offenses" by grantees: If the federal or a state EPA keeps fining a municipality for repeated violations, the offending agency must find ways to (a) pay the fines and (b) solve the problem, as opposed to just solving the problem. Coming to such a realization requires empathy, which can be seen as a focus shift from fear to love: "I recognize the problems you have, but I also recognize that my repeated punishments hurt your ability to solve your problems, so let's get together and find a solution that works to solve both problems."[4]

While the motivations for inter-governmental grant transmissions can be seen as less intense than the three broad categories exemplify in their purest form, a brief dive into state government functions, as both grantor and grantee, can reveal some of the issues that prevent better outcomes for such functions. Contracting out (to the private sector mostly, but also other governments in some cases) provide ways to overcome the lack of a role price signals play in the grants economy, structuring funding to performance that often cannot be achieved by "going it alone."

In ways, the governing by networks—the focus of the next section—has entered governmental grants through conditions. State and local agencies wanting funding from higher-level governments must show a commitment to a long-term "lifecycle" cost approach to projects as opposed to minimizing up-front costs. Transportation and water-system grants increasingly include conditions that require dedicated revenues awards (set aside by agencies, or raised through user fees, tolls, or other self-financing mechanisms) to receive grants.

While the new approach does result in "grants" operating less like their pure form, the approach has grown out of a greater realization that infrastructure should be managed consistently well to deliver its greatest value over time and doing so takes a greater commitment to finding that value both within and outside of agencies, who must know their internal capabilities and challenges in managing infrastructure risks. With that understanding, agencies are well equipped to find partnering and contracting opportunities that improve upon results agencies could achieve on their own.

Innovation in Governance: From Hierarchies to Networks

Growth in the scope of governance has also made fulfilling the demands of governance more complex and more numerous. A "top-down" approach to governance that entered contracts almost exclusively through design-bid-build (DBB) and traditional procurement arrangements has waned, leading to a more "networked" focus where government leaders develop and engage informational channels to find the greatest value in delivering services, both inside and outside of government.[5] Procuring office supplies operates mostly in the same way as decades ago, while infrastructure procurement has moved forward from DBB to new forms on contracting, management, and performance evaluation.[6]

At least in a limited sense, the new approach dovetails with entrepreneurship theory as described by Israel Kirzner.[7] Entrepreneurial activity has many forms, including "streamlining internal patterns of organization," requiring individuals with an "alertness" that helps fuel "a propensity to discover information that will be useful to them . . . a continuous discovery process."[8] While his work stressed a tendency toward equilibrium to incorporate into microeconomic theory, a government leader with a dedicated "networks" approach to facilitate resources inside and outside of government can be seen as both an entrepreneur and a director. Such leaders should possess an "alertness" to new ways of delivering value in government services through the discovery of networks that provide improved risk management opportunities.

The networked approach has moved governance to a simpler "You build it; we pay and manage it" venture, and more toward an approach that looks at the infrastructure's costs over its entire useful lifecycle, and not just its up-front construction costs. This leads to arrangements that can deliver the best outcomes on not just delivery of infrastructure, but its continued use over time. For state governments as a deliverer and overseer of services, this can be seen in their continued confrontation of deferred maintenance issues that plague highways and municipal water systems, respectively.

For highways and other projects where federal government grants were relied upon more initially, the little available comes often with the expectation that projects must have their own dedicated revenues. This creates a status quo where openness to changing opportunities to deliver, finance and maintain government infrastructure and services through resources both in and outside of government, becomes increasingly critical.

From Deferred Maintenance to Lifecycle Management: Highways and Water

Highways and municipal water are areas of critical infrastructure where state governments have significant influence, although in much different ways.

While the federal government provided most of the initial funding to build the Interstate Highway system, state governments handle the day-to-day operation of their interstate and U.S. (badge) highways. They also disburse funds collected by state and federal fuel taxes. In contrast, local or regional governments operate most water, wastewater and stormwater systems, though the state governments regulate them. States also disburse federal funds from the Drinking Water State Revolving Fund to local governments.

Contemporary discussions of the state of highways and water systems in the United States often include the term "deferred maintenance," which describes a situation where a lack of available resources and/or routine maintenance of infrastructure assets results in asset degradation that a more dedicated approach to lifecycle management could have avoided. The path dependence of governmental management provided little incentive to consider infrastructure management in terms of its full lifecycle. Under DBB contracting regimes, the agency retains the risk for the entire project, except constructing the asset(s) themselves. The agency retains risks encountered over the entire operational phase of the infrastructure lifecycle, including deferred maintenance and regulatory compliance risk.

Even with the "know-how" to manage infrastructure, agencies often lack the resources to commit to decades of consistent management to avoid deferred maintenance problems and the risk of regulatory actions, which taxpayers ultimately bear. Hard budget constraints further the incentive to focus on the short-term, day-to-day operation of infrastructure at the expense of keeping infrastructure assets a constant state of good repair. Both U.S. roads and water systems are rife with infrastructure problems resulting from deferred maintenance issues, but over time, agencies have come better to understand such problems through a more networked approach and are trying to adjust accordingly.

Private firms can often play a helpful role facilitating that transfer of focus to a more forward-looking approach, while also helping to ensure that the focus gets maintained through the useful life of the infrastructure asset(s). Contracting practices show an increased willingness of agencies to rely on private firms not just for building infrastructure—which has been the case for decades in DBB contracts—but for outsourcing the risks that come with day-to-day operations and maintenance (OM, or O&M), as well a project's financing.

Building and operating elements are often treated separately—the former usually contracted out to the private sector in the form of a DBB or DB contract, and the latter usually handled "in-house" (by the government agency itself). But with newer projects especially, the combination of infrastructure delivery and operating elements have increasingly found their way into more complex contracting agreements better equipped to handle lifecycle cost considerations, and other risks that traditional public-sector arrangements have had difficulty maintaining. While definitions vary with use, for our purposes, we'll define PPPs as long-term (20 years or more) project agreements that include both infrastructure delivery (DB) and O&M considerations, and sometimes, financing.

With that willingness to transfer additional risks to the private sector has come increased attention and guidance for avoiding further deferred maintenance and compliance issues that many state agencies face, whether from managing infrastructure directly (the case with highways), or through the oversight of management by lower-level governments (the case with water-related systems).

Highways

The primary source for highway funding, fuel taxes, serves as a proxy for the use of road surfaces themselves. Since fuel propels vehicles, the amount of fuel purchased provides a decent proxy for distance traveled. However, improved fuel economy and the introduction of alternative fuel vehicles (and a limited ability to raise fuel tax rates and broaden applicability of charges to alternative fuel vehicles) have severely "deflated" the effectiveness of fuel taxes. From 1980 to 2016, the average fuel economy of a passenger vehicle in the United States rose by about 50%, from 6.3 km per liter, to 9.4 km per liter.[9]

The diversion of fuel taxes to non-highway purposes proposed another problem confronting fuel taxes' ability to pay for roads: Eight states divert at least 20% of fuel taxes to non-road uses, while five states (NY, RI, NJ, MI, MD) divert over 30% of fuel tax revenues.[10] Arguments can be made that the transit that gets funded by some of those diverted revenues reduces reliance on roads, but perhaps with the exception of New York City, American municipalities lack the population density to make rail transit systems—whether above-ground or underground—financially viable. Additionally, transit operates with direct user fees for use, while fuel taxes only provide a rough proxy, and one of diminishing effectiveness. But while direct user fees are intended to cover the cost of providing a service, there isn't even the pretense of that being the case with transit systems in the United States. "Transit agencies do not set passenger fares based on the cost of each trip. For each dollar spent on operating costs per trip across all modes and all transit systems, 32.3 cents are recovered through fares," the U.S. Department of Transportation noted in 2020.[11]

But not all diversions even go to transit: Alaska places its fuel tax revenues in its General Fund, which all but ensures that the revenues will be used for whatever lawmakers want. While Kentucky has a lower diversion rate than many states (10.9%), the top recipients for diverted funds are the state police and secretary of states' operating budgets (93% of total diversions, combined).[12]

The increasing ineffectiveness of fuel taxes can be seen on many of the highways throughout the U.S. Assessments of American roads and bridges from professional organizations typically receive poor grades. The American Road & Transportation Builders Association (ARTBA) identifies roughly 20% of all highway miles in the United States are structurally deficient.[13] The American Society of Civil Engineers' (ASCE's) "Infrastructure Report Card" for roads from 2017 identifies a combined highway backlog total of $836 billion, stating, "the United States has been underfunding its highway system for years."[14] Highways and roads are often closed for repairs or are damaged to the point of needing to be closed. The alternatives to fuel taxes resemble direct charges for use. Adopting them without providing a lifecycle management focus to roads and highways means the current problems are likely to persist.[15]

The U.S. Department of Transportation asks agencies to incorporate lifecycle management considerations into highway construction, maintenance, and repair, and states have been finding ways to adopt more lifecycle-focused thinking into their procurement decisions.[16] But state DOT resources are limited, and can only be stretched so far, leaving agencies to make tough decisions on which projects get those resources, resulting in the backlogs.

Private-sector firms have long been used by state DOTs to undertake projects. The initial construction for the Eisenhower Interstate Highway system came mostly from DBB contracts between state agencies and private companies, financed mostly (90%) through federal funding disbursed to states.[17] Maintenance and resurfacing projects have long been handled through contracts with the private sector, too. But while contracting for construction and/or maintenance alone, and in separate arrangements may save some resources, as with private production, scale can bring even greater benefits, from a cost and risk management standpoint.

As noted above, PPPs allow multiple infrastructure project components (designing, building, financing, operating, and maintaining) to be written into a single project with a consortium of companies, also called a special purpose vehicle, made of firms dedicated to fulfilling those project components.

The expanded scope of P3 contracts (in duration, as well as in services provided) allows for a more focused approach to lifecycle-cost management than more traditional DBB and service contracting. Entering a DBB contract gives the private partner a strong incentive to stay within the asking agency's project guidelines at as low of a cost as possible, as does contracting for individual services. A private company contracting with a DOT usually has little incentive to look beyond the contract period. For service contracting, the desire to get contracts renewed does provide some incentive for added forward-thinking, but the term and scope of such projects give private firms little incentive to care about the underlying infrastructure's lifecycle.

But when the private partner is called to not just build or just maintain infrastructure, but a combination of the two, incentives change dramatically. Since the consortium will construct and operate (and possibly, finance) the infrastructure assets, it has to think about cost minimization over the PPP contract's term, often 30 years or more. Almost all PPP agreements include "handback" provisions that define conditions of infrastructure assets included in agreements, usually meaning that instead of suffering from deferred maintenance, assets remain in consistently good condition, even at the termination point of the partnership.

When looking at infrastructure projects with a more lifecycle-oriented approach to find value, the process of comparison changes from a simple cost comparison function to a more complicated net present value one. Underlying the consideration of whether or not to use a PPP versus a more traditional procurement method is a value-for-money (VfM) analysis, which strives to compare an infrastructure project in terms of what the agency can provide itself with a DBB or DB contract while handing all O&M functions (represented by what's called a "Public Sector Comparator"), versus a PPP project where both DB and O&M functions are handled by a partner.

In finding ways to deliver value, one must look not just at "bottom line" of the project's construction delivery costs but the numerous ways where value can be delivered over the project's lifecycle. For highways, this can include decisions about construction materials and approaches to repaving and resurfacing: With a full lifecycle to deliver value, spending more on the front end can mean less spending down the road. Spending too little on initial construction may mean more rehabilitative costs over time. Not completing enough routine maintenance and resurfacing can also lead to higher costs down the road, as well as more frequent closings of lanes for repairs.

In deciding how to proceed with its I-70 East project in Denver, the Colorado Department of Transportation (CDOT) ultimately chose a "DBFOM" (Design/Build/Finance/ Operate/Maintain) PPP procurement as opposed to a traditional DB, or an "in-between" DBF (Design/Build/Finance) procurement when the project was viewed over its entire lifecycle.

The VfM analysis showed the DBFOM not only offered lower estimated lifecycle costs due largely to an expected 8% in cost savings in O&M costs, but the transfer of risks to the private partner eliminated "contingency costs" in the form of overruns or change orders, which get internalized if CDOT were to retain the O&M functions. On top of the quantitative advantages of the DBFOM procurement, CDOT also noted other benefits not expressed in the VfM, including:

> Earlier completion (of the construction phase of the project); Transfer of specific project risk elements not fully captured in the contingency; Greater certainty and transparency of performance; and Additional taxes paid and economic activity generated by the private sector partner.[18]

States will continue to face problems managing their highway systems, but proliferation of networked governance and its forward-looking approach to lifecycle infrastructure management has allowed for innovative procurement and risk-management for infrastructure projects. While it will take time to fully assess the full performance of these partnerships with the benefit of hindsight, the mere availability of greater contracting and procurement options that more closely align with lifecycle management approach to infrastructure has helped shift highway procurement and operations to a more forward-looking mindset.

Water Systems

While water and wastewater (sewer/sewerage) systems are mostly under the purview of local governments, state governments play several key oversight roles: They share regulatory enforcement with federal agencies and disburse federal money to systems through the U.S. EPA's Drinking Water State Revolving Fund, which distributed $22.7 billion to over five thousand unique public water systems between 2008 and 2017.[19] Those functions mean that states play important roles in decisions that affect the construction and operation of water infrastructure, even if local governments are the ones doing the heavy lifting.

While the state's role in water systems stands in contrast to the more direct handling of highways by state DOTs, the two classes of infrastructure share some common ground with respect to practices that historically have favored the short-term over the longer-term considerations of the infrastructure's useful life. Municipal water systems typically contain "mains" (distribution pipes), pumps, and treatment plants near or past their useful life, sometimes even over a century old, especially in older cities in the eastern and midwestern United States. Many service pipes connecting mains to end users installed in the early twentieth century—6.1 million according to the American Water Works Association (AWWA)—are comprised predominantly of lead.[20] In cities with growing populations, infrastructure asset capacity can be pushed into failure if new capacity isn't produced: clean water sources and treatment facilities especially.

One key area of difference between highways and water systems (other than the level of government managing them) lies in visibility: Poor road surfaces are easy to identify, but poor water mains and sewer lines, buried underground, typically are not (at least until gushing, flooding, or smell indicate otherwise). Therefore, repair and placement of water system components often comes reactively: fixing things as they break, as opposed to preventing their breakage in the first place. The ASCE's 2017 scorecard for water infrastructure estimates 240,000 breaks in the United States every year.[13] The impact of main breaks often has spillover (sorry) effects into other types of infrastructure: The breakage can also work to damage roads, requiring additional repairs and closures. Governments that manage water systems are increasingly trying to focus on a better replacement and maintenance strategy to prevent such problems but working with limited resources can hinder agencies' abilities to do so.

But even a lack of water main breakage does not mean all is well: Building off estimates from the U.S. EPA and the AWWA, the Chicago-based Center for Neighborhood Technology estimates 2.1 trillion gallons are lost every year from leaking water mains, which comes to about 15% of all drinking water "consumed" in the United States. Monitoring the underground activity of water systems has improved with innovative technologies,[21] but fixing leaks can be costly and difficult to justify on a case-by-case basis. Therefore, many municipalities elect to replace what's broken and gushing, not what's damaged and dripping—even if the former ends up costing more.

Sourcing of water is also an issue, especially in the western United States. Some of the nation's largest western cities (Los Angeles, San Antonio) are not located near enough sources of potentially potable freshwater to meet their citizens' demands, requiring pipelines and other infrastructure—as well as the acquisition of rights to the water itself—to secure its delivery. The federal Bureau of Reclamation took action to limit states' access to water from the Colorado River following drought conditions and projections of continued poor water accumulation. If dry conditions do continue, desalination facilities become more attractive as a means of securing potable water. But few desalination facilities have emerged in the United States on the gulf and Pacific coasts—Carlsbad, California, Tampa Bay, and Alice, Texas have all successfully procured theirs. Tampa Bay opted to operate their own, while the California and Texas facilities opted to transfer more risk to the private sector in a PPP agreement. But locating water treatment facilities on coastline brings out opposition including from regulatory agencies, as the recent case of Huntington Beach, California shows.[22]

Contamination of drinking water is another issue. While water treatment facilities have become much better at identifying when problems may occur before they happen through assessing the water's "turbidity" (cloudiness), the solution often requires end users to boil their water before consuming it. Even still, outbreaks of parasites and bacteria have been better contained in the past couple of decades, largely a product of better information and detection systems, which have often required private-sector innovation, in addition to the agency-level entrepreneurship it takes to find the relevant information and relationships to secure the improvements. In 1993, Milwaukee, Wisconsin underwent the largest waterborne outbreak in U.S. history, where roughly one-fourth of area residents (403,000 out of 1.6 million) were contaminated by the *Cryptosporidium* parasite, with 69 deaths attributed to it.[23]

Wastewater systems continue to face considerable issues, too. Since many systems are built so that stormwater enters wastewater systems (often called "combined" systems), sharing the same infrastructure, wastewater treatment facilities can get inundated with inflows. When stormwater input is especially heavy, "overflows" can develop, where mixed sewage and stormwater gets discharged into waterways.[24] In 2018 alone, Harrisburg, Pennsylvania was responsible for discharging more than one billion gallons of combined sewer (sewage diluted by stormwater) into the Susquehanna River.[25] The city is hoping to negotiate with the U.S. EPA to avoid further sanctions, already under notice from state and federal regulators to limit discharges since 2015.[26]

Baltimore maintains separate systems for stormwater and wastewater, but still discharged about 260 million gallons of raw sewage in the same year.[27] Florida systems have seen their share of sewage spillage problems, too, with an estimated 1.6 billion gallons of wastewater (including over 370 million gallons of raw sewage) flowing into waterways, from over 20,000 reports of spills over roughly a decade (2009–2019).[28]

Finding better solutions to decrease sewage overflow and other wastewater system problems will require a greater deal of informational and resource networks that can be guided to finding and delivering those enhancements, as will meeting new demand that places further strain on systems. The Federal EPA and state agencies that oversee water-related systems will put upward pressure on system costs through more stringent regulation.[29] Customers will pay for all those costs at the end of the day, so finding the best tradeoffs between cost and quality is important to ensuring water customers pay as little as possible. While many costs of operating water systems are predictable, many of the costliest ones (breakage, changing regulatory guidelines) are not. When water agencies hand all their operations, maintenance, and regulatory compliance functions alone without the ability to transfer the risks associated with those functions to capable partners—private or public sector—solutions to deferred maintenance and regulatory risk problems become more difficult to overcome.

While partnered solutions (P3s leases, sales, operations and maintenance outsourcing) will necessarily include the cost of handling those risks in the rates customers paid, the comparative advantage capable partners will possess in handling those functions makes any rate increases less likely than they would have been if the agency proceeded on its own. Networked governance fosters an entrepreneurial discovery process that agencies can utilize to assure that taxpayers get the best water system management outcome. Agencies that know what functions and risks they handle well and don't handle well are best equipped to reap the gains that result from finding well-positioned partners that can improve the quality and/or cost of delivering services.

With water and transportation, the increased lifecycle focus to infrastructure has begun to deliver projects that represent improvements over the approach in the DBB era that led to deferred maintenance problems in those systems. Other areas of government services have much more fundamental problems that reflect the difficulties of finding what constitutes an effective solution.

Corrections

Unlike highways and water systems, the institutions that determine the nature of corrections in the United States exist separate from corrections itself. Police make arrests, and criminal courts (prosecutors and judges, along with lawmakers) make sentencing guidelines that largely determine how many people get incarcerated, as well as the length of incarceration. While it is true that corrections agencies can have a say in many decisions about their operations (procedures and guidelines on using force, punishment for acts while incarcerated), the populations that corrections agencies are responsible is not one of them.

Therefore, groups facing little-to-no repercussions for bad decisions dominate the determination of prison populations. Prosecutors are not fined when they wrongfully convict someone, just as police can get away using unjustifiable violence, and even, deadly, force with little-to-no punishment.[30] If a harsh judge repeatedly gives out long sentences, it is up to the corrections agencies to find space for those incarcerated. On the one hand, it does make sense that the entities in charge of sentencing need not be overly concerned with capacity restraints when doling out punishment: If the individual is guilty of crimes that laws deem punishable with incarceration, then the punishment should happen as the laws and sentencing guidelines deem. However, a push toward harsh sentencing can severely hamper corrections systems, which have clear capacity constraints.

While prison populations were low in earlier parts of the twentieth century, a growing total population, a greater number of acts defined as criminal, and a "tough on crime" mentality that saw its heyday in the 1980s to early 2000s (see figure 8.1, below) have contributed to an era of "mass incarceration" that has brought severe challenges to the corrections system. Incarceration really took off in the mid-late 1970s, reached a peak about the middle of the aughts, and has dropped a little since. Per capita rates (figure 8.1) have also dropped a little recently from a peak in the late aughts, but still are about equal in the mid-1990s. Since prison capacity is mostly fixed in the short term,

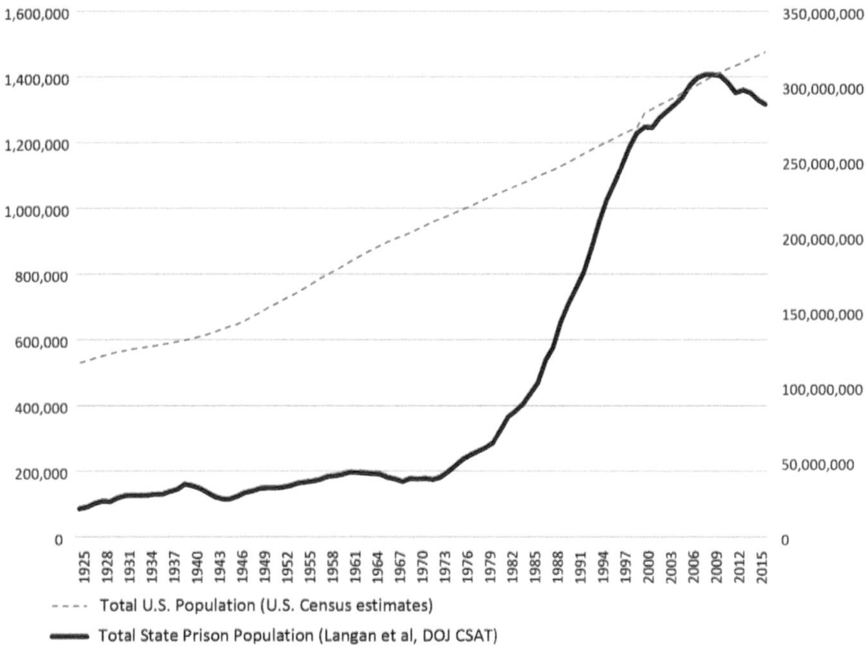

Figure 8.1 U.S. State Prison Population (Left Axis) versus U.S. Total Population (Right 1925–Present). *Source*: Created using data from U.S. Census estimates, Langan et al, and DOJ CSAT.

overcrowding in the face of such fast inmate growth would seem a threat without additional checks on incarceration, which the status quo makes difficult. While funding did increase significantly during those decades, capacity did not keep up with populations, at least until after the year 2000.[31]

And indeed, overcrowding has been, and remains a problem in many, though fewer, state corrections systems. About a decade ago (2011), the U.S. Supreme Court, in *Brown v. Plata*, ruled that overcrowding conditions in California's corrections facilities had become so dire (over 180% capacity at peak), that they constituted a violation of the U.S. Constitution's 8th Amendment protections against "cruel and unusual punishment."[32] The U.S. Department of Justice ruled similarly with respect to Alabama's state prisons in 2019.[33] As of the end of 2017, the federal Bureau of Prisons identified 24 states exceeding their minimum capacity, even as total populations dropped slightly.[34] Not all states have seen the overcrowding pressures equally, as sending inmates to other states with open capacity has been a common contracting practice for some time, which can create additional difficulties for inmates in securing visits.

But ensuring space for inmates is merely one issue in corrections. Many state correctional facilities are in poor shape, too, even if operating at acceptable capacity rates. The largest corrections facility in Kansas' state prison system, Lansing Correctional Facility, completed construction in 1868, with construction authorization coming in the first year of the Civil War (1861). The Oklahoma State Penitentiary (the largest in the state's corrections system) opened in 1908, only a year after Oklahoma became a state. Louisiana's Angola Penitentiary has been a state prison since 1901, but the facility itself dates back into the late 1800s.

As with highways and water, a lack of long-term focus has hurt correction outcomes. Since most inmates re-enter society at some point, making sure they do not return is a big issue. A 2019 United States Sentencing Commission report studied recidivism rates for 25,431 prisoners released in 2005, of which 10,004 were violent offenders. The violent offenders returned at a 63.8% rate, compared to 39.8% for non-violent offenders, with re-arrest occurring at median times of 18 months, and 25 months, respectively.[35] A 2014 report from the Bureau of Justice Statistics tracked recidivism in 30 states among 404,638 inmates finding 67.8% were rearrested within three years of release, and 76.6% rearrested within five years.[36]

Given the eventual release of inmates, the incarceration experience, in addition to atone for harmful behavior, is to prepare inmates for release. Offering therapy for mental health and substance abuse issues, as well as educational and job training provide some broad examples of ways to help ease inmates' transitions back into society. While the "tough-on-crime" crowd rejects rehabilitation as a legitimate aim for prisons, the educational, rehabilitative, and other forms of recidivism-reducing support services saw increased investments starting in the 1990s, during the "tough-on-crime" crowd's heyday. While greater focus on education, recidivism, and rehabilitation have come in more recent years, and while almost all prisons systems do provide some of these services to inmates, the extent of their offering and effectiveness remains mixed.[37]

Many nineteenth-century prisons were privately owned and/or managed, but present-day private prisons are a recent occurrence, with most present facilities being built since the late 1980s.[38] While such findings often make private prisons a target for blame as a *cause* of mass incarceration, a closer examination finds the accusation wanting. John Pfaff's work has been especially revealing, pointing out that blaming private prison companies for mass incarceration forms part of a "Standard Story" that misattributes mass incarceration's causes.[29] As private prisons handle roughly 7% of state prison populations, incarceration growth in the 1980s and 1990s is better attributed to policing, prosecutorial, and sentencing procedures compared to private prisons.[39]

The terrible state of jails and prisons has long been recognized, but the lack of improvement in terms of keeping inmates and staff safe and preventing the re-incarceration of released individuals points to a need for the innovative discovery process the networked governance approach allows. When Departments of Corrections can do little well, looking outside of the agency for PPPs and contracting opportunities provide the best chance to introduce even marginal improvement. And while prisons are mostly operated by government entities, prison services—including food services, physical and mental health care, educational and occupational programs—are increasingly handed by private entities. Whether or not those arrangements result in the improvement of outcomes rests in part on what agencies want. If an agency wants to save money on corrections health care to the point of not being willing to fund enough positions to establish a minimum standard of care—as the Arizona Department of Corrections has been accused of doing in a lawsuit—then the contract will fail to deliver good health care outcomes, even if it saves money.[40]

Improving corrections starts with the treatment of the inmate as an individual case. Most inmates will get released, so, ideally, the incarceration experience should be dedicated toward preparing the individual leave incarceration and enter a life where they have the support to avoid returning to prison. Even individuals serving without the chance of parole are better served by standards that maintain facilities that are safe and allow adequate access to health and other services.

While corrections agencies are dealt with a difficult hand in terms of the services they are expected to provide, contracting services to partners willing to provide them and be accountable to do so present ways to put corrections on a better path. While success is more elusive, a networked approach to governing provides the most promising way to bring improvements to inmate services. But first, corrections agencies must be willing to recognize the need for a more rehabilitation-focused approach to corrections and be open to finding partners that can deliver on that vision. If agencies lack the rehabilitative vision and see incarceration as mere punishment and isolation, costs without concern for quality will be the standard.

Legal or political barriers can prevent agencies from even seeking help from willing partners, too—Rikers Island jail in New York City has long been overcrowded and understaffed, but a law states that corrections duties cannot be "delegated, transferred or assigned in whole or in part to private persons or entities," preventing corrections facilities from outsourcing to the private sector even for a temporary emergency situation.[41]

Other countries have gone further down the path to utilizing the networked governance approach to corrections to improve conditions in jails and prisons: Australia and New Zealand each oversee prisons operated by private companies where the companies' awards are partially determined by their ability to reduce recidivism. The Australia contract even includes provisions that include penalties for temperatures becoming too uncomfortable in living quarters.

But even without such provisions, when a prison operator is on the hook for ensuring inmates don't return to prison after release, greater care is taken to improve conditions inside prison to foster a safer environment more conducive to reducing recidivism. Greater care is also taken after release to make sure the previously incarcerated don't come back. Ideally, providers of inmate services would be held accountable to performance guidelines consistent with a rehabilitation-focused approach to incarceration, while also being subject to regular evaluation and periodic procurement changes that ensure agencies enter the best contracting arrangements for services.

Privatization's Misguided Moral Objections

Many of the most effective ("popular") objections to privatization and outsourcing adopt arguments that marginalize the extent of private sector presence in the public sector. Some work to romanticize the work public sector workers, but more often, the practice of contracting out to the private sector in any form is deemed unethical. Private companies involved in government contracting are depicted as inferior to government, even immoral, for being profit seeking. There are cries that outsourcing prevents transparency: The American Federation of State, County and Municipal Employees (AFSCME) drafted a resolution against privatization in 2014, stating that: "Privatization does not allow transparency of the inner workings of contractors," and "the government's responsibility for the welfare of all is being eroded by replacing public functions with private, for-profit, unregulated enterprises."[42]

These sorts of objections occur, extensively, in discussions of private corrections and of water systems, especially, and do have some basis in economic literature. A much-cited work from the 1990s suggests that for-profit prison operation too strongly motivates cost cutting and/or quality reduction.[43] But the incentive to cut costs can exists for any operator, and a cost-focused agency that contracts with a private operator will get a service that emphasizes saving costs over improving outcomes.

As dehumanizing as it is to think of prisons as factories (hotels are another option), scale considerations dictate operating at as near full capacity, if possible. Critics often point to arrangements where private prisons contract on the basis of guaranteeing funding for a minimum specified number of inmates, but public-sector operators also have the same incentive to get funding for as many inmates as possible, and structure agreements with other states accordingly.

In one recent example of a state corrections system contracting with facilities out-of-state, Vermont chose to move inmates from a publicly run Pennsylvania prison to a privately run Mississippi prison. Among the reasons: Even though Pennsylvania was willing to charge Vermont less than the private prison company on a per inmate basis, Pennsylvania, unlike the private company, required payment for a minimum of 250 inmates, regardless of whether beds are empty or not. But the funding arrangement was not the only problem. Officials at the Vermont Department of Corrections had trouble finding details about several inmate deaths that occurred at the Pennsylvania facility. The state's Defender General, said of the move from Pennsylvania that to the best of his observations the inmates were "happy to get out of there."

In a previous private prison contract with a Kentucky prison, the Defender General said, "I had people in the Prisoners' Rights Office talking about Kentucky as being the best prison in the state of Vermont."[44] The company took action to correct problems. The same thing was true for the Mississippi prison. When Vermont officials objected to the prison's mail search policy, the company changed procedures.[45]

As with prisons, private companies operating water and related systems also receive moral objections based on their profiting. While lacking in substance, such appeals can be highly effective in persuading the general public. The City of Baltimore, via a 2018 referendum with a 77% approval rate, put an effective ban on private companies managing their water and wastewater systems, codified in the so-called "Water Accountability and Equity Act." Food & Water Watch, an activist organization that seeks to end all water system privatization and contracting, states on their webpage entitled "Corporate Control of Water":

> Corporations are seeking to control and restrict our increasingly scarce and polluted water supplies. But we must treat water like the priceless resource it is—and as a human right. . . . Water is essential for life, but increasingly, it is viewed as a source of windfall profits. This is unacceptable. Access to clean water should not be based on who can pay the most. . . . Food & Water Watch opposes the commodification and privatization of water in all forms.[46]

Statements like this reflect an ignorance of not just contracting practices, but also what is required to deliver drinkable water to taps. Over 50,000 municipal water systems exist in the United States, many have been run privately for long periods of time, some for over 200 years. Whether in public or private hands, potable water costs money to extract, treat, and deliver, while water systems operators have to coordinate with considerable resources to ensure clean water makes it to customers' taps. Greater utilization of the networked approach to governance works to reduce the burdens taxpayers face in funding those systems (through user fees as well as debt and government grant considerations). Declaring clean water a "right" does not eliminate those considerations. Those funds have to come from somewhere.[47]

"Polluted water" is certainly a problem system managers face, but just why it is an issue for privately run systems and not public ones is a headscratcher. The assertion that only those "who can pay the most" get access to water is beyond unfounded, unless "who" is meant to represent the vast majority of customers served by a given system. Many municipalities have programs to provide water for customers who have trouble paying for it, regardless of what type of entity runs the system.

Even for government infrastructure and services where critics like to make a moral claim for the elimination of profits, agencies are still ultimately at the helm in deciding how to deliver services. The greater use of resources outside of government that comes with the approach, and when combined with an effective monitoring and performance assessment regime, continues to provide risk management opportunities for government agencies: Moral arguments that attempt to eliminate the participation of the private sector in governance regressively eliminate potential value-enhancing relationships from taking shape.

Agencies have begun to understand how more effective risk management can be achieved by partnering with outside organizations better equipped to handle those risks. Networked governance mostly boils down to being open to new ideas in how to improve infrastructure and services that require resources outside of agencies. Objecting to such ideas on the basis of the type of entity delivering them avoids the more difficult question of why agencies would choose to partner in the first place. If there were nothing from an agency standpoint to gain from contracting, why would an agency choose to contract?

While bad actors can corrupt contracting and P3s, critics need to explain why such outcomes would be the rule, rather than exception. Pointing to profits in government contracting and exclaiming, "That's immoral!" isn't enough, especially considering the proliferation of performance-based contracting that agencies can utilize to get outcomes they desire.

CONCLUSION: CREATING GREATER VALUE IN GOVERNANCE

A central insight of Public Choice theory, put in its basest terms, is "markets fail, so do governments." At the heart of every effective decision to outsource or enter a PPP is a determination that the private sector can improve on the status quo. The decision results in a contract, as do collective bargaining agreements with public-sector workers.

Most every service contract with a private-sector entity includes performance metrics designed to align incentives between agency and private partner, with financial penalties for failing to meet the performance standards. With the right mix of standards, profits correspond with performance, and over time, agencies have taken greater opportunities to secure arrangements that do just that.

If government workers will enter contracts that reward good performance and punish bad performance, then one might conclude that the propensity for such a contract to be successful differs little from public or private sector, or maybe slightly favor the public sector because contracting with an outside entity may be more expensive than keeping work in-house (at least in terms of changing operations and developing the capacity to monitor contracts). That government workers not only look to avoid performance provisions in their collective bargaining agreements but also look to prevent any competitive forces working against them, points to a status quo that likely will result in poor performance.

For example, until a temporary repeal of Sections 52–55 of chapter 7 in Massachusetts General Laws (known as the "Pacheco Law" after its sponsor), the Massachusetts Bay Transportation Authority (MBTA) had a very limited ability to contract. The Pacheco Law, under the ruse of "protecting taxpayers," has provisions that make contracting out almost impossible. In addition to having to prove that the contract would save money (an ill-advised guideline that favors short-term costs over quality and performance), the savings have to be demonstrated by comparing costs, not to inhouse operations based on their *actual* past performance, but based on performance of inhouse operations if they were performed "in the most cost-efficient manner," a mentality similar to the one that drove the creation of Public Choice in the first place.

Why assess performance at all when it is always assumed to be perfect? And even if a proposal makes it through those (and other) trials, the state auditor has full power to deny it from moving forward.

Fortunately, MBTA did well during the temporary repeal period. It identified opportunities to improve its operations through a mission dedicated "to advance performance, not privatization." In a series of annual reports to the state legislature, MBTA identified improvements by contracting out services, and through a credible threat to contract out services.[48] In the most extreme example, MBTA's cash management operations were outsourced to Brinks. That achieved a 75% savings in the first year, with "better security and far greater transparency." By merely threatening to outsource, the MBTA was able to renegotiate with its Carmen's Union to save $200 million in a new collective bargaining agreement.

While contracting out and achieving 75% savings for a single service is certainly an outlier, the MBTA's experience provides valuable Public Choice insights into how government workers operate with little incentive to perform well: as self-interested individuals who respond to incentives, not as benevolent civil servants who are always and everywhere dedicated to providing the best available services at the lowest possible cost.[49] Instead of trying to be more efficient, unionized government workers are more likely to look to expand their ranks. While stern negotiating can push back against that mentality, credible threats to the collective bargaining status quo from outsourcing provide a better position from which agencies can work to build networks and create value to improve services. And indeed, contracting does not just help MBTA in terms of costs, MBTA's commuter rail system is privately operated, and consistently performs better than its government-operated subway system from a safety standpoint:

> The SRP (Safety Review Panel) found little evidence of the MBTA's mass transit operation establishing safety objectives, safety performance targets or safety performance indicators. Very few measures have been established to monitor safety as well as other key operational indicators. The monthly Safety reports have only one metric, "zero derailments." There are no targets or key performance indicators for other operational incidents such as collisions, fires, employee lost time injury rates and preventative maintenance. . . . The agency does not use performance monitoring tools. . . . Most of the reports can be characterized as record keeping, providing month to month trends with no analysis and causes for variance in the data reported.[50]

As for the commuter rail, the safety panel noted that the private operator wasn't just safer but operating under a more effectively regulatory regime where the company loses money for not meeting safety standards (as opposed to lacking them):

> The Panel attributes this higher level of performance to the structure provided by FRA regulations, which are clearly defined and have fiscal consequences, if not complied with. The MBTA should seriously consider immediately adopting FRA regulations for the transit operation to provide clear direction to the workforce on minimum thresholds for operational safety activities.

Privatization and contracting out are not a panacea, but on the balance, the enhanced ability to contract out to private entities for performing services as well as PPPs and other long-term risk-sharing agreements has improved governance. Similarly, adopting a governing by network approach that refocuses management and workers away from hierarchical thinking to a broader, lifecycle-focused mindset. With that mindset comes the realization that facilitating resources and guiding actions to core missions will not be successful without a continued commitment and the right mix of talent to effectively implement the network approach. The trillions of dollars needed to repair, replace, and upgrade infrastructure in the coming decades will need considerable private-sector resources to manage effectively. Agencies will need to look outside of its own resources to find the right relationships to deliver the best value for taxpayers.

If solutions do not develop, problems do not go away, and privatization, PPPs or other contracting arrangements may be revisited. The town of Long Hill, New Jersey rejected a wastewater system privatization several years ago, only to approve one a couple of years later.[51] One would almost expect that other rejections may undergo reconsideration, since the best solutions require more than in-house capabilities can deliver, and denying their utilization just keeps bad practices more entrenched.

State governments have many important roles in providing and overseeing public infrastructure and services. Over time, the risks that come with fulfilling those roles have become more difficult for state agencies to handle alone. Contracting out serves as a proven risk management tool, that allows outside resources to tackle problems that agencies have trouble managing themselves. For functions where state agencies oversee local government, encouraging competitive sourcing, PPPs, and privatization can continue to provide benefits to local governments and the states that oversee them. Even if a private option is not ultimately chosen, the competitive process is likely to improve the public sector's work, too, even if only improving performance (or its assessment) at the margins.

While opposition to privatization continues to be strong, time and history are not on their side: Banning government from contracting and partnering shuts off options to address known problems. Rejecting opportunities without an alternative means of fulfilling agency goals will work to make problems worse. The greater utilization of a more networked approach allows state agencies to better cope with factors that, in turn, demand agencies take an enhanced look both inside and outside of itself to facilitate the delivery of infrastructure and services. Contracting out provides a critical element and allows state agencies to better meet what's demanded of them, through solutions that transfer risk and utilize outside sources of capital that otherwise would not be available to agencies.

NOTES

1. U.S. Department of Transportation, "Overview of Funding and Financing at USDOT." https://www.transportation.gov/rural/toolkit/overview-funding-and-financing-usdot (Accessed: 5 July 2022).

2. Ken Boulding, et al., "Grants Economics: A Simple Introduction." *The American Economist* 16, no. 1 (Spring 1972): 19–28. https://www.jstor.org/stable/25602830

3. The consideration of negative externalities obviously can work against the extent to which the price premium constitutes a "grant" (hence the use of "may"), but the treatment here only serves to further illustrate how individuals and organizations structure their purchases of goods and services with considerations well beyond their relative prices to competitors.

4. But as David M. Konisky and Manuel P. Teodoro showed in their paper "When Governments Regulate Governments," (https://onlinelibrary.wiley.com/doi/full/10.1111/ajps.12221), agencies are more likely to take enforcement actions when private entities (such as outsourcing partners and PPP consortia discussed later) operate public infrastructure than when public agencies do so. Selective enforcement necessarily undermines the rule-of-law. If public and private entities both serve the same public function in the management and operation of public infrastructure, why should one get treated differently than the other?

5. Stephen Goldsmith and William D. Eggers. *Governing By Network*. Washington, DC: Brookings Institution (2004).

6. One may be tempted to argue that even ordering pens and paper has changed dramatically (from mail or phone order to online delivery), but in terms of the type of contract—procurement for a specified good in a given quantity—very little has changed.

7. Israel Kirzner, *Austrian Subjectivism and the Emergence of Entrepreneurship Theory*. Indianapolis: Liberty Fund (2015).

8. Ibid. 143, 147–48.

9. Bureau of Transportation Statistics, United States Department of Transportation. "Table 4-23M: Average Fuel Efficiency of U.S. Passenger Cars and Light Trucks." *BTS.gov*. https://www.bts.gov/content/average-fuel-efficiencyhttps://www.bts.gov/content/average-fuel-efficiency-us-passenger-cars-and-light-trucksus-passenger-cars-and-light-trucks.

10. Baruch Feigenbaum and Joe Hillman. "Revealing State Gas Tax Diversions." Los Angeles: Reason Foundation (2020). https://reason.org/wp-content/uploads/revealing-state-gas-tax-diversions.pdf (7/14/2020).

11. Office of Budget and Policy, U.S. Department of Transportation, "2019 National Transit Database National Transit Summaries & Trends," 24. https://www.transit.dot.gov/sites/fta.dot.gov/files/2020-12/2019-NTST-1-1_0.pdf It's important to note that the 32.3 cents figure only reflects operating costs.

12. Baruch Feigenbaum and Joe Hillman. "Revealing State Gas Tax Diversions." 15.

13. American Road & Transportation Builders Association. "Frequently Asked Questions." https://www.artba.org/about/faq/ (7/14/2020).

14. American Society of Civil Engineers. "2017 Infrastructure Scorecard: Roads." https://www.infrastructurereportcard.org/cat-item/roads/.

One should note that these two organizations actively lobby for infrastructure funding, giving them an incentive to exaggerate poor conditions. But an exaggerated problem is still a problem.

15. "OReGO: Oregon's Road Usage Charge Program." *Oregon Department of Transportation.* https://www.oregon.gov/ODOT/Programs/Pages/OReGO.aspx (7/14/2020).

16. U.S Department of Transportation. "Life-Cycle Cost Analysis Primer." August 2002.

17. Richard F. Weingroff "The Greatest Decade 1956-1966." *U.S. Department of Transportation.* https://www.fhwa.dot.gov/infrastructure/50interstate.cfm.

18. Colorado Department of Transportation. "I-70 East Corridor Project Value for Money Report" December 2013. 5.

While CDOT only considered these three delivery options, DBF, DBFO, and DBFM P3s also have been considered and/or adopted by agencies. See: Build America Bureau, United States Department of Transportation, "Public-Private Partnership (P3) Procurement: A Guide for Public Owners," March 2019. (https://www.fhwa.dot.gov/ipd/pdfs/p3/toolkit/p3_procurement_guide_0319.pdf).

19. United States Environmental Protection Agency, *Drinking Water State Revolving Fund: 2017 Annual Report.* 7.

https://www.epa.gov/sites/default/files/2018-08/documents/20th_anniversary_dwsrf_report_final_508.pdf

20. David A. Cornwell et al., "National Survey of Lead Service Line Occurrence." *American Water Works Association* (2016). https://awwa.onlinelibrary.wiley.com/doi/abs/10.5942/jawwa.2016.108.0086

21. Samer El-Zahab and Tarek Zayed, "Leak Detection in Water Distribution Networks: An Introductory Overview," *Smart Water* 4 no. 5 (2019). https://smartwaterjournal.springeropen.com/articles/10.1186/s40713-019-0017-x

22. Amy Taxin, "Agency Unanimously Rejects California Desalination Project," *Associated Press*, 12 May 2022. https://apnews.com/article/climate-california-droughts-environment-ad4fd9176850fd1c69cb330ac8841b92.

23. Phaedra S. Corso et al., "Costs of Illness in the 1993 Waterborne Cryptosporidium Outbreak, Milwaukee, Wisconsin." *Emerging Infectious Diseases.* 9 no. 4 (April 2003): 426–31. https://www.ncbi.nlm.nih.gov/pmc/articles/PMC2957981/.

24. Another way of reducing the impact of stormwater (and greater realizing the "network" approach to deliver greater value) comes in what has been deemed "community-based P3s," where private landowners implement enhancement to land management that allows for greater diversion of stormwater away from other inflow points into water and wastewater management infrastructure, rewarding actors to implement changes to those ends. (See: United States Environmental Development Agency "Financing Green Infrastructure—Is a Community-Based Public-Private Partnerships (CBP3) Right for You?" https://www.epa.gov/G3/financing-green-infrastructure-community-based-public-private-partnerships-cbp3-right-you.

25. Scott Dance, "It's Not Just Baltimore: Another City Is Sending Much More Sewage into the Chesapeake Bay, Report Says." *Baltimore Sun*, August 22, 2019. https://www.baltimoresun.com/news/environment/bs-mdhttps://www.baltimoresun.com/news/environment/bs-md-harrisburg-sewage-20190822-ayxnvjvegbglhojgcrtoyxcemq-story.htmlharrisburg-sewage-20190822-ayxnvjvegbglhojgcrtoyxcemq-story.html.

26. United States District Court for the Middle District of Pennsylvania, "CIVIL ACTION NO. 1:15-CV-291: United States of America and Commonwealth of Pennsylvania Department of Environmental Protection," Filed December 17, 2021. https://environmentalintegrity.org/wp-content/uploads/2021/12/Harrisburg-CSO-decision-Memo.pdf.

27. Ibid.

28. Daphne Chen, et al. "A Sewer Crisis in the State of Florida." *Daily Commercial*, April 14, 2019.

29. which isn't to say that the increased stringency is warranted, at least in terms of discharging sewage (or rain-diluted sewage) into bodies of freshwater. And sewage discharges are a main focus of the U.S. EPA in its wastewater system oversight, which includes a permitting system for discharges: United States Environmental Protection Agency, "National Pollutant Discharge Elimination System (NPDES)." (https://www.epa.gov/npdes) (accessed 7 July 2022).

30. which is in no way to dispute that the use of such force *can* be justifiable.

31. The Bureau of Justice Statistics' annual reports (named "Prisoners in (Year)") on incarcerated populations include many references to jails being overcrowded. The 1998 edition shows state prison populations averaging about 115% of capacity, while also noting that roughly 24,000 prisoners were held in jails because of prison crowding. U.S Department of Justice Statistics, "Prisoners in 1998," August 1999. In "Prisoners in 1990," 42 states reported operating their prisons at over 100% capacity (https://bjs.ojp.gov/content/pub/pdf/p90.pdf), but by 2005 only 23 states did. (https://bjs.ojp.gov/content/pub/pdf/p05.pdf) The 2019 edition makes no reference to state prison crowding figures, only stating "State and federal prisons may hold prisoners in county facilities or local jails to reduce crowding in their prisons." (https://bjs.ojp.gov/sites/g/files/xyckuh236/files/media/document/cpus19st.pdf).

32. *Brown v. Plata* https://www.supremecourt.gov/opinions/10pdf/09-1233.pdf.

33. U.S. Department of Justice. "Justice Department Alleges Conditions in Alabama Men's Prisons Violate the Constitution." *justice.gov*. 3 April 2019. https://www.justice.gov/opa/pr/justice-department-alleges-conditionshttps://www.justice.gov/opa/pr/justice-department-alleges-conditions-alabama-mens-prisons-violate-constitutionalabama-mens-prisons-violate-constitution.

34. Jennifer Bronson and E. Ann Carson. "Prisoners in 2017." *U.S. Department of Justice* (2019) https://www.bjs.gov/content/pub/pdf/p17.pdf.

35. United States Sentencing Commission, "Recidivism Among Federal Violent Offenders," January 2019. https://www.ussc.gov/sites/default/files/pdf/research-and-publications/research-publications/2019/20190124_Recidivism_Violence.pdfpublications/2019/20190124_Recidivism_Violence.pdf.

36. Matthew R. Durose et al., "Recidivism of Prisoners Released in 30 States in 2005: Patterns from 2005 to 2010." *U.S. Department of Justice, Bureau of Justice Statistics*. April 2014.

37. Michelle S. Phelps, "Rehabilitation in the Punitive Era: The Gap between Rhetoric and Reality in U.S. Prison Programs," *Law & Society Review*, 45, no. 1 (March 2011): 33–68.

38. The relationships between state and prison operators in this period created some terrible incentives and even worse outcomes, especially in the Jim Crow south: Operators would often "lease" inmates to companies as workers compensated only for food, shelter, and clothing. The practice was undoubtedly lucrative for states: 73% Alabama's state government revenues in 1898 came from the leasing of inmates, up from 10% merely 15 years earlier. As one would expect, death rates for inmates in states that allowed such leasing arrangements were much higher (10x) than non-lease states See: Mancini, Matthew J. *One Dies, Get Another: Convict Leasing in the American South, 1866–1928*. Columbia: University of South Carolina Press, 1996.

39. John F Pfaff. *Locked In*. New York: Basic Books. 2017. 79–104.

40. Jensen v. Shinn, No. CV-12-00601-PHX-ROS (D. Ariz. Nov. 12, 2021).

41. The Administrative Code of New York City, "§ 9-116 Three platoon system."

42. American Federation of State, County and Municipal Employees (AFSCME), "RESOLUTION NO. 65: In Opposition to Privatization," (2014). https://www.afscme.org/about/governance/conventions/resolutions-amendments/2014/resolutions/in-opposition-to-privatization.

43. Oliver Hart et al. "The Proper Scope of Government: Theory and an Application of Prisons." *Quarterly Journal of Economics* 112, no. 4 (November 1997): 1127–1161.

44. Elizabeth Murray, "Vermont Inmates Heading to Mississippi Prison with Familiar Private Operator." *Burlington Free Press*, September 19, 2018.

45. Alan J. Keays, "Mississippi Prison Reverses Mail Search Policy after Vermont Inmate Complaints." *VT Digger*, February 13, 2020. https://vtdigger.org/2020/02/13/mississippi-prison-reverses-mail-search-policy-after-vermont.

46. "Our Right to Clean, Affordable Water" *Food & Water Watch,* March 9, 2021

47. This Is no attempt to dismiss the practice of offering payment assistance for water and utilities for low-income individuals, just that the assertion of potable water and sanitary sewers as a "right" muddles the discourse of issues concerning municipal water systems.

48. Massachusetts Bay Transportation Authority. *Annual Report to the Legislature: Waiver from Provisions of Sections 52–55 of chapter 7 of Massachusetts General Laws*. September 2018. https://malegislature.gov/Bills/190/SD2757.pdf.

49. Which is precisely what the Pacheo Law's provisions assume.

50. Massachusetts Bay Transportation Authority, *Safety Review Panel: Final Report*, 9 December 2019.

51. Michelle Caffrey, "Why a N.J. Town Changed Its Mind about Selling Its Sewer System to American Water." *Philadelphia Business Journal*, January 3, 2020. https://www.bizjournals.com/philadelphia/news/2020/01/03/whyhttps://www.bizjournals.com/philadelphia/news/2020/01/03/why-a-n-j-town-changed-its-mind-about-selling.htmla-n-j-town-changed-its-mind-about-selling.html.

Chapter 9

Extending Zero-Based Budgeting to Zero-Based Regulation

James Broughel

INTRODUCTION

A common way of imposing fiscal discipline in private companies, as well as in some governments, is a process called zero-based budgeting (ZBB). The principle behind ZBB is that all expenditures be justified anew each fiscal period. Rather than assuming that spending at a particular level the previous year means the same level of spending or more spending should be authorized the next period, one assumes that zero is the relevant baseline from which spending levels are set during the budgeting process.

This paper discusses a counterpart to ZBB that could apply to the regulatory sphere, namely, zero-based regulation (ZBR). The principle behind ZBR is that periodically regulations should be justified anew, just as spending authorizations are reevaluated in a de novo manner under ZBB. The chapter will argue that ZBR has two central pillars: (1) periodic rescissions of regulations, through sunset provisions or similar mechanisms, along with (2) regulatory impact analysis (RIA) requirements. Sunset provisions are automatic expiration dates built into regulations, which trigger reevaluation of rules and determine the default setting for rules is that they cease to exist at some point in the future. RIA, meanwhile, can be used to rank and prioritize regulations according to their effectiveness. These two policies, used in concert, may have the potential to reduce costs substantially while also improving economic dynamism.

The chapter begins by explaining the key elements of ZBB, as well as its history. Next, it will show how the logic of ZBB can be extended to the realm of regulation. Governments struggling to constrain the accumulation of regulations might want to adopt a ZBR process as a means to manage regulatory volumes and ensure regulations do not outlive their usefulness. A case study of Idaho's regulatory system is provided, as Idaho is a state that has attempted to implement a regulatory review system under the banner of ZBR. The chapter concludes by discussing challenges that may arise with a ZBR model, along with recommendations about which jurisdictions might be best positioned to adopt a ZBR system.

BACKGROUND ON ZBB

ZBB is a budgeting process that was invented in the late 1960s by Peter Pyhrr, who at that time was a manager at the technology firm Texas Instruments.[1] The principle behind ZBB is simple: each fiscal period, managers should build the budget for their division from the ground up, as if starting from scratch. With traditional forms of budgeting, often referred to as incremental budgeting, budgets are set with the previous year's budget as a starting-off point. Under that system, managers of a division might request a certain percentage point or dollar increase or decrease from the previous year's baseline. The danger with incremental budgeting is that it can lock in the status quo or encourage path dependency, leading companies to consider marginal but not transformational changes.

A report from the consulting firm Deloitte defines ZBB as "a budgeting process that allocates funding based on program efficiency and necessity rather than budget history. Unlike incremental budgeting, no item is automatically included in the next budget."[2] Under ZBB, the default changes from assuming that programs should continue to exist to assuming that they should go away unless there is a good reason to keep them. In this way, programs are routinely reevaluated for their effectiveness—and routinely ended.

The National Conference of State Legislatures (NCSL) identifies three advantages of ZBB: (1) eliminating the assumption that current activities and funding will automatically continue with only minor (or incremental) changes, (2) encouraging the termination of ineffective programs, and (3) reallocating resources from lower priority programs or activities to those with higher importance.[3]

Perhaps ZBB's greatest strength is its potential for cost containment. The consulting firm McKinsey has stated that ZBB helps build a "culture of cost management" among employees.[4] Therefore, it is not surprising that ZBB is often implemented in companies during "times of economic problems, when you need to make reductions, or when you have significant and rapid technological change."[5] For this reason, it is easy to see parallels between ZBB and the economic concept of creative destruction,[6] which is the idea that modes of production, firms, and even entire sectors of the economy are periodically swept aside to make way for innovations.

Another potential advantage of ZBB is reducing gamesmanship and perverse incentives built into the budget process. There is often an incentive for managers to spend their entire budgets each year so as not to be punished with a smaller budget the following year. This phenomenon is well-documented in the federal government, where spending surges are often observed at agencies as the fiscal year draws to a close.[7] The same phenomenon exists in the private sector as well and can create considerable waste.

ZBB also includes a rigorous evaluation process for projects. According to a 2012 textbook chapter written by Peter Pyhrr, ZBB evaluation has five key elements[8]:

1. Identification of objectives
2. Evaluation of alternative means of accomplishing each activity
3. Evaluation of alternative funding levels (elimination, lower levels, current level, and increased levels)
4. Evaluation of workload and performance measures
5. Establishment of priorities

In one form of ZBB, projects are divided into "decision packages," which in turn are subdivided into "decision units." Each decision unit in a decision package is analyzed, and decision packages overall are evaluated in total and ranked. Funding requests are then made based on this information.

Evaluation of decision packages will consider factors such as the purpose or objective of the decision package, the actions to be undertaken, the costs and benefits of the package, performance measures to evaluate success, alternative means of achieving the same objectives, and the amount of benefit achieved at various levels of effort and cost.[9]

Henry Wray and Maurice McTigue argue that "evidence-based budgeting" should be combined with ZBB.[10] Analysis of projects makes ranking and prioritizing feasible. This, however, creates a tension within ZBB. ZBB is often used to reduce costs, but rigorous analysis itself can be time consuming and costly to produce.

As a result of this tension, a comprehensive ZBB evaluation of each and every decision package may be something that should take place only periodically—perhaps once every few years. Moreover, it is possible that not every decision package needs to be reviewed with the same level of analytical scrutiny. Large projects that command the most organizational resources should be scrutinized with a higher degree of rigor than smaller projects.

While ZBB has been commonly employed in the private sector, it also has its proponents in the public sector, and indeed it first gained prominence in large part due to its support by politicians. Former President Jimmy Carter implemented ZBB when he was governor of Georgia in the early 1970s.

Carter even tapped Pyhrr as a consultant as part of that effort. Then, in 1977 when he was president, Carter implemented a similar system in the federal government. By 1978, the Office of Management and Budget (OMB) had developed procedural guidelines for using ZBB in the federal budgeting process.[11]

Although ZBB was subsequently abandoned by the Reagan administration, highlighting the ephemeral nature of some management reforms at the federal level, a number of states have experimented with it in the years since. Georgia has tried a revived form of ZBB over the past decade, with annual ZBB reports now issued by the state Office of Planning and Budget.[12] Other states, including Florida, Idaho, New Hampshire, and Oklahoma, have utilized some version of the tool. A 2012 report from the NCSL notes that 17 states have used ZBB in some form over the years, and others have seriously considered it, for example, by introducing legislation.[13] All told, ZBB has been used by numerous states as well as by companies all over the world,[14] suggesting the method is well within the mainstream of modern budgeting and management processes, with adherents in both the public and private sectors.

ZERO-BASED REGULATION

The previous discussion relates to the budgeting process; however, many of the same principles related to spending also apply to regulation. Without information, the effectiveness of regulations—like government activities generally—will be difficult to judge. Moreover, a status quo bias can take hold if the default setting for regulations is that they be maintained without any changes.

Interestingly, the program evaluation criteria under ZBB (e.g., identification of objectives, evaluation of alternative means of accomplishing each activity, establishment of priorities, etc.) mirror many aspects of what is known as RIA, which is a tool used by regulators to evaluate the effectiveness of regulations. A complete RIA should consist of an assessment of the problem the regulation is intending to address, identification of different ways of solving that problem, and an evaluation of the costs and benefits of the alternatives to identify the alternative that maximizes benefits over costs.[15]

In the federal government, procedures have been in place since the 1970s that force some new regulations to be scrutinized with RIA and to undergo a quality control review by the OMB. Once regulations make it through this process, however, many are rarely scrutinized with the same degree of rigor ever again, nor are they routinely updated. One 2018 study finds that 68% of federal regulations have never been updated.[16]

Thus, not only is the default for regulations that the status quo should prevail unless a compelling case is presented otherwise, but also periodic review generally is a relatively rare phenomenon. Periodic rescissions of regulations could help initiate a shift in mindset that would move the regulatory process away from promoting the status quo and toward promoting dynamism and change. Periodic rescissions could be achieved by mandating that regulations be refiled on a scheduled basis or by implementing sunset provisions, which attach expiration dates to regulations. A key advantage of these mechanisms is that they force a periodic review. Moreover, they can leverage an existing system to scrutinize new rules (as happens under OMB review at the federal level) and extend this review process to existing rules. In other words, with sunset provisions and periodic rescission requirements, there is not a need for an entirely new retrospective review process atop procedures for new regulations. Rather, the same process can be used for both purposes.

Sunset provisions have several additional advantages. Academic research has found that they may be associated with lower levels of regulation.[17] Seventeen states already have some form of sunset provision for regulations, demonstrating their practicability.[18] New Jersey, for example, has a sunset review process for regulations whereby rules expire automatically seven years after they are adopted unless they are readopted by the regulating agency.[19] Roughly 35% of regulations filed each year are readoptions, most of which are amended in some way from their original form,[20] meaning they are being updated perhaps to reflect changing circumstances. The state of North Carolina requires that rules be reviewed every 10 years.[21] Rules that are not reviewed or that are deemed no longer necessary expire according to a schedule set by the state Rules Review Commission, an executive agency that reviews and approves regulations adopted by state agencies.[22] Regulations deemed necessary as part of the North Carolina review process can be readopted as if they were new rules.[23]

While both sunset provisions and regulatory analysis requirements are relatively common, they are rarely utilized in conjunction to deliberately change the default mindset for regulations. Idaho is a state that has defied this norm, so we turn to its unique regulatory system next.

ZBR IN IDAHO

Idaho has combined periodic rescissions of regulations with regulatory analysis requirements and has done so under the banner of ZBR. Interestingly, Idaho's experiment with a ZBR model may have begun in an unlikely place: at the state Board of Pharmacy (BoP). The BoP oversees pharmacy regulations in the state and is charged with protecting public health, safety, and welfare.[24] Beginning in 2017, innovative reforms at the BoP were undertaken that would eventually spread to other agencies across the state. The national media began to take notice when, in 2019, the state allowed its entire regulatory code to sunset for the first time in state history.[25]

The Idaho BoP began its experimental regulatory reform by measuring the amount of pharmacy regulations in place. Idaho statutes and regulations relevant to the practice of pharmacy were collected, as they stood on July 1, 2017. These documents were then analyzed using text analysis, and the results were eventually published in an academic journal article written by the then executive director of the BoP, Alex Adams.[26] The analysis finds that there were 37,882 words in regulations relating to the practice of pharmacy. This was up from 26,698 in 1996—an increase of 42%.

As in many other jurisdictions, regulatory creep was occurring at the BoP. In fact, by the word count measure, the practice of pharmacy was more regulated than either nursing or medicine at that time. About 16% of Idaho's pharmacy regulations related to occupational licensing, 44% to professional practice standards, 19% to facility standards, and the remaining portion to board governance and general provisions.[27] Idaho also had another 20,003 words dedicated to the practice of pharmacy in statute.[28]

Using these numbers as a baseline, the staff at the BoP implemented a "repeal and replace" strategy. In early 2018, the BoP received approval from the legislature for a full repeal of board rules.[29] As the agency worked on repealing the old code, it was simultaneously writing a new and simpler set of rules to replace the old one. Not all regulations were repealed, of course. Many stayed in place in largely the same form. However, by repealing the agency's chapter in its entirety, the BoP was able to start from scratch, selecting rules that made sense to maintain while also respecting statutory obligations, and at times rewriting rules to improve readability, clarity, and efficiency.

The result was a more streamlined and easy-to-follow set of instructions for state pharmacies. Initially, the board oversaw a 55% reduction in word count and a 62% decrease in regulatory restrictions. During this time, six categories of licensure were eliminated.[30] By May 2021, the word count had declined 74%, relative to 2017. This significant reduction in the number of words in Idaho's pharmacy rules is illustrated in figure 9.1.

The reforms at Idaho's BoP are impressive in their own right. For example, the light-touch regulatory environment may have played a role in drawing national corporations to the area and creating jobs.[31] However, this turned out to be only the beginning of an even more ambitious set of reforms implemented statewide. The approach taken at the BoP was soon emulated across the entire state, and interestingly, the reforms again took place under the direction of Alex Adams. By 2019, Adams had moved on from his role as

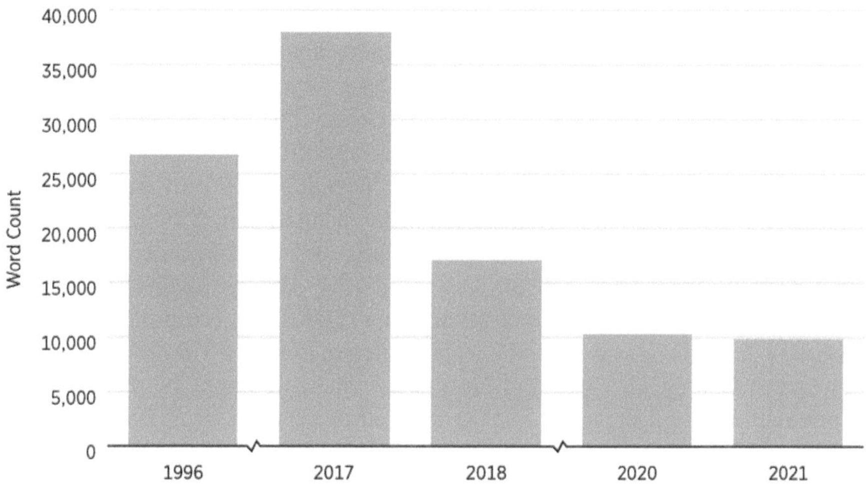

Figure 9.1 Word Count of Idaho Board of Pharmacy Regulations. *Source*: Author's calculations based on Adams, "Transitioning Pharmacy to 'Standard of Care' Regulation"; Idaho State Board of Pharmacy, News, March 2018; and personal communications with DFM Administrator Alex Adams on May 31, 2020, July 7, 2020, and March 31, 2022.

executive director of the BoP to become administrator of the state Division of Financial Management (DFM), tapped for the position by the new governor, Brad Little. The DFM in Idaho is the equivalent of the state budget office, akin to the OMB at the federal level. Much like the OMB, the DFM plays an oversight role in the regulatory process, as well as having other responsibilities.

Idaho kicked off a round of regulatory reforms in early 2019, soon after Governor Little took office, with the signing of an Executive Order dubbed the "Red Tape Reduction Act."[32] The order required that two regulations be repealed or significantly simplified each time a new regulation is added. The order also designated rules review officers to lead red tape reduction efforts within the state agencies and for them to work in coordination with the director of the DFM.

Idaho's reforms began simply enough and were, at least initially, not so different from other red tape reduction efforts that were going on at the federal level or in other states around that time.[33] However, the situation changed dramatically in April 2019. Idaho is a somewhat unique state in that each year all its regulations sunset, unless reauthorized for an additional year by an act of the legislature.[34] Usually reauthorization occurs as a matter of regular business, but not in 2019. Because of infighting between the different legislative chambers, the legislature ended its session without having passed an administrative code reauthorization bill.[35] This unexpected turn of events created an unprecedented opportunity to institute reforms like those undertaken at the state BoP, except in this case on a larger scale.

By failing to reauthorize the code, the state legislature set off a chain of events to repeal and replace the entire administrative code in Idaho—in essence, starting state regulations from a base of zero. Like when the BoP repealed its entire rulebook a few years prior, this did not mean that all regulations went away. Rather, it created an opportunity to remove unnecessary clutter that had accumulated over past decades and to rewrite rules that needed to be maintained in simpler and clearer language.

All told, 19% of rule chapters, 10% of pages, and 19,000 regulatory restrictions were allowed to expire on July 1, 2019.[36] The remaining rules were extended through the issuance of emergency regulations promulgated by the executive branch. The governor's office later claimed that in 2019 it cut or simplified 75% of all rules and eliminated 250 rule chapters, 1,804 pages of regulations, and close to 31,000 regulatory restrictions.[37] By 2022, the governor claimed to have cut or simplified 95% of Idaho regulations.[38] As a result of these reforms, Idaho became the least regulated state in the nation by some measures.[39]

The sunsetting process was viewed as so successful that Governor Little quickly moved to institutionalize the 2019 reforms and to make them a part of regular governance in Idaho. In early 2020, Little signed another regulatory reform Executive Order, this one aptly named "Zero-Based Regulation,"[40] which set up a process whereby agencies would have to review their rules on a five-year revolving basis. The review process would begin with agencies formally issuing a rulemaking repealing their existing chapter from the administrative code. The repeal rule would then be followed by issuance of another rulemaking, a replacement rule that, if necessary, re-implements the relevant chapter, hopefully with improvements. Agencies were encouraged to update rules only in years in which a relevant chapter was being reviewed under the ZBR Executive Order. The rest of the time, a moratorium would be in place. Finally, new economic analysis requirements were enacted to ensure a retrospective analysis would be undertaken when regulations were re-proposed.[41]

This ZBR approach was later extended to regulations waived or suspended during the coronavirus pandemic. In June 2020, Governor Little signed Executive Order 2020-13, titled "Regulatory Relief to Support Economic Recovery."[42] That order directed agencies to promulgate rules removing regulations waived or suspended during the pandemic. An exemption process was set up to maintain necessary regulations, if need be, but the default was that regulations would be removed from the code unless a sound reason could be demonstrated to support keeping them.

The Idaho reforms were significant, but the experience of other states has demonstrated that they need not be viewed as an isolated event that is unlikely to be repeated. One other notable example of a jurisdiction that has experimented with something approximating ZBR is Rhode Island. At the end of 2018, Rhode Island allowed its entire regulatory code to sunset. The expiration was not due to legislative infighting in this case but rather a deliberate overhaul of the state Administrative Procedure Act, which coincided with moving the state's rules into a new online system.[43] Rhode Island has a requirement for periodic refiling of regulations,[44] and a statewide refiling requirement was put in place to facilitate the development of an online administrative code. Notably, both Rhode Island and Idaho have refiling requirements that take place on a five-year schedule, which differs somewhat from a traditional sunset provision. Given that these states have very different political environments, this suggests that streamlining regulations to improve the business environment need not be a partisan endeavor.

POTENTIAL CONCERNS ABOUT ZBR

Several concerns might be raised about ZBR, some of which mirror concerns sometimes raised about ZBB. One concern relates to cost—that is, ZBR could require significant time and effort from regulators as well as financial resources, and therefore it may not be worth implementing. This concern is most likely to be valid if cost savings have already been squeezed out of the system by other means. However, it is unlikely to be valid if a jurisdiction, like the United States presently, does not conduct periodic reviews on a consistent basis.

The regulators themselves might be an impediment to implementing ZBR. Bureaucrats are agents with their own goals, which are often in conflict with the goals of their political principals.[45] Indeed, the somewhat mixed track record of ZBB in the states may be evidence of this. A few states have abandoned using the management system over the years, sometimes citing the amount of work needed to produce detailed reports as a leading reason.

Regulators also may feel threatened when their activities are closely scrutinized and may argue that "my agency is different" and should be exempted from reviews or sunset provisions. Such concerns are understandable. Any change in routine is likely to be resisted; it is human nature to dislike being held accountable for one's performance. However, regulators, as well as legislators, must be willing to do the hard work of checking whether the regulations they've written are achieving the stated objectives. If they do not, the public can have little confidence that policies are achieving their intended outcomes.

The key challenge is aligning the incentives and motivations of regulators with the objectives of a ZBR program. In Idaho, the expertise of regulators was leveraged to make major changes on a tight schedule. Had regulators not been on board, the situation could have turned out very differently. Many regulators were skeptical when they heard the state's sunset provision would be exercised across the entire administrative code, but they came around and saw value in the review process after it was completed. Consequently, getting buy-in from regulators and having them see the value of conducting evaluations are critical for ensuring that they support larger (or more sustained) evaluative efforts in the future.[46] Idaho even gave awards to regulators and agencies that were most successful in cutting red tape.[47] Starting a small pilot program at a handful of agencies or initiating reviews using a limited number of programs at first can also help build support for a larger regulatory review effort.

A related concern is whether states have the resources and talent available to produce regulatory analysis at a level of competency adequate to inform regulatory reviews. Whereas the federal government employs many PhD economists whose primary focus is producing RIA—and even so the analysis can be lacking in terms of rigor or objectivity—states have fewer resources to devote to such tasks. They may find it difficult to offer competitive employment packages to economists, especially given the demand for their work in the private sector, the academy, and the federal government.

There are several responses to these concerns. As to cost, the cumulative costs of regulation tend to dwarf the relatively much smaller costs of employing staff to conduct reviews. One recent study estimates that the costs of federal regulations alone (not counting state regulations) could be about $4 trillion annually.[48] Another study estimates the costs could be as high as $39 trillion annually.[49] If a regulatory review process can reduce some of these costs by even a tiny percentage, it will likely pay for itself many times over. Moreover, there is considerable agreement among scholars that administrative costs do not just burden the private sector, but also interfere with the effectiveness of government programs by inhibiting access.[50]

States also do not need to produce the kind of lengthy analyses often seen at the federal level for their analysis to be useful. Some scholars criticize federal regulatory analysis for being too complex and inaccessible when a more back-of-the-envelope analysis could prove just as useful.[51] Idaho has put an emphasis on limiting the number of words an agency can issue through regulation. While a relatively blunt measure, this can force the agency to consider tradeoffs more than it otherwise would (as words must often be reduced before more can be added). Other simplifications to analyses are also available, such as dispensing with the complicated practice of assigning dollar values to nonmarket outcomes.

In general, different regulatory programs deserve different levels of scrutiny depending on their level of importance. Smaller, less costly projects or programs should receive simpler, less rigorous analysis, whereas larger projects should be analyzed with more rigor. For similar reasons, it probably does not make sense to sunset or force the rescission of the entire regulatory code each year. Idaho's staggered review process under its 2020 "Zero-Based Regulation" Executive Order operates on a five-year schedule, with roughly 20%nt of chapters reviewed and therefore repealed each year. Setting up a staggered time schedule can help avoid overwhelming regulators.[52]

One concern sometimes raised about sunset provisions is that some regulations take a long time to calibrate properly, and it may not make sense to have to revisit these regulations frequently. Many environmental rules in Idaho, for example, were designed to ensure state primacy in certain areas, and sometimes it took years to strike the right balance between environmental concerns and industry needs. Having to constantly relitigate these battles may not always make sense, meaning some regulations probably should be exempted from sunset procedures.

A final concern regarding ZBR is whether reforms can scale. Just because large reductions in the volume of rules have been achieved in small states like Idaho and Rhode Island, it does not mean similar reforms will be successful at the federal level. Here, the jury is still out, and experimentation will likely be needed at the federal level for ZBR to demonstrate its practicality. Nevertheless, there does seem to be sufficient evidence at this point to suggest ZBR can work in other small states and in a variety of political environments. This may suggest ZBR can work in smaller countries, too, such as in Europe.

CONCLUSION

Milton Friedman once stated that there is "nothing so permanent as a temporary government program."[53] In the same way, regulations often seem as though they are bestowed with a kind of immortality. ZBR changes this dynamic by changing the default setting for regulations such that they are mortal and thus not everlasting, which is likely to promote dynamism and growth. Governments interested in promoting an efficient, low-cost regulatory system should therefore consider adopting the ZBR model of governance.

In the near term, a ZBR approach is probably most likely to be enacted at the state level. States may be more incentivized to enact policy reforms because they need to compete with other states to bring in business. Moreover, there tends to be more policy consensus at the state level than at the federal level due to less political polarization. The reforms in Idaho and Rhode Island did not become a partisan punching bag, likely because these states tend to be fairly monolithic in their outlooks.

Reforms may be possible at the federal level as well, though making them long-lasting could prove challenging. Institutionalized regulatory reforms are relatively rare at the federal level, especially given the general need to enact them through executive actions as opposed to legislatively.[54] Although it is possible to achieve substantial reforms through executive actions, the factors that contribute to executive order longevity are myriad,[55] and even those orders that are not repealed outright by a future administration are often not complied with or prioritized to the same extent.

One lesson that can be learned from Idaho is that it is important to have a champion of regulatory reform at the top. It was probably not a coincidence that the head of the state BoP, Alex Adams, would later go on to be head of the state budget department when a similar model of reforms was implemented statewide. Having a single, highly motivated, and influential advocate of regulatory reform can be a crucial ingredient to success, though this may only be one important ingredient of many. Other potential key elements likely include generating regulator buy-in from the outset and perhaps some prior experience demonstrating the practical feasibility of repealing a section of code, such as through a pilot program.

A ZBR approach may create discomfort for those who benefit from the inertia of having regulations exist in perpetuity. It may also create some additional costs for the government. However, the costs of not reviewing regulations for their effectiveness, which is essentially the norm in the United States, are far scarier to fathom, especially given the growth of regulations across time and the high estimated cumulative costs of regulations. Those who care about fiscal accountability and results should therefore think favorably about ZBR, just as many already think favorably about its close cousin, ZBB.

NOTES

1. David Kesmodel, "Meet the Father of Zero-Based Budgeting," *Wall Street Journal*, March 26, 2015.
2. Deloitte, *Zero-Based Budgeting: Zero or Hero?*, 2015.
3. Ronald Snell, *NCSL Fiscal Brief: Zero-Base Budgeting in the States* (Washington, DC: National Conference of State Legislatures, 2012).
4. Shaun Callaghan, Kyle Hawke, and Carey Mignerey, *Five Myths (and Realities) about Zero-Based Budgeting* (McKinsey & Company, October 1, 2014).
5. Kesmodel, "Meet the Father of Zero-Based Budgeting."
6. Joseph Schumpeter, *Capitalism, Socialism and Democracy* (1942; repr., New York: Harper Perennial, 2008), 84.
7. Jason J. Fichtner, "Curbing Wasteful Year-End Federal Government Spending: Reforming 'Use It or Lose It' Rules" (Testimony before the Senate Committee on Homeland Security and Governmental Affairs, Mercatus Center at George Mason University, Arlington, VA, September 20, 2017).

8. Peter Pyhrr, "Zero-Based Budgeting," in *Handbook of Budgeting*, ed. William R. Lalli, 6th ed. (Hoboken, NJ: Wiley, 2012).

9. Pyhrr, "Zero-Based Budgeting."

10. Henry Wray and Maurice McTigue, "A Process for Examining the Budget of an Agency within a Federal Department" (Mercatus on Policy, Mercatus Center at George Mason University, Arlington, VA, July 2015).

11. Snell, *NCSL Fiscal Brief.*

12. "Zero-Based Budgeting," Georgia Governor's Office of Planning and Budget, accessed May 12, 2022, https://opb.georgia.gov/budget-information/budget-documents/zero-based-budgeting.

13. Snell, *NCSL Fiscal Brief.*

14. Deloitte, *Zero-Based Budgeting: Global Perspectives and Lessons Learned*, 2018.

15. For a more in-depth description of RIA, see James Broughel, "A Primer on Regulatory Impact Analysis" (Mercatus Policy Brief, Mercatus Center at George Mason University, Arlington, VA, May 2022).

16. William D. Eggers and Mike Turley, "The Future of Regulation: Principles for Regulating Emerging Technologies," *Deloitte Insights*, June 19, 2018.

17. Russ Sobel and John Dove, "Analyzing the Effectiveness of State Regulatory Review," *Public Finance Review* 44, no. 4 (2016): 446–77.

18. Brian Baugus, Feler Bose, and James Broughel, "A 50-State Review of Regulatory Procedures" (Mercatus Working Paper, Mercatus Center at George Mason University, Arlington, VA, April 2022).

19. N.J. Rev. Stat. § 52:14B-5.1 (2011).

20. Brian Baugus, Feler Bose, and James Broughel, "Cutting Red Tape in the Garden State: New Jersey's Regulatory Reform Program under Governor Chris Christie" (Mercatus Working Paper, Mercatus Center at George Mason University, Arlington, VA, May 2018).

21. N.C. Gen. Stat. § 150B-21.3A (2021).

22. "Rules Review Commission," North Carolina Office of Administrative Hearings, accessed June 14, 2022, https://www.oah.nc.gov/rules-division/rules-review-commission.

23. N.C. Gen. Stat. § 150B-21.3A(c)(2)g (2021).

24. "About Us," Idaho State Board of Pharmacy, accessed May 12, 2022, https://bop.idaho.gov/about-us/.

25. See Kevin Williamson, "Idaho's Deregulatory Revolution," *National Review,* May 19, 2019; "Idaho Quits Worrying about Snails," *Wall Street Journal*, June 28, 2019; Keith Ridler, "Idaho Governor Has Unfettered Chance to Cut State Rules," Associated Press, April 17, 2019; and James Broughel and Krista Chavez, "Idaho Is the Least Regulated State and a Model for the Rest of the Country," *The Bridge,* January 2, 2020.

26. Alex Adams, "Transitioning Pharmacy to 'Standard of Care' Regulation: Analyzing How Pharmacy Regulates Relative to Medicine and Nursing," *Research in Social and Administrative Pharmacy* 15, no. 10 (October 2019): 1230–35.

27. Adams, "Transitioning Pharmacy to 'Standard of Care' Regulation."

28. Adams, "Transitioning Pharmacy to 'Standard of Care' Regulation."

29. Idaho State Board of Pharmacy, News, March 2018, https://nabp.pharmacy/wp-content/uploads/2016/06/Idaho-Newsletter-March-2018.pdf.

30. Idaho State Board of Pharmacy, News, March 2018.

31. See, for example, Kate Talerico, "This Amazon-Owned Company Says It Will Bring 500 Jobs to Boise Area by 2021," *Idaho Statesman,* June 10, 2020; and Jessica Taylor, "Boise's New Pharmacy Tech Training Center Opens," Idaho News 6, November 12, 2019.

32. Idaho Exec. Order No. 2019-02 (January 21, 2019).

33. For more on contemporary regulatory reform efforts, see James Broughel, "The Mighty Waves of Regulatory Reform: Regulatory Budgets and the Future of Cost-Benefit Analysis," *Business, Entrepreneurship & Tax Law Review* 3, no. 2 (2019): 206–23.

34. Idaho is not totally unique in this regard. Utah has a similar law. See Utah Code Ann. § 63G-3-502(2) (2022).

35. James Broughel, "Idaho Repeals Its Regulatory Code," *The Bridge,* May 9, 2019.

36. Cynthia Sewell (@CynthiaSewell), "Idaho @GovernorLittle announces more regulatory cuts on the horizon in Idaho. Goal: 55%–60% may be cut by end of year. #IDpol #IDleg," Twitter, July 19, 2019, 1:35 p.m., https://twitter.com/CynthiaSewell/status/1152270706714894336.

37. Idaho Exec. Order No. 2020-01 (January 16, 2020).

38. "Cutting Red Tape," Idaho Office of Governor, accessed May 12, 2022, https://gov.idaho.gov/cutting-red-tape/.

39. Broughel and Chavez, "Idaho Is the Least Regulated State."

40. Idaho Exec. Order No. 2020-01 (January 16, 2020).

41. Idaho Exec. Order No. 2020-01 (January 16, 2020). In practice, this would be forward looking "prospective analysis" for the replacement rule, though it served a retrospective function for rules being reissued.

42. Idaho Exec. Order No. 2020-13 (June 22, 2020).

43. James Broughel, "The Mighty Waves of Regulatory Reform."

44. R.I. Gen. Laws §§ 42-35-4.1 & 4.2 (2016).

45. Rachel Augustine Potter, *Bending the Rules: Procedural Politicking in the Bureaucracy* (Chicago: University of Chicago Press, 2019).

46. Joseph S. Wholey, *Evaluation—Promise and Performance* (Washington, DC: Urban Institute, 1979).

47. A similar approach was taken in British Columbia, Canada. See Laura Jones, "Cutting Red Tape in Canada: A Regulatory Reform Model for the United States?" (Mercatus Research, Mercatus Center at George Mason University, Arlington, VA, November 2015).

48. Bentley Coffey, Patrick A. McLaughlin, and Pietro Peretto, "The Cumulative Cost of Regulations," *Review of Economic Dynamics* 38 (2020): 1–21.

49. John W. Dawson and John J. Seater, "Federal Regulation and Aggregate Economic Growth," *Journal of Economic Growth* 18, no. 2 (2013): 137–77.

50. Pamela Herd and Donald P. Moynihan, *Administrative Burden: Policymaking by Other Means* (New York: Russell Sage Foundation, 2019); and Cass R. Sunstein, “Sludge Audits,” *Behavioural Public Policy* (2020): 1–20.

51. Christopher Carrigan and Stuart Shapiro, “What’s Wrong with the Back of the Envelope? A Call for Simple (and Timely) Benefit–Cost Analysis,” *Regulation & Governance* 11, no. 2 (June 2017): 203–12.

52. That said, Rhode Island was able to sunset its entire code in 2018 without seeming to overload its regulatory system. This may have been due to responsible coordination across agencies by the state’s budget department, which oversaw the agency response to the sunset.

53. Milton Friedman and Rose D. Friedman, *Tyranny of the Status Quo* (New York: Houghton Mifflin Harcourt, 1984), 115.

54. Andrew Rudalevige, “Beyond Structure and Process: The Early Institutionalization of Regulatory Review,” *Journal of Policy History* 30, no. 4 (August 2018): 577–608.

55. Sharece Thrower, “To Revoke or Not Revoke? The Political Determinants of Executive Order Longevity,” *American Journal of Political Science* 61, no. 3 (July 2017): 642–56.

Part III

FISCAL FEDERALISM

Chapter 10

Government Growth, Institutional Erosion, and the Fiscal Squeeze

Nebraska as a Case Study

Michael D. Thomas and Diana W. Thomas

INTRODUCTION

This chapter offers a case study of the state of Nebraska and of the institutional and ideological changes underpinning increasing budgets and fiscal pressures at the state level over the last century. The case study substantiates the phenomenon of the fiscal squeeze of state budgets between increasing fiscal responsibilities for local public goods production and ever greater levels of federal influence over policy priorities in the state. We identify the erosion of the institutions that define fiscal federalism as a major factor creating this squeeze. Empirically, paying for local public goods like school funding, health-care funding, and pension funds, to name a few, has strained the ability of the state to keep balanced budgets. At the same time, federal mandates make it impossible for states to focus on local priorities to manage expenditures, but they come with limited guarantees for federal funding and therefore create additional budgetary pressures. Although in the past federal government grants have been a reliable and increasingly important source of funding, there is rising uncertainty over whether the federal government will be able to continue to aid the various programs that were shaped by federal government policy to the same degree.

The growth of government over the last century has received much attention and study. Various theories explaining the phenomenon have been advanced, from preference-based descriptions of government as a luxury good[1] to an institutional explanation of the growth of government as a ratchet effect of political crises.[2] At the same time, governments at the local, state, and federal level are facing severe and systematic budget deficits and, in extreme cases, fiscal crises and default.

Rather than offering a broad explanation for government growth and the related fiscal malaise, we use a case study of the state of Nebraska over the last 100 years and offer an overview of the micro-foundations of institutional and ideological changes underpinning the macro-phenomenon of government growth and fiscal deficits. Put differently, this chapter provides a theoretical exploration of existing empirical trends underpinning government budgets at the state, local, and federal level. We identify the erosion of the institutions that define fiscal federalism[3] as a major factor enabling government growth and identify one important fiscal consequence of this 100-year trend in how public finance institutions are organized. The specific consequence we focus on is what we call the fiscal squeeze of state budgets: states, like Nebraska, have remained fiscally responsible for decisions that are now made at the level of the federal government. Empirically, paying for local or municipal expenditures like school funding, health-care funding, and pension funds has strained the ability of many states to keep balanced budgets and avoid debt or default. Although in the past federal government grants have been a reliable and increasingly important source of funding, there is rising uncertainty over whether the federal government will be able to continue to aid states in financing the programs that were shaped by federal government policy to the same degree as before.[4] Federal government budgets are increasingly under pressure from entitlement programs and rising levels of inflation are threatening to erode federal grants to states. To account for these pressures, the various state budgets and programs will face much-needed reform, or state taxes will have to continue to rise as a proportion of income. Walczak (2016) offers some suggestions for tax reform in Nebraska in particular, he concludes that policy should expand the tax base and lower the rates to retain revenue neutrality and promote growth.

An emerging literature on fiscal sociology[5] and entangled political economy[6] seeks to bridge the gap between static models of traditional public finance and the realities of entangled government budgets. We seek to contribute to this literature by offering the case of Nebraska's fiscal situation as an example of a larger trend of financial responsibilities shifting from municipalities to states and decision-making authority being turned over from states to the federal government. This separation of decision-making from budgetary responsibility has resulted in a budgetary squeeze for the state of Nebraska and may be a generalizable phenomenon. The next section briefly defines the idea of the *budgetary squeeze* and details the movement of responsibility from the local level of government to the state as well as the problems created by federal transfers to states when they come with mandates about how to carry out those duties. After we define the squeeze phenomenon, we offer Nebraska as an example before we conclude.

THE SQUEEZE DEFINED

Almost all U.S. states are currently facing budgetary pressures in some form.[7] We have argued elsewhere that this general trend is the result of fiscal centralization at the federal level which leaves local government with less discretion over spending as spending rises and means of collecting revenue falls, we call this the *fiscal squeeze*.[8] Among the three levels of government, each has their own means of revenue collection and is tasked with setting spending priorities. In theory, spending and revenue collection at the three levels are compartmentalized and can be analyzed independently.[9] In line with the literature in institutional public finance, we argue that in practice, revenue collection and spending on the three levels is interrelated, and trends at each level can be traced back to general phenomena dominating the public finance landscape.

The first component of the squeeze of state budgets is that fiscal responsibilities have shifted from the local level to the states. Relatively straightforward fiscal models historically constrained the ability of politicians at the local levels to spend more because local ability to raise revenue was limited. In Nebraska, for example, the sole source of revenue for both state and local governments was property taxes for the first roughly 100 years of the state's existence. From the perspective of taxpayers, spending priorities were clearly divided and attributable to either the state or local portions of the property tax, and the strict division prevented the state from taking on tasks that were local in nature.

Since mid-twentieth century, there has been a general shift in revenue collection authority from local governments to the state level. Concerns about equity in the middle of the twentieth century both at the federal and state levels justified a movement away from a constrained fiscal model of largely locally funded public goods provision. To allow for greater levels of transfers from relatively wealthy to relatively poor districts, revenue collection at the state level increased. The advent of the automobile had resulted in wealthier households moving to suburban communities, which left urban areas relatively poorer. At the same time, increased mobility allowed non-paying individuals from neighboring communities to take advantage of amenities financed by local property taxes. The resulting economic segregation and increased concerns over free-rider problems led to calls for a greater involvement of state governments in financing public goods that were previously municipally funded. In addition, municipalities expanded in size to solve the problem of internalizing spillover effects that accrued to ever-larger geographic areas. The unfortunate consequences of larger municipalities and greater state involvement in funding local public goods were threefold: There were aggravated fiscal commons problems[10]; there was a greater fiscal illusion[11]; and monitoring costs increased.[12]

As the scale of these polities grew, citizens confronted a more complex array of governance organizations, and they faced an increased cost of monitoring the fiscal institutions of their particular municipality. State governments were not only more complex in terms of organization and budgets, but state capitols are also geographically further away than city or county governments from affected individuals, which made monitoring by fiscally concerned citizens difficult. Ultimately the revenue and spending models in most states were changed so substantially that their budgets were placed on an unsustainable path.

The second component of the squeeze is the federal influence on state policy. The federal government has increasingly used regulation, intergovernmental grants, and matching funds to influence state policy. Over the twentieth century, activists called attention to the negative spillover effects of economic activity both in terms of environmental damage as well as consumer health and safety. They used these concerns to justify an increase in federal regulation that affected an ever-greater share of economic life in the states. In addition, arguments about the relatively greater level of expertise of politicians and bureaucrats at the federal level formed the basis for greater federal involvement in state policy through mandates regarding health and welfare policy in particular. The short-term bargain of adopting federal priorities in exchange for funding has come with time and repetition to limit the states' ability to determine their own priorities.

These two components leave state governments in a difficult position. State budgets have been squeezed between federal mandates, which remove the states' ability to set their own priorities, and greater responsibility for the financing and provision of local public goods. As a result, states have taken on financial responsibility for a much greater scope of programs, which they cannot execute competently without federal expertise and guidance. We explore this trend in greater detail for the state of Nebraska below.

NEBRASKA: SPILLOVER EFFECTS AND INEQUALITY—THE SHIFT FROM LOCAL TO STATE

As discussed in the previous section, the shift of program and funding responsibility from the local to the state level was, in large part, justified and motivated by concerns over justice and equality. In the state of Nebraska, these concerns were expressed in two particular ways. The first concern over equality was expressed in the context of education funding and more specifically concerns over inequality in education funding between rural, suburban, and urban school districts. The second concern over justice and equality was expressed in the context of taxation policy and more specifically the fact that state revenue was sourced solely from property taxes which were paid mostly by farmers in rural districts and left non-property-owning individuals essentially free from the burden of state taxes. We explore the history of these two concerns in greater detail below.

Education

Prior to 1967, school districts in Nebraska were funded exclusively through local property taxes. In 1967, Nebraska's legislature passed a new funding bill, which, for the first time, allowed for redistribution of revenue between districts. The School Foundation and Equalization Act (LB 448 1967) was not just motivated by local considerations. It was part of a broader movement across different states to create more equal schooling for students independent of where they happened to live. The Nebraska bill included foundational aid to all school districts based on enrollment, as well as equalization aid to redistribute toward lower-income districts.[13] Finally, the 1967 bill also included incentive aid to allow school districts to hire better trained teachers and experiment with summer and other programs. This was the first move intended to homogenize school districts in the state and equalize outcomes for students. The program redistributing funds between the school districts in the state was financed by state taxes. In addition to redistributing funds from suburban to more urban school districts, LB 448 also promised to redistribute funds to rural school districts with lower per-pupil expenditure. Despite these rather significant changes of educational policy at the state level, local property taxes for education stayed roughly the same.[14] The combined tax burden to finance education on Nebraska's taxpayers increased, however, and with the state's funding for school districts came some new programs reflecting the priorities of state senators as opposed to local educators including the previously mentioned summer programs and increased teacher quality.

One additional aspect of the 1967 bill, LB 448, was that it grouped schools into districts with and without high schools. The specific goal of this classification was to make it harder for residents to avoid taxes by moving to school districts without high schools. Homes in districts without a high school had lower property taxes because they merely funded elementary schools. This caused problems as some property owners were treating the low property tax districts as tax havens. In 1987, districts without a high school were merged with other districts that had a high school.[15] This law also pushed back against the Tiebout (1956) competition that had led to people moving to districts without high schools.

Since the 1960s, calls have grown for the state to play an even larger role in redistributing resources among localities by contributing to local schools. Despite all these early changes and the continued calls for equalized revenue for school districts, Nebraska remained among the states with the greatest level of inequality in spending among school districts. In 1988, Nebraska commissioned a report to study the efficiency of their educational spending. The state collected twice as much property tax per student as the U.S. average ($2,918 to $1,570 annually) and gave half as much state aid to school districts ($842 to $1,675).[16] The Syracuse report, named after the 1988 grant writer's university, suggested that the number of school districts should be dramatically reduced (from 891 to 95—there are 93 counties in Nebraska), there should be an increase in state aid to local areas, and property tax should be further supplemented by other sources of revenue. All these suggested changes would help to make districts less reliant on local property taxes and, as a predicted result, equalize education outcomes for students from different school districts.

In addition to the changes at the state level discussed above, Nebraska's biggest urban area surrounding the city of Omaha experienced a host of other policy changes and challenges directed at more educational funding and, by implication, outcome equality. As many other areas of the country, the Omaha area had experienced a significant expansion of its metropolitan areas with the rise of local mass transit and the automobile over the course of the early twentieth century. Families who had both lived and worked in downtown Omaha moved to the newly emerging suburban areas around the city as the cost of commuting to the city for work decreased. This trend to abandon the downtown residential areas leaving only workplaces behind became the justification for the annexation of neighboring towns starting in the early twentieth century. Annexations continued throughout the twentieth century, with the most recent annexation of several neighborhoods on the north-western border of the city in 2018. As Omaha has expanded in scale, so have most aspects of its governance structure, except for schooling.

Throughout the history of the city annexing neighboring towns, newly integrated school districts have remained separate entities. Because the growing municipality combined neighborhoods with vastly different socioeconomic profiles and property values, the distinct school districts had significantly different revenue profiles and, over time, inequality of public services became more obvious in the unified, expanded city. The rise of the automobile meant that those who could afford to live in the areas to the south and west of Omaha were moving to suburbs where property values were rising quickly. The areas of town they left behind saw property values tank and with them funding for schools. The perception in the Omaha Public Schools (OPS) school district, was that the urban school district was in crisis due to economic segregation.[17]

The incorporation of new cities on the outskirts of Omaha without a simultaneous merging of school districts meant that the city's school district was "landlocked" and had to find a way to tax the people who had escaped into surrounding areas, a classic spillover argument. Annexation of the surrounding school districts seemed like a plausible remedy that would help to shore up the local government revenue portion of the eroding budget, while also forcing an equalization of the now more segregated districts.

The dynamic came to a head starting in 2005. OPS invoked a line of text from previous legislation, "One city, one district" and argued that the natural course of events would have allowed Omaha city schools to expand south and west as the city grew. In the absence of this expansion, the Omaha metro area's 11 school districts exhibited a familiar pattern: The central city schools were decaying as whiter and more affluent families moved to the suburbs. To push back on this development, Omaha Public Schools promoted the creation of a *Learning Community,* which would treat all 11 school districts in the Omaha area as a common school district with a separate governing board, in order to create a regional tax base and enact policy to redistribute from relatively well-off to less well-off districts in the Omaha area. The Nebraska legislature passed the requisite laws to establish such a learning community over three consecutive legislative sessions starting in 2008.[18]

The only obstacle for OPS in its fight for greater equalization of district revenue in Nebraska was the question of the constitutionality of collecting funds from one municipality and spending them in another. This practice had been interpreted as a "state use" which was prohibited by precedent based on the 1954 state law LB 701, also known as the Duis Amendment,[19] which, in effect, prohibited the state from using a property tax to raise state revenue. Schools on the outskirts of Omaha challenged the one-city, one-district notion based on this precedent. The suburban school districts lost their appeal in 2012. Following these developments, each of the school districts in Omaha were charged a common levy ($0.05 per $100 of taxable property ~ $75 a year for a home valued at $150,000).

Together, the early changes establishing equalization of education funding at the state level through LB 448 and the creation of the Learning Community with its common levy for the school districts in the city of Omaha have pushed in the direction of greater redistribution between school districts and ultimately a shift of revenue generation from the local (property tax) to the regional (common levy) and state (income tax) levels in line with the fiscal squeeze as we have defined it above. These developments have threatened the distinct spheres of local spending and state spending in the state of Nebraska with little improvement in terms of improving equality in education outcomes. Nebraska's black-white achievement gap, for example, has remained stubbornly unchanged since at least 1990 when black students scored, on average, 28 points lower on their fourth grade National Assessment of Education Progress reading quiz than white students as compared to a 26-point gap in 2015, the most recent year for which data was available.[20]

Taxes

In line with the changes in school district financing, the tax system in Nebraska changed as municipalities increased in size and school district financing became a cross-district issue over the course of the twentieth century. Historically, the state of Nebraska was limited to property taxes as well as a head tax as its sole sources of revenue, as were most other U.S. states. Having a straightforward source of government revenue provided clarity and accountability and acted like a disciplinary mechanism.

From the very beginning of Nebraska statehood, the state operated with a very simple tax system that combined state property taxes with a head tax. Because of its simplicity, Nebraska's constitution was initially strong on fiscal restraint as suggested by the public finance literature more broadly.[21] By focusing on a single source of tax revenue at both the local and state level (both property taxes), the problem of fiscal illusion was minimized, taxpayers could accurately assess the tax prices of the government services they received, and government expansion was therefore limited by mostly accurate assessments of the relative costs and benefits of different programs to the individual taxpayer. A local property tax paid for things like schools and police, and there was a state property tax to run the operations of the state government.

With the expansion of the set of priorities given to governments at the local, state, and federal level as part of the Great Society programs, however, a shift of decision-making authority from the local to the state and federal levels resulted in aggravated commons problems (i.e., there was a greater number of potential beneficiaries and a more dispersed cost structure), an expansion of the scope of government. In most states, these developments resulted in a push for a parallel increase in the complexity of the tax structure to finance the newly identified priorities. As Wagner (1976) shows, increasingly complex tax/revenue structures come with greater potential for fiscal illusion and a separation of the actual cost of government from the benefits generated by government funded public goods.

In an attempt to keep the state government's ability to tax residents contained, voters in Nebraska approved LB 701, the previously mentioned Duis Amendment, in the 1954 General Election, which stipulated that in the event that the state should implement a more complex income or sales tax system, the state general property tax would be automatically eliminated. In 1965 the Nebraska legislature introduced the first state income tax system, thereby triggering the Duis amendment and eliminating the state-level property tax. Business interests from across the state, who were opposed to the income tax, quickly drafted a referendum petition to repeal the new income tax. But farm interests similarly initiated a petition to remove the property tax provision from the constitution. On November 8, 1966, voters approved both petitions, leaving the state without any tax revenue. This situation forced the 1967 legislature to produce a new revenue bill that would return the state to a situation of having a stable source of revenues. The solution the legislators designed introduced a first-ever income and sales tax system for the state of Nebraska, which was signed into law by Governor Norbert Tiemann in 1967, who had actively sought to bring the situation to a head by encouraging both farm and business interests to promote action that triggered the Duis amendment.[22]

There are excellent reasons to reconfigure a tax code. One is simply to structure the tax more equitably. Generally, a tax on a particular item or class of items, like a property tax, will have distortive effects that increase with the elasticity of the tax. A property tax is largely considered an inelastic tax, meaning there are few substitutes that can be used to decrease one's reliance on owning property. If property taxes are charged at a state level, the only way that someone could escape the tax is to leave the state. Equity concerns might influence a policymaker to broaden the tax base by including more things that are taxable and then lower the rate so that the total tax bill is spread out over more items.

When Nebraska moved away from the state property tax, it did so completely.[23] The use of income and sales taxes in its place had the feature of providing broader tax base than the state property tax. The problem was that it introduced an added level of complexity in administering, collecting, and understanding the tax code. In addition, the move toward greater and more complex taxation at the state level did not come with a reduction in local taxation. The tendency for spending to go to higher levels of government (local to state, state to federal) while having less than a one-to-one decrease in spending at the lower level was pointed out by Jack Osman (1966).[24]

The developments regarding both education financing and the structure of the tax system in the state of Nebraska over the twentieth century have left the state with a much more complex system of revenue collection as well as more, and more complex, government spending. The primary justification for the increased complexity of education spending was a desire for greater equalization of education funding across school districts with different socioeconomic profiles. Yet it is unclear that school district funding or outcomes are significantly more equal over time. In fact, Nebraska remains among the states with the highest white-black achievement gap in terms of test scores for both reading (7th greatest achievement gap) and mathematics proficiency (6th greatest achievement gap) in 4th grade in the nation.[25] Overall, the state has taken on a greater role in funding and regulating education, which used to be an exclusively local issue. This historical anecdote offered here provides an example of the first theoretical leg of the fiscal squeeze of state budgets through a movement of responsibility and spending from the local to the state level. In what follows, we discuss the second part of the squeeze, which considers the fiscal dynamics between the state of Nebraska and the federal government.

FEDERAL TO STATE: THE SECOND PART OF THE SQUEEZE

Nebraska is a net recipient of federal tax dollars based on a Rockefeller Institute report from 2021.[26] The $1.04 received per dollar sent to the federal government places Nebraska at the lower end of states receiving federal tax transfers from other states (rank #41). This is a good position to be in, but as the federal budget position weakens (increased entitlement spending like social security, Medicare, and Medicaid) the pressure on states to fund greater amounts of these expenditures increases, which will ultimately result in a greater overall tax burden in the states because of the empirical phenomenon that federal expenditures in a state do not result in reductions in state spending, termed the flypaper effect.[27]

Mandates are often used to create equitable conditions for citizens among jurisdictions. Generally speaking, a higher level of government sets standards that must be met by lower levels of government. It makes sense that some uniformity exist among different parts of the same state or country, but mandates can be divided into two general categories depending on how they are financed. Funded mandates are specifically tied to expenditure at the level of government where the mandate is imposed. An unfunded mandate is a mandate that must be followed even without expenditure from the imposing level; this could be partially funded or totally unfunded. A state which requires an after-school program but does not earmark spending in the budget for it creates an unfunded mandate on a local government. Federal mandates for many programs including Medicaid come with funding already earmarked. Examples of categories of mandates include general civil rights, discrimination, emergency aid (disaster relief), mandatory auditing Procedures, homeland security, and Social Security and disability.

Federal programs set mandated levels of either spending or outcomes that then have to be met by states. As federal budgets decrease (either by explicit cuts or by failure to adjust for inflation) the states' obligations rise. In January

2013, Governor Dave Heineman wrote about the impact on Nebraska of one mandate in particular, Medicaid:

> The most significant challenge in enacting a biennial budget for 2013–2015 will be the financing of the Medicaid program in Nebraska. I have placed the highest priority on financing education, but the requirements presented by the current Medicaid program and the implications of new federal mandates cause an explosive demand for state resources.[28]

After years of dispute and consecutive governors opposed to the expansion (current governor Pete Ricketts and his predecessor Dave Heineman) Medicaid expansion, originally part of the Affordable Care Act, was approved by voters in 2018 and distribution of funds began in fall 2020[29]. Fiscal conservatives in Nebraska had originally argued that to approve Medicaid expansion was too expensive for the state, especially given that the federal government only committed to funding 90% of state expenditures. State officials also worried that Medicaid transfers from the federal government would fall below 90% of spending in the foreseeable future.

Empirically, Medicaid expenditure in the state of Nebraska increased from 10.5% of state revenue in 2000 to 15.6% in 2017. Nebraska's Medicaid expenditures did not deviate significantly from the trend across the 50 states, even though Nebraska delayed Medicaid expansion in the wake of the Affordable Care Act until 2018. Medicaid funding from own-source revenue as opposed to federal grants and aid increased in all 50 states between 2000 and 2017. The figure below shows the trend for Nebraska as well as the average of all 50 states. Nebraska's expenditures are in line with the prediction of the fiscal squeeze theory that states are spending increasing amounts of their own tax resources on federally designed programs. Analysis by the Pew Charitable Trust suggests that the increase in spending of state revenue on Medicaid in particular is the result of higher enrollment resulting primarily from Medicaid expansion.

Infrastructure expenditures are another budget item that historically received a lot of attention and funding from the federal government but are increasingly becoming a state issue. In an effort to get ahead of the problem, Nebraska recently raised its gas tax, which suggests the state is taking greater control of its own infrastructure and relying relatively less on USDOT.

CONCLUSION

Nebraska, like other states around the country, is always at risk of fiscal problem because of the dynamic we have presented here and elsewhere[30] that results in a squeeze of state resources. Nebraska has long benefited from a

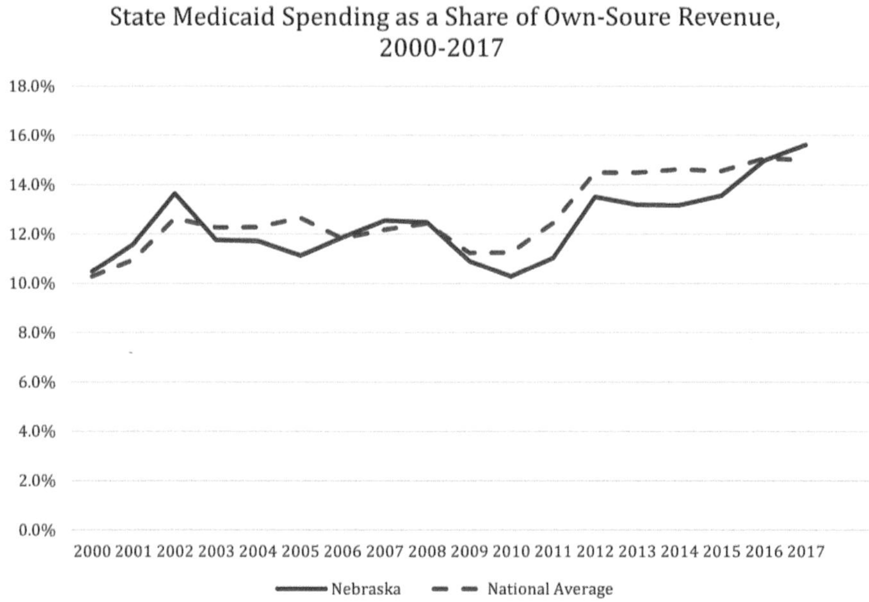

Figure 10.1 State Medicaid Spending as a Share of Own-Source Revenue, 2000–2017. *Source*: Pew Charitable Trust, "Fiscal 50: State Trends and Analysis," State Medicaid Spending, January 2020.

relatively good financial position,[31] but the expansion in the scope of tasks the state now manages has the potential to undermine the ability of the state to set priorities and limit spending when needed. This is occurring everywhere as a result of two pressures. The first pressure is to accommodate more spending at the state level that has traditionally occurred at the local level. This is a response to a concern over inequality in spending among local jurisdictions, particularly with regard to schooling. The second pressure comes from the federal government, which encourages an increase in spending, as suggested by the example of Medicaid spending discussed above, by offering partially funding for an expansion of existing programs or the creation of popular new programs. A reduction of federal support for state spending is likely to occur as pressures on the federal budget increase due to entitlement spending increases and inflation pressure. The way forward is to set realistic priorities for spending at the state level. Nebraska is in a better position to manage this task than other states, because it is in a relatively healthy fiscal position. Reforms that increase efficiency are possible, including setting priorities in health care and exploring school choice options. These reforms will help keep Nebraska's fiscal house in order and avoid the looming crisis brought on by changing budget circumstances.

NOTES

1. Tyler Cowen, "Does Technology Drive the Growth of Government?" In Joshua Hall and Bryan Khoo (Eds.), *Essays on Government Growth.* New York: Springer International Publishing, 2021.

2. Robert Higgs, *Crisis and Leviathan: Critical Episodes in the Growth of American Government*, Oxford: Oxford University Press, 1987.

3. Wallace E. Oats, "An Essay on Fiscal Federalism," *Journal of Economic Literature* 37, no. 3 (1999): 1120–1149.

4. Center on Budget and Policy Priorities, "Federal Aid to State and Local Governments" *Policy Basics*, (April 19, 2018). https://www.cbpp.org/research/state-budget-and-tax/federal-aid-to-state-and-local-governments.

5. Richard E. Wagner, *Fiscal Sociology and the Theory of Public Finance: An Exploratory Essay.* New Thinking in Political economy series. New York: Edward Elgar, 2007.

6. Roger Koppl and Steve Horwitz (eds.), *Entangled Political Economy.* New York: Emerald Group Publishing Limited, 2014.

7. Eileen Norcross and Olivia Gonzalez, Ranking the States by Fiscal Condition, *Mercatus Working paper* (June 2016). http://mercatus.org/sites/default/files/Norcross-Fiscal-Rankings-2-v2_1.pdf.

8. Diana W. Thomas and Michael D. Thomas, "The Fiscal Squeeze: Budgets Between Fiscal Illusion, Fiscal Commons, and the Tyranny of Experts," In Hebert and Thomas (eds.), *Emergence, Entanglement, and Political Economy.* New York: Springer, 2020.

9. Morton Grodzins, *The American Political System: A New View of Government in the United States.* Chicago: Rand McNally.

10. Ringa Radula, "Governing Budgetary Commons: What we can learn from Elinor Ostrom," *European Journal of Law and Economics* 30 (2010): 201–221; Richard E. Wagner, *Deficits, Debt, and Democracy: Wrestling with Tragedy on the Fiscal Commons.* New York: Edward Elgar, 2012.

11. James M. Buchanan and Richard E. Wagner, *Democracy in Deficit: The Political Legacy of Lord Keynes,* Indianapolis: Liberty Fund, 1977; Richard E. Wagner, "Grazing the Federal Budgetary Commons: The Rational Politics of Budgetary Irresponsibility." *Journal of Law and Politics* 9 (1992): 105–119.

12. Daniele Coen-Pirani and Michael Wooley, "Fiscal Centralization: Theory and Evidence from the Great Depression," *American Economic Journal: Economic Policy* 10, no. 2 (2018): 43.

13. Mike Dulaney, "The History of the Nebraska Tax Equity and Educational Opportunities Support Act. Dissertation," (2007). http://www.ncsa.org/dr-michael-dulaney.

14. Michael Wasylenko and John Yinger, "Nebraska Comprehensive Tax Study: Summary and Recommendations," *Occasional Paper, Maxwell Graduate School of Citizenship and Public Affairs* (June, 1988).

15. Mike Dulaney, "The History of the Nebraska Tax Equity and Educational Opportunities Support Act. Dissertation," (2007). http://www.ncsa.org/dr-michael-dulaney.

16. See "The History of the Nebraska Tax Equity and Educational Opportunities Support Act (TEEOSA)" available at http://schoolfinance.ncsa.org/teeosa-policy-history.

17. Paul A. Jargowsky, "Take the Money and Run: Economic Segregation in US Metropolitan Areas," *American Sociological Review* 61, no. 6 (1966): 984–998.

18. Matthew L. Blomsted, "The Legislative Purposes and Intent of the Common Levy in Nebraska's Learning Community," *Digital Commons University of Nebraska Lincoln* (Spring, May 2013). https://digitalcommons.unl.edu/cgi/viewcontent.cgi?article=1142&context=cehsedaddiss.

19. Mary Margaret Simpson, *A Profile of Nebraska's Community College System*, Nebraska Technical Community College Association, 1985.

20. U.S. Department of Education, Institute of Education Sciences, National Center for Education Statistics, "National Assessment of Educational Progress" (NAEP), 2019. https://www.nationsreportcard.gov/profiles/stateprofile/overview/NE?cti=PgTab_GapComparisons&chort=1&sub=RED&sj=NE&fs=Grade&st=MN&year=1992R2&sg=Race%2FEthnicity%3A+White+vs.+Black&sgv=Difference&ts=Cross-Year&tss=2019R3&sfj=NP

21. Buchanan and Wagner, *Democracy in Deficit.*

22. Frederick C. Luebke, "Tiemann, Taxes, and the Centennial Legislature of 1967: Beginning Nebraska's Second Century," Nebraska History 71 (1990): 106–120.

23. Mary Margaret Simpson. *A Profile of Nebraska's Community College System*, p. 4.

24. Eileen Norcross and Frederic Sautet, "Institutions Matter: Can New Jersey Reverse Course?" *Mercatus Working Paper* (2009). http://mercatus.org/publication/institutions-matter-can-new-jersey-reverse-course; Anderson, John E. and Eric C. Thompson. "Property Taxes in Nebraska: Past, Present, and Future." Platte Institute for Economic Research. (2014). http://www.platteinstitute.org/research/detail/property-taxes-in-nebraska-past-present-and-future

25. U.S. Department of Education, "National Assessment of Educational Progress."

26. Laura Schultz, "Giving or Getting? New York's Balance of Payments with the Federal Government," SUNY Rockefeller Institute of Government (2021). https://rockinst.org/wp-content/uploads/2021/01/2021-Balance-of-Payments-Report-web.pdf.

27. Robert P. Inman, "The Flypaper Effect," *NBER Working Paper* 14579 (2008).

28. Dave Heineman, "Executive Budget in Brief," January 2013, http://budget.nebraska.gov/das_budget/budget13/brief.pdf.

29. Grant Schulte, "Expanded Medicaid begins in Nebraska after years of dispute," Associate Press. (September 30, 2020). https://apnews.com/article/legislature-campaigns-nebraska-medicaid-572e3ac9bc92b5a88d58654486bcb724.

30. Diana W. Thomas and Michael D. Thomas, "The Fiscal Squeeze: Budgets Between Fiscal Illusion, Fiscal Commons, and the Tyranny of Experts," In Hebert and Thomas (eds.), *Emergence, Entanglement, and Political Economy*. New York: Springer, 2020.

31. Eileen Norcross, "Ranking the States by Fiscal Condition: Nebraska," *State Fiscal Rankings Mercatus Center* (2018). https://www.mercatus.org/publications/1-ranking-states-fiscal-condition-nebraska.

REFERENCES

Anderson, John E. and Eric C. Thompson. "Property Taxes in Nebraska: Past, Present, and Future." *Platte Institute for Economic Research.* (2014). http://www.platteinstitute.org/research/detail/property-taxes-in-nebraska-past-present-and-future.

Blomsted, Matthew L. "The Legislative Purposes and Intent of the Common Levy in Nebraska's Learning Community." *Digital Commons University of Nebraska Lincoln* (Spring, May 2013). https://digitalcommons.unl.edu/cgi/viewcontent.cgi?article=1142&context=cehsedaddiss.

Buchanan, James M. and Richard E. Wagner. *Democracy in Deficit: The Political Legacy of Lord Keynes*. Indianapolis: Liberty Fund, 2000[1977].

Center on Budget and Policy Priorities. "Federal Aid to State and Local Governments" *Policy Basics*. (April 19, 2018). https://www.cbpp.org/research/state-budget-and-tax/federal-aid-to-state-and-local-governments.

Coen-Pirani, Daniele and Michael Wooley. "Fiscal Centralization: Theory and Evidence from the Great Depression." *American Economic Journal: Economic Policy 10*, no. 2 (2018): 39–61.

Cowen, Tyler. "Does Technology Drive the Growth of Government?" In Joshua Hall and Bryan Khoo (Eds.), *Essays on Government Growth.* New York: Springer International Publishing, 2021.

Dulaney, Mike. "The History of the Nebraska Tax Equity and Educational Opportunities Support Act. Dissertation." (2007). http://www.ncsa.org/dr-michael-dulaney.

Grodzins, Morton. *The American Political System: A New View of Government in the United States*. Chicago: Rand McNally.

Higgs, Robert. *Crisis and Leviathan: Critical Episodes in the Growth of American Government.* Oxford: Oxford University Press, 1987.

Heineman, Dave. "Executive Budget in Brief." *State of Nebraska* (January 15, 2013). https://budget.nebraska.gov/das_budget/budget13/brief.pdf.

Inman, Robert P. "The Flypaper Effect." *NBER Working Paper* 14579 (2008).

Jargowsky, Paul A. "Take the Money and Run: Economic Segregation in US Metropolitan Areas." *American Sociological Review* 61, no. 6 (1966): 984–98.

Koppl, Roger and Steve Horwitz (eds.) *Entangled Political Economy.* New York: Emerald Group Publishing Limited, 2014.

Luebke, Fredrick C. "Tiemann, Taxes, and the Centennial Legislature of 1967: Beginning Nebraska's Second Century." *Nebraska History* 71 (1990): 106–20.

Norcross, Eileen. "Ranking the States by Fical Condition: Nebraska" *State Fiscal Rankings Mercatus Center* (2018). https://www.mercatus.org/publications/1-ranking-states-fiscal-condition-nebraska.

Norcross, Eileen and Olivia Gonzalez. Ranking the States by Fiscal Condition. Mercatus Working paper. (June 2016). http://mercatus.org/sites/default/files/Norcross-Fiscal-Rankings-2-v2_1.pdf.

Norcross, Eileen and Frederic Sautet. "Institutions Matter: Can New Jersey Reverse Course?" *Mercatus Working Paper* (2009). http://mercatus.org/publication/institutions-matter-can-new-jersey-reverse-course.

Oats, Wallace E. "An Essay on Fiscal Federalism." *Journal of Economic Literature* 37, no. 3 (1999): 1120–49.

Osman, Jack W. "The Dual Impact of Federal Aid on State and Local Expenditures." *National Tax Journal* 19, no. 4 (1966): 362–71.

Radula, Ringa. "Governing Budgetary Commons: What we can learn from Elinor Ostrom." *European Journal of Law and Economics* 30 (2010): 201–21.

Simpson, Mary Margaret. *A Profile of Nebraska's Community College System.* Nebraska Technical Community College Association, 1985.

Schulte, Grant. "Expanded Medicaid begins in Nebraska after years of dispute." *Associate Press*. (September 30, 2020). https://apnews.com/article/legislature-campaigns-nebraska-medicaid-572e3ac9bc92b5a88d58654486bcb724.

Schultz, Laura. "Giving or Getting? New York's Balance of Payments with the Federal Government." *SUNY Rockefeller Institute of Government* (2021). https://rockinst.org/wp-content/uploads/2021/01/2021-Balance-of-Payments-Report-web.pdf.

Thomas, Diana W. and Michael D. Thomas. "The Fiscal Squeeze: Budgets Between Fiscal Illusion, Fiscal Commons, and the Tyranny of Experts." In Hebert and Thomas (eds). *Emergence, Entanglement, and Political Economy.* New York: Springer, 2020.

Tiebout, Charles. "A Pure Theory of Local Expenditures." *Journal of Political Economy* 64, no. 5 (1956): 416–24.

U.S. Department of Education, Institute of Education Sciences, National Center for Education Statistics, "National Assessment of Educational Progress" (NAEP), 2019. https://www.nationsreportcard.gov/profiles/stateprofile/overview/NE?cti=PgTab_GapComparisons&chort=1&sub=RED&sj=NE&fs=Grade&st=MN&year=1992R2&sg=Race%2FEthnicity%3A+White+vs.+Black&sgv=Difference&ts=Cross-Year&tss=2019R3&sfj=NP.

Walczak, Jared. "A Twenty-first Century Tax Code for Nebraska." *Tax Foundation* (August 18, 2016). http://taxfoundation.org/article/twenty-first-century-tax-code-nebraska.

Wagner, Richard E. "Revenue Structure, Fiscal Illusion, and Budgetary Choice." *Public Choice 25* (Spring 1976): 45–61.

Wagner, Richard E. "Grazing the Federal Budgetary Commons: The Rational Politics of Budgetary Irresponsibility." *Journal of Law and Politics 9* (1992): 105–19.

Wagner, Richard E. *Fiscal Sociology and the Theory of Public Finance: An Exploratory Essay*. New Thinking in Political economy series. New York: Edward Elgar, 2007.

Wagner, Richard E. *Deficits, Debt, and Democracy: Wrestling with Tragedy on the Fiscal Commons*. New York: Edward Elgar, 2012.

Wasylenko, Michael and John Yinger. "Nebraska Comprehensive Tax Study: Summary and Recommendations." *Occasional Paper, Maxwell Graduate School of Citizenship and Public Affairs* (June, 1988).

Chapter 11

Fiscal Federalism and State Budgeting

Chris Edwards

INTRODUCTION

The federal government has a large presence in many state policy activities, including education, housing, and transportation. That presence is facilitated by grant-in-aid programs, which are subsidies to state and local governments accompanied by top-down regulations.

Federal aid spending was $721 billion in 2019, which was distributed through more than 1,300 separate programs.[1] In 2020 and 2021, aid for the states soared by hundreds of billions of dollars as Congress responded to the COVID-19 crisis and recession.

State and local governments have become dependent on federal aid, but the aid system produces irresponsible policymaking. It encourages excessive and misallocated spending. It reduces accountability for failures while generating costly bureaucracy and regulations. It stifles policy diversity and undermines democratic control of government.

Cutting federal aid would improve the performance of federal, state, and local governments. The idea that federal experts can efficiently solve local problems with rule-laden subsidy programs is misguided. Decades of experience in many policy areas show that federal aid often produces harmful results, and it displaces state, local, and private policy solutions.

It is true that the states face fiscal challenges during recessions because they are generally required to balance their budgets. But state governments can plan ahead for downturns by building large rainy-day (budget stabilization) funds and by shifting to more stable tax bases.

This study describes the advantages of cutting federal aid. It discusses ten reasons why it is better to fund state and local activities with state and local revenues rather than with aid from Washington. Shrinking the aid system would improve American governance along many dimensions. State governments can reform their fiscal systems so as not to be so reliant on Washington for ongoing funding or for bailouts during recessions.

GROWTH IN FEDERAL AID

Under the Constitution, the federal government was assigned specific limited powers, and most government functions were left to the states. To ensure that people understood the limits on federal power, the Framers added the Constitution's Tenth Amendment: "The powers not delegated to the United States by the Constitution, nor prohibited by it to the States, are reserved to the States respectively, or to the people." The amendment embodies federalism, the idea that federal and state governments have separate policy areas and that proper federal activities are "few and defined," as James Madison noted in *Federalist 45*.

The federal government generally kept out of state and local affairs for the first century and a half of the nation. But in recent decades, Congress has increasingly intervened in state and local activities with aid programs. The number of aid programs rose from 463 in 1990 to 653 in 2000 despite promises by Republicans in 1995 to "return power to our states and our people," as Senate Majority Leader Bob Dole promised, and to "return money, power and responsibility to the states," as House Budget Committee chair John Kasich said.[2] The number of federal aid programs jumped to 967 by 2010 and then to 1,386 by 2018.[3]

Federal aid spending was $721 billion in 2019, and then soared in 2020 as Congress responded to the COVID-19 crisis and recession with large subsidy packages.[4] The large federal subsidies turned out to be unneeded as state tax revenues have soared since 2020 generating substantial budget surpluses in most states. The largest federal aid program is Medicaid, which accounts for more than half of overall aid. Other large aid programs are for highway funding, school breakfast and lunches, rental housing, and K–12 education.

Federal aid spending is misguided. Experience has shown that federal aid and related regulations are not effective at solving state and local problems. The following ten sections describe reasons aid programs should be repealed. After that, sections on rainy-day funds and state tax bases discuss how state governments can handle economic downturns by themselves, rather than relying on costly federal handouts.

AID CAUSES EXCESSIVE SPENDING

Supporters of federal aid often talk as if state governments lack resources to fund their programs, while the federal government has endlessly deep pockets. But every dollar of federal aid that supports state and local programs ultimately comes from taxpayers who live in the 50 states. There is no special, costless source of money that funds the federal budget.[5]

It is true that the federal government has a greater ability to run deficits than state governments, which gives the illusion of deep pockets.[6] But the fact that the federal government can run large deficits is an argument against the aid system, not for it. By pushing funding for state activities up to the federal level, the aid system biases American government in favor of imprudent deficit financing. It is better to fund state spending activities at the state level because state governments must generally balance their budgets and limit their debt issuance.[7]

The aid system inflates the political benefits of spending. With a state-funded program, state policymakers must balance the benefit of the spending with the cost of raising taxes to pay for it. But if a program is partly funded with federal aid, both federal and state policymakers can claim credit for the spending yet are only responsible for part of the tax cost. In this way, aid programs increase the ratio of the local political benefits of spending to the tax costs, thus inducing excess spending.

Many federal aid programs include a matching feature to stimulate added state funding of an activity. Since the beginning of the aid system a century ago, a common match has been 50–50, meaning that for every dollar the federal government spends on a program, recipient states must chip in a dollar of their own. When the federal match is open-ended, states can endlessly expand programs and draw additional federal cash. Matching aid stimulates higher state spending than nonmatching aid.[8] The Medicaid program is a good example of how federal matching aid balloons overall spending and undermines incentives for restraint.

AID DISTORTS SPENDING ALLOCATIONS

Supporters of aid hope that federal experts can efficiently allocate funds to high-value activities across the nation. But there is no reason to think that federal officials are better able than state officials to effectively target resources for education, housing, transportation, and other activities.

For one thing, the allocation formulas used in aid programs are blunt tools that do not measure need very well. Highway aid formulas are biased against states that have larger highway systems and more highway use, and thus biased against states with greater needs.[9] Some states with growing populations consistently get shortchanged. Texas, for example, has accounted for an average of 10% of gas taxes paid into the federal highway account over the past decade but has received only 8% of the spending from it.[10] One study found that the deadweight or inefficiency losses from federal highway aid misallocation was 40% of the value of the spending.[11]

Numerous studies find that politics explains aid allocations, not economics.[12] In theory, aid should be targeted to the neediest states or targeted to fix interstate externalities. But according to an Advisory Commission on Intergovernmental Relations (ACIR) study, "the record indicates that federal aid programs have never consistently transferred income to the poorest jurisdictions or individuals. Neither do most existing grants accord with the prescriptions of 'externality' theory."[13] And the ACIR noted, "the logrolling style . . . through which most grant programs are adopted frequently precludes any careful 'targeting' of fiscal resources."[14]

One can see this bias with federal aid for airports, which is tilted toward smaller, rural airports and away from the largest airports where it would generate the most benefit.[15] There has been a similar bias in homeland security aid, whereby rural areas with low terrorism risks have received an unduly large share of the grants, which in the years after 9/11 resulted in much low-value spending.[16]

For 2019, the federal budget provides estimates broken down by state for $666 billion of federal aid spending.[17] The 10 highest-income states received $2,354 per capita while the 10 lowest-income received $2,068. Medicaid's allocation formula is based on state per capita income, so poorer states receive a higher federal match rate. However, the match has encouraged wealthier states to expand Medicaid more than poorer states, so wealthier states end up getting relatively more dollars.[18] There are similar patterns in other programs. A U.S. News and World Report investigation into federal school aid found that "billions of dollars end up in districts that are richer on average, while many of the nation's poorest districts receive little Title I funding."[19]

Federal aid induces states to spend more on federally subsidized activities, and less on other activities that state residents may value more. Consider urban transit. Since the 1970s, federal aid for transit has been mainly for capital costs, not for operations and maintenance. That has induced dozens of cities to purchase systems with big up-front costs, which usually means expensive rail systems rather than cheaper bus systems, even though the latter are usually more efficient, more flexible, and safer.[20] The number of U.S. cities with rail transit has grown from 8 in 1975 to 42 today, and the construction costs of nearly all these new systems were subsidized with federal aid.[21]

One consequence of the bias toward rail is that many cities, such as New York and Boston, are now getting stung by huge rail maintenance costs years after federal aid induced them to build the systems. U.S. transit systems have deferred maintenance costs of more than $90 billion, and systems across the nation are suffering from breakdowns, delays, and safety hazards.[22]

A recent boondoggle in Albuquerque, New Mexico, illustrates how federal aid induce cities to spend on ill-suited systems. City leaders sprang for an expensive $133 million electric bus system because federal subsidies covered more than half of the costs. But the *Los Angeles Times* reports that the "project resulted in parts of what's now Central Avenue being ripped up to host dedicated lanes for the electric buses, which are currently out of commission and have so many problems that [Mayor] Keller freely calls them 'a bit of a lemon.'"[23] Residents did not want the buses, local businesses hated them, and dozens of businesses along the dedicated bus route have closed. Federal aid generated problems, not solutions.

Federal aid induces state and local governments to make decisions that are divorced from the actual needs of their own citizens. A classic example was the urban renewal or "slum clearing" of the mid-twentieth century that used billions of federal aid dollars to bulldoze poor neighborhoods in favor of grand development schemes.[24] A 1963 analysis of these federally driven projects found, "Wholesale clearance of slum areas and pillar-to-post relocation of the families who lived there have generated wide discontent. Members of racial and ethnic minorities who have seen the slum buildings they occupied replaced by luxury apartment houses have grown resentful of city planning that rarely seems to make adequate provision for their needs."[25] At the time, urbanist Jane Jacobs said of these projects, "This is not the rebuilding of cities. This is the sacking of cities."[26]

One infamous federally funded project in the early 1980s was the demolition of the Poletown neighborhood of Detroit. The City of Detroit condemned more than 1,300 homes over 465 acres and removed 4,200 people through eminent domain so that General Motors could build a new plant. The city demolished 143 businesses and 16 churches.[27] Economist William Fischel argues that the Poletown expropriation would not have happened without hundreds of millions of dollars of federal grants and loans as well as state subsidies.[28] Local politicians would be much more cautious before proceeding with grandiose and harmful projects if they had to balance the expected benefits with local tax costs.

AID GENERATES BUREAUCRACY

The federal aid system has long generated large government bureaucracies. In 1980, an ACIR report on federalism concluded that the aid system is a "bewildering maze" in which the federal government's role has become "more pervasive, more intrusive, more unmanageable, more ineffective, more costly, and above all, more unaccountable."[29] At the time, there were

434 aid programs; today there are 1,386. More recently, the Government Accountability Office said, "the federal grant system continues to be highly fragmented, potentially resulting in a high degree of duplication and overlap among federal programs."[30]

Aid programs need legions of administrators, accountants, consultants, and lawyers to prepare and review applications, draft program plans and procedures, file reports, submit waivers, audit recipients, litigate disagreements, and comply with regulations. The federal rules for each aid program can run to thousands of pages. The federal administrative costs of aid programs range from a few percent of the value of the aid to more than 10%. On top of the federal costs are state and local administrative costs. Bureaucracy expert Paul Light very roughly estimated that 4.6 million state and local government jobs exist to handle federal regulations—both the rules tied to federal aid programs and direct federal mandates for environmental, labor, and other social policies.[31]

Consider the large bureaucracy for the federal aid program Community Development Block Grants (CDBGs). The GAO found that local governments spent an average of 17% of CDBG funds on administration.[32] Or consider federal aid for K–12 schools that flows from the federal government to state bureaucracies, then to local school agencies, and then to schools. A study of Wisconsin found that state-level administration consumed about 7% of the federal aid flowing through to local school agencies.[33]

The Obama administration handed out $4.3 billion in Race-to-the-Top school grants to selected states.[34] The state applications for Race-to-the-Top were generally more than 600 pages long, which needed large teams of state employees to complete.[35] Or consider the federal Assistance for Arts Education Development and Dissemination program. In 2018, it awarded $12 million to school boards in 22 grants out of 96 applications received.[36] Each application was more than 50 pages in length.[37] That is a large paperwork effort for a small amount of federal money.

In sum, funding state and local programs from Washington adds a large bureaucratic cost that would be avoided if state and local governments funded their own programs.

AID CREATES WASTE AND ABUSE

Many federal aid programs suffer from high levels of waste, fraud, and abuse. State administrators have little incentive to reduce such costs because the funds come "free" from Washington. At the same time, members of Congress have little incentive to reduce waste in aid programs because all federal spending in their districts is seen as a political positive.

The largest aid program, Medicaid, has huge amounts of erroneous and fraudulent spending, referred to as "improper payments." The GAO estimates that $37 billion in Medicaid spending in 2017 was improper, which was 10% of the program's total cost.[38] As a matching program, the incentive for state administrators to reduce Medicaid waste is low because they would need to find more than two dollars of waste to save state taxpayers one dollar. Indeed, the states themselves abuse Medicaid with dubious schemes to inflate the matching dollars they receive from Washington.[39]

The school lunch and breakfast programs are subject to widespread abuse as families take benefits they are not eligible for. The improper payment rate for school lunches is 16% and for breakfasts 25%.[40] Local governments do little verification of recipient eligibility because they have no incentive to.[41] Indeed, school administrators have been caught illegally inflating the number of children receiving benefits.[42] When federal auditors have examined applications in detail, they have found that about half of them claim excessive benefits.[43]

Government infrastructure funded by federal aid is plagued by cost overruns. Boston's huge Big Dig highway project more than quadrupled in cost from $2.6 billion to $14.6 billion, of which $8.5 billion came from the federal government.[44] Cost overruns are common on small projects as well. In Arlington, Virginia, the local government built a single bus shelter that cost $1 million, whereas a "typical bus shelter costs between $10,000 and $20,000" noted the *Washington Post*.[45] Arlington chose to build a Taj Mahal bus shelter—which has heated floors—because the federal and state governments were paying 80% of the costs.[46]

Urban transit has suffered from bloated costs since the 1960s, when private systems were taken over by city governments and the federal government began pouring in subsidies. Construction cost overruns averaged 43% on 64 major rail projects tracked by the federal government since 1990.[47]

The unneeded imposition of federal bureaucracy on local infrastructure projects undermines sound management. The GAO points to the "fragmented approach as five DOT agencies with 6,000 employees administer over 100 separate programs with separate funding streams for highways, transit, rail, and safety functions. This fragmented approach impedes effective decision making."[48] New York's World Trade Center rail station, which was completed in 2015, doubled in cost from $2 billion to $4 billion. A *Wall Street Journal* investigation pointed to bureaucratic delays and complexities: "In public and private clashes," federal, state, and local government agencies "each pushed to include their own ideas, making the site's design ever more complex, former project officials said. These disputes added significant delays and costs to the transit station."[49]

In sum, state administrators do not treat federal money in a frugal manner, and the involvement of multiple levels of governments in projects adds costs, complexity, and delays.

AID BURIES THE NATION IN REGULATIONS

Since the first aid program in 1862 for land-grant colleges, the federal government has imposed on states complex rules for operating programs and for detailed reporting to Washington. The aid system includes regulations that are tied to particular programs, as well as regulations that apply to a broad range of programs, which are called cross-cutting regulations. The latter type greatly increased in the 1960s and 1970s as the federal government imposed dozens of labor, environmental, safety, and other social requirements on aid recipients.[50]

Federalism expert John Kincaid says that during the 1960s and 1970s, the "conditions of aid, mandates, preemptions, and federal court orders experienced unprecedented increases. Consequently, state and local governments took on the mantle of administrative arms of the federal government."[51]

The rules tied to federal aid raise state and local costs. For example, the Davis-Bacon Act's labor rules require that workers on federally funded construction projects be paid "prevailing wages," generally meaning higher union wages. These rules increase wage costs on highway projects by an average of 22%, while also slowing projects and piling paperwork on contractors.[52]

Federal environmental rules tied to aid push up construction costs and cause delays. A report for the Obama administration found that the average time to complete federal environmental studies for infrastructure projects increased from 2.2 years in the 1970s to 6.6 years more recently.[53] The number of federal environmental laws and executive orders that transportation projects must comply with increased from 26 in 1970 to about 70 today.[54]

Similarly, regulations that accompany aid from the Federal Emergency Management Agency (FEMA) raise local costs. The federal Assistance to Firefighters Grants total more than $600 million a year. A few years ago, San Diego was ready to break ground on two new fire stations funded by local revenues. Then the city heard that they could apply for a federal grant to pay for the buildings. The city eventually received the federal aid, but their new stations were far behind schedule and cost $2.2 million more than otherwise because of aid-related regulations.[55] Aid-tied regulations are a negative for the states and a negative for the U.S. economy.

AID UNDERMINES DIVERSITY

Residents of each state may have different preferences for policies on education, highways, transit, and other items. They may have different views on taxes and spending. In America's federal system, state and local governments can maximize value by tailoring policies to the preferences of their residents.[56] At the same time, individuals can improve their own lives by moving to jurisdictions that suit them best.

Federal aid and related regulations undermine such beneficial state policy diversity. A good example was the 55-mile-per-hour national speed limit that was enforced between 1974 and 1995 by federal threats of withdrawing highway aid. Such one-size-fits-all rules destroy value because they ignore state variations in geography, traditions, and resident preferences.

President Reagan's 1987 executive order on federalism noted, "The nature of our constitutional system encourages a healthy diversity in the public policies adopted by the people of the several states according to their own conditions, needs, and desires. In the search for enlightened public policy, individual states and communities are free to experiment with a variety of approaches to public issues."[57] But the states cannot be free to experiment if Washington is calling the shots.

Reagan was a conservative, but diversity through federalism should be a social ideal championed by liberals as well. It was liberal Supreme Court Judge Louis Brandeis who said that with federalism each state can "serve as a laboratory; and try novel social and economic experiments without risk to the rest of the country."[58] Unfortunately, most policymakers on the left have become strong supporters of the federal aid system even though it undermines diversity and local choice.

Brandeis put his finger onto something important—it is less risky to pursue policy experiments at the state level than at the federal level. Federalism expert Adam Freedman notes, "When states are in charge, policy mistakes are localized," but "when the federal government is in charge, mistakes are Big Mistakes."[59] By contrast, he writes, with decentralization, "the failures stay local while the successes go national," as states freely copy good ideas from other states.[60]

A good example of a Big Mistake was federal aid for high-rise public housing projects in the mid-twentieth century. Those projects are now widely regarded as a policy disaster.[61] The projects encouraged crime and social dysfunction, and government housing authorities allowed buildings to deteriorate rapidly. Why did many major American cities bulldoze neighborhoods in "slum-clearing" operations and erect unsightly concrete fortresses for the poor? Because the federal government was paying for it and promoting it.

Another example of a Big Mistake generated by federal aid is light-rail transit. Since the 1970s, federal aid has induced dozens of cites to install these expensive systems even though they are less efficient and flexible than buses. In city after city, aid-backed rail systems have had large construction cost overruns, a fraction of the riders originally promised, and severe maintenance problems.[62] Many cities would not have made the mistake without the subsidies from Washington. Instead, they would have explored less-expensive transportation options better tailored to local circumstances.

AID REDUCES FREEDOM

The structure of American government is based on subsidiarity, meaning that "responsibility rests first with the lowest authority, the individual; then, if necessary, with local, state, and finally national officials."[63] At the nation's founding, that structure "maximized liberty by keeping authority as close to the individual as possible."[64]

In discussing how federalism would restrain government power, James Madison said, "a double security arises to the rights of the people. The different governments will control each other; at the same time that each will be controlled by itself."[65]

More recently, the idea that federalism undergirds our freedoms was articulated in a 1987 Executive Order by President Ronald Reagan. The order was aimed at restraining federal overreach and stated, "Federalism is rooted in the knowledge that our political liberties are best assured by limiting the size and scope of the national government. . . . The people of the States are free, subject only to restrictions in the Constitution itself or in constitutionally authorized Acts of Congress, to define the moral, political, and legal character of their lives."[66]

Alas, we have strayed far from the Founders or even Ronald Reagan's vision of a decentralized federation. The federal government has used aid programs to expand into many areas that should be left to states, businesses, charities, and individuals. That expansion is creating a top-down bureaucratic society that is alien to American traditions. Cutting federal aid and related regulations would reverse the tide. It would expand freedom by limiting government power and moving its exercise closer to the people.

AID WEAKENS DEMOCRACY

One of the casualties from the growth in federal aid has been democracy. With aid programs, policy decisions are often made by unelected officials in

Washington rather than by elected officials locally. Aid programs move decisions away from the nation's more than 500,000 elected state and local officials to thousands of unknown and inaccessible federal agency employees.

In theory, the 535 elected members of Congress oversee aid programs, but they have delegated much of their power to the federal bureaucracies. If you do not like a policy in your child's public school, you can voice your concern to local officials. But if the policy was imposed by Washington, you will have a hard time making your concerns known.

Furthermore, the sheer size of the federal government works against democratic involvement. There is empirical evidence that "both citizen influence and effort increase as the size of the government declines."[67] The federal budget is 100 times larger than the average state budget, so federal policymakers only have a fraction of the time that state policymakers would have to handle any citizen concerns about a particular program.

The federal government controls a substantial share of state policy. Federal aid accounts for one-quarter of state and local government revenues.[68] Another measure of control comes from a study that looked at the share of all state agencies across the nation that receive at least some federal aid. That share increased from one-third in the mid-1960s to four-fifths today.[69]

In the United States, state leaders do not control a substantial part of their own governments anymore. "Citizens are effectively disenfranchised" because of the aid system, noted former U.S. Senator James Buckley.[70] A similar view about aid comes from Richard Epstein and Mario Loyola: "When Americans vote in state and local elections, they think they are voting on state and local policies. But often they are just deciding which local officials get to implement the dictates of distant and insulated federal bureaucrats, whom even Congress can't control."[71]

Many state employees really "work for" the federal government because that is who funds their salary in full or in part. State agencies know that "even if only a small percent of an employee's salary or program resources comes from federal aid, loss of that portion can result in a job loss or program cutback."[72] Federal aid is the tail that wags the dog in terms of program control.

Former Nebraska Governor Ben Nelson expressed his dismay at the limitations of his office: "I honestly wondered if I was actually elected governor or just a branch manager of the state of Nebraska for the federal government."[73] The U.S. Constitution guarantees to each state a "Republican form of government," meaning a representative democracy, but that promise is undermined when the states are just "branch managers."[74] In his book on federalism, Adam Freedman says that the rise of federal aid and related regulations is an "assault on democracy because the point of such measures is to coerce states into doing things that their voters do not want, or at least would not be willing to pay for themselves."[75]

AID DESTROYS ACCOUNTABILITY

Federal aid requirements have spawned the creation and expansion of state and local government agencies. Agencies relying on aid often have substantial autonomy from state elected officials, and so aid has horizontally fragmented state governments.[76]

At the same time, federal aid has jumbled American government vertically. Originally, the three levels of government were like a tidy layer cake with each layer handling separate functions. Citizens knew whom to praise or blame for policy actions. But with the rise of aid, American government has become like a marble cake with responsibilities mixed across layers.[77] Federal, state, and local governments now play intermixed roles in such areas as education, housing, and transportation.

In his 1983 budget message, Reagan argued, "during the past 20 years, what had been a classic division of functions between the federal government and the states and localities has become a confused mess."[78] Reagan was right, and the confused mess has made it harder for citizens to hold politicians accountable. Today's marble cake structure of government allows politicians to point fingers of blame at other government levels when failures occur. That was clear in the aftermath of Hurricane Katrina in 2005, and it was evident during the water crisis in Flint, Michigan, a few years ago. When every government has a hand in an activity, no government takes responsibility for failures.

Budget expert James Capretta noted, "Medicaid's current federal-state design also undermines political accountability. Neither the federal government nor the states are fully in charge. As a result, each side has tended to blame the other for the program's shortcomings, and neither believes it has sufficient power to unilaterally impose effective reforms."[79]

Similarly, the ACIR noted that the aid system "has become too big, too broad, and too deep for effective operation or control. Where all responsibilities are shared, no one is truly responsible. And, if everyone is responsible for everything, none can fulfill their obligations."[80] Finally, political scientist Steven Teles noted, "The complexity of our grant-in-aid system makes the actual business of governing difficult and wasteful."[81]

AID CROWDS OUT STATE AND PRIVATE ACTIVITIES

The federal government often appears to play a crucial role when state and local governments and the private sector are not addressing a public need. But that is the case only because the federal government has displaced or "crowded out" state, local, and private efforts.

For better or worse, the states have usually led the way on expansions in government services over the past century, but then the federal government moves in and displaces them.[82] Modern limited-access highways, for example, were pioneered by the states before the federal government passed the Interstate Highway Act of 1956. The Pennsylvania Turnpike opened in 1940, and its success prompted more than a dozen states to launch their own superhighway programs.[83] The states were already weaving together their highways into a larger national system before the 1956 federal highway law.[84]

Federal efforts displace state efforts, but federal subsidies also induce the states to displace the private provision of services. For example, the expansion of federal aid crowded out the provision of private highway bridges. A 1932 survey found that nearly two-thirds of 322 toll bridges in the United States were privately owned, notes Robert Poole.[85] But then federal and state governments began handing out subsidies to government-owned bridges during the 1930s, and that put private bridges at a competitive disadvantage. Because private bridge owners did not receive subsidies, many of them succumbed to government takeovers.

Urban transit systems in most American cities were privately owned and operated until the 1960s, but then the private share fell rapidly. Of the systems in the 100 largest U.S. cities, the private share fell from 90% in 1960 to just 20% by the late 1970s.[86] The rise of automobiles undermined transit; transit firms had difficulty cutting costs because they were unionized; and local governments resisted allowing transit firms to end unprofitable routes. The nail in the coffin for private transit was the Urban Mass Transportation Act of 1964, which provided federal aid to government-owned bus and rail systems. That encouraged state and local governments to take over private systems, and a century of private transit in America came to an end.[87]

A similar thing happened in aviation. About half of U.S. airports were privately owned in the early years of commercial aviation in the 1920s and 1930s. The main airports in Los Angeles, Miami, Philadelphia, Washington DC, and other cities were for-profit business ventures. These airports were successful and innovative, but they lost ground from unfair government competition. City governments could issue bonds exempt from federal tax to finance their own airports, giving them a financial edge over private airports. Private airports had to pay taxes while government airports did not. The federal government began handing out aid to government-owned airports during the New Deal, and then the Airport Act of 1946 began regular federal aid funding of government-owned airports. Today, virtually all U.S. commercial airports are in government hands.

Federal aid has encouraged the states to crowd out private provision in other areas. The expansion of Medicaid has crowded out private health care. Estimates vary, but roughly every two persons added to the program has reduced private health coverage by one person.[88] Medicaid long-term care aid has induced many families who would have otherwise paid privately to take advantage of government benefits.[89] Similarly, local public schools have long crowded out private schools, and federal aid has exacerbated the problem.

STATES NEED LARGE RAINY-DAY FUNDS

The crisis of 2020 prompted the federal government to shower states with hundreds of billions of extra dollars in aid for health care, education, and other state and local activities. As it turned out, state and local government revenues have soared since 2020, and the extra aid from Washington was mainly unneeded. According to the U.S. Bureau of Economic Analysis, total state and local tax revenues in second quarter 2022 were up 21% from before the pandemic in first quarter 2020.[90]

Looking ahead, state and local governments should not rely on extra federal aid during downturns, as the federal budget itself is in crisis with record-high debt levels. Economic downturns can be a large blow to the states because they operate within statutory and constitutional rules that require them to balance their general fund budgets.[91] However, the states can handle these blows by reining in excess spending and building large rainy-day funds in anticipation of downturns.

During boom years, state policymakers should be saving a share of tax revenues in these funds to be available during a downturn or crisis. The states use a variety of rules and mechanisms for deposits into, and withdrawals from, their rainy-day funds.[92] Large rainy-day funds are viewed favorably by bond rating agencies and thus tend to boost a state's credit rating and reduce borrowing costs.[93]

The National Association of State Budget Officers tracks data on state rainy-day funds. Going into the recession in 2020, rainy-day fund balances totaled 8.7% of annual general fund spending for the states as a whole, up from 4.8% going into the last recession in 2008.[94] Rainy-day funds are a portion of "total balances," which are the accumulated state funds left over after spending. Total balances are a broader cushion for state budgets, and they averaged 12.1% of annual spending going into this recession.

The sizes of rainy-day funds varies widely. In 2020, they totaled 10% or more of annual spending in 18 states, but they totaled less than 5% in 11 states.[95] Among these less-prudent states, New Jersey, Pennsylvania, Illinois, and Kansas had saved virtually nothing in their rainy-day funds going into 2020, even after a decade-long economic expansion.

Energy producing states tend to have boom-bust economies, and governments in those states are vulnerable because they often rely on severance taxes (on energy extraction) for revenue. However, many of those states—including Alaska, North Dakota, Texas, and Wyoming—knew their vulnerability to downturns and planned ahead, and they went into 2020 with quite large rainy-day funds.

In sum, states that were prudent and built large rainy days going into this recession will have an easier time budgeting over the next year or two. But recent events should be a warning to all state governments to plan ahead and build large rainy-day funds because crises and recessions usually happen without warning.

STATES SHOULD ADOPT STABLE TAX BASES

State governments raised $1.09 trillion in tax revenues in 2019. Sales taxes were 46% of the total, individual income taxes were 38%, corporate income taxes were 5%, and other taxes were 11%.[96] To reduce a boom-bust cycle in their budgets as the economy expands and contracts, state policymakers should move toward sources of tax revenue that are more stable across economic cycles.

Income tax revenues are more volatile than sales tax revenues. During the Great Recession, state personal income tax revenues fell 12%, and state corporate income tax revenues fell 18% from the peak in 2007 to the trough in 2009.[97] State sales tax revenues fell just 9% during that period. An Urban Institute study looking at state revenues found that "the corporate income tax tends to be the most volatile source of tax revenue; the personal income tax, which includes the highly unpredictable capital gains tax, is a close second."[98] A related problem is that forecasts for future income tax revenue are more error-prone than forecasts for sales taxes, which makes state budget planning more difficult.[99]

The Urban Institute study noted that states have become more dependent on volatile revenue sources since the 1970s as the share of revenues from income taxes has risen while the share from sales taxes has fallen.[100] A Federal Reserve study also found that state revenues have become more volatile over time.[101] A chart of annual changes in sales and income tax revenues over the decades clearly shows greater fluctuations in the latter.[102] Within the income tax base, the Federal Reserve study found that investment income (dividends, interest, and capital gains) is far more volatile than wage income.[103]

Progressive personal income taxes that have higher rates on top earners are more volatile than proportional or flat-rate systems. That is because incomes at the top end are heavily weighted by investment and business income, which fluctuate strongly with economic ups and downs. During the last recession, federal adjusted gross income of the top 1% fell 34% between 2007 and

2009, which compared to just a 6% drop in adjusted gross income for the other 99% of taxpayers.[104]

The volatility of high-end incomes creates a major budget problem for states that have highly progressive income tax structures, such as New York and California. In New York, the top 1% of earners pays about 41% of state income taxes, and in California, the top 1% pays about 50% of state income taxes.[105] In 2019, income taxes accounted for 64% of New York's overall tax revenue and 61% of California's. When the investment and business income of the top 1% drops during a recession in states such as these, it generates a major budget crisis.

During the last recession, California's personal income tax revenues plunged 20% in 2009, which compared to just a 9% fall in the other 49 states.[106] California's top personal income tax rate of 13.3% is the highest in the nation. An analysis by California's legislature found that the state's personal income tax revenues are about five times more volatile than overall personal income because of the income tax system's graduated rate structure and other design features.[107] Within income taxes, capital gains taxes are particularly volatile.[108]

Pew Charitable Trusts examined tax revenue volatility between 1998 and 2017 and found that California had the fifth highest out of the 50 states. The three states with the most volatile revenue systems were the energy producers Alaska, North Dakota, and Wyoming, which rely heavily on severance taxes.[109]

In the Pew analysis, South Dakota has the least revenue volatility among the 50 states. South Dakota does not have a personal income tax, and sales taxes account for 83% of state tax revenues.[110] During the last recession, South Dakota's total tax revenues did not fall—they were flat for a couple years and then started rising again. Thus, states wanting to be better prepared for the next recession should transition away from income taxes and rely more on sales taxes.

Aside from being a more stable revenue source, sales taxes are less harmful to economic growth than income taxes because they do not tax the return to saving and investment.[111] The Tax Cuts and Jobs Act of 2017 created a further incentive to move away from income taxes, particularly systems with progressive structures. The law capped the federal deduction for state and local taxes at $10,000, which had the effect of increasing the tax burden particularly on high earners living in high-tax states. The reform means that millions of middle- and higher-income households have a stronger incentive to move to a lower-tax state.

As explored in a Cato Institute study, state policymakers should rethink their tax codes in today's era of heightened interstate tax competition.[112] High-rate individual income taxes and corporate income taxes make less sense than sales taxes because of the greater harm caused to the economy and the reduced stability for state budgets.[113] As it turned out, state income tax revenues soared in recent years despite the health crisis, and capital gains tax revenue increased as the stock market rose. However, the stock market was down in 2022 and income and capital gains tax revenues may decline substantially if the economy goes into recession. State governments should make plans to shift away from income and capital gains taxes toward more stable consumption-based taxes.

CONCLUSION

The federal aid system is a roundabout way to fund state and local activities that the deficit-ridden federal government cannot afford. The aid system does not deliver efficient public services, but rather delivers bureaucracy, overspending, and federal micromanagement. It undermines policy diversity and political accountability. With larger rainy-day funds and more stable tax bases, the states should be able to handle economic downturns without the gushers of poorly targeted aid from Washington.

It is understandable that federal policymakers are eager to try and fix the nation's ills. But they should appreciate that the states can handle domestic policies by themselves and that federal intervention is usually counterproductive. Americans want more responsive and effective government, and they can get it by devolving power to the states and reviving competitive federalism.

NOTES

1. This is a fiscal year estimate from the *Budget of the U.S. Government, FY2021, Analytical Perspectives* (Washington, DC: Government Printing Office, 2020).

2. Quoted in Kenneth Jost, "The States and Federalism: Should More Power be Shifted to the States?," *CQ Researcher*, September 13, 1996.

3. The figure for 2018 is based on my analysis of the Catalog of Federal Domestic Assistance (CFDA), which is available at https://beta.sam.gov (formerly www.cfda.gov). I included programs of type A, B, and C for state, local, and tribal governments, while excluding programs for private-sector recipients. Programs with zero obligations were excluded. The Congressional Research Service provided a count for 2017 of 1,319. See Robert Day Dilger, "Federal Grants to State and Local Governments: A Historical Perspective on Contemporary Issues," Congressional Research Service, R40638, May 7, 2018.

4. Data for 2019 from *Budget of the U.S. Government, FY2021, Analytical Perspectives* (Washington, DC: Government Printing Office, 2020).

5. A study by a liberal thinktank arguing against President Trump's proposed aid cuts said, "State and local governments do not have the funds to replace the magnitude of funds that could be lost through cuts." Yet the federal government is running massive deficits and does not "have the funds" either. See Iris J. Lav and Michael Leachman, "At Risk: Federal Grants to State and Local Governments," Center on Budget and Policy Priorities, March 13, 2017.

6. Federalism expert John Kincaid notes, "Just as grants create the illusion of free money for state and local taxpayers, federal deficit spending encourages state and local officials to try to shift costs to the federal government because it appears to be costless and because state and local officials face comparatively hard budget constraints in the forms of constitutional or statutory tax, expenditure, and borrowing limits." John Kincaid, "The Eclipse of Dual Federalism by One-Way Cooperation Federalism," *Arizona State Law Journal* 49, no. 3 (Fall 2017): 1075. The first book about the new and growing federal aid system published in 1928 captured the political appeal of federal funding: "The voters have clamored loudly for better standards of service—more and better schools, more and better teachers, more and better roads. At the same time they have voiced no less insistently their demand for lower taxes. State legislators . . . have cast about for new sources of revenue. One the richest finds has been the federal treasury." Austin F. Macdonald, *Federal Aid: A Study of the American Subsidy System* (New York: Thomas Y. Crowell Company, 1928), p. 5.

7. In addition to legal limits on debt issuance, state budgeting is disciplined by credit ratings on state bond debt. Some states have large unfunded obligations in their worker retirement plans and thus are not fiscal saints. However, state and local debt and unfunded obligations is a smaller problem than federal government debt and unfunded obligations. Also, some states are quite prudent and have very low debt and unfunded obligations.

8. Shama Gamkhar and Wallace Oates, "Asymmetries in the Response to Increases and Decreases in Intergovernmental Grants: Some Empirical Findings," *National Tax Journal* 49, no. 4 (December 1996): 501–12.

9. Pengyu Zhu and Jeffrey R. Brown, "Donor States and Donee States: Investigating Geographic Redistribution of the U.S. Federal-Aid Highway Program 1974–2008," *Transportation* 40, no. 1 (January 2013): 203–27.

10. Author's calculation for 2006 to 2015 of the HTF's highway account. See Federal Highway Administration, "Highway Statistics 2015," August 2016, Table FE-221B.

11. This is Inman's interpretation of Knight's statistical results. Robert P. Inman, "The Flypaper Effect," National Bureau of Economic Research Working Paper no. 14579, December 2008. Brian Knight, "Parochial Interests and the Centralized Provision of Local Public Goods," National Bureau of Economic Research Working Paper no. 9748, June 2003.

12. Some studies that have found political biases in aid allocations include: Dino P. Christenson, Douglas L. Kriner, and Andrew Reeves, "All the President's Senators: Presidential Copartisans and the Allocation of Federal Grants," *Legislative Studies Quarterly* 42, no. 2 (May 2017); Thomas A. Garrett and Russell S. Sobel, "The Political Economy of FEMA Disaster Payments," *Economic Inquiry* 41, no. 3

(July 2003): 496–509; David Albouy, "Partisan Representation in Congress and the Geographic Distribution of Federal Funds," National Bureau of Economic Research Working Paper no. 15224, August 2009; and Pengyu Zhu and Jeffrey R. Brown, "Donor States and Donee States: Investigating Geographic Redistribution of the U.S. Federal-Aid Highway Program 1974–2008," *Transportation* 40, no. 1 (January 2013): 203.

13. Advisory Commission on Intergovernmental Relations, "The Federal Role in the Federal System: The Dynamics of Growth," no. A-86, June 1981, p. 94.

14. Advisory Commission on Intergovernmental Relations, "The Federal Role in the Federal System: The Dynamics of Growth," no. A-86, June 1981, p. 106.

15. Clifford Winston, "On the Performance of the U.S. Transportation System: Caution Ahead," *Journal of Economic Literature* 51, no. 3 (September 2013): 790.

16. Dean E. Murphy, "Security Grants Still Streaming to Rural States," *New York Times*, October 12, 2004. And see Chris Edwards, "Terminating the Department of Homeland Security," DownsizingGovernment.org, Cato Institute, November 1, 2014.

17. *Budget of the U.S. Government, FY2020, Analytical Perspectives* (Washington, DC: Government Printing Office, 2019), Table 17-4.

18. Joseph Antos, "The Structure of Medicaid," in *The Economics of Medicaid,* ed. Jason J. Fichtner (ArlingtonVA: Mercatus Center, 2014), p. 9.

19. Lauren Camera and Lindsey Cook, "Title 1: Rich School Districts Get Millions Meant for Poor Kids," *U.S. News and World Report,* June 1, 2016.

20. Randal O'Toole, *Romance of the Rails: Why the Passenger Trains We Love Are Not the Transportation We Need* (Washington, DC: Cato Institute, 2018), Chapter 13.

21. Randal O'Toole, *Romance of the Rails: Why the Passenger Trains We Love Are Not the Transportation We Need* (Washington, DC: Cato Institute, 2018), pp. 165, 168, 215.

22. Randal O'Toole, *Romance of the Rails: Why the Passenger Trains We Love Are Not the Transportation We Need* (Washington, DC: Cato Institute, 2018), p. 213. And see the transit section of www.infrastructurereportcard.org.

23. Gustavo Arellano, "Albuquerque's $133-Million Electric Bus System Is Going Nowhere Fast," *Los Angeles Times*, February 17, 2019.

24. The Housing Act of 1949 launched a large federal effort of urban renewal, slum clearing, and public housing projects.

25. W. B. Dickinson Jr., "Urban Renewal Under Fire," *CQ Researcher* (formerly *Editorial Research Reports*), August 21, 1963.

26. Jane Jacobs, *The Death and Life of Great American Cities* (New York: Random House, 1961), p. 4.

27. James T. Bennett, *Corporate Welfare: Crony Capitalism that Enriches the Rich* (New Brunswick, NJ: Transaction Publishers, 2015), Chapter 5.

28. William A. Fischel, "Before Kelo," *Regulation* 28, no. 4 (Winter 2005): 32–35.

29. Advisory Committee on Intergovernmental Relations, "The Federal Role in the Federal System: The Dynamics of Growth," December 1980, Introduction. This is the "In Brief" summary volume.

30. Government Accountability Office, "Federal Assistance: Grant System Continues to Be Highly Fragmented," GAO-03-718T, April 29, 2003.

31. Paul C. Light, "Fact Sheet on the New True Size of Government," Brookings Institution 2003. And see Paul C. Light, *The True Size of Government* (Washington, DC: Brookings Institution, 1999), pp. 26–36.

32. Government Accountability Office, "Community Development Block Grants: Program Offers Recipients Flexibility but Oversight Can Be Improved," GAO-06-732, July 2006, p. 14.

33. Mike Nichols, *Federal Grant$tanding: How Federal Grants Are Depriving Us of Our Money, Liberty and Trust in Government—and What We Can Do about It* (Wisconsin: Badger Institute, 2018), p. 69.

34. Patrick McGuinn, "From No Child Left Behind to the Every Student Succeeds Act: Federalism and the Education Legacy of the Obama Administration," *Publius: The Journal of Federalism* 46, no. 3 (2016): 396.

35. For example, California's application was 606 pages in length and Colorado's was 762 pages.

36. This program is CFDA 84.351D. Information on it is at https://innovation.ed.gov.

37. This figure is from a sampling of applications for 2014. Recent award applications are not posted.

38. Government Accountability Office, "Medicaid: Further Action Needed to Expedite Use of National Data for Program Oversight," GAO-18-70, December 2017.

39. Health care provider taxes are a widely criticized example, but there are also other dubious schemes. Regarding provider taxes, see Brian C. Blase, "Medicaid Provider Taxes: The Gimmick That Exposes Flaws with Medicaid's Financing," Mercatus Center, February 2016.

40. Government Accountability Office, "School-Meals Programs: USDA Has Enhanced Controls, but Additional Verification Could Help Ensure Legitimate Program Access," GAO-14-262, May 2014, p. 15.

41. Government Accountability Office, "School-Meals Programs: USDA Has Enhanced Controls, but Additional Verification Could Help Ensure Legitimate Program Access," GAO-14-262, May 2014, p. 9. A scandal in Chicago Public Schools made this clear. See Monica Eng and Joel Hood, "School Free-Lunch Program Dogged by Abuses at CPS," *Chicago Tribune*, January 13, 2012.

42. Monica Eng and Joel Hood, "School Free-Lunch Program Dogged by Abuses at CPS," *Chicago Tribune*, January 13, 2012.

43. U.S. Department of Agriculture, Office of Inspector General, "FNS -National School Lunch and School Breakfast Programs," April 2015, p. 4.

44. Chris Edwards and Nicole Kaeding, "Federal Government Cost Overruns," DownsizingGovernment.org, Cato Institute, September 1, 2015.

45. Patricia Sullivan, "Arlington County to Hire Independent Contractor to Review $1 Million Bus Stop," *The Washington Post*, June 24, 2013.

46. Chris Edwards, "Update on Arlington's $1 Million Bust Stop," DownsizingG overnment.org, Cato Institute, June 26, 2013.

47. Randal O'Toole, *Romance of the Rails: Why the Passenger Trains We Love Are Not the Transportation We Need* (Washington, DC: Cato Institute, 2018), p. 217.

48. Government Accountability Office, "Opportunities to Reduce Potential Duplication in Government Programs, Save Tax Dollars, and Enhance Revenue," GAO-11-318SP, March 2011, p. 48.

49. Eliot Brown, "Complex Design, Political Disputes Send World Trade Center Rail Hub's Cost Soaring," *The Wall Street Journal*, September 3, 2014.

50. David B. Walker, *The Rebirth of Federalism: Slouching toward Washington* (New Jersey: Chatham House Publishers, 1995), p. 238.

51. John Kincaid, "The Eclipse of Dual Federalism by One-Way Cooperation Federalism," *Arizona State Law Journal* 49, no. 3 (Fall 2017): 1070.

52. James Sherk, "Repealing the Davis-Bacon Act Would Save Taxpayers $10.9 Billion," Heritage Foundation, February 14, 2011.

53. AECOM and Build America Investment Initiative for the Department of the Treasury, "40 Proposed U.S. Transportation and Water Infrastructure Projects of Major Economic Significance," December 2016, p. 7.

54. Associated General Contractors of Alaska, *The Alaska Contractor*, Fall 2012, p. 10.

55. Chris Edwards, "The Federal Emergency Management Agency: Floods, Failures, and Federalism," DownsizingGovernment.org, Cato Institute, December 1, 2014.

56. Economist Wallace Oates notes that even aside from the possibility of inter-jurisdictional migration, the optimal level of public services will vary from place to place because preferences vary from place to place. But Oates and other economists favoring aid believe that that factor is balanced by other factors favoring centralized provision. Wallace E. Oates, "An Essay on Fiscal Federalism," *Journal of Economic Literature* 37, no. 3 (September 1999): 1124.

57. Executive Order no. 12612.

58. *New State Ice Co. v. Liebmann*, 285 U.S. 262 (1932).

59. Adam Freedman, *A Less Perfect Union: The Case for States' Rights* (New York: Broadside Books, 2015).

60. Adam Freedman, *A Less Perfect Union: The Case for States' Rights* (New York: Broadside Books, 2015), p. 235.

61. For example, see D. Bradford Hunt, *Blueprint for Disaster: The Unraveling of Chicago Public Housing* (Chicago: University of Chicago Press, 2009).

62. Randal O'Toole, *Romance of the Rails: Why the Passenger Trains We Love Are Not the Transportation We Need* (Washington, DC: Cato Institute, 2018).

63. Roger Pilon, "Federalism, Then and Now," *inFocus Quarterly* (Washington, DC: Jewish Policy Center, 2015), p. 4.

64. Roger Pilon, "Federalism, Then and Now," *inFocus Quarterly* (Washington, DC: Jewish Policy Center, 2015), p. 4.

65. James Madison, Federalist no. 51.

66. Executive Order no. 12612.

67. Wallace Oates quoting Robert Inman and Daniel Rubinfeld in Wallace E. Oates, "An Essay on Fiscal Federalism," *Journal of Economic Literature* 37, no. 3 (September 1999): 1138.

68. U.S. Bureau of Economic Analysis, National Income and Product Accounts, Table 3.3, https://apps.bea.gov/itable/index.cfm.

69. Chung-Lae Cho and Deil S. Wright, "Perceptions of Federal Aid Impacts on State Agencies: Patterns, Trends, and Variations Across the 20th Century," *Publius: The Journal of Federalism* 37, no. 1 (Winter 2007): 111.

70. James L. Buckley, *Saving Congress from Itself: Emancipating the States and Empowering Their People* (New York: Encounter Books, 2014), p. xii.

71. Richard A. Epstein and Mario Loyola, "The United State of America," *The Atlantic*, July 31, 2014.

72. John Kincaid, "The Eclipse of Dual Federalism by One-Way Cooperation Federalism," *Arizona State Law Journal* 49, no. 3 (Fall 2017): 1074.

73. Quoted in Stanley Kurtz, "The Politics of the Administrative State," www.nationalreview.com, January 8, 2018.

74. The Founders thought that a republican form of government had popular rule, the rule of law, and was not a monarchy. Edwin Meese, Matthew Spalding, and David F. Forte, *The Heritage Guide to the Constitution* (Washington, DC: Regnery Publishing, 2005), p. 282.

75. Adam Freedman, *A Less Perfect Union: The Case for States' Rights* (New York: Broadside Books, 2015), p. 219.

76. Chung-Lae Cho and Deil S. Wright, "Perceptions of Federal Aid Impacts on State Agencies: Patterns, Trends, and Variations Across the 20th Century," *Publius: The Journal of Federalism* 37, no. 1 (Winter 2007).

77. The marble cake metaphor was coined by political scientist Morton Grodzins.

78. Ronald Reagan, "Budget Message of the President," *Budget of the U.S. Government, Fiscal Year 1983* (Washington, DC: Government Printing Office, February 1982), p. M22.

79. James C. Capretta, "A New Safety Net: Medicaid," American Enterprise Institute, February 2017.

80. Advisory Commission on Intergovernmental Relations, "The Federal Role in the Federal System: The Dynamics of Growth," no. A-86, June 1981, p. 95.

81. Steven M. Teles, "Kludgeocracy in America," *National Affairs*, Fall 2013.

82. Richard Nathan provides many examples in Richard P. Nathan, "Updating Theories of American Federalism," in *Intergovernmental Management for the Twenty-First Century* (Washington, DC: Brookings Institution, 2008). Adam Freedman also provides numerous examples in Adam Freedman, *A Less Perfect Union: The Case for States' Rights* (New York: Broadside Books, 2015).

83. Robert W. Poole, Jr., *Rethinking America's Highways: A 21st-Century Vision for Better Infrastructure* (Chicago: University of Chicago Press, 2018), p. 7.

84. Robert W. Poole, Jr., *Rethinking America's Highways: A 21st-Century Vision for Better Infrastructure* (Chicago: University of Chicago Press, 2018), p. 35.

85. Robert W. Poole, Jr., *Rethinking America's Highways: A 21st-Century Vision for Better Infrastructure* (Chicago: University of Chicago Press, 2018), p. 40.

86. Randal O'Toole, *Romance of the Rails: Why the Passenger Trains We Love Are Not the Transportation We Need* (Washington, DC: Cato Institute, 2018), p. 136.

87. Transportation Research Board—National Research Council, Special Report no. 258, *Contracting for Bus and Demand-Responsive Transit Services: A Survey of*

U.S. Practice and Experience (Washington, DC: National Academy Press, 2001), p. 35.

88. Chris Edwards, "Medicaid Reforms," DownsizingGovernment.org, Cato Institute, May 1, 2018.

89. Mark Warshawsky, "Mark Warshawsky: Millionaires on Medicaid," *Wall Street Journal*, January 6, 2014.

90. U.S. Bureau of Economic Analysis, National Income and Product Accounts, Table 3.3.

91. National Conference of State Legislatures, "State Balanced Budget Provisions," October 2010. In some states, the rules are loose, but all states generally balance their budgets based on tradition as well as interpretations of the formal rules.

92. For a discussion of the state rules, see Jared Walczak and Janelle Cammenga, "State Rainy Day Funds and the COVID-19 Crisis," Tax Foundation, April 7, 2020.

93. Barb Rosewicz, Justin Theal, and Joe Fleming, "States' Financial Reserves Hit Record Highs," Pew Charitable Trusts, March 18, 2020.

94. National Association of State Budget Officers, "The Fiscal Survey of States," Spring 2020, Table 24.

95. National Association of State Budget Officers, "The Fiscal Survey of States," Spring 2020, Table 26.

96. Census Bureau, "Annual Survey of State Government Tax Collections," 2019. The Census groups gross receipts taxes with sales taxes.

97. Bureau of Economic Analysis, National Income and Product Accounts, Table 3.20, https://apps.bea.gov/itable/index.cfm.

98. Kim S. Rueben and Megan Randall, "Revenue Volatility: How States Manage Uncertainty," Urban Institute, November 27, 2017.

99. Donald J. Boyd and Lucy Dadayan, "State Tax Revenue Forecasting Accuracy," Rockefeller Institute of Government, September 2014, Figure 1.

100. Kim S. Rueben and Megan Randall, "Revenue Volatility: How States Manage Uncertainty," Urban Institute, November 27, 2017.

101. Rick Mattoon and Leslie McGranahan, "State Tax Revenues over the Business Cycle: Patterns and Policy Responses," Federal Reserve Bank of Chicago, *Chicago Fed Letter*, June 2012.

102. Rick Mattoon and Leslie McGranahan, "State Tax Revenues over the Business Cycle: Patterns and Policy Responses," Federal Reserve Bank of Chicago, *Chicago Fed Letter*, June 2012, figure 2. See also figure 2 in Lucy Dadayan and Donald J. Boyd "Volatility in State Tax Revenues; Mounting Fiscal Uncertainties," Rockefeller Institute of Government, September 2017.

103. Rick Mattoon and Leslie McGranahan, "State Tax Revenues over the Business Cycle: Patterns and Policy Responses," Federal Reserve Bank of Chicago, *Chicago Fed Letter*, June 2012, Figure 3.

104. Erica York, "Summary of the Latest Federal Income Tax Data, 2020 Update," Tax Foundation, February 25, 2020.

105. Justin Garosi and Jason Sisney, "Top 1 Percent Pays Half of State Income Taxes," California Legislative Analyst's Office, December 4, 2014. And see New

York State, Department of Taxation and Finance, "Analysis of 2014 Personal Income Tax Returns," Table 21.

106. Census Bureau, "Annual Survey of State and Local Government Finances," www.census.gov/programs-surveys/gov-finances.html.

107. California Legislative Analyst's Office, "CalFacts 2018," p. 12.

108. Capital gains taxes are usually included in tallies of individual income taxes, but whether gains are properly considered income or not is subject to debate. See Chris Edwards, "Advantages of Low Capital Gains Tax Rates," Cato Institute Tax and Budget Bulletin no. 66, December 2012.

109. Mary Murphy, Akshay Iyengar, and Alexandria Zhang, "Tax Revenue Volatility Varies Across States, Revenue Streams," Pew Charitable Trusts, August 29, 2018.

110. Census Bureau, "Annual Survey of State Government Tax Collections," 2019, www.census.gov/programs-surveys/stc.html.

111. Chris Edwards, "Taxing Wealth and Capital Income," Cato Institute Tax and Budget Bulletin no. 85, August 2019.

112. Chris Edwards, "Tax Reform and Interstate Migration," Cato Institute Tax and Budget Bulletin no. 84, September 2018.

113. State corporate income taxes are perhaps the most inefficient sources of state revenue. Corporate investment is highly elastic across jurisdictions, and the state corporate tax raises little revenue compared to its high compliance costs. See Chris Edwards, "State Corporate Income Taxes Should Be Repealed," Cato Institute Tax and Budget Bulletin no. 19, April 2004.

Chapter 12

Give People a Vote That Counts, and They Will Vote for Fiscal Responsibility

Dwight Lee

INTRODUCTION

Voting is obviously an essential feature of a political process constrained by "the consent of the governed," a constraint stated in the Declaration of Independence, and which guided the founders at the Constitutional Convention in 1787. The founders made clear, however, that more than voting is needed if there is to be reasonable hope that government will use its coercive powers responsibly. Those constraints put substantive restrictions on what the federal government can do no matter how many voted for it to be done, and procedural requirements dispersed governing powers over three different branches of government and the states.[1] The purpose was for the executive, legislative, and judicial branches of the federal government to limit themselves by making it possible for the decisions of each branch to be negated or modified by decisions in the other two. Indeed, the only federal officeholders that voters could elect directly were members of the U.S. House of Representatives, with senators being chosen by their state legislatures until the 17th Amendment allowed voters to elect them directly in 1913. The president and vice president have never been elected directly by popular vote, but by electors chosen by the states as specified in Article II, Section 1 of the Constitution. This process was altered somewhat by Amendment 12 in 1804, which is referred to as the Electoral College even though that term is not found in the Constitution.[2] Federal judicial appointments are made by the president subject to the advice and consent of the Senate. Terms such as "the tyranny of the majority" and "the violence of majority faction" were commonly used by John Adams, James Madison and Alexander Hamilton and other founders to justify their unwillingness to rely solely on voters to limit irresponsible government actions.

The recently developed branch of economics known as public choice has expanded our understanding of why we can't depend solely on voting to restrain government actions. Public choice economics begins with the observation that as the size of the electorate increases, it becomes less likely that any one vote will determine the election's outcome. This has two troublesome consequences. The first is that voters have little motivation to become informed on political issues and candidates because there is by now only the tiniest probability that an individual vote will have any effect on the decisions being made. Voters may know, for example, that maintaining air quality is more important to them and their families than saving a nickel a gallon on gasoline. But the decision each makes on where to buy gasoline is 100% decisive, and their decision on which political candidate to vote for has effectively no influence on what environmental policies are enacted. Thus we can expect voters to be far more informed on where to get the cheapest gasoline than on which candidates' policy proposals are more effective at reducing air pollution. This explains why the evidence is overwhelming that most voters have little information about candidates' positions on the issues and even less on the issues themselves, a phenomenon which we refer to as rational voter ignorance.[3] This ignorance makes it easy for politicians to convince large numbers of voters that, for example, social injustice can be reduced by spending more money on new and existing government programs, subsidies, and transfers, although these already comprise well over 60% of the federal budget. As this chapter is being written, well over a year before the next presidential election in November 2020, aspiring presidential candidates are promising unprecedented increases in federal spending for a host of noble sounding policies that, of course, can be funded by increasing taxes on the rich. Seldom do these politicians say anything about increasing the federal debt and passing it on to those yet unborn.[4]

Even uninformed voters aren't always completely naïve about such promises. Most surely suspect that the middle class will pay for much of any new government spending, and some may make the connection between the steady stream of budget deficits and the increasing federal debt that is being shifted to future generations. But this brings us to the second problem resulting from the miniscule probability that one vote will determine the outcome of an election. Many voters have been convinced that voting for candidates who favor expanding compassionate-sounding government programs and spending will help society's victims and punish their victimizers. They believe that this is the moral thing to do. Those voting for such programs will have no sense of responsibility for the unfortunate effects of their votes or the costly failures of the programs voted for. Their intentions are pure and noble and, anyway, an individual vote is only slightly more likely to determine what programs are enacted than a wish upon a star. Because of the miniscule probability of a single vote determining an election's outcome, voters are primarily motivated by the expressive satisfaction they receive from supporting a political outcome instead of by the instrumental satisfaction from expecting their vote to determine the outcome. Public choice economists refer to this as *expressive voting.*

Of course, many voters criticize government spending as excessive and express concern about federal debt, yet most would resist any move to reduce programs that benefit them and be thrilled when they are expanded. Why shouldn't conservatives feel good about voting for politicians who promise to expand government spending that benefits them when they know they will have to continue paying for the government spending progressive voters like? Lately politicians who in the past at least promised to reduce the federal budget deficit have largely dropped even the pretense of being fiscally conservative. Politicians in both parties know that once voters identify with a party or candidate they feel good about voting for, they are not strongly influenced by the particular policies their favored candidate supports.[5] With neither Republican nor Democratic politicians interested in reducing federal spending, expressive voters with very different political preferences can be thought of as two herds of lemmings voting to continue stampeding toward the same fiscal abyss with little awareness or sense of responsibility for the disaster that lies ahead.

Voting is only part of the problem, however. Many of the prevailing mores and understandings that empowered the Constitution to prevent government from going beyond reasonable limits have eroded over the years as more problems, real or imagined, are seen to justify government action. Critical to the Constitution's ability to limit government was not only requiring a reasonable level of agreement by the three branches of the federal government to exercise power, but also sharing of fiscal responsibility by state and local governments. For the United States' first 140-plus years, the federal government's peacetime tax receipts and expenditures were less than state and local tax receipts and expenditures, with federal spending never greater than 3.5% of GDP. Furthermore, the federal government did not engage in deficit spending except during wartime and sometimes during economic downturns. During the downturns, the deficits were due to reductions in tax receipts, not expenditures to pump up the economy. Indeed, after the Civil War the federal budget was in surplus from 1866 to 1893, and the debt incurred during the war was almost eliminated.

This fiscal responsibility of the federal government started to break down during the progressive era beginning in the late nineteenth century, as public opinion began slowly shifting in favor of the federal government taking on more activities. However, taxing and spending were greater at the state and local level than at the federal except during major wars until the great depression and it was close until after World War II. Though federal taxing and spending declining after World War II, spending has never since fallen below state and local levels.[6] For reasons that will become clear in this chapter, the increased concentration of taxation and spending at the federal government created incentives for more taxing, spending, and waste at all levels of government. Rationally ignorant and expressive voters do not explain all of this increased concentration, but the concentration does exacerbate the problems of such voting. The purpose of this chapter is to consider an admittedly radical constitutional reform that would fundamentally change political incentives in ways that greatly increase the ability of voters to impose fiscal discipline on all levels of government. And by voters, I mean those who vote both with their ballots and with their feet.

REVERSE REVENUE SHARING

I refer to my proposal as "reverse revenue sharing," and I have discussed it elsewhere.[7] Here I reintroduce the idea with particular attention to its effects on voting. Under this proposal, *all tax revenue is raised within the states, and each state must transfer the same percentage of its tax revenue to the federal government*. The percentage could be legislative adjusted in a true emergency, such as a legislatively declared war, as opposed to a ridiculous executive order to increase federal spending to reduce inflation before an upcoming election, and war would have to be determined at a constitutional level, but no state would be able to have its percentage reduced without the percentage for all states being reduced the same amount. A reasonable percentage would be in the range of 35 to 40%, which was about the percent of total government tax revenue the federal government raised during the first 140 plus years after the ratification of the U. S. Constitution.[8]

An obvious advantage of reverse revenue sharing is that it would increase the competition among the states, motivating them to tax more efficiently and do a better job providing services that their citizens value at lower cost than they do now. True, states already face competition as people vote with their feet by choosing to move to a state they believe would provide them a better economic climate. The problem is that this competition is now seriously attenuated by having to carry the largest portion of their tax burden with them—their federal tax burden. A less obvious advantage of reverse revenue sharing is that the information conveyed through votes (both with ballots and feet) would motivate state governments and the federal government to do a much better job of providing citizens with the government services they most value at far less cost than they do now.[9] I distinguish only between state and federal government and largely ignore local government and their taxes, although local taxing and spending decisions are important. I assume that states can structure the fiscal relationships between state and local government as they choose in response to the additional competition for residents and tax bases.

Voting with our ballots is important, with the caveats discussed above. As opposed to voting with ballots, however, when we vote with our feet our own decisions are 100% decisive. That overcomes the two distortions when voting with our ballots—rational voter ignorance and expressive voting. Since we are sure to get what we vote for when voting with our feet, the motivation is strong to become informed on the likely consequences of our votes. When mistakes will be made, state politicians will see people correcting those mistakes by taking their taxable efforts and assets elsewhere. Those politicians will also notice that influencing the decisions of foot voters with emotional rhetoric is not nearly as effective as it is with those voting with their ballots.

Reverse revenue sharing not only motivates more responsible and informed voting by raising the instrumental payoff to voting with our feet, it also dramatically alters the incentives for federal and state politicians to respond to the information transmitted by that voting to make more socially responsible taxing and spending decisions. As the next section shows, politicians at the federal level will become more responsible by doing less. Below we will see that reverse revenue sharing may result in state politicians doing more, but whether they do more or less, they will do it in ways that are far more creative and fiscally responsible than they are doing now. As my title promises, give people a vote that counts and they will vote for fiscal responsibility, and this means that politicians are far more likely to provide it.

MORE FISCAL RESPONSIBILITY AT THE FEDERAL LEVEL

Under reverse revenue sharing, the federal government would be motivated to restrict its spending to the efficient provision of those services which are most appropriately provided by a central government. There would be a strong incentive to avoid using federal money to help pay for services best provided by state and local governments or left to private provision. With the federal government dependent on a fixed percentage of the tax revenue the states raise, Congress would recognize the folly of providing federal money to help state governments pay for such things as bike paths, community swimming pools, public schools, street repairs, light-rail systems and diversity bureaucracies. If states don't think such things are worth financing with their own taxes, then why should the federal government fund them? Of course, many things are worth states spending money on, often in conjunction with local governments, such as education, police and fire protection, and highways. Under reverse revenue sharing the federal government would not be motivated to provide financial assistance for such things, since doing so would reduce the amount states raised in taxes, thus reducing the federal government's only source of revenue.

The federal government would be motivated to efficiently provide genuine public goods with nationwide benefits; such goods are not in the interest of any one state or consortium of states to finance. Such public goods would enhance the country's general productivity, which would be the most effective way for the federal government to increase its revenue. The opposite side of this coin would be strong federal resistance to maintaining, much less expanding, the host of income transfer programs that are the fastest-growing components of the federal budget, and a major source of reduced economic efficiency.

Well over 60% of the federal budget consists of money taken from some people in taxes and transferred to others. It is often the case that the transfers go back and forth between the same groups of people, leaving all of them worse off than if they could give up their transfers in return for not having to pay the taxes to finance the transfers to the others. The taxes to finance transfers invariably cost more than the revenue raised because of the deadweight loss (or excess burden) of taxation. This deadweight loss has been estimated to cost the economy in the range of \$0.30 to \$0.50 every time the federal government collects an additional dollar in tax revenue.[10] This deadweight loss is the result of distortions created by the tax that motivate people to make investment and consumption decisions that create less value than the decisions they would have made without the tax. And this doesn't include the rent-seeking costs that are spent to get and/or qualify for transfers, which can result in no net gain even for successful rent-seekers.[11] Also, the transfers are commonly used to finance activities that produce less wealth than would have been produced if the money had remained in the private sector and spent in response to market prices not distorted by political taxes and transfers. For example, consider federal transfers such as those paying farmers for growing cotton in the desert; that subsidize firms to produce corn-based ethanol, which does nothing to reduce global warming; that bail out companies that are too big to fail, thus making them even bigger the next time they fail; or that create dependency by the poor on government transfers by reducing the amount they receive if they make an effort to work their way out of poverty.

These transfers and subsidies are almost always the result of rent-seeking by organized interest groups that has been especially effective at the federal level. Federal politicians are now ideally positioned to make exchanges with interest groups with both capturing benefits—political contributions for politicians, and subsidies and transfers for interest groups—by spreading the costs thinly over the entire population. Under reverse revenue sharing, federal politicians would no longer see advantage in reducing the general economic productivity with special-interest subsidies and transfers when the only means of increasing federal revenue is by increasing productivity, not reducing it. They would also lose their enthusiasm for claiming with a straight face that they can lower the cost of healthcare, college tuition, green energy, electric cars, or bullet trains by increasing the subsidies they receive.

PROVIDING BETTER STATE SERVICES AT LOWER COSTS

Reverse revenue sharing would also create incentives for state governments to spend more selectively and efficiently. First, the need for state governments to raise more than a dollar to spend a dollar in their state would serve as a serious constraint on funding such projects as mass transit systems that cannot cover their operating costs, metropolitan highway systems to alleviate traffic congestion without also imposing highway tolls, building sports coliseums and stadiums for rich owners of professional sports teams with taxpayer dollars, and funding public schools directly rather than through educational vouchers.

With all taxation taking place at the state level, wasteful spending arising from special-interest influence would put a state at a noticeable disadvantage in the competition with other states. When, as is currently the case, the federal government raises most of the tax revenue, differences in tax burdens between the states are less important in deciding where to live and do business than they would be if states decided the entire tax burden. State taxes would probably rise under reverse revenue sharing because states would pick up some formerly federally funded programs. But the overall tax burden would surely drop because all tax revenue would be raised and spent in a far more competitive environment than is currently the case. Currently the federal government's transfers to the states serve to suppress the tax competition among states below what it would otherwise be. These transfers often come with mandates or incentives for the states to maintain or increase their own tax revenue. One can reasonably think of this arrangement as a tax cartel between the federal and state governments that makes it easier for all levels of government to squeeze more money out of taxpayers.

Not all state and local projects that are wasteful now would be eliminated or even scaled back under reverse revenue sharing because they would be provided at lower costs. One way the cost of state services can be reduced is through tax reform that lowers the deadweight loss of raising tax revenue to pay for those services. Few state tax systems are as convoluted or do more to distort economic decisions as the federal tax system, but they could still be significantly improved by the incentive of reverse revenue sharing. The problem with improving current tax codes is not lack of knowing how to do it. Any moderately intelligent seventh grader could come up with a better tax structure than those most states currently have. A broad base with low marginal tax rates is a good general rule, but one advantage of reverse revenue sharing is that each state is left to work out their own tax reforms given their situations and the feedback they receive from the competition between states.

State taxes and expenditures would quickly improve once reverse revenue sharing abolished the federal tax system. Without the federal tax, state taxpayers would be unable to reduce federal taxes by some percentage of their state and local taxes. This federal tax break artificially lowers the cost for states to increase taxes. Consider trash collection, tennis courts, golf courses, swimming pools, and parks provided and paid for by local taxes. And education shouldn't be overlooked. Better K–12 education at lower social costs cannot be achieved by allowing taxpayers to shift part of their state's education cost to taxpayers in other states. Without this tax distortion, public schools would face more competition from private schools, and the political ability of educational unions to resist school choice would be greatly weakened. The incentive for all state governments to raise the quality and lower the cost of all the services they provide increases as the competition they face from other states increases.

Today, each state competes against other states by rent-seeking for the federal government to spend more money on goods, services, and jobs in their state than their citizens pay in federal taxes. This attempt by states to free ride off the tax payments of other states is a clear example of negative-sum competition. It requires using labor and resources to capture existing wealth instead of increasing it. Even when a state wins the competition, it typically receives money for projects that cost more than they are worth to its taxpayers. But that doesn't eliminate a state's enthusiasm for entering such negative-sum competition. Taxpayers realize that they will be paying the same amount in federal taxes regardless of how much they get back. If Atlanta, for example, had not received federal spending for a downtown light-rail streetcar that has done more to motivate jokes than to provide useful transportation, some other city would be having all the laughs with a free ride on federal taxes paid by Georgians.

This negative-sum rent seeking among states would quickly be reduced and would probably cease entirely. Federal politicians would realize that funding state projects would cost them votes because such projects would be less valuable to their constituents than the public goods they could no longer provide.

With the federal government providing public goods primarily benefiting all states, as discussed in the previous section, each state would have an incentive to reduce its contribution to the funding of those goods, since that would have little effect on the general benefits provided, and each would benefit from the entire reduction in its contribution. The only way a state can achieve such a beneficial free ride under reverse revenue sharing, however, would be by reducing expenditures on wasteful state services and funding those services that are worth more than they cost as efficiently as possible, thus reducing both the tax revenue being raised and the amount sent to the federal government. We can expect more privatization of services, more school choice, and less union influence on the pay and perks of state employees, to name a few cost-saving possibilities that state and local politicians will find far more appealing than they do now.

WOULD REVERSE REVENUE SHARING STARVE GOVERNMENT?

Given the fiscal irresponsibility that characterizes our current political arrangement, any change that increases the fiscal responsibility of political decisions will be seen by political activists as "starving" government. Once large numbers of people learn to see governments at every level, particularly at the federal level, as the means of providing them benefits at the expense of others, any suggestion for internalizing these negative externalities will be widely resisted as unjust and unacceptable. Internalizing negative political externalities is another way of describing reverse revenue sharing.

But that explains why reverse revenue sharing would not reduce the amount of wealth available to accomplish desirable and noble objectives. Quite the contrary, given the incentives to leave more resources in the private sector and eliminate many of the externalities that create government waste, there would be more wealth produced and better use made of that wealth. Despite the impression so many people have, reducing the size of government is not the same thing as reducing desirable things for which politicians excel at taking credit.

Consider the noble objective of reducing poverty. The most effective way to reduce poverty has always been by producing more wealth, not transferring existing wealth from the rich to the poor. With this in mind, it is important to acknowledge that government can play an important role in poverty reduction by establishing an environment in which markets can flourish by doing such things as protecting private property, enforcing the rules of voluntary exchange, establishing means of adjudicating disputes, providing basic infrastructure, securing our borders against military invasion, and protecting citizens from domestic crime. Doing those things is far more effective at (1) providing the poor with the incentives and opportunities to improve their economic well-being with productive efforts, while also (2) enhancing their sense of purpose and dignity, which is seldom achieved by receiving an unearned monthly check from a government agency. Does anyone who understands that consumption comes before production really believe that poverty would be less in America today if the federal government had started the War on Poverty in 1870 with the same percentage of GDP and the same terms as in 1964? The stipulation at the time was that recipient payments would be significantly reduced for those who improved their own economic well-being, and that would be wealth-destroying in any era.[12]

People tend to forget that public welfare crowds out private charities that would otherwise be helping the poor.[13] As Milton Friedman pointed out, "the heyday of laissez-faire, the middle and late nineteenth century in Britain and the United States, saw an extraordinary proliferation of private eleemosynary organizations and institutions."[14] And private charities are better at motivating recipients to appreciate the help they receive, and feel an obligation to make the best of it to help themselves, than does the promise of a steady check from an impersonal government bureaucracy.

The federal government has important responsibilities, such as providing national defense and controlling pollution that extends over several states, but which could be done better and at less cost if political arrangements provided the government decision-makers with strong incentives to consider the cost effectiveness of their efforts. Reverse revenue sharing would provide such incentives. It would also give the federal government strong incentives to quit spending on many of the things that governments shouldn't be doing, or which would be better done by the states.

CONCLUSION

Clearly, moving to a fiscal arrangement such as reverse revenue sharing would be controversial. People have made decisions that make sense only under the assumption that the federal government will continue to maintain spending on existing programs at current or increasing levels, which it cannot do under the proposed rules. Reverse revenue sharing is one of the efficient ways to end the federal government's unsustainable fiscal practices, even if it would upset some plans.[15]

People notice immediately when they stop receiving "free" or subsidized goods and services they've come to expect. It takes them longer to recognize that they are paying less in taxes to pay for "free" and subsidized goods for others. Eventually, however, it would be noticed under reverse revenue sharing that the payoff from producing more wealth through productive market activity has risen and the payoff from capturing existing wealth through wasteful political activity has fallen.

I don't deny that a transition to reverse revenue sharing would create social conflict. So will the unsustainability of existing federal fiscal practices. The current path of federal fiscal recklessness and identity politics is increasingly pitting more groups against each other in negative-sum political competition that elevates the level of political and social conflict. The inevitable result of trying to continue delusionary federal fiscal policy will be increasingly hateful clashes between interest groups and social justice advocates as government starts defaulting on promises that have become seen as righteously deserved entitlements.

My proposal is radical, and it will be dismissed by many as too radical to be taken seriously. Yet I present it with far more seriousness than should be given to political promises that government will soon adopt fiscal responsibility. This is not because I believe reverse revenue sharing is the only, or even the best, possible proposal for effective fiscal reform. For one thing, it doesn't address critical concerns, such as the federal government resorting to regulations to force state and local governments to finance spending programs, or having the Federal Reserve buy treasury bonds to continue finance the existing level of federal spending, although it's not clear why anyone would buy treasury bonds from a federal government that could borrow freely, but that depends on someone else to pay its bills. I would welcome other proposals for motivating more responsible fiscal policy at the federal and state levels, or for improving reverse revenue sharing.

There are three reasons for taking the arguments for reverse revenue sharing seriously even though it would depart radically from the usual political and fiscal arrangements. First, it forces consideration of fundamental distortions in current fiscal arrangements that will soon have to be addressed to avoid a fiscal collapse. Second, our Constitution served us well for over 140 years and could continue to do so if somehow we can start restoring the political norms of acceptable government fiscal responsibilities that existed through the nineteenth century and into the twentieth. Third, politicians from both major parties could help restore those political norms by immediately acknowledging their joint fiscal recklessness and uniting in efforts to make responsible policy adjustments before the federal fiscal crisis begins to manifest truly painful symptoms. But the response I recommend may not happen. So I have put forth my argument for reverse revenue sharing in the same spirit that motivated Milton Friedman (1982, pp. xiii–xiv) to express what he saw as a basic function of academics:

> There is enormous inertia—a tyranny of the status quo—in private and especially government arrangements. Only a crisis—actual or perceived—produces real change. When that crisis occurs, the actions that are taken depend on the ideas that are lying around. That, I believe, is our basic function: to develop alternatives to existing policies, to keep them alive and available until the politically impossible becomes politically inevitable.

I would add that putting forth politically infeasible policies, such as the one just discussed, may increase the probability of less politically infeasible proposals, better than those they would replace, becoming feasible.

NOTES

1. See: Wandred, K. (2019).
2. A group of electors was referred to as a college at the time.
3. See: Somin (2016).
4. This doesn't mean that these candidates are unconcerned about the dangers of excessive federal debt. For example, Elizabeth Warren (2019) is concerned that private debt is likely to lead to a recession or worse and that she will address the problem by canceling student loan debt, reducing the cost of household debt, and mobilizing the industrial base with a 2 trillion dollar investment in her Green Manufacturing Plan. She never mentions government debt as a problem even though all her recommendations would directly increase the federal debt except for those that increase the cost of doing business, which will likely indirectly increase the federal debt. Fairness compels me to point out that few politicians in Washington from either party seem concerned about the increasing federal debt. See Davidson and Hilsenath (2019).
5. Based on numerous studies Mason (2018, pp. 20–21) states "more often than not, citizens do not choose which party to support based on policy opinion; they alter their policy opinion according to which party they support." Of course, this is consistent with rationally ignorant voters not knowing much about what policies their favored candidates will support if elected, or what the effect of those policies will be if enacted.
6. See: Michael Schuyler, "A Short History of Government Taxing and Spending in the United States," Tax Foundation (2014), Table 1. https://taxfoundation.org/short-history-government-taxing-and-spending-united-states/.
7. See: Dwight Lee, "A Case for Fiscal Federalism," *Intercollegiate Review* 31, no. 1 (1996): 37-45, as well as J. R. Clark and Dwight Lee, "Tax Reform as a Discovery Process," in *For Your Own Good: Taxes, Paternalism, and Fiscal Discrimination in the Twenty-First Century*, ed. Adam Hoffer and Todd Nesbit (Arlington, VA: Mercatus Center), 289–302.
8. The one exception to the prohibition of federal taxation concerns wars. But for federal taxation to be used to finance a war it would have to be declared by both branches of Congress, as now stated (but routinely ignored) in Article I, Section 8,

Clause 11. What is now referred to as the commerce clause (Article I, Section 8, Clause 3) would prevent states from imposing tariffs on, or otherwise restrict, the importation of commercial goods and services from other states. In addition to Lee (1985) another article by Clark and Lee (2018) make use of some of the same arguments discussed here for the purpose of focusing attention on tax reform.

9. There are some parallels between my discussion and that of Tiebout (1956). Tiebout considers local governments and argues that they are very sensitive to citizen's preferences. He doesn't consider, however, any fundamental change in the location of taxation as I do with reverse revenue sharing, which is critical to the efficiencies I discuss.

10. Browning, Edgar K., *Stealing from Each Other: How the Welfare State Robs Americans of Money and Spirit* (Westport, Connecticut: Praeger, 2008).

11. See: Tullock (1975) for an explanation and examples.

12. Even if welfare programs are doing more to reduce poverty in American than increase it, there are serious concerns as to how sustainable they are. See: https://www.nytimes.com/roomfordebate/2015/07/30/the-next-50-years-for-medicare-and-medicaid/medicare-and-medicaid-are-unsustainable-without-quick-action.

See also: Autor (2011).

13. See: Schansberg, (1996). See also Tanner (2003).

14. See: Friedman (2002, p. 190).

15. See: John Merrifield and Barry Poulson (eds), *A Fiscal Cliff* (Washington, DC: Cato Institute, 2020).

REFERENCES

Autor, D. (2011). The unsustainable rise in the disability rolls in the United States: Causes, consequences and policy options. NBER Working Paper No. 17697, (December).

Browning, E. (2008). *Stealing from Each Other: How the Welfare State Robs Americans of Money and Spirit* (Westport, CT: Praeger).

Clark, J. R. and Lee, D. (2018). Tax reform as a discovery process. In Hoffer, Adam and Todd Nesbit (eds.), *For Your Own Good: Taxes, Paternalism, and Fiscal Discrimination in the Twenty-First Century* (Arlington, VA. Mercatus Center): 289–302.

Davidson, K. and Hilsenath J. (2019). Washington puts aside fears and embraces debt. *Wall Street Journal* (June 14): 1 & 11.

Friedman, M. (2002). *Capitalism and Freedom* (Chicago: University of Chicago Press): pp. xiii–xiv.

Lee, Dwight (1985). Reverse revenue sharing: A modest proposal. *Public Choice,* 45 (3): 279–89.

Mason, L. (2018). *Uncivil Agreement: How Politics Become Our Identity* (Chicago: The University of Chicago Press).

Schansberg, E. (1996). *Poor Policy: How Poor Government Policy Harms the Poor* (Boulder, CO: West Press, Inc.).

Somin, I. (2016). *Democracy and Political Ignorance* (Stanford: Stanford University Press).

Tanner, M. (2003). *The Poverty of Welfare: Helping Others in Civil Society* (Washington, DC: Cato).

Tiebout, Charles M. (1956). A pure theory of local taxation. *Journal of Political Economy* 64 (5): 416–24.

Tullock, Gordon (1975). The transitional gains trap. *Bell Journal of Economics* 6 (2): 671–78.

Wandred, K. (2019). What features of the U.S. Constitution had distrust of a democracy (updated May 10). https://www.theclassroom.com/features-constitution-distrust-democracy-20581.html.

Warren, E. (2019). The coming economic crash—and how to stop it. *Medium Election 2020* (July 22). https://medium.com/@teamwarren/the-coming-economic-crash-and-how-to-stop-it-355703da148b.

Chapter 13

Florida's Fiscal Conservatism

Randall G. Holcombe

INTRODUCTION

The twentieth century was characterized by government growth at all levels of government. While government spending growth in the United States has slowed since the 1990s, governments continue to spend more than they collect in tax revenues, resulting in financial stress which is felt especially acutely at the state and local levels, where governments cannot print their own money to finance their debts.[1] The state of Florida stands out as an example of fiscal conservatism and fiscal responsibility. Inflation-adjusted state government expenditures per person in 2020 are at the same level they were in the mid-1990s, Because of income growth, state government expenditures are a shrinking share of income. State government debt has also declined substantially in the 2010s, albeit after a big increase during the Great Recession in the previous decade.

FACTS ABOUT FLORIDA'S FISCAL CONSERVATISM

Figure 13.1 summarizes the main fact behind Florida's fiscal conservatism: Inflation-adjusted state government appropriations per person were at about the same level at the end of the 2010s as they were in the mid-1990s.[2] Appropriations per person in the 2019–2020 budget were $4,583.72 (in 2020 dollars). Inflation-adjusted appropriations per person in 1994–1995 were $4,727.95. State government expenditures were slightly lower in 2020 than they were 25 years earlier, after adjusting for inflation and population growth. In an era when government expenditures seem to continually rise

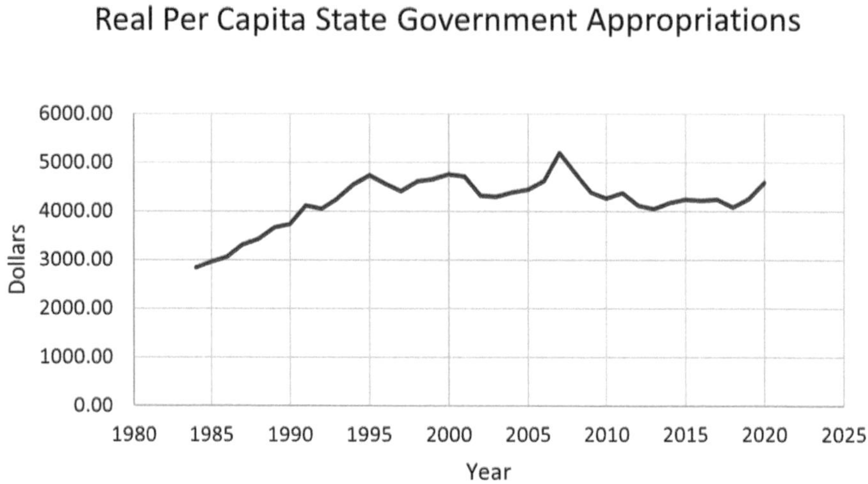

Figure 13.1 Real Per Capita State Government Appropriations. *Source*: Table 1, Column 3.

everywhere, Florida offers a rare example of not just slow growth, but expenditure reduction.[3]

Because of income growth over the period, state government spending as a share of income has fallen from more than 11% in 1995–1996 to 8.4% in 2017. Figure 13.1 shows that this has not always been the case. Appropriations were rising steadily until the mid-1990s before they leveled off for a quarter of a century. Inflation-adjusted appropriations per person were $2,828 in 1983–1984 and rose to $4,728 in 1994–1995, an increase of 67% in just over a decade. In light of that history, it is all the more remarkable that Florida has been able to hold the line on expenditures for a quarter of a century. For the United States as a whole, state government expenditures per person, adjusted for inflation, increased by 40.6% from 1994–1995 to 2017–2018.

Florida's local governments have not been as fiscally conservative as its state government. They have grown at about the same rate as the national average. When comparing total expenditures across states, it may be more appropriate to compare state and local expenditures because the ratio of state to state and local expenditures varies considerably across states. Spending in some states is much more centralized than in others. In 2015 Florida's state and local expenditures per person ranked fourth from the lowest among states, with Arizona, Tennessee, and Georgia the only states that spent less.[4] In 1997, Florida's state and local expenditure was 92.8% of the national average. By 2015 Florida's state and local expenditure was 80% of the national average. The national average of inflation-adjusted state and local government spending per person rose by 29.6% from 1997 to 2015, while it rose by 11.8%

in Florida. Inflation-adjusted per-person state government expenditure in Florida fell from $4,400 to $4,231 during that period, so all of the increase in Florida's state and local expenditures was due to an increase in local expenditures. The approximately flat level of state government expenditures was not due to a shift of expenditures from the state to the local level. Combined, state and local expenditures grew less than half as much as the national average.

Florida also has been fiscally conservative in its issuance of debt. Figure 13.2 shows inflation-adjusted gross state debt through 2017. The figure shows a sharp increase in debt as the housing bubble peaks and then bursts, but then a sharp decline after 2008. Figure 13.1 shows a peak in appropriations around the same time as the state (and nation) slid into recession. Florida's state government, which receives substantial revenue from documentary stamp fees that are assessed when real estate is sold, suffered because of the decline in real estate prices and sales. But Figure 13.2 shows that the state did not allow the resulting increase in debt to linger. Debt in 2017 was at about the same level it was in 2005.

Florida's $28.82 billion in state government debt in 2017 comes out to $1,392 per person. Five states have lower levels of debt per person than Florida, placing it among the lowest states in debt. Florida's state government pension plan was 79% funded in 2016, ranking it 13th among states. More than half of the states had pension plans that were less than 50% funded. Unfunded pension liabilities are a major source of fiscal stress for state governments. Florida also ranks fourth from the bottom in state government employees per capita.[5]

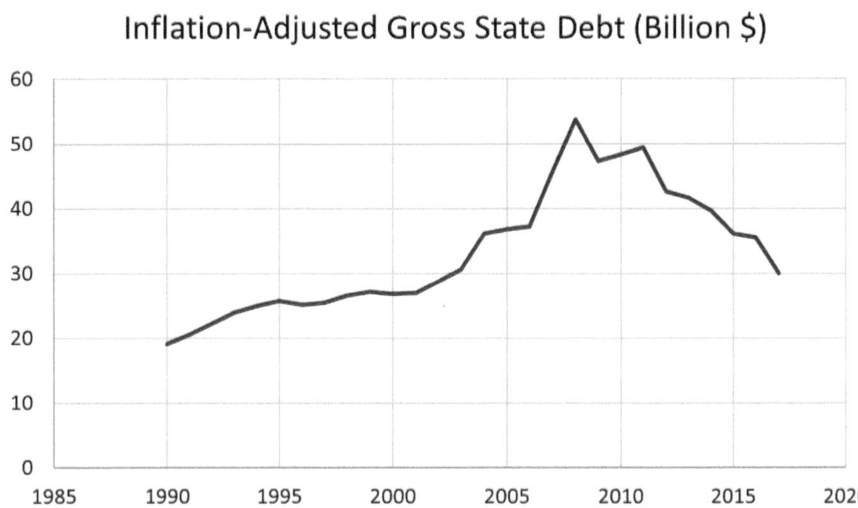

Figure 13.2 Inflation-Adjusted Gross State Debt (Billions $). *Source*: United States Census Bureau, Annual Survey of State Government Finances.

The basic facts about Florida's fiscal conservatism are documented in these two graphs. Florida's state government has not increased inflation-adjusted expenditures per person for a quarter of a century and has held the

Table 13.1 Florida's State Government Appropriations

Year	*Appropriations (Billion $)*	*Real Per Capita Appropriations ($)*	*Annual Change (%)*
1983–84	11.9	2,828	
1984–85	13.3	2,951	4.35
1985–86	14.7	3,054	3.48
1986–87	16.6	3,297	7.98
1987–88	18.5	3,427	3.95
1988–89	21.3	3,667	6.99
1989–90	23.2	3,729	1.68
1990–91	27.7	4,107	10.15
1991–92	28.9	4,045	−1.50
1992–93	31.7	4,244	4.92
1993–94	36.5	4,542	7.01
1994–95	38.8	4,728	4.10
1995–96	39.1	4,556	−3.64
1996–97	39.8	4,400	−3.42
1997–98	43.3	4,605	4.66
1998–99	45.4	4,656	1.11
1999–00	48.7	4,755	2.13
2000–01	51.0	4,703	−1.10
2001–02	48.5	4,314	−8.27
2002–03	50.3	4,287	−0.62
2003–04	53.5	4,381	2.18
2004–05	57.3	4,441	1.37
2005–06	63.1	4,619	4.02
2006–07	73.9	5,188	12.30
2007–08	71.5	4,772	−8.01
2008–09	66.2	4,381	−8.20
2009–10	66.5	4,256	−2.84
2010–11	70.5	4,373	2.73
2011–12	69.1	4,110	−6.00
2012–13	70.0	4,042	−1.67
2013–14	74.1	4,166	3.06
2014–15	77.0	4,231	1.58
2015–16	78.7	4,217	−0.34
2016–17	82.3	4,234	4.13
2017–18	82.4	4,083	−3.58
2018–19	88.7	4,248	4.04
2019–20	99.1	4,584	7.91
2020–21	93.2	4,206	−8.00
2021–22	101.5	4,221	0.89

Source: Appropriations compiled from annual budget reports in the *Tallahassee Democrat*. Real Per Capita Appropriations and the Percentage Change were calculated by the author using population data from the Census Bureau and CPI statistics from the Bureau of Labor Statistics.

line on state government debt. Figure 13.1 was composed from the data that appears in table 13.1. The table documents the substantial increases in the budget prior to 1996: 8% in 1996–1997; 7% in 1998–1999; more than 10% in 1990–1991; and 7% in 1993–1994. The trend changes abruptly in 1995–1996 with two consecutive decreases and a leveling off of expenditures afterward. The 2006–2007 budget year stands out because of the 12% increase, but it is followed by two consecutive years of 8% decreases. One other thing that stands out is the final year in the table, which saw an increase of almost 8%.

The 2019–2020 fiscal year is noteworthy because it was the first year of Governor Ron DeSantis's term. The 2020–2021 budget fall by almost 8% and under Governor DeSantis has modest increases of less than 1% per year over the next two years. It appears that the change in political leadership had little impact on Florida's fiscally conservative state budgeting.

MAJOR BUDGET PRIORITIES

The three areas of education, Medicaid, and transportation constitute more than 70% of the state's budget, and represent areas that are high priorities in state spending. Table 13.2 shows a history of these three areas as a percentage of Florida's total state government budget. One thing that stands out in looking at these figures is that Medicaid has taken an increasing share of the state's budget over the decades. Another thing that stands out is that as Medicaid expenditures have increased as a share of the state's budget, these other two categories have not decreased.

Medicaid expenditures were slightly more than 10% of Florida's state government expenditures in the 1990–1991 fiscal year and nearly tripled to 30% in the next two decades. Medicaid expenditures increased by 47% from the 1990–1991 fiscal year to the 1995–1996 fiscal year—a period of only five

Table 13.2 Florida's Education, Medicaid, and Transportation Expenditures as a Percentage of Total State Government Expenditures

Year	*Education*	*Medicaid*	*Transportation*
2017/18	26.7	32.1	12.8
2016/17	28.1	33.1	11.9
2015/16	28.4	32.2	12.1
2010/11	28.2	30.0	9.4
2005/06	27.6	23.8	12.9
2000/01	28.2	15.7	13.0
1995/96	23.8	15.3	11.9
1990/91	25.4	10.4	7.3

Source: National Association of State Budget Officers

years. It would be easy to conclude that the increase in Medicaid expenditures during that period was the major cause of total expenditure increases over that period that are shown in figure 13.1. Yet total expenditures leveled off after the 1995–1996 budget year, even as Medicaid expenditures increased by 96% to 30% of the state budget by 2010–2011. Despite an increasing share of the state budget going to Medicaid, inflation-adjusted total state expenditures per person did not rise.

The fact that the state government was able to hold the line on total state spending even as rising Medicaid expenditures squeezed the budget reinforces the evidence on Florida's fiscal conservatism. Meanwhile, despite rising Medicaid expenditures, spending on education and transportation were not reduced as a share of the budget. Education expenditures fluctuated around 27% of state expenditures through most of the history shown in table 13.2, and transportation expenditures have remained around 12%.

Note that when Medicaid expenditures showed substantial increases from 1990–1991 to 1995–1996, not only did total expenditures rise, education expenditures were crowded out and fell from 25.4% of total spending to 23.8%. As Medicaid spending continued to rise through 2010–2011, not only did total spending level out, education bounced back to 28.2% of the budget—higher than it was in 1990–1991. It has remained at about that level since, although with a slight decrease in the most recent fiscal year shown in the table. These figures show that Florida's state government has been able to hold the line on expenditure increases, even when pressured by rising Medicaid expenditures. The major spending categories of education and transportation have not seen spending cuts despite the increases in Medicaid spending.

These figures also show the threat that Medicaid expenditures represent to state government budgets, in Florida and in all states. Medicaid expenditures rose from slightly more than 10% of state government spending in Florida in 1990–1991 to about a third of state government expenditures in 2017–2018. Despite that increase, Florida remains in good fiscal condition, but many states face serious fiscal problems. Controlling Medicaid expenditures must be one of the things states need to do to get their finances under control.

STATE GOVERNMENT PENSION LIABILITY

One of the fiscal challenges facing many states is unfunded state government pension liabilities. According to the Pew Charitable Trusts, Florida is in relatively good shape with regard to its pensions, although the state's pensions are not fully funded. Florida's state government pension plans were 79% funded in 2016, according to Pew,[6] compared to a national average of 66%. South Dakota and Wisconsin stand out in this category because their state government pension plans are approximately fully funded. Five states have pension plans that are less than 50% funded. Kentucky, at 31%, and Illinois, at 36%, are at the bottom. Another eight states have pension plans less than 60% funded, so 13 states in total are funded at less than 60%.

Those states face additional budgetary challenges because in addition to having to meet current expenditures, they will have to also pay for these unfunded liabilities in the future unless they default on their pension promises. While Florida could improve in this area, the state is above the national average and far from facing a pension crisis.

One thing Florida has done to try to limit its pension liabilities is establish an optional investment plan as an alternative to the state's defined-benefit pension plan. The investment plan is a defined-contribution pension plan that leaves the state with no unfunded liabilities for pensions in that plan. The state's defined-benefit plan, as is the case with most states, pays retirees a pension based on their salaries when they were working and the length of time they were employed and enrolled in the plan. States have run into pension funding problems because they have not set aside enough money to pay the promised pensions, leaving unfunded liabilities. Florida's recently introduced defined-contribution plan puts money into an investment account for those who participate, and their pension amounts are determined by how much is in their accounts when they retire. There is no unfunded liability.

There has been some effort on the part of legislators to require that all new hires enroll in the defined-contribution plan, but they have not been successful, and new hires have the option of enrolling in either plan. Most choose the defined-benefit plan, so at this point, the introduction of the defined-contribution plan has had a minimal effect on Florida's unfunded pension liabilities. Because the legislature has a long history of fiscal conservatism, one would expect continuing attempts on the part of the legislature to push more state employees—and maybe all of them—into the defined-contribution plan.

While Florida is not facing a crisis in unfunded pension liabilities, a move toward defined-contribution plans rather than defined-benefit plans is something all states should consider to gain control of their pension liabilities. The private sector has made major moves in this direction, and governments have been slow to follow. The problem with defined-benefit plans in the public sector is that current legislatures have a substantial incentive to offer increasingly generous pension benefits without raising contributions or taxes. Doing so promises spending in the future, when current workers retire, so it costs nothing now and passes on the liability to future legislatures. Pay increases, which a defined-contribution plan would effectively implement, take money out of the current budget. Politically, it is tempting to offer higher defined-benefit pensions, which cost nothing now, rather than pay increases. This has produced the crisis of unfunded pension liabilities that many states face.

Defined-contribution pension plans overcome this problem because pension funding occurs in the current budget year rather than being a promise to pay in future years.

FLORIDA'S SALES TAX

Because Florida is one of a few states that does not have a personal income tax, Florida's state government relies heavily on its sales tax as the state's major source of state tax revenues. The state sales tax rate is 6%, and local governments have the option of adding to it, which most parts of the state have done (local sales taxes do not generate additional state revenues). While intended as a retail sales tax, many retail sales are not taxed, including groceries, medical supplies, and rent payments. Meanwhile many non-retail sales are taxed, including office equipment and building supplies. Florida is not unique in this regard. All states exempt some retail purchases and tax some non-retail purchases, as Ring (1989) has noted.

One ongoing issue in Florida politics is whether the sales tax should be extended to services. When it was originally implemented, the sales tax was described as a tax on the retail sale of tangible goods. While the tax base has been extended to some services by specifically legislating that those services be taxed (parking services and skybox rentals are two), broadening the tax base to include all services has been a controversial issue for decades. In 1987 then-Governor Bob Martinez pushed a bill through the legislature that taxed all services, including non-retail professional services like legal services, accounting services, advertising, and consulting services, as Hellerstein (1988) describes. The tax was met with considerable opposition, resulting in its repeal that same year. As a compromise, the state sales-tax rate was increased from 5% to 6%, where it has remained for more than three decades.

Despite not having a personal income tax, Florida's sales-tax rate is moderate compared with most states. Fifteen states have higher state sales-tax rates, and when including allowable local option sales taxes, 27 states have higher combined state and local sales-tax rates. This is further evidence of Florida's fiscal conservatism.

One issue many states are grappling with is whether or how to apply sales tax to the online purchases made by the state's residents. One possible way to deal with this is addressed in the Streamlined Sales Tax Project (SSTP), which is a proposed multi-state agreement in which states that participate in the SSTP require sellers in their states to remit sales taxes on purchasers from other participating states, as discussed by Einav, Knoepfle, Levin, and Sundaresan (2014) and Bruce, Fox, and Luna (2015). As of 2019, 23 states had joined the SSTP, but Florida was not among them. However, Florida did join the nation-wide trend and began collecting sales tax on the on-line purchases of Florida residents on July 1, 2021.

States that tax on-line sales obviously stand to gain revenues, and strong support for the taxing those sales comes from business lobbies who want their out-of-state competitors to have to collect sales taxes as in-state businesses do. But for in-person sales, sales taxes are collected in the seller's jurisdiction, not the buyer's. A California resident who goes to New York and makes a retail purchase pays New York sales tax, not California sales tax. Why should it be different for online sales? Why should the Californian who buys from a New York seller be required to pay California sales tax if the purchase is made on-line but New York sales tax if the purchase is made in person? The answer is that business lobbies do not want to have in-state businesses taxed; they want taxes placed on their out-of-state competitors.

Arguments like the one in the previous paragraph have little relevance to actual tax law, which is designed based on political pressures rather than economic reasoning (even though economic reasoning can play a role in shaping political pressures). Business interests lobby to have taxes placed on their competitors—thus in-state sellers lobby to place taxes on out-of-state sales, even though for most sales the tax is paid in the seller's jurisdiction, not the buyer's. Florida's resistance to taxing on-line sales kept tax revenues lower, thereby lowering government expenditures, for Florida residents. Ultimately, the state's business interests won this battle when the state began taxing on-line sales in 2021.

More generally, Florida's relatively moderate sales tax rate—especially considering the absence of a personal income tax—its reluctance to broaden the sales tax base, and its absence of a rate increase in more than three decades, have all contributed to the state's fiscal conservatism.

FLORIDA'S INTANGIBLE PROPERTY TAX

Florida's intangible property tax was established in 1972 as a tax on the holdings of stocks, bonds, and other intangible assets. Bank accounts were excluded from the tax base. The rate varied over the years from 50 cents per $1000 of intangible property to $2 per $1000. The tax was understandably unpopular with Florida's fiscal conservatives, and when Jeb Bush was elected governor in 1998, he referred to the tax as the "seniors and savers tax," and advocated its repeal. The tax was repealed in 2007, just prior to the end of Bush's second term as governor. The repeal of this tax, even as inflation-adjusted state government expenditures per person had been approximately constant for more than a decade, is yet more evidence of the state's fiscal conservatism. While Governor Bush advocated the repeal of the tax, he did not have the power to do so himself, but did so with the cooperation of Florida's fiscally conservative legislature.

PARTY POLITICS AND THE STATE BUDGET

Florida has a reputation for being a swing state, not solidly leaning toward either the Republican or Democratic party. There are slightly more registered Republicans than Democrats, but 28.7% of voters are registered as independents or affiliated with minor parties. Florida was a solidly Democratic state in 1983, where the data in table 13.1 begins, both in terms of those who held office and in terms of registered voters, but a decade later it began its shift toward the Republican party. Despite being a swing state in national elections, Florida has had a Republican governor and both houses of the state legislature have had a Republican majority since 1998.

The shift away from the Democratic party mirrors what was happening in other southern states. The South was solidly Democratic prior to the 1980s, but southern Democrats were always more fiscally conservative than northern Democrats. Democratic Governor Bob Graham was in office during the first years in the table 13.1 data with a solidly Democratic legislature behind him. After being term-limited out of office, he was replaced by Republican Bob Martinez, elected in 1986. The legislature remained Democratic, and some missteps on tax policy resulted in his being a one-term governor,[7] replaced by Democratic Governor Lawton Chiles, who was elected in 1990 and served through 1998.

During Chiles's terms in office the legislature flipped from Democratic to Republican, with the House becoming majority Republican after the 1994 election and the Senate following two years later. Republican Jeb Bush was elected governor in 1998, and both the governorship and both houses of the legislature have remained solidly Republican since.

One could make a (weak) case that Florida's switch from a solidly Democratic state to a solidly Republican one was a factor in its fiscal conservatism, but several counterarguments weigh against the case. First, this party switch was common to southern states in general, not just Florida, but other southern states have not seen the same fiscal conservatism. Second, the Florida electorate remains divided. Florida voters have supported the winning presidential candidate in nine of the last 11 presidential elections.[8] But Republicans tend to be more fiscally conservative than Democrats, so it is likely the case that if the state government was not controlled by Republicans, the state would not have gone a quarter of a century without a long-term increase in expenditures.

FACTORS SUPPORTING FISCAL CONSERVATISM

Several factors explain why Florida has been so fiscally conservative for the quarter of a century preceding 2020. The previous section considered the effect of having a Republican governor along with a solidly Republican legislature, and while Republicans tend to be more fiscally conservative than Democrats, Florida is not the only solidly Republican state, and voter registrations show about the same number of registered Democrats as Republicans in Florida. The general perception of Florida as a swing state suggests that while a Republican state government is likely a factor, it cannot be considered a complete explanation.

Another factor may be that Florida has many retirees. Older people may tend to be more fiscally conservative and also may have lower demands for state and local government services, even though they are high consumers of federal government services, such as Social Security and Medicare. Together with Florida, Arizona and Nevada, two other states that attract a substantial number of retirees, are three of the five states that have the lowest state and local government spending.[9]

Florida has no state or local personal income tax, and the state's constitutional barrier to income taxes is another factor that might contribute to its fiscal conservatism. Personal income taxation is prohibited in the state's constitution, which requires 60% voter approval to amend, so it is very unlikely that Florida will ever tax personal income. The unlikelihood that an income tax amendment could succeed means that there is very little interest, even from those who would like a state income tax, to attempt one. Deprived of that revenue source, the state government might find it more difficult to raise revenue, which helps keep government expenditure low.[10]

While the lack of a state income tax seems like a plausible factor leading to fiscal conservatism, seven states have no personal income tax, and while four of those states (Florida, Nevada, South Dakota, and Texas) are in the lowest half of states in state and local government expenditures per person, three (Alaska, Washington, and Wyoming) are in the highest half. The lack of a state income tax does not necessarily lead to fiscal conservatism, but surely it plays a role, in that when people migrate from one state to another, fiscally conservative individuals are more likely to favor states without income taxes.

Another factor that Holcombe (2015) suggests may play a role is legislative term limits. Florida places a limit of eight years on Senators, Representatives, and the governor. The limit says that if a legislator has been in that office for eight years, that person's name cannot appear on the ballot for that office in the next election. It does not prevent term-limited legislators from running for other offices, and does not prevent them from running again in a future election. But it does prevent them from running again from the office they currently hold if they have been in office for eight years.

Legislative term limits were enacted by a citizen-initiative constitutional amendment that passed in 1992, when the term-limit clock began running. That meant that legislators already in office could continue to run and serve in the office until 2000. Note, referring to figure 13.1, that prior to term limits, there was an upward trend in inflation-adjusted state government expenditures per person, and that the leveling off in expenditures seems correlated with the passage of term limits. While this is suggestive, California also has term limits and is among the least fiscally conservative states. Term limits alone do not bring with them a fiscally conservative state government.

As just noted, Florida also allows its state constitution to be amended by citizen initiative, one of eight states to do so.[11] Two others are California and Massachusetts, states that cannot be viewed as fiscally conservative, so again, the availability of citizen initiatives to amend the state constitution cannot be the determining factor that pushes a state to fiscal conservatism. Florida is the only state that has (1) no state income tax, (2) term limits on its legislature, and (3) the availability of citizen initiatives to amend its constitution. These are all factors that might push a state government toward fiscal conservatism, but these factors may just coincidentally line up that way. These institutional factors, combined with a solidly Republican state government, might tilt Florida in that direction.

TERM LIMITS AND POLITICAL ORGANIZATION

The Speaker of the House and President of the Senate have a substantial amount of power in Florida, amounting to more than is the case at the federal level, for example. All staff positions in the legislature technically report to and are employees of those leaders in their respective chambers, and those leaders have control of the legislative agenda, so bills from legislators will only be considered if the Speaker or President decide to hear them.[12] It is barely an exaggeration to say that when legislation is being considered, negotiations are among three individuals: the governor, Speaker of the House, and President of the Senate.

Legislators, including the Speaker and President, face term limits, and the custom in both Houses has been to appoint the Speaker and President in the last two years of their terms. Representatives are elected for two-year terms, and Senators for four-year terms, so term limits mean that Representatives serve at most for four terms and senators at most for two. Future Speakers and Presidents serve for six years as members and for their final two years as the heads of their respective chambers.

The members who will eventually lead their chambers are typically chosen well before their terms as Speaker or President, which illustrates one reason term limits make a difference. Reelection is viewed as enough of a sure thing that legislators confidently choose their next leaders of their chambers even when those leaders must be reelected to the legislature to serve their final terms as leaders.

Once in command of their respective chambers, they know they will be term limited out of office once their current terms end, so there is no pressure on them to be reelected, and if they were driven even in part by their ideologies to run in the first place, there is nothing standing in the way of their acting to further their ideological views in their final terms. And with term limits, legislators know when they are elected that they will only be in office for eight years, so they are not looking at their current positions as possible lifetime occupations. Once their leadership positions are over, they can run for a different office or move into the private sector.

The solid Republican majorities in both Houses tend to choose members with conservative ideologies to lead their chambers, so a combination of conservative values and the absence of electoral pressures can push leaders who already have fiscally conservative inclinations to resist compromising on budgetary issues. They will not lose their leadership positions and have no concerns about reelection, so members who want to pad the budget with pork barrel projects are in a weak bargaining position relative to the leaders in their chambers.

LAND USE POLICY IN FLORIDA

A conservative ideology tends to favor smaller government, and recent land use policy in Florida has reflected this conservatism as well. Florida was one of the leading states in implementing statewide growth management and land use policies when the state passed its Growth Management Act in 1985, which required every local government in Florida to draw up a comprehensive plan consistent with the state government's comprehensive plan.[13] Plans were to be reviewed by the state's Department of Community Affairs to determine if they conformed with the requirements of the Act. The Act gave local governments a five-year lead time, so the first local plans were submitted to the state in 1990, and many of them were rejected. The view held by some was that the Department of Community Affairs was using criteria that went well beyond what the Act specified to reject those plans, while others applauded the Department's strict enforcement to manage the state's rapid growth.

The 1985 Act was passed when the state government was solidly Democratic, with a Democratic governor and Democratic majorities in both houses of the legislature. Its implementation was occurring as the state government was shifting from Democratic to Republican, which may have led to some dissatisfaction with the state government's heavy-handed role. In addition, some aspects of the Act were leading to counterproductive results according to the Act's proponents, who sought amendments to it.[14] The Act was amended several times, always bringing with it some controversy.

When Governor Rick Scott assumed office in 2011, one of the first things he did was to abolish the Department of Community Affairs, and along with it, statewide land use planning. Florida had gone from being one of the leaders in statewide land use planning to having none at all. The demise of statewide land use planning is once again consistent with a conservative attitude toward government that has occurred along with Florida's fiscal conservatism.

Florida still has a substantial amount of land use planning, because in the quarter century during which state-wide land use planning was in effect, local land use planning bureaucracies were created to comply with the state's regulations. Local governments now have their own growth management departments that were created as a result of the 1985 Act, and that have remained after state-wide land use planning was abolished. In addition, local governments coordinate their efforts through regional development councils. These local bureaucracies are the legacies of the state's efforts and land use planning, so government land use planning bureaucracies remain active in Florida, but not at the state level.

Florida's push toward limiting the reach of state government with regard to land use policy suggests a conservative government consistent with its fiscal conservatism. This points toward a state government that has, for a quarter of a century, favored limited government in many dimensions. Seen in this way, Florida's fiscal conservatism is one component of a more generally conservative state government.

CONCLUSION

This chapter discusses the fact, shown in figure 13.1, that for a quarter of a century dating back to 1995, Florida's inflation-adjusted state government expenditures per person have been approximately constant. In an era when government spending growth is the norm, a government that has had no spending growth in a quarter of a century is noteworthy. As figure 13.1 also shows, the decade prior to 1995 showed the steady growth in government expenditures that has been the norm for most governments, most of the time, since the beginning of the twentieth century. If readers take one thing away from this chapter, it should be simply that this has happened. Government growth is not inevitable.

The chapter further supported that simple fact by providing evidence of the state's fiscal conservatism in several other dimensions. Florida has no personal income tax, has not increased its sales tax rate in three decades, and has kept the sales tax base approximately unchanged, although there is some tinkering with the base in every legislative session. Florida has repealed its intangible property tax, has not added other taxes to its tax portfolio, has an adequately funded (though not fully funded) state pension system that is better funded than the average state, and has been conservative, in the sense of supporting limited government, in other areas beyond just its fiscal conservatism. A second takeaway from the chapter is that the absence of state government expenditure growth has not been an accident, and is not due to failed attempts to boost the state's expenditures. It has been the product of a fiscally conservative government.

The chapter speculates on reasons why Florida's state government has been so fiscally conservative for a quarter of a century, and why it has been successful at holding the line on state government expenditures. Speculation is the operative word here. There are many factors that point toward reasons the state government has been fiscally conservative, but it is unclear how much any of these factors have contributed, individually or together, to produce a fiscally conservative government.

Legislative institutions may play a role. With legislative term limits, people who compete for those offices know they can only hold those positions temporarily, which might affect both who chooses to run for seats in the state legislature, and their attitudes toward government after they are elected. Since the establishment of term limits, both Houses of the legislature have been led by individuals in their final two years of their eight-year maximum terms, so they have no concerns about opposition from other legislators or about reelection (although they may choose to run for other offices). Further, the Speaker of the House and President of the Senate are very powerful in Florida, so it is not much of an exaggeration to say that state government policy is dominated by negotiations among three individuals: the Speaker, the President, and the governor (who is also term-limited).

In addition to these institutional factors, while Florida is considered a swing state nationally, during the quarter of a century in which the state government has been so fiscally conservative, the legislature and the governor's office have been solidly Republican. Add to this the substantial population of retirees in the state and the fact that fiscally conservative state is likely to attract fiscally conservative in-migrants and there are good demographic reasons why Florida might lean toward fiscal conservatism.

A number of factors might be behind Florida's fiscal conservatism, and while some were considered here, the causal factors remain an open question. But it is clear that Florida's fiscal conservatism over a quarter of a century has been a choice made by Florida's legislature and governors, and it is remarkable that in an era of government growth, Florida stands out for its history of a quarter of a century in which inflation-adjusted state government expenditures per person have not grown.

NOTES

1. Technically, the federal government does not print its own money either. The Federal Reserve Bank creates new money by buying U.S. government bonds, which amounts to the same thing.

2. Florida's state budget is stated as a level of appropriations rather than expenditures, but appropriations are a close approximation for expenditures. They are not identical because money is sometimes appropriated from one fund to another, and the budget document is opaque enough that it is not clear to anybody how much this is. The consensus is that it is small enough that appropriations is a good measure of expenditures.

3. Taking a more global perspective, many nations have had declines in government spending as a share of GDP since the 1990s, including the "big-government" Scandinavian countries and (not surprisingly) Russia. Even in the United States, federal government spending as a share of GDP is in the neighborhood of where it was in the early 1990s. Holcombe (2019) discusses some details.

4. Data in this paragraph is from U.S. Census Bureau Survey of State and Local Government Finances, 2017.

5. Data from U.S. Census Bureau 2014 Annual Survey of Public Employment & Payroll Data.

6. Pew Charitable Trusts, *The State Pension Funding Gap: 2016*. Philadelphia: Pew Charitable Trusts, 2018, 17th edition, Chapter 14.

7. The legislature wanted to increase spending, and because Florida has consistently maintained a balanced budget, needed more revenues to do so. Governor Martinez proposed extending the sales tax to services as a method of increasing revenue, which passed the legislature and was signed into law. The services tax had strong opponents, pushing Governor Martinez to almost immediately recommend repealing it and instead raising the state sales-tax rate from 5% to 6%, which also passed. Thus, Martinez managed to antagonize everyone in the state. The opponents of the services tax were angry that he pushed to have it adopted and only backed off under substantial pressure, and the proponents of the services tax were angry at its repeal. See Hellerstein (1988) for some details.

8. The two exceptions were in 1992 when Florida's electoral votes went to George H. W. Bush but Bill Clinton won the election and in 2020 when Florida's electoral votes went to Florida resident Donald Trump but Joe Biden won..

9. Idaho spends the least per person, followed by Georgia. Data is from the U.S. Census Bureau's State and Local Government Snapshot.

10. Brennan and Buchanan (1980) argue that limiting the number of tax bases a government can tax can act as an effective constraint on government spending.

11. The others are Arizona, Arkansas, California, Colorado, Illinois, Massachusetts, and Michigan.

12. One example of the exercise of this power came when the President of the Senate, early in the 2000s, wanted a specific piece of legislation on tax reform passed early in the legislative session. One senator voted against the legislation, and the President of the Senate promptly fired all of that senator's staff. In another case in the House, a Representative voted against a bill the Speaker wanted passed and was removed from all of his committee assignments.

13. The process is described in Holcombe (2001).

14. For example, to encourage urban infill, the Act specified low densities for development outside of urban areas. This prompted low-density development in less-developed areas, encouraging urban sprawl—one of the things the proponents of the original Act hoped to prevent.

REFERENCES

Brennan, Geoffrey, and James M. Buchanan. *The Power to Tax: Analytical Foundations of a Fiscal Constitution*. Cambridge: Cambridge University Press, 1980.

Bruce, Donald, William F. Fox, and LeAnn Luna. "E-tailer Sales Tax nexus and State Sales Tax Policies." *National Tax Journal* 68, no. 3S (September 2015): 735–66.

Einav, Liran, Dan Knoepfle, Jonathan D. Levin, and Neel Sundaressan. "Sales Taxes and Internet Commerce." *American Economic Review* 104, no. 1 (January 2014): 1–26.

Hellerstein, Walter. "Florida's Sales Tax On Services." *National Tax Journal* 41, no. 1 (March 1988): 1–18.

Hellerstein, Walter. "Florida's Sales Tax on Services." *National Tax Journal* 41, no. 1 (March 1988): 1–18.

Holcombe, Randall G. *Florida's Fiscal Policy: Responsible Budgeting in a Growing State*. Arlington, VA: Mercatus Center at George Mason University, 2015.

Holcombe, Randall G. "Growth Management in Action: The Case of Florida." Chapter 8 in Randall G. Holcombe and Samuel R. Staley, eds., *Smarter Growth: Market-Base Strategies of Land-Use Planning in the 21st Century*. Westport, CT: Greenwood, 2001.

Holcombe, Randall G. "Is Government Growth Inevitable?" Chapter 30 in Roger D. Congleton, Bernard, Goffman, and Stefan Voigt, eds., *Oxford Handbook of Public Choice*. Oxford: Oxford University Press, 2019: 588–603.

Pew Charitable Trusts, *The State Pension Funding Gap: 2016*. Philadelphia: Pew Charitable Trusts, 2018.

Ring, Raymond J., Jr. "The Proportion of Consumers' and Producers' Goods in the General Sales Tax." *National Tax Journal* 42, no. 2 (June 1989): 167–79.

Schuyler, Michael. "A Short History of Government Taxing and Spending in the United States." Tax Foundation Fiscal Fact No. 415 (February 2014).

Index

About the Editors

Barry W. Poulson is emeritus professor of economics at the University of Colorado. He has been visiting professor at several universities including the Universidad Autónoma de Guadalajara, University of North Carolina, Cambridge University, Konan University, and Universidad Carlos Tercera. He is the author of numerous books and articles in the fields of economic development and economic history. He has served as president of the North American Economics and Finance Association, and is advisor to the Task Force on Tax and Fiscal Policy for the American Legislative Exchange Council. His current research focuses on fiscal policies and fiscal constitutions.

John Merrifield was on the faculty of the University of Texas at San Antonio for 32 years. He retired from teaching and faculty meetings to devote additional time to critical research issues, and to have more time with his wife and "high-maintenance" teenage adopted boys. He is associate editor for the *Nonpartisan Education Review*, past editor for *Journal of School Choice*, and has authored or edited five books, 56 peer-reviewed journal articles, and several chapters in his primary teaching and research fields of Education Economics, Public Finance, Urban and Regional Economics, and Environmental and Natural Resource Economics.

About the Contributors

James Broughel is an economist who specializes in regulatory reform, cost-benefit analysis, and the impact of regulations on economic growth. He is author of the book *Regulation and Economic Growth: Applying Economic Theory to Public Policy*. His writing has appeared in popular outlets such as the *Wall Street Journal*, the *Los Angeles Times*, and the *Washington Post*. He received his PhD in economics from George Mason University and his BA and MA in economics from Hunter College of the City University of New York.

Chris Edwards occupies the Kilts Family Chair in Fiscal Studies at the Cato Institute and is the editor of DownsizingGovernment.org. He is a top expert on federal and state tax and budget issues. Before joining Cato, he was a senior economist on the congressional Joint Economic Committee, a manager with PricewaterhouseCoopers, and an economist with the Tax Foundation.

Erick M. Elder joined UA Little Rock in 1996 after receiving his PdD from the University of Pittsburgh. His areas of specialization are statistics, macroeconomics, and international economics. He is actively engaged in academic research and has published articles on topics including government deficits, executive options, trade patterns after NAFTA, Social Security, state budget stabilization funds, and public pensions. He teaches MBA-level and undergraduate Statistics, Principles and Intermediate Macroeconomics, and International Economics. Finally, he serves as a litigation consultant for the plaintiff and defense in the area of forensic economics for 15 years estimating economics damages in personal injury and wrongful death cases.

Olivia Gonzalez is an economist at the Small Business Administration and a Mercatus Frederic Bastiat Fellow. She has published research on economic development, fiscal health, and zoning. She is the co-author of the Mercatus Center's *Ranking the States by Fiscal Condition* report. Her research has been featured in media outlets such as the Tribune News Service, U.S. News & World Report, Planetizen, *City Journal*, and various local newspapers across the United States. She earned her BS and MA in economics at George Mason University, where she is currently a PhD candidate.

Randall G. Holcombe is DeVoe Moore Professor of Economics at Florida State University. He received his PhD in economics from Virginia Tech, and taught at Texas A&M University and at Auburn University prior to coming to Florida State in 1988. He is also Senior Fellow at the James Madison Institute, a Tallahassee-based think tank that specializes in issues facing state governments, is Senior Fellow at the Independent Institute in Oakland, California, and is a Research Fellow at the Law & Economics Center at George Mason University. He served on Florida Governor Jeb Bush's Council of Economic Advisors from 2000 to 2006, and is past president of the Public Choice Society and the Society for the Development of Austrian Economics. He is the author of twenty books and more than 200 articles published in academic and professional journals. His books include *Political Capitalism: How Economic and Political Power Is Made and Maintained* (2018) and *Coordination, Cooperation, and Control: The Evolution of Economic and Political Power* (2020).

Jeremy Horpedahl is an associate professor of economics at the University of Central Arkansas. He teaches courses in public finance, economic history, and introductory economics courses. He is also the director of Arkansas Center for Research in Economics, with his research focusing on state and local tax policy. He received his PhD in economics from George Mason University in 2009. His research has been published in peer-reviewed journals including *Public Choice*, *Econ Journal Watch*, and *Constitutional Political Economy*. His popular writings have been published in the *Arkansas Democrat-Gazette,* the *Chicago Tribune, Real Clear Policy,* and US News & World Report. He has appeared on NPR's *Marketplace* as well as many television and radio programs in Arkansas.

Dwight Lee is an emeritus professor of economics at the University of Georgia and is Affiliated Visiting Faculty Fellow in the Institute for the Study of Political Economy at Ball State University. He has taught at the University of Colorado at Boulder, Virginia Tech, George Mason University, University of Georgia, and Southern Methodist University. He received his PhD in economics from the University of California, San Diego.

Veronica Lucero is an attorney in private practice. She has researched, written about, and litigated cases under state constitutional anti-subsidy provisions.

Matthew Mitchell is a Senior Fellow in the Centre for Economic Freedom at the Fraser Institute and a Senior Research Fellow at the Knee Center at West Virginia University. His research focuses on economic freedom and institutional barriers to prosperity.

Anne Philpot is a former legal research associate at the Mercatus Center. She holds a JD from George Mason University Scalia Law School.

Thurston Powers is a graduate of NYU Wagner Graduate School of Public Service, where he studied public policy analysis. He has worked for the Yankee Institute for Public Policy as a policy analyst and at the American Legislative Exchange Council as a research manager.

Jonathan Riches is the vice president for litigation at the Goldwater Institute's Scharf-Norton Center for Constitutional Litigation and General Counsel for the Institute. He litigates in federal and state trial and appellate courts in several areas of constitutional law, including taxpayer protection cases.

Thomas Savidge is the research director of the Center for State Fiscal Reform at the American Legislative Exchange Council. He works on economic issues facing state and local governments with a focus on tax and fiscal policy. He earned his bachelor's degree in political science and philosophy from SUNY New Paltz and his master's degree in public policy from George Mason University.

Austill Stuart received his bachelor's in economics from Auburn University and his master's in economics from George Mason University. After over a decade living inside the DC Beltway, he returned to his hometown of Mobile, Alabama in late 2021, where he currently resides.

Diana W. Thomas, professor of economics, Creighton University, and director, Institute for Economic Inquiry, Creighton University.

Michael D. Thomas, associate professor of economics, Creighton University, and student programs director, Institute for Economic Inquiry, Creighton University.

Gary A. Wagner currently holds the Acadiana Business Economist Endowed Chair at the University of Louisiana at Lafayette. His research interests range from regional economics to state and local public finance issues, with a particular focus on tax structures and economic development, borrowing costs, and pension systems. He has authored or co-authored more than 60 professional articles and reports and has delivered more than 300 presentations to public audiences on national and regional economic conditions. He holds a PhD in economics from West Virginia University. Prior to joining the University of Louisiana at Lafayette, he was vice president and senior regional officer for the Federal Reserve Bank of Cleveland.

www.ingramcontent.com/pod-product-compliance
Ingram Content Group UK Ltd.
Pitfield, Milton Keynes, MK11 3LW, UK
UKHW041450071026
15587UKWH00010B/744

9 781666 932034